Java™ For Dummies, 3rd Edition

W9-AZJ-987

Cheat Sheet

`<APPLET>` Tag

Tag Structure:

```
<APPLET attributes>
appletparameter tags
alternate HTML
</APPLET>
```

Example:

```
<APPLET CODE="LivingLinks.class"
WIDTH=100 HEIGHT=100>
<PARAM NAME="image"
VALUE="animalsButton.gif">
<PARAM NAME="effect" VALUE="Warp">
<PARAM NAME="soundDir" VALUE="audio/
animals/">
<PARAM NAME="inSound"
VALUE="dolphinSqueak.au |
lionRoar.au | rooster.au">
<PARAM NAME="links" VALUE= "Dolphins
= http://www.dolphin.com | Lions =
http://www.lion.com | Roosters =
http://www.rooster.com">
<B>If you can read this, you're
visiting without a Java-savvy
browser! </B>
This page requires a Java-savvy
browser...
<A HREF="http://
www.netscape.com">GET ONE!</A>
</APPLET>
```

Java Plug-In `<OBJECT>` Tag for Internet Explorer on Windows

```
<OBJECT classid="clsid:8AD9C840-
044E-11D1-B3E9-@ca
00805F499D93"
width="200" height="200"
align="baseline"
codebase="http://java.sun.com/
products/plugin/@ca
1.1/jinstall-11-
win32.cab#Version=1,1,0,0">
<PARAM NAME="code"
VALUE="MyApplet.class">
```

```
<PARAM NAME="codebase" @ca
VALUE="http://
www.AnyValidWebAddress.org/">
<PARAM NAME="type"
VALUE="application/@ca
x-java-applet;version=1.1">
<PARAM NAME="anyParameter"
VALUE="parameter value">
```

Sorry, this browser doesn't support the Java Plug-in!
`</OBJECT>`

Java Plug-In `<EMBED>` Tag for Netscape Navigator on Windows and Solaris

```
<EMBED type="application/x-java-
applet;version=1.1"@ca
width="200" height="200"
align="baseline"@ca
code="MyApplet.class"
codebase="http://
www.AnyValidWebAddress.org/"
anyParameter ="corresponding
parameter value"
pluginspage="http://java.sun.com/
products/plugin/@ca
1.1/plugin-install.html">
<NOEMBED>
Sorry, this browser doesn't support
the Java Plug-in!
</NOEMBED>
</EMBED>
```

Five Best Java Resources on the Web

Java For Dummies Support site:
www.mantiscorp.com/JavaForDummies

The Sun Java Web Site: java.sun.com

Mantis Java Links: www.mantiscorp.com/java

Gamelan: www.gamelan.com

The IDG Java Resource site:
www.idgbooks.com/rc/java

...For Dummies: #1 Computer Book Series for Beginners

Java™ For Dummies, 3rd Edition

Cheat Sheet

Required and Optional Applet Attributes

Within your <APPLET> tags, some attributes are required, others give you room to play around. However, you'll never be able to use either of the two new Java 1.1 attributes when hooking up an original Java 1.0 applet because Java 1.1 attributes aren't supported by older Java 1.0 applets (they're only supported by Java 1.1 and Java 1.2 applets)— so be careful when weaving your Java-powered pages!

Attribute	Description
Required Attributes	
CODE	This attribute specifies the name of the applet file to imbed in your page. (**Note:** The CODE attribute is not used if the Java 1.1 OBJECT attribute described below is used.)
HEIGHT	This attribute specifies the height of your applet in pixels.
WIDTH	This attribute specifies the width of your applet in pixels.
Optional Attributes	
PARAM	Not an <APPLET> tag attribute, actually, but an optional tag that itself has two required attributes (NAME and VALUE). You can use any number of <PARAM> tags to customize an applet, as long as the applet you're dealing with supports them.
CODEBASE	This attribute specifies the base URL for your applet. The applet itself must be located relative to this URL. If CODEBASE isn't specified, the applet is expected to reside in the same directory as the Web page itself.
ALIGN	This attribute specifies where your applet is placed on the page in respect to the text around it; this attribute can be one of the following nine alignments: left, right, top, texttop, middle, absmiddle, baseline, bottom, and absbottom.
ALT	This attribute specifies alternate text to be displayed by Java-savvy browsers that are incapable of executing the applet for whatever reason. Note that this text is seen *only* by Java-savvy browsers, as it falls within the opening <APPLET> tag, which all non-Java browsers skip over. If you want to communicate with non-Java browsers, do so by using *alternate HTML*.
NAME	This attribute specifies the symbolic name of your applet, allowing other applets imbedded in the same page to locate your applet by name. This attribute is used only when applets on a page communicate with one another, something most applets don't do.
HSPACE	This attribute specifies the horizontal space surrounding your applet.
VSPACE	This attribute specifies the vertical space surrounding your applet.
Java 1.1 and 1.2 Attributes	
ARCHIVE	Available only with applets created using Java 1.1 and Java 1.2 or later, this attribute is used to specify one or more Java archives (JARs), assuming the applet actually takes advantage of JAR files (special-purpose archives introduced with Java 1.1). If multiple JAR files are required, they must be separated by a comma.
OBJECT	Available only with applets created using Java 1.1 and Java 1.2 or later, this attribute is used to specify the name of a "serialized" applet file, as opposed to the non-serialized applet file (standard Java class file) specified through the CODE attribute. Because serialized applet files are actually special versions of standard applets, the CODE attribute is not necessary when the OBJECT is used. When the CODE attribute is used, the OBJECT attribute is not used.

...For Dummies: #1 Computer Book Series for Beginners

JAVA™
FOR
DUMMIES®
3RD EDITION

by Aaron E. Walsh

IDG Books Worldwide, Inc.
An International Data Group Company

Foster City, CA ♦ Chicago, IL ♦ Indianapolis, IN ♦ New York, NY

Java™ **For Dummies**,® **3rd Edition**

Published by
IDG Books Worldwide, Inc.
An International Data Group Company
919 E. Hillsdale Blvd.
Suite 400
Foster City, CA 94404
www.idgbooks.com (IDG Books Worldwide Web site)
www.dummies.com (Dummies Press Web site)

Library of Congress Catalog Card No.: 98-87435

ISBN: 0-7645-0417-7

Printed in the United States of America

10 9 8 7 6 5 4 3 2 1

3B/RV/QZ/ZY/IN

Distributed in the United States by IDG Books Worldwide, Inc.

Distributed by Macmillan Canada for Canada; by Transworld Publishers Limited in the United Kingdom; by IDG Norge Books for Norway; by IDG Sweden Books for Sweden; by Woodslane Pty. Ltd. for Australia; by Woodslane (NZ) Ltd. for New Zealand; by Addison Wesley Longman Singapore Pte Ltd. for Singapore, Malaysia, Thailand, Indonesia and Korea; by Norma Comunicaciones S.A. for Colombia; by Intersoft for South Africa; by International Thomson Publishing for Germany, Austria and Switzerland; by Toppan Company Ltd. for Japan; by Distribuidora Cuspide for Argentina; by Livraria Cultura for Brazil; by Ediciencia S.A. for Ecuador; by Ediciones ZETA S.C.R. Ltda. for Peru; by WS Computer Publishing Corporation, Inc., for the Philippines; by Unalis Corporation for Taiwan; by Contemporanea de Ediciones for Venezuela; by Computer Book & Magazine Store for Puerto Rico; by Express Computer Distributors for the Caribbean and West Indies. Authorized Sales Agent: Anthony Rudkin Associates for the Middle East and North Africa.

For general information on IDG Books Worldwide's books in the U.S., please call our Consumer Customer Service department at 800-762-2974. For reseller information, including discounts and premium sales, please call our Reseller Customer Service department at 800-434-3422.

For information on where to purchase IDG Books Worldwide's books outside the U.S., please contact our International Sales department at 650-655-3200 or fax 650-655-3297.

For information on foreign language translations, please contact our Foreign & Subsidiary Rights department at 650-655-3021 or fax 650-655-3281.

For sales inquiries and special prices for bulk quantities, please contact our Sales department at 650-655-3200 or write to the address above.

For information on using IDG Books Worldwide's books in the classroom or for ordering examination copies, please contact our Educational Sales department at 800-434-2086 or fax 317-596-5499.

For press review copies, author interviews, or other publicity information, please contact our Public Relations department at 650-655-3000 or fax 650-655-3299.

For authorization to photocopy items for corporate, personal, or educational use, please contact Copyright Clearance Center, 222 Rosewood Drive, Danvers, MA 01923, or fax 978-750-4470.

is a trademark under exclusive license to IDG Books Worldwide, Inc., from International Data Group, Inc.

About the Author

Aaron E. Walsh is President and CEO of Mantis Development Corporation, a Boston-based software development firm specializing in advanced multimedia and network technologies, and an international best-selling author for IDG Books Worldwide, Inc.

Formerly the manager of Boston College's Advanced Technology Group (ATG), Aaron was lead software architect and engineer for a number of advanced technology projects developed at Boston College, including robust client/server technologies that pre-date the World Wide Web. While at Boston College, Aaron also wrote the core software system for Eagle Eyes, a research project that allows users to navigate their personal computer through eye movement alone. Under development for over four years, Eagle Eyes was selected as a finalist in Discover Magazine's 1994 Awards for Technical Innovation.

In 1992, Aaron co-founded Mantis Development Corporation, where he currently leads development of advanced software technologies based on the Java programming language developed by Sun Microsystems, Inc. He is the author of several articles for *MacTech Magazine* (formerly *MacTutor*) and *Dr. Dobb's Programming Journal,* and has written a number of books for IDG Books Worldwide, including *Destination Multimedia, Java For Dummies, Foundations of Java Programming for the World Wide Web,* and the *Java Bible.* In addition, Aaron teaches Java software development for Boston College's College of Advancing Studies.

Aaron is also the chairman of the Virtual Reality Modeling Language (VRML) Universal Media Element Library (UMEL) working group, a formal VRML Consortium research group. With an immediate mission to "increase the realism of VRML worlds and decrease network downloads by defining a small, cross-platform library of locally resident media elements (textures, sounds and VRML objects) and a uniform mechanism by which VRML content creators can incorporate these media elements into their worlds," Aaron believes that the technology brought to fruition by his group will ultimately offer significant advantages to the entire World Wide Web.

ABOUT IDG BOOKS WORLDWIDE

Welcome to the world of IDG Books Worldwide.

IDG Books Worldwide, Inc., is a subsidiary of International Data Group, the world's largest publisher of computer-related information and the leading global provider of information services on information technology. IDG was founded more than 25 years ago and now employs more than 8,500 people worldwide. IDG publishes more than 275 computer publications in over 75 countries (see listing below). More than 90 million people read one or more IDG publications each month.

Launched in 1990, IDG Books Worldwide is today the #1 publisher of best-selling computer books in the United States. We are proud to have received eight awards from the Computer Press Association in recognition of editorial excellence and three from *Computer Currents'* First Annual Readers' Choice Awards. Our best-selling *...For Dummies*® series has more than 50 million copies in print with translations in 38 languages. IDG Books Worldwide, through a joint venture with IDG's Hi-Tech Beijing, became the first U.S. publisher to publish a computer book in the People's Republic of China. In record time, IDG Books Worldwide has become the first choice for millions of readers around the world who want to learn how to better manage their businesses.

Our mission is simple: Every one of our books is designed to bring extra value and skill-building instructions to the reader. Our books are written by experts who understand and care about our readers. The knowledge base of our editorial staff comes from years of experience in publishing, education, and journalism — experience we use to produce books for the '90s. In short, we care about books, so we attract the best people. We devote special attention to details such as audience, interior design, use of icons, and illustrations. And because we use an efficient process of authoring, editing, and desktop publishing our books electronically, we can spend more time ensuring superior content and spend less time on the technicalities of making books.

You can count on our commitment to deliver high-quality books at competitive prices on topics you want to read about. At IDG Books Worldwide, we continue in the IDG tradition of delivering quality for more than 25 years. You'll find no better book on a subject than one from IDG Books Worldwide.

John Kilcullen
CEO
IDG Books Worldwide, Inc.

Steven Berkowitz
President and Publisher
IDG Books Worldwide, Inc.

Eighth Annual
Computer Press
Awards ≥1992

Ninth Annual
Computer Press
Awards ≥1993

Tenth Annual
Computer Press
Awards ≥1994

Eleventh Annual
Computer Press
Awards ≥1995

Dedication

To my nephew Dane, with love. You did it!

Author's Acknowledgments

With thanks to Tim Berners-Lee for inventing the World Wide Web, and to Sun Microsystems for giving it a serious jolt of life with Java.

Special thanks to Barbara Mikolajczak, whose dedicated and diligent work in so many areas made the original *Java For Dummies* book and all subsequent revisions of it possible, and to everyone at Mantis Development Corporation (www.mantiscorp.com). In particular I'd like to thank David Ruxton, Igor Svibilskiy, Jeff Orkin, and Jeff Lynch for their significant contributions to the Living Desktop application, the LivingLinks applet, and many other Java applets provided on CD-ROM (with additional thanks to Jeff Orkin for Celebrity Painter and the LivingLinks Editor). I would also like to thank Robert Wade, who wrote the majority of JavaScript code found in the original book and Appendix B of this revision.

To Bill Wellington, Adam Gupta, and Yeji Hong for their work on the Java "CookBook" Web pages provided on CD-ROM, and Baiju Paul Mathews, Sanjeev Dasgupta, and Scott Clark for creating special effect plug-ins for the LivingLinks applet. Thanks to Alex Garbagnati for the Marquee applet, and to Frank Imbarro for the use of his mobile office at the most crucial times.

I'd also like to extend special thanks to Rich Burridge, the technical editor for this revision of *Java For Dummies*. In addition to thanking Rich for his fine work on this and other projects we've worked on together, I'd like to congratulate him and his wife Lynea on their first child (who, as fate would have it, is expected to launch into this world at about the same time this book hits the stands!).

To the good folks at IDG Books and Dummies Press (www.dummies.com) for making this book possible in the first place. I would like to thank my editor Brian Kramer, especially, for all of his work on the manuscript and for keeping this revision on track. To Mary Bednarek for giving the thumbs-up to my original *Java For Dummies* proposal, and to Joyce Pepple for putting the pedal to the metal when we needed it most (by the way, Nathan's agreed to take the lead in the Java For Dummies musical, and the comedy troupe's about ready to tour. I'm still working on the sock puppets). I'd also like to thank Carmen Krikorian and Marita Ellixson for all their work on the CD-ROM.

Finally, I'd like to thank my families, old and new alike, for everything.

Publisher's Acknowledgments

We're proud of this book; please register your comments through our IDG Books Worldwide Online Registration Form located at http://my2cents.dummies.com.

Some of the people who helped bring this book to market include the following:

Acquisitions, Editorial, and Media Development

Project Editor: Brian Kramer

Acquisitions Editor: Joyce Pepple

Copy Editors: William A. Barton, Constance Carlisle, Tamara Castleman, Kathleen Dobie, Stephanie Koutek, Phil Worthington

Technical Editor: Richard Burridge

Media Development Editor: Marita Ellixson

Associate Permissions Editor: Carmen Krikorian

Editorial Manager: Leah P. Cameron

Media Development Manager: Heather Heath Dismore

Editorial Assistant: Donna Love

Production

Associate Project Coordinator: Tom Missler

Layout and Graphics: Lou Boudreau, Linda M. Boyer, J. Tyler Connor, Angela F. Hunckler, Drew R. Moore, Anna Rohrer, Brent Savage, Janet Seib, Deirdre Smith

Proofreaders: Christine Berman, Kelli Botta, Nancy Price, Rebecca Senninger, Janet M. Withers

Indexer: Sharon Hilgenberg

General and Administrative

IDG Books Worldwide, Inc.: John Kilcullen, CEO; Steven Berkowitz, President and Publisher

IDG Books Technology Publishing: Brenda McLaughlin, Senior Vice President and Group Publisher

Dummies Technology Press and Dummies Editorial: Diane Graves Steele, Vice President and Associate Publisher; Mary Bednarek, Director of Acquisitions and Product Development; Kristin A. Cocks, Editorial Director

Dummies Trade Press: Kathleen A. Welton, Vice President and Publisher; Kevin Thornton, Acquisitions Manager

IDG Books Production for Dummies Press: Michael R. Britton, Vice President of Production and Creative Services; Beth Jenkins Roberts, Production Director; Cindy L. Phipps, Manager of Project Coordination, Production Proofreading, and Indexing; Kathie S. Schutte, Supervisor of Page Layout; Shelley Lea, Supervisor of Graphics and Design; Debbie J. Gates, Production Systems Specialist; Robert Springer, Supervisor of Proofreading; Debbie Stailey, Special Projects Coordinator; Tony Augsburger, Supervisor of Reprints and Bluelines

Dummies Packaging and Book Design: Robin Seaman, Creative Director; Jocelyn Kelaita, Product Packaging Coordinator; Kavish + Kavish, Cover Design

♦

The publisher would like to give special thanks to Patrick J. McGovern, without whom this book would not have been possible.

♦

Contents at a Glance

Cartoons at a Glance

By Rich Tennant

page 7

page 47

"Well, this is festive – a miniature intranet amidst a swirl of Java applets."

page 245

"I don't mean to hinder your quest for knowledge, however it's not generally a good idea to try to download the entire Internet."

page 285

"You know, I've asked you a dozen times not to animate the torches on our Web page!"

page 311

Fax: 978-546-7747 • E-mail: the5wave@tiac.net

Table of Contents

Introduction

As if the World Wide Web isn't reason enough to do cartwheels down the street, the globe is now ablaze with the fire of a different flavor: *Java*. Nope, I'm not talking about the life-giving beverage (without which this book could not have been possible). I'm referring to the Java that has tens of millions of people around the world abuzz — a fresh blend of technologies that bring the Web to life with dazzling animation, pulse-pounding sound, and full-blown interactivity, the likes of which the online community has never seen. And, if electrifying the Web weren't enough, Java is on the verge of revolutionizing the traditional desktop computer software world as well. Talk about an ambitious cup o' Joe! With this book, you're poised to plunge headfirst into the most exciting craze ever to sweep the face of the Earth.

About This Book

One of the wonderful things about Java is its universal appeal; all Web surfers can add a dash or two of Java to their Web pages, bringing their Web sites to life with little effort. Although that capability alone may be enough to keep you satisfied, Java recently began to flow off the Web and invade the desktop. And that's exactly what this book shows you how to do — not only create state-of-the-art Web pages using Java, but also bring your desktop computer to life with Java programs that live outside of the Web.

This book tells you where Java fits into the Internet, why Java exploded onto the Web, how it oozed onto the desktop, and how Java promises to change the way you learn, work, and play. Of course, discovering this neat stuff about Java is only the beginning. The real purpose of this book is to show you how to get your fill of the following two tasty flavors of Java:

- **Java applets:** Miniature applications that bring your Web pages to life with sound, action, and interactivity.
- **Java applications:** Java-powered programs that run on your desktop computer just as other programs do but that are generally souped up to take advantage of Java's special capabilities.

Yep, this book offers everything you need to know to inject your pages and desktop with the appropriate flavor of Java. As icing on the cake (or cream in your coffee, if you prefer), I show you the best places on the Web to satisfy the constant Java cravings you're sure to get. Brace yourself — you stand a good chance of becoming a serious Java addict.

A Few Assumptions

Although the title of this book reads ...*For Dummies,* I'd bet dimes to donuts that you're no fool. You wouldn't be reading this book if you were. This book helps you make sense of Java and assumes that you already know a little bit about using the Web and creating Web pages. But don't worry if you're not a major Web-head.

Even if you've never seen Java in action before, you're going to be just fine. And even if that *is* the case, the only thing that you really need is a computer that can run a Java-savvy Web browser (for details, see Chapter 2). Assuming that you're comfortable using your computer, you're soon likely to find yourself surfing the seas of Java on the World Wide Web, creating your very own Java-powered pages, and hooking up Java applications on your desktop computer. To use the information in this book, I do assume that you're comfortable performing any of the following tasks:

- ✔ Copying files and creating directories (or *folders*).
- ✔ Using an online service or a direct Internet connection.
- ✔ Browsing and creating pages on the World Wide Web.

The CD-ROM that comes with this book contains a directory of Internet Service Providers (ISPs) that support Java-savvy browsers, as well as a special ISP "kit" that can get you up and running with AT&T WorldNet Service — a well-respected, Java-loving ISP — in no time flat. (See Appendix C for a guide to using this CD-ROM.) And Chapter 2 shows you how to set yourself up with a Java-savvy browser even if the online service you already use doesn't offer one.

How to Use This Book

I wrote this book to make creating Java-powered Web pages easy, and to show you how to take Java off the Web and bring it down to your desktop. I organized the book in a modular fashion, which enables you to find the information you need without needing to read the entire book from start to finish. You can just cruise through the Table of Contents for the specific information that interests you. If you're comfortable using the Web already, for example, but don't yet have a Java-savvy browser, you can jump right to Chapter 2.

If you're already surfing the Web with a Java-ready browser, however, you needn't bother with Chapter 2 at all. Instead, you may jump right to Part II, where you actually hook up your own Java-powered pages — starting with a crash course in HTML. If, on the other hand, you don't want to deal with applets at all, you can always start with Part III and begin creating Java applications. But if you're hard core, you may choose to leap into both applets and applications with reckless abandon. Think of that course as a double shot of espresso with a cappuccino chaser; you're wired for days!

But suppose that you're brand-spanking-new to Java, or you want a nice, detailed overview of everything from soup to nuts. Consider then starting at the very beginning (a very good place to start) and working your way through the book from there. Not only is this approach easier on the heart, but you also discover many cool things about the Internet, the Web, and Java. You're sure to impress friends, relatives, and in-laws at your next backyard barbecue.

Regardless of where you begin or where you end, from time to time, you're going to run across text that `looks like this example`. I use this style to represent code or other text exactly as you find it on-screen. Such text may represent a Web address or certain lines of code that you use to weave Java into your own Web page. In both cases, be careful to enter the text exactly as I show it — even your use of uppercase and lowercase letters must match the text I provide to you . . . unless, of course, I tell you otherwise!

Often, the lines of code you need to type are pretty long. In fact, every once in a while you'll come upon code in this book that you're supposed to type as one long line, but, because a printed page only has so much room, the line of code appears as two or more lines as the following snippet of code illustrates:

```
<APPLET CODE="Marquee" HEIGHT=25 WIDTH=450 ALT="This is a
        cool applet -- too bad you can't see it!"
        HSPACE=10
        VSPACE=25>
```

The indented lines of code appearing after the initial line of code indicate that they're all part of the same line. As such, you can type the preceding example as one line even though it's been separated into different lines in order to fit on a printed page in this book.

At times, where you're required to type in text other than code, it looks **like this bold little example**.

And because I assume that you're already comfortable surfing the Web, I've removed the `http://` from Web addresses altogether — today's browsers don't actually need it. So why clutter things up with `http://` if you don't even need it?

How This Book Is Organized

I organized this book into five parts, each part capable of standing on its own. If you want, however, you can read through one part and into the next one. Heck, you can even read this book from front to back, if you're so inclined. Although each chapter in this book can stand on its own, reading straight through can be a lot of fun, too. Take your pick!

Part I: Caught in a Web of Intrigue

In Part I, you find out exactly why everyone on the Web these days seems to be scrambling for a taste of Java. You discover what the Web really is and its relationship to the Internet and Java. Here you find out how to get your hands on a Java-savvy browser and how to prepare it for some of the coolest Java sites on the Web.

Part II: It's Applet Pickin' Time!

In Part II, you get your hands on Java applets, the most flexible form of Java you can find. I show you how to find and distinguish between the original Java 1.0 applets and the latest crops of Java 1.1 and Java 1.2 applets, and how to weave each type of applet into your Web page, customizing the little darlings to fit your needs. In this part, you create dazzling, living Web pages for the entire world to experience.

Part III: Application Overdrive: Bringing Java to the Desktop

In Part III, you find out about applications, Java's powerful, stand-alone alternative to applets. Discover how Java desktop applications differ from their Web-oriented applet counterparts. In this part, you discover how to pluck Java applications off the Web and install them on your desktop computer. You also find out how to customize and fine-tune your Java-powered applications.

Part IV: The Part of Tens

Part IV lists the top places on the Web to find Java help when you need it most, as well as where to locate Java applets for your Web pages and some nifty, kick-butt Java applications for your desktop. With access to the very best Java joints on the Net, your cup runneth over. And just in case your Java percolator goes on the fritz, Part IV also describes the top Java snafus you may face at one time or another.

Part V: Appendixes

Okay, I know what you're thinking: "Where does this guy get off calling some appendixes a *part?*"

Sure, Part V doesn't have any actual chapters in it, but it's packed with useful information nonetheless! Among its goodies are the following handy items:

- ✔ *Appendix A* guides you through the many and varied resources available on the Internet for Java-lovers. From e-zines and support areas to search engines and newsgroups, this appendix promises to keep you plugged into Java.

- ✔ *Appendix B* gives you a quick taste of *JavaScript,* English-like commands that you can use to control how your browser behaves. Specifically, this appendix explains how Java and JavaScript are related, and how you can weave the two together in your pages for a double-dose of caffeine.

- ✔ *Appendix C* is your road map to the CD-ROM that comes with this book. Look here for all the information you need to locate the applets, applications, sample Web pages, utilities, and other goodies jam-packed on the CD-ROM. Between the book you now hold in your hands and the CD-ROM that comes with it, you'll be off and running with Java in no time. Not bad, huh?

Icons Used in This Book

If you're like me, reading nothing but straight text is a killer. After a while, your eyes start to twitch and your mind starts to wander. That's why many books are full of illustrations — to break up the text and give you something to look at as you're reading.

This book is no different. Each chapter contains pictures to help you make sense of the material (and to keep your eyes from bugging out). But this book has another important graphical element: Each chapter is brimming with icons that highlight specific information. In fact, I organized the icons in this book so that you can skim through the text and find much of the most important information at a glance!

The information beside this icon can save you time, money, or both.

This icon alerts you to other ...*For Dummies* books that relate directly to the discussion at hand — books that are worth taking a gander at if you want to find out more about the current topic.

This icon marks stuff that you should tuck away in the back of your mind — you're sure to need it at some point in the near future.

If you're interested in the nitty-gritty, if you like tech talk, or if you're really into the material you're reading, check out the information next to the Technical Stuff icons. Although this info isn't absolutely necessary to get the job done, it does make interesting bedtime reading and is sure to make you an instant hit at your next company party.

Whenever the discussion involves stuff that you can find on the CD-ROM that comes with this book, you see this icon. If you find this icon, you can put down the book (assuming, of course, that you can tear yourself away from the thrill-a-minute pace) and pop in the CD-ROM to get your hands on the subject of the moment. Does life get any better?

What good would a book dealing with the Web be without a goodly supply of Web addresses? Not much, which is why this icon appears from time to time to supply you with the freshest and most exhilarating Web nuggets related to Java. Don't be shy: Fire up your Web browser and give 'em a whirl.

Never ignore this icon! Even if you skip the other icons, this baby is one that you *don't* want to miss. Trust me. If you ignore a warning, chances are frighteningly high that something bad will happen to you, your computer, or your Web pages. To avoid a self-inflicted meltdown, be sure to read every warning you come across very carefully.

So — Off You Go!

You're still reading this Intro? Jeez, get the lead out and get on with it! A dazzling, exciting new world awaits, and you're holding the key. So what are you waiting for? Go get your jolt of Java!

Part I
Caught in a Web of Intrigue

The 5th Wave   By Rich Tennant

MIDTOWN

WHERE'S THE DANG DOOR?!

WebSite DESIGN Co.

C'mon in!

OUR AWARDS

In this part . . .

Tired of feeling left out of the online craze? Starting to suspect that keeping up with Internet buzzwords is a full-time job? Want to know exactly what Java is and how it fits into the whole World Wide Web? If so, then Part I is the place for you to get your feet wet. This part brings you quickly up to speed with Java and its role on the Web and even shows you how to get your hands on a Java-savvy browser so that you can view Java-powered pages for yourself.

Chapter 1

A Thirst for Java

First it was the Internet. Then the World Wide Web. And just as you thought you could safely remove the cotton from your ears, another buzzword — Java — rings out loud and clear. Java has exploded onto the scene, promising to change the way you learn, work, and play. But what is Java? And, to be just a tad bit cynical, aren't all the other buzzwords promising the same thing, too?

For answers to these questions, you must take a closer look at each buzzword so that you can separate fact from fiction amid all the surrounding hype. Fortunately, I happen to have my official technology tour-guide hat and buzzword microscope handy. Follow me.

The Internet: Where Everything Started

The Internet was developed shortly after World War II. Its purpose was to provide U.S. government officials with a reliable means of communication capable of transmitting electronic messages even in a nuclear attack. From there, the Internet grew into today's granddaddy of computer networks — a vast, globally connected system of computers and people. Unfortunately, the Internet's always been a royal pain to use.

Because using the Internet required a significant amount of computer expertise, it was off-limits to the masses for the first 20 years or so of its existence. Most folks could only sit idly by and listen half-heartedly as others gushed about the joys of connecting to the Internet: "Zap!" as they sent electronic mail to their more savvy friends on the other side of the globe. "Zing!" as they scoured the data-rich ether, digging up timely nuggets of information to impress their bosses. "Pow!" as they bought and sold countless and varied items over the wire without leaving the comfort of their home computers. "Shazam!" as they shed pounds of excess weight thanks to the delicious, fat-free recipes to which only those on the Internet were privy.

And so life on the Internet went. Zap! Zing! Pow! Shazam! The "Net" was tremendously exciting and paid great dividends to those who had access and knew how to use it. But, sadly, it offered squat to the rest of us.

Welcome to the Web

The World Wide Web, commonly known as *the Web,* is to the Internet what hot fudge, whipped cream, and sprinkles are to vanilla ice cream: sheer heaven. The traditional, plain-vanilla Internet is cryptic and difficult to navigate. Although it offers a load of information, you need a suite of special software programs and detailed knowledge of each program just to scratch the surface of what's out there. The World Wide Web, however, sits on top of the plain-vanilla Internet, turning it into a sumptuous, decadent treat.

By using the Web, you can now instantly access and easily understand what was once nearly impossible to find and terribly confusing to use. Instead of forcing you to master a new tool for each type of information out there, the Web gives you access to everything through one simple tool — a Web browser. And where the Internet is cryptic and text-based, the Web is a rich and attractive blend of text, images, and sound. The difference between the two is like that between night and day or, more accurately, like the difference between newspaper and television. Essentially, the same information is available regardless of how you get it. The Web just makes getting it easier.

To get the whole scoop on the Internet, take a peek at *The Internet For Dummies,* 4th Edition, by John R. Levine, Carol Baroudi, and Margaret Levine Young (IDG Books Worldwide, Inc.).

Web pages: The building blocks

All the information that you can access by using the Web you actually find in documents, or *files.* You're probably familiar already with the concept of files; whenever you use any computer program, document, graphic, or message, you deal with files.

In standard computer programs (such as word processors and graphic-design programs), you typically view the information (graphics, text, or whatever) one file at a time in each window. On the Web, however, you can access many different files at once from within a single window, as illustrated in Figure 1-1. A special file known as a *Web page* may point to (or *reference*) other files that contain any combination of text, images, animation, and sound.

Web pages don't just appear all by themselves. Just as you need a word processor to view text files and a graphics program to view image files, you need a Web program to view Web files. This program, called a *Web browser,* displays the files that abound on the Web, enabling you to navigate the Web's vast contents. You may say that the browser is your vehicle or, better yet, your surfboard for surfing the Web. (Chapter 2 covers Web browsers in mind-boggling depth.)

Surveying Web sites

Web sites are collections of interlinked Web pages, much as a book is a collection of printed pages that a binding holds together. Notice, however, that the pages a site contains needn't contain related information. The subject matter a page contains has nothing to do with its capability to link to other pages. As a result, the pages of a Web site can cover a diverse array of subjects.

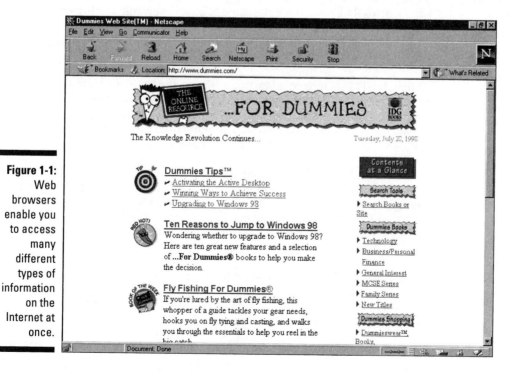

Figure 1-1: Web browsers enable you to access many different types of information on the Internet at once.

Although its creators are likely to dedicate a soccer site, for example, entirely to that sport, and a corporate site, such as a clothing store, is likely to contain pages relating to its product line, whether all the pages in a site stick to the topic is up to whoever creates the site (or owns the company). The soccer site can just as easily contain pages about knitting and macramé. For that matter, a clothing store site may even contain a few pages describing how to throw a memorable cocktail party.

Think of the Web as a giant filing cabinet, with each site as a manila folder inside the cabinet. Web pages, in turn, are documents inside these manila folders. Nothing prevents you from stuffing a mishmash of unrelated documents inside the folder, and nothing prevents a site from containing a bizarre combination of pages. Thus; the nature of the Web.

Hypertext Markup Language (HTML)

You create most Web pages by using a special language known as *Hypertext Markup Language* (HTML). This language enables you to organize text, graphics, animation, and sound into documents that a browser can understand. HTML is the glue that holds the Web together — the language that makes hypertext and hypermedia possible.

While the vast majority of Web pages are created using nothing more than HTML, new Web-based languages such as the Virtual Reality Modeling Language (VRML) and the Extensible Markup Language (XML) arrived in recent years. As a result, it's technically possible to create Web pages that don't contain a single line of HTML, although non-HTML Web pages are few and far between.

Although HTML is indeed a language, it's not the type of programming language that you typically associate with computers and software development. You don't need to study for years or earn a college degree to master HTML. Instead, HTML is a relatively friendly markup language that practically everyone can begin using within a day or two.

Markup languages define a formal set of rules and procedures for preparing text for electronically interpretation and presentation. In using HTML, for example, you surround text and references to files with special directives known as *tags*. You use tags to specify how the text or files are to appear when viewed in a Web browser — that is, to "mark up" the document in a way that the Web browser understands.

Using tags to mark up a document for electronic publication is easy. You can take a standard word processor document, add a dash or two of HTML, and — *voilà* — you create a Web page. Not bad, considering that creating a simple page can take just a few minutes.

In truth, a Web page is nothing more than a text file that contains references to any number of image, animation, and sound files that the browser retrieves, assembles, and displays as someone accesses that page. All files are stored independently of the pages in which they appear — that is, the Web pages that display the files don't also store them inside themselves. Instead, HTML merely *references,* or points to, these files, telling the browser exactly where to find them so that it can go out and get the files when it displays the page.

Figure 1-2 shows a portion of the HTML source code that creates the Web page appearing earlier in this chapter (refer to Figure 1-1). HTML may seem like gibberish at first, but after you spend a few days getting to know the language, it all starts making perfect sense. If mastering the language seems too daunting a task for you, however, you're probably happy to know that special–purpose tools exist to enable you to create Web pages without knowing a spec of HTML. But if you want a *really* dazzling Web page — one that you can gloriously enhance with Java — you do need to know a bit more about HTML.

Although Chapter 3 of this book starts you on your way with HTML, it's just a sip. To drink in all that HTML has to offer, check out *HTML For Dummies,* 3rd Edition, by Ed Tittel and Stephen N. James (IDG Books Worldwide, Inc.).

Figure 1-2:
Hypertext
Markup
Language
(HTML) is
the glue
that holds
the Web
together.

```
Source of: http://www.dummies.com/ - Netscape

<!DOCTYPE HTML PUBLIC "-//IETF//DTD HTML//EN">
<html>

<head>
<title>Dummies Web Site(TM)</title>
<meta http-equiv="Content-Type"
content="text/html; charset=iso-8859-1">
<META name="description" content="...For Dummies&reg; books, online resource for user-friendly co
ers.">
<META name="keywords"
content="books, dummies, for dummies books, idg books, idg, computer books, books online, online
s, online shopping, book resources">

</head>

<body bgcolor="#FFFFFF">
<div align="center"><center>

<table border="0" width="544">
    <tr>
        <td colspan=2><img  src="http://www.dummies.com//images/mastb.gif" valign="bottom" width=
<tr><td valign=top>The Knowledge Revolution Continues...</td>
<td align=right valign=top><font
        color="#808080" size="2">  Tuesday, July 28, 1998  </font></td>
    </tr>

</table>
</center></div><div align="center">
<p>
<center>

<table border="0" cellpadding="0" cellspacing="0" width="540">
```

Java: Caffeine for the World Wide Web

Although the Web is an incredible invention, unlike anything the world has seen before, it does have shortcomings. As the Web matures, myriad innovations are sure to address these shortcomings. Because Java is one such innovation that addresses many of the Web's current failings, it's become a red-hot topic.

About the time the World Wide Web was hatching in a particle-physics lab in Switzerland (way back in the early 1990s), California-based Sun Microsystems was embarking on an advanced-technology odyssey of its own. Although developed separately and, initially, for entirely different purposes, the World Wide Web and Sun's Java came together nearly four years later. Jointly the two innovations hold the promise of a second information revolution: a truly interactive Web.

Java is a programming language that enables software developers to create special little programs known as *applets*. Unlike the software programs that you use on your personal computer, applets live inside Web pages. If a Web browser encounters a page containing applets, something special happens. If the browser is *Java-savvy* (that is, if it understands what applets are and knows how to deal with them), it downloads the applets and hands them off to your computer to run. If the browser isn't Java-savvy, it simply ignores all the applets it encounters and displays Web pages without them.

Because applets are actually little software programs, you can program them to do just about anything. How a given applet behaves is up to the software developer who creates it. Java applets, for example, can play sounds, animate images, and enable you to interact with Web Pages in ways that were impossible before Java. Although the capabilities of applets range far and wide, as do the capabilities of standard software programs, Java applets all have one thing in common: They enhance the traditional Web built on standard HTML alone, bringing an otherwise static medium to life!

Although Java was one of the first and most significant enhancements to the Web, it's not the only way to bring pages to life. Today, many new technologies exist that liven up the Web. Dynamic HTML (DHTML) and the Extensible Markup Language (XML) are two such examples, and worth finding out more about. If you're interested in delving into Dynamic HTML or XML, pick up a copy of *Dynamic HTML For Dummies* by Michael I. Hyman and *XML For Dummies* by Ed Tittel, Norbert Mikula, and Ramesh Chandak (both published by IDG Books Worldwide, Inc.).

The Java language enables developers to create full-blown desktop applications, too, and not just applets that live in Web pages. Java's first and most important success, however, was realized on the Web. So the Web's the natural place to start exploring Java technology. To find out more about Java applications themselves, turn to Part III.

Thanks to miraculous little Java applets, Web pages can contain interactive games, spreadsheets, paint and draw capabilities, and just about anything else you now do on your computer. But the magic is that you don't access these features by using software programs that reside on your home computer; instead, you do so across the World Wide Web — as do millions of other people who are free to access the same Web pages at exactly the same time.

Delivering dynamic content

Before Java burst onto the scene, the Web was limited to *static content.* By *static,* I mean that the Web was designed to display information that doesn't change as you view it. Of course, static content is ideal for information such as magazine articles, recipes, tax forms, and the like, but it's woefully inadequate for *dynamic content* that changes over time such as constantly updated stock market prices or live news coverage.

Java overcame this natural limitation of the Web because it easily and efficiently delivers dynamic content over the Internet. Without Java, you can best describe standard HTML Web pages as snazzy electronic magazines and brochures. You can see images and text, but before Java came along, nothing could change or move, nor could you truly interact with what you saw. Life in the early days of the Web was . . . well, blah.

After people started injecting Java into Web pages, however, those pages truly came to life: Regularly updated stock-market ticker tapes slide across pages; buttons dance and sing; images jump around; and sound and music pour over the ether and out your computer speakers.

Introducing interactivity

Dynamic content is only half the battle against the war on static information. With dynamic content alone, you have little more than a computerized (and considerably slower) version of television and radio. To be of real use in the information age, information must be interactive.

Alternative routes to interactivity

Although a few nonstandard ways exist for providing interactivity on the Web, the only *standard* mechanism is known as the *Common Gateway Interface (CGI)*. Unfortunately, CGI is difficult to weave into Web pages and terribly limited in its capability to deliver interactivity — so limited, in fact, that most people don't consider CGI-enhanced pages truly interactive at all.

The main use of CGI is to enable you to enter text information on the Web through *forms*. By using CGI, you can type information into forms, as you do in using a search engine (for example, Yahoo!, Lycos, or AltaVista) or registering for a product. Although forms such as these examples aren't at all interactive, you can also use CGI for a more interactive purpose: to create image maps. *Image maps* are images containing different areas that you can click to hyperlink to separate URLs, thereby enabling visitors to click various sections of an image to access different places on a Web site. Web designers often use image maps as navigation toolbars in Web sites.

Although such capabilities are useful, that's about all you can do with CGI in terms of interactivity: Create forms and image maps. Java, on the other hand, can create forms, image maps, and much more. In addition, Java is much faster than CGI. As a result, Java is likely to make CGI obsolete in the near future.

If traditional Web pages, which people create using only standard HTML, don't support dynamic content, you can bet your sweet sanity that the content they deliver isn't interactive either. No, the best that the Javaless Web can offer is hyperlinked content. *Hyperlinked content* is text (or *hypertext*) and images (or *hypermedia*) that you can click and then jump to other pages of information. Sure, hyperlinked content is convenient, but it's a far cry from interactive content, my friend.

Without Java, and relying solely on standard HTML, you can only view information and click hyperlinked text and images to visit more information on the Web. You can't interact with that information. But interactivity is the key to compelling content. You don't want to merely *see* cool stuff coming across the wire — you want to add to it, change it, and work with it. You want to *interact* with it (see Figure 1-3).

The applet shown in Figure 1-3 is called Celebrity Painter and is available on the CD-ROM that comes with this book (refer to Appendix C). Celebrity Painter enables you to combine the faces of famous celebrities, meaning you can construct wacky and weird composites such as the one shown in this figure. You can weave the Celebrity Painter applet into your own Web pages (see Part II for details on creating Java-powered pages).

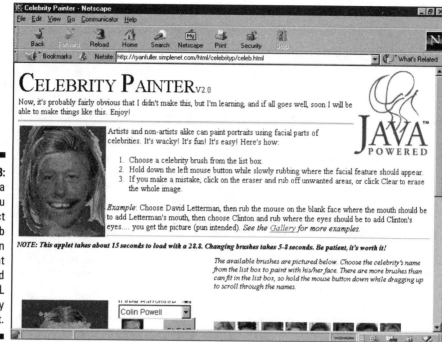

Figure 1-3:
Java
enables you
to interact
with Web
pages in
ways that
standard
HTML
simply
does not.

A confession: Interactivity is really nothing new to you and your personal computer, although you may not have thought much about it. Have you ever played a video game, drawn or painted an image, created an electronic slide show in a presentation package, recorded or altered sound or music, or done anything other than read, view, or listen to data on your personal computer? If so, you interacted with that data.

Interacting with data is something that everyone who uses a personal computer takes for granted. But the standard Web itself, without enhancements, is incapable of providing a truly interactive experience, relegating you to the role of passive viewer. With Java, which is the ultimate Web enhancement, you're in control — you're part of the action.

Delivering executable content

The key to Java's early success was its capability to deliver executable content over the Web. *Executable content* is what enables Web pages to contain dynamic and interactive content, where previously everything was static and lifeless. To understand executable content, you must understand what *execution* means. In the real world, executions are rare; life without parole is much more common. In the computer world, however, executions occur all the time.

Whenever you run a computer program, you're said to be "executing a piece of software." To write a letter, you must execute a word processor. To send electronic mail, you execute an e-mail package. Want to play a game? Paint a graphics image? Crunch a spreadsheet? Execute. Execute. Execute.

By *executing* a program, you effectively tell your computer to follow all the instructions that make up the program itself. *Programs* are really nothing more than a bunch of instructions that tell the computer how to present information and handle user input. Every program has its own set of instructions, specific to the task or set of tasks that it performs. After you execute a program, the computer carries out its instructions.

Your browser recognizes the applets that a particular Web page contains as something much more than static content. Rather than trying to display an applet, the browser hands it off to the personal computer and says, "Here's a little program, buddy — execute it!" This executable content is what Java is really all about. Executable content enables you to embed tiny programs in your Web pages so that, if someone accesses your page, the programs do their magic on your visitor's computer. As a result, dynamic and interactive content becomes a reality.

Because Java applets download directly to a user's personal computer and execute as actual software programs, applets can do just about anything you can imagine. Think of how many different programs are available for your personal computer. Now consider that Java enables people to embed the same type of programs in Web pages. You can perhaps understand now why such a buzz surrounds this new technology. Suddenly, anything that you can imagine — and much of what you can't imagine — becomes possible.

You may think at first that applets provide the perfect opportunity to invade your system with viruses, worms, or Trojan horses (all of which can infiltrate your computer system and cause you and your system grief in one way or another). Java, however, was designed from the get-go with security in mind. True, it's not foolproof. (Never say "Never!") But circumventing the various security checks that Java applets must pass through before they can execute on your computer would be incredibly difficult. Creating malicious or deceitful applets, therefore, would be quite a feat. For more information about applets and security issues, however, see Chapter 2.

Okay, So It's Not Perfect — Yet!

Okay, so I'm a Java zealot. I admit that. But I'm also open-minded enough to admit that Java isn't 100 percent perfect. (Shhh . . . it's our little secret.)

In truth, Java has come a very long way since it was first introduced, although it still has a fair distance to go before it's the be-all-end-all that the early hype led many Web users to believe. Originally, for example, applets couldn't print. Yes, it's a sad but true fact: The original crop of applets to hit the Web had no way of sending information to a printer! They simply weren't given that kind of power until recently — and for good reason. Would you want an applet that you didn't really trust taking over your printer? Not a chance, and so the original crop of applets had heavy-duty security restrictions placed on them.

Java was designed with security in mind, so applets don't get all the power of full-blown applications. After all, do you *really* know who's behind every Web page that you visit? Of course not; that's the beauty of the Web — you can click yourself dizzy, visiting countless sites using little more than your mouse. You never need to wonder about such questions as "Who created this page?" and "Can I trust the people behind this site?"

The reason that you can surf the Web just as freely as a hippie lived during the '60s comes down to one thing: lack of privilege. Web pages have no right nor capability to do anything at all with your computer. They can only appear on a Web browser — and that's about it. If you print a Web page today, your Web browser actually does the work — the page itself has no clue what's going on. It just sits around looking pretty.

The engineers at Sun originally made Java as limited in its knowledge of your computer as a Web page itself. They effectively lobotomized early Java applets to prevent them from doing anything beyond running inside a Java-savvy browser. Smarter capabilities have been built into Java since the good ol' days of yore, however, so you'll soon encounter applets that can print, store files on your computer, and even read the contents of files residing on your own hard drive.

Don't freak out quite yet! The kind engineers who built these smarter capabilities into Java understand how rogue applets may abuse such privileges and wreak serious damage on an unsuspecting system. So those same engineers devised a sophisticated set of checks and balances that enable you, the end user, to precisely control what level of access Java applets get to your computer.

Thanks to the security features built into the very fabric of Java, only you can grant applets intimate access to your computer. If you don't give an applet explicit access to your computer, it has no way of doing damage. And, because you're likely to give applets such access only if you really trust the party on whose Web page they appear (unless you're a technomasochist and love the abuse), the chance of granting a potentially dangerous applet access to your computer is pretty low.

Spilling the Beans: Java is Everywhere

Although the combination of Java and the World Wide Web is relatively new, it was such a perfect mix that it's already revolutionized the world of communications as we know it, as millions of Web users, or *Webbers,* can eagerly tell you. The excitement is particularly amazing considering that the first wave of Java-powered Web pages were rather primitive compared to what's really possible today.

Whenever someone asks me, "Hey, Aaron, what are the chances of the Boston Red Sox winning the World Series in your lifetime? And just out of curiosity, what does Java hold in store for the Web?" I have a canned answer waiting in the wings: "None and everything."

The Red Sox don't seem to have much hope. But with Java, you're dealing with a fresh technology and facing an absolutely unlimited field of dreams. Most of the Java applets that you find on the Web today are primarily from the first crop to hit the Internet, with only a small portion — a second and third generation of applets — actually showing Java's potential. In fact, most of the applets that you run into today aren't mind-blowing. But those new applets are becoming more compelling every day, and literally hundreds of thousands — and soon millions — of people from around the world are diving into Java.

By the year 2000, the vast majority of Web pages are certain to look and act nothing like they did a few years ago — or even as they do today for that matter. By then, you can expect the lion's share of Java-powered pages to have the same visual appeal as the best CD-ROM titles on the market today. And you can expect the same degree of interactivity, if not more. If you see Java on the Web and can remember what life was like before its advent, you can truly understand how Java has transformed the Web and computing as we know them. And the best is still to come.

To use my favorite analogy, compare the Web today to the state of television after it was first invented. The television that first reached into homes was terribly crude by today's standards. The picture quality was poor at best and wasn't even in color. To change the station, you needed to extract yourself from the cozy couch cushions to shuffle over and turn the knob. You didn't even have much of a selection compared to the hundreds of channels that you can get today through cable and satellite.

From a futurist's point of view, you can say the same for today's Java and the World Wide Web. They're generally crude compared to what's in store, but they're going to explode in complexity overnight — guaranteed. Computer technology advances at an astounding, sometimes unbelievable rate. Approximately every two years, computers double in speed and power while the software you run on them becomes more sophisticated, more appealing, and more packed full of features. Astonishing as it may seem, Java's been moving at an even faster pace, thanks to a global initiative and breakneck effort under way by millions of developers to make the Web as fast, smooth, and attractive as television — yet with the interactivity you expect from today's best CD-ROM titles.

By merely reading this book, you're standing knee-deep in a true revolution. Just look around and you're going to see great gains and enormous changes taking place in the next few years. This book shows you how to contribute your own musket to the charge by adding Java to your very own Web pages and installing your very own Java desktop applications. As you begin to add Java to your own pages and install Java applications on your computer, you may become aware of other Web pages that also make use of this irresistible technology — or bump into others who've also installed Java on their desktops. Already, Java is changing the way people learn, work, and play.

Martian Java

On July 4, 1997, Java landed on Mars — literally. The mobile Mars rover, called *Pathfinder*, landed on the surface of the red planet that day, powered in part by Java. Thanks to Java-powered applets on the Web, some 40 million earthlings peeked in on the rover each day during the first few weeks of our visit to the Martian planet.

And, thanks again to Java, you have the amazing capability to remotely control a Pathfinder simulator set against Mars' surface — using photographs sent back to earth from the real Pathfinder. You can, in essence, drive your own little rovers around Mars, checking out the terrain from the comfort of your office cubicle.

If you're itchin' to see the red planet for yourself, check out the java.sun.com/features/1997/july/mars.html Web site.

A Tonic for All Web Ills?

The Web was just the beginning of the world's relationship with Java. If you look hard enough, however, you see Java spilling out of the Web into all aspects of your life. Because the Java technology is so rich in breadth and depth, you can't limit it to the Web alone. You're likely to see it everywhere in the very near future, if not today: TVs, VCRs, appliances, and all other electronic consumer devices are ideal candidates for the Java invasion.

Today, the Java rush is on. Unlike any previous technology other than the Web itself, Java has ignited the world in a blaze of excitement and anticipation. Every day, thousands of programmers around the globe create new and exciting Web pages that feature content never before possible. As millions of people just like you and me load premade Java applets into their pages, we're adding fuel to the Java fire.

Soon, the majority of Web pages are going to take advantage of Java's executable content capabilities. After all, why have dead pages if you can bring your Web site to life?

Chapter 2

Java-Savvy Browsers

*B*efore you dive head first into Java, you must obtain and install a *browser* — the software that connects you to the Web. This chapter answers all your lingering questions about browsers: What's the difference between an ordinary browser and a Java-savvy browser? Which browser should you use? And how do you enable Java in your browser?

Browser, Smowser: What's the Big Deal?

Without a Web browser, you must navigate the Internet the old-fashioned way — by using a specialized tool for each type of information that you want to retrieve. You have no way of viewing graphical Web pages without a browser, which means that you miss the benefit of hyperlinks — *hypertext* (words with links to other Web pages) and *hypermedia* (images or movies with links) — to make navigation a snap. And if you can't use hyperlinks, you must manually retrieve each piece of information that you want, which means that you must find out where the information resides on the Web and then figure out how to get there. Without a Web browser, however, you're probably not even going to bother surfing the Web at all, because doing so takes so much time and effort — which is exactly why so many people avoided the Internet in its early days. Before Web browsers, the Internet was just too difficult and time-consuming for most people to bother with.

Not only is finding the specific piece of information you want nearly impossible without a browser, but even if you actually do manage to locate the document, you also must know what tool to use to retrieve it. And after you manage to copy, or *download,* the document to your own computer, you must figure out which program to use to view it. And even if you have a rough idea of the document's format, you must own a software program capable of displaying documents in that particular format.

Thanks to Web browsers, however, you don't need to worry about such difficulties. Instead of needing to know exactly where a file resides on the Internet, you can follow a hyperlink to that file — or better yet, you can use a sophisticated tool known as a *search engine* to find what you're looking for instantly. (See Appendix A for all the grisly details.) And after the link or search engine locates the information you want, the browser displays that information immediately — you don't need to bother downloading and saving files to your computer for use with yet another piece of software. A browser displays text, graphics, and animation and plays sounds as it encounters them.

You also can save information to your own computer for later use, if you want to. You can, however, access information on the Web simply by navigating from hyperlink to hyperlink without ever manually downloading anything to your computer. And, because Web browsers combine the functionality of several traditional Internet software programs, you don't need to understand a whole new set of tools to get the information you need. Just select a hyperlink, and the browser does the rest.

The Kilroy of the '90s

If you're like me, tearing yourself away from your computer is virtually impossible after you actively begin prowling the Web to look for Java applets and applications. You can *always* find another link to try or another site to visit. You soon while away your waking hours basking in the warm, comfortable glow of your computer monitor.

Your relationships with friends, relatives, and loved ones soon give way to the eternal bond that you form with Duke, the official Java mascot. A surprising number of Java developers use this adorable little creature if they need a graphics image and don't have one handy. Looking something like a Corn Nut carrying a red beach ball, Duke is sure to appear somewhere in your quest for fire.

This rakish devil appears to have infiltrated the Web. He's been spotted dancing, tumbling, waving, and operating a jackhammer, among other things. And lucky for us: Early mornings, long days, late nights, and weekends spent Java-surfing — mastering the subtle art of cruising the Web in search of cool Java applets and applications — may otherwise be a solitary endeavor. Thanks to Duke, however, you have a friend on the Web (and a Java-induced friend, at that).

Okay, So I Need a Web Browser — But What's a Java-Savvy Browser?

You probably know by now that you can't surf the Web if you don't have a browser — but do you know that not all browsers are the same? To view pages containing Java applets, you need to obtain and install a *Java-savvy* browser. Because Java applets are actually tiny programs that people embed inside Web pages (see Chapters 1 and 4 for details), the browser that you use must understand how to deal with such unique content. As a Java-savvy browser accesses Web pages, it automatically downloads and executes all Java applets inside the page. If you use a non-Java-savvy browser to view a page containing Java applets, the browser simply ignores the applets. After all, only Java-savvy browsers recognize applets and know how to download and execute them. If a non-Java-savvy browser comes across an applet, it simply goes, "Huh?" and skips right over it.

Without a Java-savvy browser, expect to be sorely disappointed visiting Java-applet-enhanced Web sites, because you can't see or interact with the applet-enhanced portions of the page. If you're using a Java-savvy browser, however, a dazzling world of Web-page wonders is just a few mouse clicks away.

Not all computer systems, however, can run Java-savvy browsers. Currently, users of the following systems can cash in on the Java craze:

- Intel-based machines running Microsoft Windows NT, Windows 95, Windows 98, or Windows 3.1.
- Apple Macintosh (and Power Macintosh) machines running System 7.5 or later.
- Sun SPARC-based machines running Solaris 2.3 or later.
- Silicon Graphics machines running Irix 5.2 or later.
- Systems running IBM AIX.
- Systems running DEC Digital UNIX.
- Systems running Linux.

The Many Flavors of Java-Savvy Browsers

A few years ago, Java-savvy browsers were scarce — Java was brand-spanking-new at that time. Today, however, the story is entirely different — Java is an incredibly hot commodity these days, with just about everyone who uses the Web clamoring for access to it. As a result, most companies that make browsers have added support for Java to their products. The question of the day is, "What flavor of Java-savvy browser is best for me?"

Choosing a Java-savvy browser is a little like choosing a pet — it's largely a personal decision. You have several browsers from which to choose, each slightly different from the others in features and appearance. You can choose currently from the following three leading Java-savvy browsers:

- ✔ Netscape Navigator
- ✔ Microsoft Internet Explorer
- ✔ HotJava from Sun Microsystems

If you have a choice, you may consider using the latest version of Netscape Navigator. Because Navigator is still the most popular browser in the world (although Explorer is catching up fast), you can't go wrong by choosing this market leader. Not only do you get the most advanced browser on the market, but you're likely to find that a bunch of your fellow Webbers are using it, too.

In some cases, you don't have a choice of browsers. If you're connecting to the Web through a commercial online service, such as America Online, CompuServe, or Prodigy, you may not have the option of choosing a browser other than the one that your service provides (which, right now, is usually Internet Explorer).

Regardless of the browser you choose, as long as it's Java-savvy, you don't need to worry about having the right tool for the job — if your browser's Java-savvy, it's up to the task at hand.

HotJava

The world's first Java-savvy browser, HotJava, was created by the same company that created Java (see Figure 2-1). HotJava was developed by the Sun Microsystems Java Software group, specifically to showcase its Java technology. For Sun, creating the first Java-savvy browser was, in fact, a necessity.

After Sun developed Java, it built a brand-new Web browser, one capable of displaying non-Java Web pages as well as those embedded with Java applets. Written entirely in Java, HotJava was a technological marvel at the time it was released. (See the accompanying sidebar "Applets versus applications.") It displayed standard Web pages and could also handle the executable content delivered in applet form.

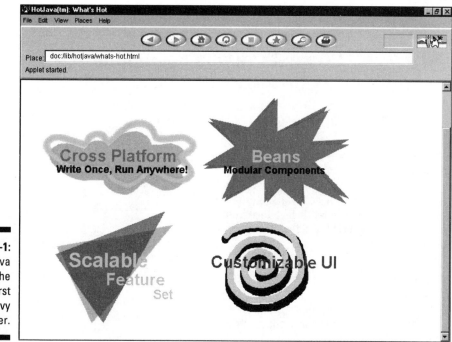

Figure 2-1:
HotJava
was the
world's first
Java-savvy
browser.

HotJava was the first browser that *learns* about the Web as it browses, which means that, if HotJava encounters information or protocols it doesn't understand, it dynamically learns how to deal with them. Instead of requiring a browser software upgrade every time new technology comes along — which seems to happen nearly every day — HotJava extends itself on the fly through an innovative feature known as *handlers*. Handlers are kinda like brain implants that Java-savvy browsers call on to handle new information or protocols. Whenever someone develops a new protocol or type of content for the Web, he or she can also develops a corresponding Java handler. Then, if a Java-savvy browser comes across the unknown content or protocol, it instantly learns how to cope with it by using the corresponding handler.

Note: Although HotJava was the first Java-savvy browser, it certainly isn't the most popular. Netscape Navigator and Microsoft Internet Explorer are, by far, the browsers that most people use. But HotJava remains significant nonetheless.

Applets versus applications

The Java technology, rich in breadth and depth, doesn't just bring Web pages to life. Java can, in fact, do much more, as you find out in Part III of this book.

In essence, Java is a new software-development language. By using Java, you can create any software program that you can imagine — and many that you couldn't begin to dream of before Java was invented. In fact, the HotJava browser was developed through use of the Java language!

HotJava is actually an application and not an applet, meaning that it doesn't exist inside a Web page. Unlike applets, which are tiny programs that you embed in Web pages, Java applications are just like any other software program that you use. You execute Java applications the same way that you execute any other programs on your computer.

Unlike standard applications, however, Java applications are often deeply enmeshed with the Internet, because the Java language makes developing network products, such as HotJava, relatively easy. Standard software-development languages, such as C and Pascal, were invented long before the Internet exploded in popularity. As a result, creating network-capable products in such languages is painstaking and tedious if you compare them to what the Java programming language offers.

The Java language, invented only a handful of years ago, was designed with networks in mind. As a result, programs that you develop by using Java automatically understand how to connect to the Internet, retrieve information from it, and send information across it. This capability is why applets and applications, the two types of software programs that you can create in the Java language, so deeply intertwine with the Internet and the World Wide Web.

Sun never intended for HotJava to compete head to head with mainstream browsers. HotJava was originally intended as (and has remained) a *concept browser,* designed to showcase the Java technology and to prompt other browser vendors to include support for Java in their products. Clearly, the concept was a hit. After HotJava's introduction, all major browser vendors rushed back to the drawing board to make their products Java-savvy. Today, HotJava continues to lead the pack in terms of pure technological Java prowess, and the other browsers continue to follow this modern-day Pied Piper.

Netscape Communicator and Navigator

Netscape Navigator was developed by Netscape Communications Corporation, which is consistently on the cutting edge of browser technology. Navigator, in fact, is largely responsible for the massive buzz surrounding the Web. In the good old days (about three years ago!), Netscape's primary claim to fame was its Navigator browser. Today, things are a little different. Navigator has given way to a product known as *Communicator,* which has more bells and whistles than you can shake an electric stick at.

Communicator is actually a set of products, of which the Navigator browser is one part. By using Communicator, you can browse the Web with the latest, slickest version of Navigator; create and publish your own Web pages, courtesy of Composer; send and receive e-mail using Messenger; conduct live chats over the Internet; and much more. Undoubtedly, Communicator is an impressive collection of software products that you use expressly for communicating over the Internet. In fact, Netscape Communicator 4.5 (the latest and greatest version of the product) provides so many cool ways to communicate that I wish I had more friends and a larger family with whom to communicate.

To get Navigator up and running, you need to understand the three different groups of controls visible at the top of the browser window, as shown in Figure 2-2.

Personal Toolbar   Navigation Toolbar   Location Toolbar

Figure 2-2:
The three
toolbars in
Navigator.

Navigator: Blowing past Mosaic

When Netscape Navigator was introduced way back in December 1994, it was several times faster than the predominant browser of the time, NCSA Mosaic. In addition, Navigator was more flexible in the types of data and protocols it understood. Without a doubt, Navigator was the Cadillac of Web browsers. Bursting ahead of NCSA Mosaic, Navigator took an early lead in the browser race and never looked back; today, Mosaic is so far behind the times that most people don't even know that it's still available. Within the first nine months of its release, more than ten million people were using the Navigator to browse the Web. Millions more have made Navigator their browser of choice since then, thanks to its superior speed and flexibility.

These three groups of controls consist of the following toolbars:

- ✔ **Navigation Toolbar:** These buttons correspond to the Navigator commands that you use most frequently.

- ✔ **Location Toolbar:** The Location Toolbar enables you to view addresses (URLs) or type URLs manually (in the Location text area) so that you can connect directly to a Web page if you know its corresponding URL. The Bookmark button provides quick and easy access to your favorite Web sites. By using this button, you can also *bookmark* a specific site after you visit it, which then enables you to return to that site at a later time without needing to remember or type the entire URL. In addition, a What's Related button on the far right-hand side of this toolbar gives you quick and easy access to Web pages that are similar in content to the one that you're currently viewing.

- ✔ **Personal Toolbar:** These buttons provide quick access to a few of the most useful sites on the Web, helping you navigate its vast contents.

By default, these three controls appear on the Navigator browser from top to bottom (refer to Figure 2-2) in order of significance; you're likely to use the Navigation Toolbar the most, followed by the Location Toolbar and then the Personal Toolbar. Of course, this rule isn't set in stone; it's just an educated guess based on experience and what each feature offers. You're free to rearrange and move the toolbars as you see fit, which means you can customize the order in which they appear to best suit your needs.

If you find that you aren't using one (or more) of the Navigator controls, you can remove it entirely from the screen by deselecting it from the Options menu. Removing a group of controls from the screen gives you more space to view Web pages. For the most space possible, remove all three groups of controls from the screen. Because all features are accessible via keyboard or menu commands, you don't lose their functionality at all; you just can't see them on the browser window and don't have handy access to these commands.

Navigation Toolbar

The Navigator Navigation Toolbar consists of several buttons that correspond to the browser's commands you use most commonly. Each of these items is also available through a menu item, so you can access them either way. The Navigation Toolbar offers the following features:

✔ **Back and Forward:** Of the available Navigation Toolbar buttons, you probably use the Back and Forward buttons the most. Clicking these buttons (which correspond to options in the Go menu) enables you to revisit pages that you encounter during your current Web-surfing session. To return to the page you visited immediately before the one you're currently viewing, click the Back button. After you arrive at that page, you can return to the page where you clicked the Back button by clicking the Forward button.

You can click Back and Forward several times in a row to revisit pages farther back (or forward) in your current surfing session. If, for example, you want to revisit a page that you encountered five pages ago, just click the Back button five times. But you're better off simply selecting that page from the Go menu instead of clicking Back over and over (or you can even click and hold your mouse down for a few seconds over the Back button for faster access to the menu items displayed in the Go menu)! The Go menu takes you directly to the page that you select, whereas the Back button stops at each page in between the one that you want to view and the one you're currently viewing.

✔ **Reload:** Clicking the Reload button reloads the current page, retrieving it from the Web as if you're connecting to the page for the first time. This option helps if you're viewing a page that's jumbled because it didn't transmit all its data correctly. Simply click Reload, and presto — the page comes in fresh from the Web.

✔ **Home:** Clicking the Home button takes you directly to the startup Web page. By default, this page is the Netscape Communications Corporation home page, although you can set it to any page that you want (by choosing Edit➪Preferences to open the Preferences dialog box and changing the Navigator item that appears there).

✔ **Search:** Clicking the Search button takes you to Navigator's search engines, which enable you to search the Web for topics that interest you. You can search for Web pages relevant to the information that you're looking for by typing keywords in the Search text boxes (such as **car**, or **iguana**, or **Pig Latin**) and then clicking the Search button. You can also use the search engine's category hyperlinks to help narrow down your search or even search the online Yellow Pages by clicking that link.

✔ **My Netscape:** Clicking the My Netscape button takes you to a special area on Netscape's Web site called, fittingly, My Netscape. The My Netscape area is a Web page that you can customize to show information that is of interest to you and you alone.

✔ **Print:** Clicking the Print button is equivalent to choosing File⇨Print. Both actions enable you to send a Web page to your printer (if you have a printer).

✔ **Security:** Clicking the Security button shows you detailed information relating to the security features of Navigator. To find out more about security, choose Help⇨Help Contents from the Navigator menu bar and then click the Security link that appears. I talk more specifically about security later in this chapter.

✔ **Stop:** One of the toolbar buttons that you use most often, Stop instructs the browser to stop loading the current page. If you find that a page is taking an excessive amount of time to load, you can click the Stop button and then choose Reload, forcing the browser to establish a brand-new connection to the page.

Location Toolbar

The Navigator Location Toolbar appears by default just below the Navigation Toolbar (see Figure 2-3). As you may guess, you use the Bookmarks button to save *bookmarks,* or shortcuts, to your favorite Web pages. If you encounter a page that you want to bookmark, just click this button and choose the Add Bookmark item from the pop-up menu that appears under your cursor. Navigator then *bookmarks* the name of the page, and it appears in a list along with any other pages that you may have previously bookmarked. To visit a bookmarked page, simply click the Bookmarks button and choose that page from the pop-up list of Web pages that appears.

Figure 2-3:
The
Navigator
Location
Toolbar
features the
Bookmarks
button
and the
Location
area.

Bookmarks Location: file:///C|/WINDOWS/DESKTOP/Barb - File/JFD/helloworld/TestMediaHello.htm   What's Related

To the right of the Bookmarks button is the Location area (also known as a Netsite area), which serves two purposes: It tells you where you are by displaying the URL of the current page, and it enables you to quickly access a page by typing the page's corresponding URL. To connect to a Web page by using the Location area, simply type the URL for that page and press Enter on your keyboard.

To the right of the Location area is the What's Related button. When you click the What's Related button, a pop-up list appears that contains the names of Web pages that are similar in content to the one you're currently viewing. To visit a related page, simply choose its name from the What's Related pop-up menu. The concept behind the What's Related button is simple, really: Why spend a lot of time and effort using a search engine when what you're looking for is conceptually related to a page that you're already viewing?

Personal Toolbar

The Navigator Personal Toolbar, as shown in Figure 2-4, provides quick access to some of the more useful sites on the Web, helping you to navigate the Web's vast contents. Although each of its buttons connects you to a valuable site, perhaps the most interesting is the New&Cool button. Clicking this button reveals two menu items: New and Cool.

✔ Selecting the New item takes you to a Web page on Netscape's site that contains a list of brand-spanking-new sites that you may consider visiting. In addition to providing hyperlinks to these new sites, the good folks at Netscape actually take the time to rate these new sites on a scale of 1 to 10.

✔ Selecting the Cool item takes you to a page on Netscape's site dedicated to, well, "cool" Web pages. If you're curious as to just what makes a site cool, all you have to do is visit a few of these pages and you'll be in the know. So far the Cat Scan Contest is my favorite cool site. Hey, who hasn't wanted to press their pet feline into an image scanner and upload the resulting picture to the Web at one time or another?

Figure 2-4:
The Navigator Personal Toolbar includes cool links to useful sites.

Customizing your browser

To get the most out of your new Java-savvy browser, you can customize it to fit your personal needs and interests. To customize Navigator or Explorer, use the various items that appear in the dialog box after you choose Edit⇨Preferences (in Navigator) or View⇨Options (in Explorer). These items include ways to customize your browser, from changing the color and style of hyperlinks to setting a startup Web page and even to disabling the automatic loading of images for a dramatic speed increase while browsing the Web.

To find out about the many ways in which you can customize your browser, choose Help⇨Help Contents from the menu bar. This action opens the online Help manual, where you find everything that you can ever want to know about your browser!

If you're new to Navigator or want to find out more about the Navigator product, you should use the Help menu on the main menu bar. Choose Help⇨Help Contents (the first item in the Help menu) as the first place to start — and you even receive detailed instructions on how to use Java within Navigator. But don't bother with the Help menu if you're anxious to get going with Java; just read "Pedal to the Medal — Enabling Java" later in this chapter.

Microsoft Internet Explorer

Although Navigator has reigned supreme since first exploding onto the Web scene, Microsoft is hard at work trying to steal a little of the thunder, if not the entire storm, that Navigator has generated.

Microsoft Internet Explorer is now a major player in the Java-savvy browser market since introducing Internet Explorer 3.0 several years ago. Every new Windows 95 and Windows 98 computer comes with Internet Explorer built in, which means that millions of new computer buyers potentially become new Internet Explorer users at the same time. What else would you expect from the company that brought you Windows, Word, Excel, PowerPoint, Encarta, and a raft of other award-winning software products?

Thanks to the muscle Microsoft can flex in striking deals, Explorer is beginning to replace the non-Java-savvy browsers that many online services provide.

The fact is that Internet Explorer is a great browser. Concerning Java support, Microsoft claims that Internet Explorer is significantly faster than Navigator in running applets. I tend to believe this claim because the Java-powered Web pages that I view while using Internet Explorer seem to download faster and run at a slightly higher speed than the same pages do in Navigator. (Applets that produce animations, for example, appear faster and are smoother looking if you view them with Internet Explorer rather than with Navigator.) Navigator, however, is no slouch either — the difference between the two is almost negligible, and you probably don't notice any increase in performance in Internet Explorer unless you're paying close attention.

The user interface for Internet Explorer is much the same as that of Netscape Navigator, although the terminology that each browser uses is slightly different (see Figure 2-5). Navigator, for example, uses the term *Navigation Toolbar* to describe the toolbar that contains navigational buttons, such as Back, Forward, and Stop; Internet Explorer uses the term *Standard Buttons Toolbar* instead. Functionally, these two toolbars are more or less the same, with only minor differences between the two. But first, take a moment to review Table 2-1, which lists the names of the three basic toolbars available in each browser.

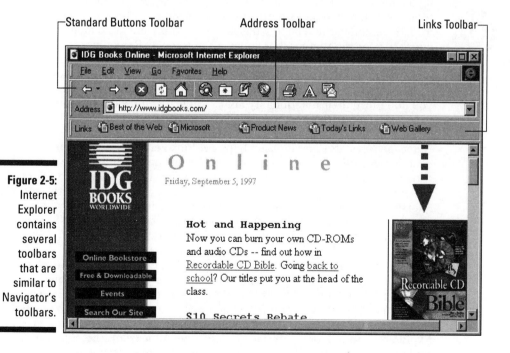

Figure 2-5: Internet Explorer contains several toolbars that are similar to Navigator's toolbars.

Table 2-1	The Three Basic Toolbars
Netscape Navigator	*Internet Explorer*
Navigation Toolbar	Standard Buttons Toolbar
Location Toolbar	Address Toolbar
Personal Toolbar	Links Toolbar

Just as with Navigator, the Internet Explorer toolbars appear in order of significance; you're likely to use the Standard Buttons Toolbar most often, followed by the Address Toolbar, and then the Links Toolbar. Of course, how you use these toolbars is entirely up to you. You may find that the Address Toolbar is the most useful to you — or even the Links Toolbar. You can, therefore, rearrange the Internet Explorer toolbars in the order that best fits your needs. To arrange your toolbars, simply click the thin vertical line that appears at the far left of a toolbar and drag it to the position where you want to locate that toolbar. After you release the mouse button, the toolbar moves to that place on-screen; other toolbars automatically reposition to accommodate the one you move.

If you find that you really don't use one (or more) of the Internet Explorer toolbars, you may remove it from the screen entirely. Choose View⇨Toolbars from the menu bar and simply deselect from the Toolbars dialog box the check box for the toolbar that you want to remove. Removing a toolbar from the screen gives you more space for viewing Web pages. For the most space possible, remove all three toolbars from the screen. Because the features each toolbar offers are accessible via keyboard or menu commands too, you don't lose their functionality at all; you just can't see them on the browser window.

Netscape Navigator and Internet Explorer look very much the same, and each browser offers a similar set of toolbars for navigating the Web. Although the toolbars each browser uses are very similar, however, they're not exactly the same. Because I discuss the Navigator toolbars in the section "Netscape Communicator and Navigator," earlier in this chapter, I give you a closer look in the following sections, to help you see where the differences lie among the toolbars that Internet Explorer offers.

Note: Although not set in stone, Internet Explorer 5.0 will likely feature the same toolbars, buttons, and menu items as those you find in Internet Explorer 4.0 (the most current shipping version of the product). From what I've seen of Internet Explorer 5.0, which was available in an early beta test form as this book goes to print, it's almost exactly the same as Internet Explorer 4.0 from a user interface perspective. Unless Internet Explorer 5.0 undergoes a radical toolbar, button, and menu item overhaul, the user interface descriptions for Version 4.0 that follow will also apply to Version 5.0 of the browser.

Standard Buttons Toolbar

The Internet Explorer Standard Buttons Toolbar contains several buttons that correspond to the browser commands that you use most commonly. Each of the following commands is also available through a menu item, so you can access them either way:

✔ **Back and Forward:** Of the buttons on the Standard Buttons Toolbar, the Back and Forward buttons are probably the ones that you use the most. You can click these buttons (which correspond to options in the Go menu) to revisit pages that you've already seen during your current Web-surfing session. To return to the page you visited immediately before the one you're currently viewing, click Back. After you arrive at that page, you can return to the page where you clicked the Back button by clicking Forward.

You can click Back and Forward several times in a row to revisit pages farther back (or forward) in your current surfing session. If, for example, you want to revisit a page that you saw five pages ago, just click the Back button five times. But you're better off simply selecting that page from the Go menu instead of clicking Back over and over! The Go menu takes you directly to the page that you select, whereas the Back button stops at each page in between the one you want and the one you're currently viewing.

✔ **Stop:** One of the buttons on the toolbar that you use most often, Stop instructs the browser to stop loading the current page. If you're at a page that's taking too long to load, click the Stop button and then choose Refresh, which forces the browser to establish a brand-new connection to the page.

✔ **Refresh:** Clicking the Refresh button reloads the current page, retrieving it from the Web as if connecting to it for the first time. This option helps if you're viewing a page that's jumbled because the data it contains didn't transmit entirely. In this case, simply click Refresh, and presto — the page comes in fresh from the Web.

✔ **Home:** Clicking the Home button takes you directly to the startup Web page. By default, this page is the Microsoft home page, although you can set it to any page that you want (by choosing View⇨Options to open the Options dialog box).

✔ **Search:** Clicking the Search button displays Internet Explorer's search engines, such as the NetFind search engine, which enable you to search the Web for topics that interest you. Using search engines such as NetFind, you can scour the Web for pages that relate to the information you're seeking by simply typing keywords (such as **car**, **iguana**, or **Pig Latin**) and then clicking the engine's Find button.

- ✔ **Favorites:** Internet Explorer's Favorites are the equivalent of Netscape Navigator's bookmarks. Clicking the Favorites button enables you to view and access all the Web addresses (URLs) that you add to this menu, if any. (Notice that clicking the Favorites buttons enables you only to view and access Web sites. To *add* a new favorite, you must choose Favorites⇨Add to Favorites from the menu bar.)

- ✔ **History:** Clicking the History button shows a listing of all the Web pages you recently visited, enabling you to quickly return to a previously visited site, even if you haven't bothered to add it to your Favorites. To visit a Web page that appears in the History list, simply click its name.

- ✔ **Channels:** Clicking the Channels button displays the various Web sites that may broadcast directly to your personal computer. In the same way that television shows broadcast over the airwaves, Internet Explorer gives Web site developers the capability to customize their pages for broadcast over the Internet. By clicking the Channels button, you can view and subscribe to these Web broadcasts.

- ✔ **Print:** Clicking the Print button is equivalent to choosing File⇨Print. Both actions send a Web page to your printer (if you have a printer).

- ✔ **Font:** Clicking the Font button displays a pop-up menu that enables you to either increase or decrease the text size that Internet Explorer uses to display Web pages. If Web pages are too difficult to read because of the size of the text, click the Font button and increase or decrease the font size accordingly. The pop-up menu that appears also contains items that enable you to specify a particular alphabet to use in displaying Web page text. (The default is a font known as Western alphabet.)

- ✔ **Mail:** Clicking the Mail button opens a pop-up menu from which you can choose to send or read e-mail. (That's assuming, of course, that you've configured Internet Explorer to deal with e-mail. If not, you can click the Mail button, which leads you through the process of hooking up Internet Explorer's e-mail capabilities.)

Address Toolbar

The Internet Explorer Address Toolbar (as shown in Figure 2-6) appears by default just below the Standard Buttons Toolbar. Just as does the Location area in the Netscape Navigator Location Toolbar, the Internet Explorer Address Toolbar serves two purposes: It tells you where you are by display- ing the URL of the current page, and it enables you to quickly access a page by typing the page's URL. To connect to a Web page by using the Address Toolbar, simply type the URL for that page and press Enter on your keyboard.

Figure 2-6:
The
Address
Toolbar
displays the
current
URL.

Links Toolbar

Similar to the Navigator Personal Toolbar, the Internet Explorer Links Toolbar
contains a variety of buttons that give you quick access to some of the more
useful sites on the Web to help you navigate the Web's vast contents (see
Figure 2-7). Although each of these buttons connects to a valuable site,
perhaps the most interesting button is Best of the Web. Clicking this button
takes you to some of the, well, best sites on the World Wide Web.

Figure 2-7:
The Links
Toolbar
connects
you to
valuable
Web sites.

| Links | Best of the Web | Microsoft | Product News | Today's Links | Web Gallery |

If you're new to Internet Explorer 4.0 or if you want to find out more about
the product, try using the Help menu on the main menu bar. I strongly
suggest that you check out the Help menu first: It is, without a doubt, the
first feature of Internet Explorer with which you want to become familiar,
because it provides direct access to all the online Help documents and
guides that you need to get the most out of Internet Explorer.

Finding a Browser on the Web

If you already use the Web, you don't have a problem getting your hands on
a Java-savvy browser. Because all browsers are available on the Web, you
can simply connect to one of the sites I list in Table 2-2 to download your
Java-savvy browser of choice. After you download the new browser to your
personal computer, installing it is a snap.

Browser vendors give away their products online to get customers such as you to use them; they make their money by licensing the same products to large companies (such as Internet Service Providers — ISPs). The catch, however, is that technical support usually doesn't come for free. If you want to call or e-mail the vendor with questions or problems, you usually must pay a fee. As a general rule, browsers are trouble-free, so before you slap down cold, hard cash for technical support, test-drive the puppy for a while to see whether you really need any support.

Table 2-2	Java-Savvy Browsers on the World Wide Web		
Browser	*Version*	*Supported Platforms*	*Web Address*
Netscape Navigator	2.0, 3.0, 4.0, 4.5	Windows NT/95/98, Macintosh, Sun Solaris, Silicon Graphics, and most flavors of UNIX	(home page) `home.netscape.com/;` (download page) `home.netscape.com/ comprod/mirror/ client_download.html`
Microsoft Internet Explorer	3.0, 4.0, 5.0	Windows NT/95/98, Macintosh	(home page) `www.microsoft.com/;` (download page) `www.microsoft.com/ ie/msie.htm`
HotJava	1.0, 1.1	Windows NT/95/98, Sun Solaris SPARC-based machines	`java.sun.com/ products/hotjava/`

If you don't already use the Web, you should set up an Internet account at some point. After all, why bother creating Java-powered Web pages if you can't share them with the world when you're done? Sure, you can keep them to yourself or even place your Web pages on a private, self-contained network (also known as an intranet), but why not go the extra mile and make them available to the world via the Web? In general, you can gain access to the World Wide Web in either of the following two ways:

✔ Through an ISP.

✔ Through a commercial online service, such as America Online, CompuServe, or Prodigy.

If you're in the market for an ISP, you really need to choose one that not only gives you access to the Web, but also enables you to create your own Web pages. Although most service providers automatically grant their customers the right to create personal Web pages, not all providers do.

Providing access to the Internet is a booming business. With literally thousands of service providers from which to choose, making sense of the myriad offerings can be a bit daunting. To help cut to the chase and get you on the Web in short order, the CD-ROM that comes with this book includes a listing of several top-rated service providers. (See Appendix C for details about using the *Java For Dummies,* 3rd Edition, CD-ROM.)

Pedal to the Metal — Enabling Java

To get off the ground and get cooking with Java, you must ensure that you configure your browser correctly to deal with Java applets. Although Navigator and Explorer both come with Java already on, future versions of these browsers may not have this option all ready to go. (Java is always enabled in HotJava, so you can't disable Java support even if you wanted to when using this browser.) And if you share your computer with others, someone may accidentally disable Java!

You may begin to suspect that Java is disabled if everything seems dead as you surf the Web. Because applets don't execute if your browser's Java support is off, Java-powered pages appear dull and lifeless. If you ever happen on pages that you're sure contain Java applets, yet nothing exciting or cool happens, your browser's Java option is probably disabled. The following list tells you how to know for certain:

✔ If you're using Netscape Navigator 4.5, the only way to know for sure whether Java is disabled on your browser is to choose Edit⇨Preferences from the menu bar. The Preferences dialog box appears, enabling you to customize various settings.

To view your Java settings, select the Advanced list item from the list of names that appears, which is at the left side of the Preference dialog box. Several options then appear in the right side of the dialog box (see Figure 2-8). These options include two check boxes that you can use to enable or disable Java and JavaScript. If you want to tap into the full power of Java, make sure that both these items are selected, and then click the OK button displayed at the bottom of the Preferences dialog box. (For more information on JavaScript, see Appendix B.)

✔ Internet Explorer 4.0 users, on the other hand, can determine whether their browser is ready to view Java-powered pages by checking the browser's Security Zones settings. You access these settings by choosing View⇨Options from the menu bar. The Options dialog box appears, as shown in Figure 2-9. Select the Security Zones tab of the dialog box, select the Custom radio button option, and then click the Settings button. Upon clicking the Settings button a new dialog box called

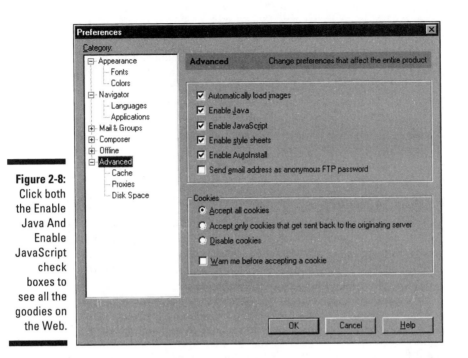

Figure 2-8:
Click both
the Enable
Java And
Enable
JavaScript
check
boxes to
see all the
goodies on
the Web.

Security Settings appears. Scroll down the list of settings options that appear in the Security Settings dialog box (as shown in Figure 2-10) until Java appears in the list; click the Java item. You should see an option to disable Java, which you can use to turn support for Java on or off (clicking this radio button disables Java).

From what I've seen of Internet Explorer 5.0, users of this version of the browser enable and disable Java in exactly the same was as those using Internet Explorer 4.0.

If you use Internet Explorer 4.0 or 5.0, keep in mind that options settings are based on *zones,* or areas, of Web content — general categories that Explorer uses to describe the types of Web content you're likely to encounter. (Figure 2-9 shows the four zones.) The Internet zone is the default zone if you view Internet Explorer options, although you can specify unique settings for three additional zones: Local intranet zone, Trusted sites zone, and Restricted sites zone. If you want to completely disable Java support, you must do so for each zone (that is, you must disable Java four different times — one for each zone that appears under the Security Zones tab of the Options dialog box). Choose Help⇨Help Contents while running Internet Explorer for more information on zones.

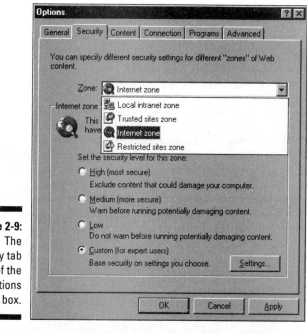

Figure 2-9:
The
Security tab
of the
Options
dialog box.

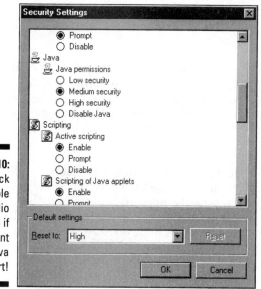

Figure 2-10:
Don't click
the Disable
Java radio
button if
you want
Java
support!

Applet Security: Playing Safely in the Sandbox

Although Java applets greatly enhance Web pages thanks to their ability to deliver executable content (see Chapter 1 for details), they also pose a serious security threat to your computer. In truth, any form of executable content (such as Java or Microsoft ActiveX, an alternative to Java) poses some level of security concern because executable content is program code that runs, or executes, inside a Web browser. As with any code, unrestricted executable content can delete or otherwise damage files on your computer.

Fortunately, Java was built from the ground up with security in mind. The jolly engineers who invented Java were sharp enough to recognize the potential damage that unrestricted executable content could wreak. To prevent unscrupulous and malicious programmers from abusing Java, serious restrictions were placed on applets. As a result, programmers who use the Java language to develop applets can't perform dangerous acts such as accessing your hard drive without first obtaining permission to do so.

Unlike Java applets, which are restricted in a number of ways, Java applications are free to do anything they like — delete files on your computer, create files for their own purpose, and even connect to the network without restriction. As a result, you must be extremely careful when installing Java applications (or any application, for that matter). Turn to Chapter 13 for more about Java applications.

Unfortunately, the severe security restrictions imposed on the original crop of applets also made it difficult to create powerful programs. That is to say, the very restrictions placed on applets crippled them from the get-go due to applets' inability to read or store information in files residing on your hard drive or to make connections to a network host other than the one they reside on.

Happily, several improvements have been made with respect to Java security over the years. In an attempt to solve the shortcomings of the original language, new and improved security measures are now available with the latest crop of applets. Whereas Java 1.0 applets have the most extreme security restrictions imposed on them, later versions of the language are more relaxed. Specifically, Java 1.1 and Java 1.2 allow applets to step out of the security "sandbox" as the following sections explain.

Java 1.0: Sandbox restrictions

Applets created with the original version of Java live entirely in a security "sandbox." As Chapters 13 and 14 discuss, Java 1.0 applets (applets written using versions 1.0, 1.0.1 and 1.0.2 of the Java language) aren't allowed to reach outside of the browser in which they run. They are, instead, forced to play inside an imaginary sandbox conceptually represented by your browser. Java 1.0 applets also cannot make a network connection to any host other than the one on which they reside. An applet residing at www.mantiscorp.com, for example, can only make a network connection to that host. It cannot connect to another host such as www.dummies.com.

Java 1.1: All-or-nothing "trust" through signatures

Java 1.1 (which covers versions 1.1, 1.1.1, 1.1.2, 1.1.3, 1.1.4, 1.1.5, and 1.1.6 of the language!) introduced the concept of "trust" through the use of digital signatures. The concept is simple: You can trust applets that you know to be harmless, as well as those that come from a reliable and trustworthy source. Trusted applets can step out of the sandbox, meaning they can access files on your hard drive and make network connections to hosts other than the one they reside on. Untrusted applets, on the other hand, must play inside the sandbox.

Of course, before you can trust an applet, you first must have some way of knowing where it comes from. Enter the notion of a digital signature. Similar to a notarized signature in the real world, *digital signatures* offer a reliable way to identify a person or entity (such as a company). Instead of being inscribed with pen and ink, applets can be inscribed with an electronic code. This code, or digital signature, is *encrypted* (scrambled in such a way that renders it unreadable by humans) and tamper-proof.

Applets bearing a digital signature are said to be *signed.* Signed applets, in essence, offer the computer equivalent of an alibi; they tell you where an applet comes from (the distributor) and who created it (the applet developer). If you can trust either the developer or the distributor of an applet, it stands to reason that you can trust the applet itself.

Unfortunately, Java 1.1 security is an "all-or-nothing" concept. After you trust an applet, it's free to do whatever it wants. A trusted applet that needs only to read a file on your computer, for example, also has complete and unbridled access to your system and the network. Because security in Java 1.1 is based on an all-or-nothing level of trust, the level of security granted to applets written with this version of the language applets is often overkill compared to what they truly need.

Trust no one!

By default, your Web browser is highly suspicious of executable content such as Java applets. As a result, applets that attempt to perform unauthorized activity are stopped dead in their tracks and are often accompanied by a message in the browser status area that says "Security Exception Encountered". Naturally, however, you sometimes come upon applets that are trustworthy (see Java 1.1 and Java 1.2 for a discussion of trust). In such cases, you can choose to trust an applet that your browser would otherwise see as a security threat.

While you may be tempted to trust every applet that you come upon in the wild (out on the Web, that is), don't do it! In fact, never trust an applet unless you're 100 percent certain that it's harmless.

Each Web browser is different in how it deals with trusted applets. To find out how to trust applets using your own browser, select Help⇨Help Contents and look for topics related to security. Keywords such as "security," "signature," and "trust" will lead you in the right direction. But be warned: Trust applets at your own risk!

Java 1.2: Levels of trust

Java 1.2, the latest and greatest version of the language due in late 1998, picks up where Java 1.1 security leaves off. You can grant Java 1.2 applets different *levels* of trust, offering a significant advantage over the all-or-nothing nature of Java 1.1 (see preceding section). You can grant an applet that needs to read a file on your computer that privilege only and no more (that is, you can grant the applet the right to read files on your computer, but prevent it from creating new files or making network connections). Furthermore, Java 1.2 features such finely grained levels of security that you can specify precisely what file that applet can read.

To find out more about Java 1.2 security and how you can implement it in your browser (Java 1.2 wasn't supported by browsers at the time this book went to print), visit:

```
java.sun.com/security/
```

Part II
It's Applet Pickin' Time!

The 5th Wave   By Rich Tennant

©RICHTENNANT

EXIT

IRIC F

"Well, this is festive— a miniature intranet amidst a swirl of Java applets."

In this part . . .

Ready to apply the latest Java applets to your own Web page? Part II walks you through designing a Java-powered Web page, finding suitable applets, and customizing them to meet your needs. You don't need to learn the ins and outs of Java programming to be the proud owner of a sleek, personalized Java-powered Web site. This part explains how you can benefit from the labor of others — legally! You can also find out what makes an applet an applet and pick up just enough HTML to put applets on your Web page and create Web pages that satisfy non-Java-savvy Web surfers as well.

Chapter 3

HTML and the <APPLET> Tag

In This Chapter

▶ Understanding what HTML has to do with Java

▶ Marking up documents with HTML

▶ Looking at standard and nonstandard HTML

*T*o weave Java applets into your Web pages, you must first know the basics of the *Hypertext Markup Language (HTML)*. You can now find software tools that enable you to create incredibly sophisticated Web pages without knowing a thing about HTML, but if you want a *Java-powered* Web page, you still need to know a thing or two about HTML. Here's why:

✔ Most of today's HTML-generation tools aren't designed with Java in mind. Instead of enabling you to drag-and-drop applets right into your pages (as is the case with images), most HTML-generation tools deal with applets the old-fashioned way — they force you to type the applet information by hand.

✔ Webbers using non-Java browsers invariably visit your Java-powered pages. In this case, the non-Java browser has no idea how to deal with applets and shows the user nothing but blank, empty space instead of your wonderful applet. Chapter 4 tells you how to use HTML to provide "alternative" content for these poor souls.

HTML Basics

Hypertext Markup Language is the glue that holds all Web pages together; without it, Web pages couldn't exist. Although the name *Hypertext Markup Language* sounds a little intimidating, HTML is really a cream puff. It's something that everyone can figure out how to use in a day or two. If you know how to use a word processor, you can create Web pages by using HTML. In essence, Web pages are really nothing more than plain ol' text documents that you enhance with HTML.

This chapter covers just enough HTML information to wet your whistle, giving you the information you need to inject Java into your Web pages. If you really want to get the most that HTML offers, I highly recommend that you sashay on down to your local bookstore and plunk a few bucks on the counter for *HTML For Dummies,* 3rd Edition, by Ed Tittel and Steve James (IDG Books Worldwide, Inc.). Because HTML and Java applets go hand-in-hand, *HTML For Dummies* is the perfect companion to this book.

Marking it up

By using HTML, you can convert any blasé text document into a hypermedia tour de force, complete with hypertext and hypermedia links to any object on the World Wide Web. But you're not limited to enhancing existing text documents — you can create razzle-dazzle Web pages from scratch using this flexible markup language.

Markup language? Yes indeed. HTML is a *markup language,* meaning that it's not one of those complex programming languages that computer scientists discuss, using cryptic jargon and lots of math. HTML is not something you use to create a software program, such as a word processor or a video game. Instead, it's a friendly language with the express purpose of creating Web pages.

Java, on the other hand, is actually a full-blown programming language that you can use to create applets or applications. Whereas Java applets "live" in Web pages, Java applications look and act like standard desktop applications. I examine the differences between Java applets and applications in detail in Part III.

HTML 4.0: The latest and greatest

HTML 4.0 — a brand new version of HTML — is the latest and greatest revision of the Hypertext Markup Language to appear on the Web. It incorporates a large number of the most popular nonstandard tags in a noble effort to bring browsers into *parity* with one another, meaning they all support the same suite of HTML tags and therefore all display the same Web page in exactly the same way (provided, of course, that all browsers support HTML 4.0). In fact, HTML 4.0 supports a new tag called <OBJECT> that may eventually replace the <APPLET> tag, because it's designed specifically to weave executable content into Web pages.

Unfortunately, not all Web browsers will immediately support HTML 4.0 and the <OBJECT> tag. HTML 4.0 is so new that browser vendors need some time to incorporate it into their products. As a result, our good friend <APPLET> is still the only way to go when it comes to weaving Java applets into Web pages.

Marking up text is really nothing new. Think for a moment about how you highlight a word or phrase in a word-processor document and then apply a special format to it. You can change the font type and size; specify bold, italic, or underlined; and even change the color of the highlighted text. In essence, you're *marking up* a document. But instead of going onto the Web, where browsers view them, word-processor documents usually remain on a personal computer, where you view them using a word processor.

Generally speaking, a *markup language* is a formal set of rules and procedures that you use to prepare text for electronic interpretation and presentation. In the case of HTML, you create documents to present on the World Wide Web, where browsers interpret them. After preparing the documents for the Web, you apply special keywords, or *tags,* to portions of the text — that is, you "mark up" text by using tags.

Playing tag

Tags are the fundamental building blocks of HTML. You apply tags to parts of a text document to specify how browsers are to interpret that text and the document itself. Do you want portions of the text to appear big, small, bold, or in italics? How about making a word or phrase hyperlink to another Web page? And don't forget hypermedia. Why not add a few nice-looking graphics to the document to jazz it up a bit and make a few of these graphics link to other places on the Web? By using HTML tags, you can accomplish all these tasks and more.

HTML tags are very easy to create and use. They're nothing more than a keyword (or even a single letter) inside a pair of less-than (<) and greater-than (>) characters. To indicate the beginning of bold text, for example, HTML uses the tag <B>. You simply add the *opening tag* <B> at the beginning of any text that you want browsers to display as bold, as shown in the following example:

```
This text isn't bold . . . <B> but this text is!
```

Easy enough, huh? If you view it with a browser, all the text appearing after the <B> tag is bold.

But how about turning *off* the bold format? That's easy, too; simply create a *closing tag* by putting a forward slash mark before the HTML keyword that you want to turn off. To turn off the bold format, for example, you place the tag </B> after the last piece of text that you want to appear bold, as follows:

```
This text isn't bold . . . <B> but this </B> text is!
```

In the preceding code line, I specify that the words *but this* are bold. All the other words appear as normal text because they fall before the opening <B> tag or after the closing </B> tag. Pretty simple stuff, isn't it? The following structure forms the basis of HTML:

✔ You specify the opening tag with the keyword inside (<>).

✔ The closing tag (assuming that this particular tag even requires a closing tag — not all do) is the same keyword but with a slash before it (</>).

Although you're free to enter tags in uppercase or lowercase, I recommend that you always use uppercase letters to make the tags easier for you to read. Although <b> and <B>, for example, mean the same thing to your browser, the tag in uppercase stands out more. As you're reading through reams of HTML code, lowercase tags have a way of disappearing into the text, whereas those in uppercase seem to jump right out at you.

In HTML, you can't include any spaces between the <> characters and the text inside them. If you type < B>, the browser doesn't know what you mean because a space appears before the B. To create a tag, squish the <> characters right up against whatever you put inside them. No spaces allowed!

Working with HTML documents

If a Web page is nothing more than a text document that you mark up with a bunch of HTML tags, how does the Web browser know the difference between the two? What happens, for example, if a browser comes across a regular text file? And, better yet, what happens after a browser encounters a document full of HTML tags?

Consider the following poem:

```
Mountain Twilight
Iron clouds
have moved east.
The mountain is
a black silhouette
the lake
a gold and lavender
bowl of twilight.
                -TFW
```

Clearly, the preceding poem has no HTML tags, making it nothing more than standard text. Suppose that a browser comes across the document containing this poem. How does it display the document? The answer to that question depends on the browser that's viewing the document. Depending on how they're designed, browsers use one of the following two different methods of identifying an HTML document:

✔ By checking the document's filename for an HTML or HTM extension.

✔ By determining whether the document contains HTML tags.

Because you have no surefire way of knowing which method a particular browser may use to view your Web document, you should use both methods of identification.

If you store the preceding poem (which contains no HTML tags) in a file with a TXT extension, for example, every browser recognizes it as a plain text document and displays the contents as plain text (see Figure 3-1). In fact, even if this file's extension is ABC, the browser treats its contents as plain text because the text itself contains nothing special to tell the browser otherwise. If, however, the file contains more than just text and includes HTML tags, some browsers actually disregard the extension and display the document as if it has an HTML extension.

Because not all browsers go the extra distance and bother to look inside the files they display for the presence of HTML tags, giving your pages the correct extension is critical. Whenever your Web files contain HTML tags (which they almost always do, unless you need to display plain text), they should also have the HTML extension (or HTM, for computers that can handle only three-letter extensions). The HTML file extension is the standard way of telling browsers to expect HTML code inside.

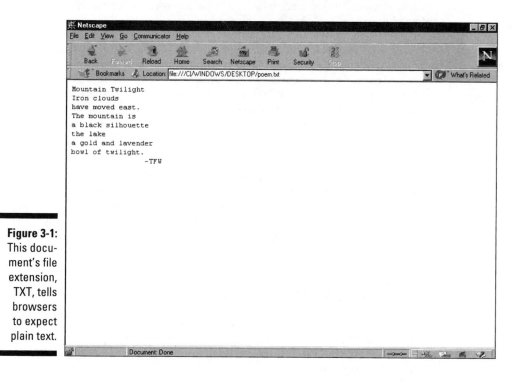

Figure 3-1:
This document's file extension, TXT, tells browsers to expect plain text.

If plain text resides in a file displaying the HTML extension, browsers treat that text as if you'd marked it up with HTML. But in the case of the preceding poem, no HTML tags are present. As a result, if this document has the HTML extension, everything in it jumbles together, as shown in Figure 3-2.

Creating an HTML document involves more than just saving text in a file that displays an HTML extension. For a text file to truly function as an HTML document, you must, at a minimum, enclose the text in that document in opening <HTML> and closing </HTML> tags, as the following example shows:

```
<HTML>
Mountain Twilight
Iron clouds
have moved east.
The mountain is
a black silhouette
the lake
a gold and lavender
bowl of twilight.
                -TFW
</HTML>
```

If these two tags are present, together with an HTML extension, any browser knows immediately to treat whatever's between these tags as HTML instead of as plain text.

Although, technically, you don't need to store HTML documents in files displaying the HTML (or HTM) extension, people almost always do so. Rarely, if ever, do you encounter an HTML document on the Web with a different extension. Because extensions are a way of identifying the file to which you append them, storing HTML documents in files with anything other than an HTML (or HTM) extension doesn't make much sense.

Getting the text in order

Now, you may think that the presence of the opening and closing <HTML> tags should make a big difference in how a browser displays your document, but it doesn't! The opening <HTML> tag just tells the browser, "Hey, you're dealing with an HTML file — keep your eyes open for more tags from now on." The closing </HTML> tag, on the other hand, just says, "Okay, you've reached the end of the HTML file — you don't see any tags from here on out."

In effect, the opening <HTML> and closing </HTML> tags just define the beginning and ending of the file. What falls between these two tags is what matters. And because nothing but plain text falls between these two tags in the poem example, the browser doesn't do anything special with it. HTML doesn't even recognize *carriage returns* (that is, paragraph marks) the way that your word processor does. Instead, you must supply carriage returns the HTML way — as tags.

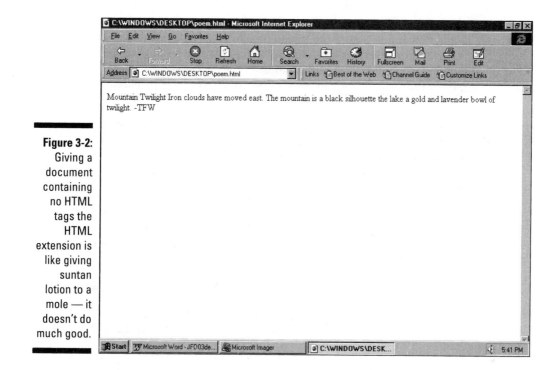

You can indicate carriage returns in two ways in HTML. If you want the browser to recognize the carriage returns as they actually occur in the text, you can surround the entire poem (between the opening and closing HTML tags) with the opening <PRE> and closing </PRE> tags. These tags, which mark text as *preformatted information,* tell the browser to expect word-processor-style carriage returns, as the following example shows:

```
<HTML>
<PRE>
Mountain Twilight
Iron clouds
have moved east.
The mountain is
a black silhouette
the lake
a gold and lavender
bowl of twilight.
                -TFW

</PRE>
</HTML>
```

Although this approach does the trick, as Figure 3-3 shows, it may not give you exactly what you're hoping for. Because the browser assumes that preformatted information is special text, it displays that text in a special, monotype font that looks different from the surrounding text (it looks like typewriter text). As a result, text appearing between the opening <PRE> and closing </PRE> tags looks different than other HTML text looks.

Because of this font variation, Web page authors often scrap the <PRE> tags and use the *line-break*
 tag or the *paragraph-break* <P> tag instead. A line break acts much like a single carriage return, forcing the text following it to begin on a new line; a paragraph break acts like a couple carriage returns, adding a line of blank space between it and the text following it. (These two tags don't require a closing companion tag because they simply tell the browser to insert a paragraph break or line break wherever they appear.)

Here's how the poem looks if you use the line- and paragraph-break tags instead of the <PRE> tag:

```
<HTML>Mountain Twilight <P>Iron clouds <BR>have moved
        east.<BR>The mountain is<BR>a black
        silhouette<BR>the lake<BR>a gold and
        lavender<BR>bowl of twilight.<BR>-TFW</HTML>
```

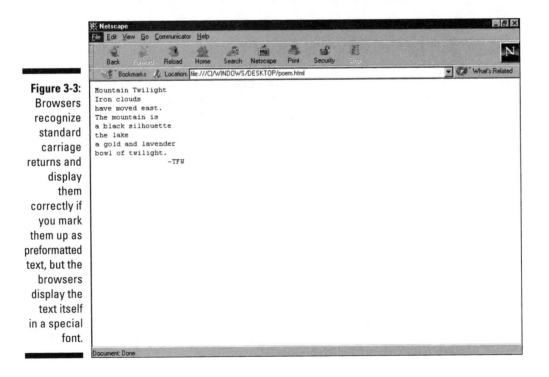

Figure 3-3: Browsers recognize standard carriage returns and display them correctly if you mark them up as preformatted text, but the browsers display the text itself in a special font.

Notice in this code example that I removed the word-processor-style carriage returns that previously came between the lines of the poem. Because I no longer have the poem marked up as preformatted information, browsers ignore all word-processor-style carriage returns anyway. You're free to include them, however, in your HTML *source code* — that's what you call these lines of commands, or code — just to make the text easier for you to read, as in the following example:

```
<HTML>
Mountain Twilight <P>
Iron clouds <BR>
have moved east.<BR>
The mountain is<BR>
a black silhouette<BR>
the lake<BR>
a gold and lavender<BR>
bowl of twilight.<BR>
                -TFW
</HTML>
```

The results of both examples (with or without carriage returns) look the same, as shown in Figure 3-4. But take a look at the last line. Instead of appearing to the far right, the text (-TFW) is left-aligned, just as the other text is. The browser disregards the spaces before the text.

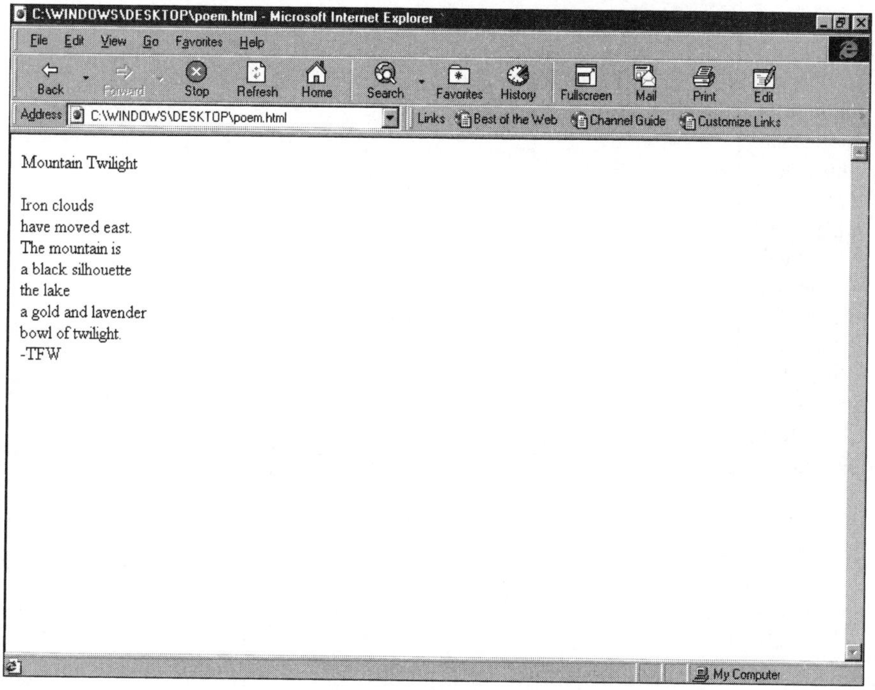

Figure 3-4:
You can't use multiple spaces to align text without using the <PRE> tag.

By marking the last line as preformatted information, browsers keep the spaces intact (see Figure 3-5). And because this last line is not part of the poem but rather is the initials of the author, having it appear in a different font is actually desirable in this case, as the following example demonstrates:

```
<HTML>
Mountain Twilight <P>
Iron clouds <BR>
have moved east.<BR>
The mountain is<BR>
a black silhouette<BR>
the lake<BR>
a gold and lavender<BR>
bowl of twilight.<BR>
<PRE>                    -TFW </PRE>
</HTML>
```

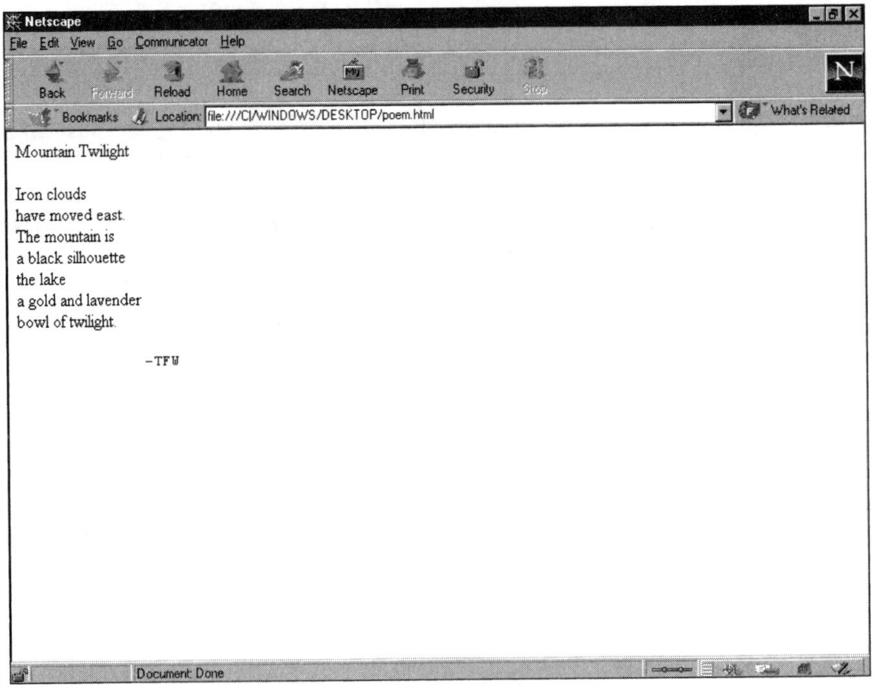

Figure 3-5:
If you mark them as preformatted information, the spaces preceding the author's initials appear exactly as they do in the HTML source code.

Standard HTML's more advanced features

The "Mountain Twilight" example in the preceding section shows how HTML markup tags function to format text so that browsers can view it. HTML has many tags and structures (other than the ones I discuss in the preceding sections) that you can use to create cool Web pages. The following bulleted list gives you an idea of some other important HTML functions and characteristics:

- You can use *nested tags* to apply more than one type of formatting to the same text. (You can, for example, place one set of opening and closing tags, such as <I> and </I> to denote italics, inside a different set of opening and closing tags, such as <B> and </B> for bold.) For both bold and italic, you place tags as follows:

```
<B><I>moved east</I></B>
```

- You can organize your text into logical, easy-to-read sections by using tags for different levels of headings. For a bold, italic level 3 heading, you'd follow this example:

```
<H3><B><I>moved east</I></B></H3>
```

- You can supply certain HTML tags with *attributes* (special keywords that help qualify how the tag acts). To include a graphic image on your Web page, use the image tag <IMG> with the source (SRC) attribute:

```
<IMG SRC="coolgraphic.gif">
```

- You can include hyperlinks to any other type of object residing on the Web. (See the nearby sidebar "Linking to relative and absolute URLs.") For a link to another Web document, include the URL for the document inside the anchor tag <A>. To make the word *lakes* a hyperlink to a lake Web site, you follow this example:

```
<A HREF="http://www.bodiesofwater.org/lakes.html"> lakes
        </A>
```

- You can further format your Web page by grouping items into bulleted lists, aligning text and images, creating special characters (such as copyright and trademark symbols), and including horizontal rules.
- And, of course, you can include exciting Java applets in your Web page by using the <APPLET> tag. (I show you how in Chapter 4.)

The evolution of HTML

HTML is a constantly evolving language, with developers adding new tags all the time to keep up with the demands of Web publishers and Webbers. HTML originally offered only a relatively small set of tags. But millions of Web page developers around the world quickly outgrew those initial offerings, requiring the addition of new features to the language.

TECHNICAL STUFF

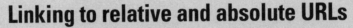

Linking to relative and absolute URLs

You can use HTML to create hyperlinked text and images — words and pictures that you can click to call new information to the screen. You need only the following two things to create hyperlinks:

✔ The object that's to serve as your link (for example, a word, phrase, image, or animation file).

✔ The location (URL) of the object to which you want the link to lead.

Suppose that you want to link the word *lakes* to a distant Web site dedicated to large bodies of water. As long as you know the URL for the site, you're all set. Your code may look as follows:

```
<A HREF="http://
   www.bodiesofwater.org/
   lakes.html"> lakes </A>
```

Here, the word *lakes* now associates with a Web page by the combination of the <A> anchor tag with a *hypertext reference* attribute (HREF="") containing a URL (http://www.bodiesofwater.org/lakes.html). As a result, you've enhanced the opening <A> tag with the special information that's necessary to create a hyperlink, making the tag much longer than most other tags.

Although this tag is quite long, the browser treats it as just another opening tag. This tag, however, creates a hyperlink reference for the text that follows. The browser treats all text

following this opening tag as a hyperlink until it encounters a closing </A> tag. In this example, only the word *lakes* is a hyperlink, although I could just as easily place an entire chunk of text — such as "Check out my awesome lake photo, dudes!" — inside the <A> and </A> tags instead. Hey, this is HTML — we can mark up any amount of text that we want.

Whenever a Webber clicks the word *lakes*, the browser connects to the associated Web page. This connection is known as an *absolute reference* because it supplies the exact (or *absolute*) URL for the information to which it refers. Both text and image hyperlinks, however, can utilize *relative* references.

Relative references, sometimes known as *partial addresses* because they're not complete URLs, create links to information that you find relative to the location of the Web page containing the reference itself. Objects that you specify by using a relative URL must be located in the same directory as the Web page containing the HTML code itself. Thus, if you use a relative URL reference, you don't specify the complete URL in your tag. If the LAKES.HTML document to which you want to link the word *lakes* resides in the same directory as your Web page, you may use the following relative reference instead:

```
<A HREF="lakes.html">lakes</A>
```

In many respects, you can think of HTML as a software product: New features (tags) appear, problematic and unused ones disappear, and developers prepare a new release for public consumption. Unlike a software product, however, HTML doesn't simply become available (or *go golden*) based on one company's belief that it's ready for release. Instead, each new version of HTML goes through a rigorous evaluation process before it becomes a standard.

The HTML tags that I discuss in this chapter are a fraction — a very *small* fraction — of the ones available for use. And not all browsers support all tags, so make sure that you take care in crafting your Web pages to ensure that you use standard HTML tags that all browsers understand.

To accommodate users with browsers that don't support all tags, you should enhance your applets with standard HTML (see Chapter 4). Including standard HTML in your Java-powered Web pages enables both Webbers who use Java-savvy browsers and those who aren't so fortunate to get the most out of your site. If you don't provide such an alternative, those with non-Java browsers may turn away from your site, thinking that you just don't know how to create cool Web pages.

Chapter 4

Learning to Love the <APPLET> Tag

In This Chapter

▶ Closing the gap between HTML and Java applets

▶ Introducing the <APPLET> tag

▶ Making sense of Java 1.1 and Java 1.2 <APPLET> tag enhancements

The <APPLET> tag, which you use to embed Java applets in Web pages, is the mother of all nonstandard tags (see Chapter 3 for details on standard and nonstandard HTML tags). Depending on the applet that you're embedding, and to what extent you choose to customize that applet (see Chapters 8 and 9), you can construct either a relatively simple or exceptionally complex <APPLET> tag.

In this chapter, you find out how to create your own Java-powered pages. You weave applets into your Web pages by using the <APPLET> tag and find out how to use <APPLET> tag parameters to customize applets. Along the way, you see the new features introduced with Java 1.1 and Java 1.2. So what are you waiting for? Let the weaving begin!

Constructing the <APPLET> Tag

The <APPLET> tag is a *compound tag,* which means it has several parts; you may include additional information related to the tag between the first portion of the opening tag (<APPLET) and the closing brace of the opening tag (>). However, only a few of these pieces of information are mandatory. Specifically, CODE, HEIGHT, and WIDTH are required parts of all <APPLET> tags, as the section "The opening <APPLET> tag" explains.

Whether you have to provide anything other than these three bare minimum parts depends entirely on the applet you are configuring. Some applets make heavy use of all parts of the <APPLET> tag; others need only the required parts, and the only way to know what your applet requires is to read the documentation that comes with it (see Chapter 8 for details).

The following code gives a simplified look at the four main parts of the <APPLET> tag:

```
<APPLET attributes>
applet parameters
alternate HTML
</APPLET>
```

Squeezing applets into tiny JARs

Some applets rely on a number of files, such as images, sounds, and even other bytecode files that a programmer creates — each of which your browser must download over the network to your computer before it can use them. As you may suspect, downloading each of the files that an applet needs takes time, especially because the browser has to make a *network connection* — a special request — for each one. When Java first came on the scene, the browser had to download every file that an applet needed one at a time, meaning a unique network connection had to be created and then closed for each file.

Java has matured quite a bit since then. Today, the most current crop of Java-savvy browsers can download all the files an applet needs by using a single network connection. There's a catch, however: The developer first must assemble these files and then compress them into a *Java Archive* (JAR for short). A JAR file is essentially a compressed archive that contains the files an applet uses. You can download a JAR in considerably less time than it takes to download each file separately.

A developer may choose not to take advantage of JAR files because only the latest versions of browsers understand them. However, JARs have gained in popularity since they were first introduced in Java 1.1, and I imagine they'll soon become more widely used than class files in the next few years.

Of course, JAR files don't come for free as far as the <APPLET> tag is concerned. You must specify every JAR file that an applet needs via the ARCHIVE attribute, (which I cover at the end of this chapter). When an applet makes use of a JAR, or more than one JAR (yep, applets can use multiple JARs), the ARCHIVE attribute comes into play. If you don't properly specify JAR files by using the ARCHIVE attribute, the browsers have no way of knowing what to download — other than the applet file specified in the CODE attribute. The ARCHIVE attribute does not replace the CODE attribute; rather, these two attributes work hand in hand (as this chapter explains).

The opening <APPLET> tag

As with all tags, both standard and nonstandard, the <APPLET> tag begins with an opening tag. And like many other tags, the opening tag supports a number of *attributes* — information that enhances the way the applet looks or acts when a browser runs it.

Placing the required attributes

Attributes are keywords that tell browsers to do something special when they encounter a tag; in the case of the <APPLET> opening tag, this something is a bit more complex than with most other tags. Although many opening tags consist of nothing more than a letter or two (<B>, <I>, <BR>, and so forth) and no attributes whatsoever, the <APPLET> tag requires that you provide the initial part of the opening tag (<APPLET>) *and* at least three attributes that together tell the browser the name of the applet and how much space the applet will take up when displayed:

```
<APPLET CODE="Marquee" HEIGHT=25 WIDTH=450>
```

This example specifies an applet named Marquee. The opening tag's CODE attribute identifies the file that contains the applet. The HEIGHT and WIDTH attributes of the opening tag tell the browser how much space the applet requires in the Web page. In this case, the applet takes up 25 pixels in height and 450 pixels in width.

Using quotation marks

Notice that quotes surround the name of the applet file, Marquee, but not the height and width values. Although quotes are not absolutely necessary when dealing with the CODE attribute, you often see strings of characters enclosed in quotes because of the potential for spaces in applet names. An applet named Ticker Tape, for example, contains a space in its name, as opposed to an applet called TickerTape, which doesn't. (Numeric values, such as height and width, never have spaces in them.)

Surrounding strings with quotes ensures that the browser knows exactly what to look for, even if spaces are included. For example, if you leave off the quotes on an applet *parameter* — a piece of information that modifies how an applet looks or acts — named Background Color, the browser sees only the characters leading up to the first space. In this case, the browser sees only the first word, *Background,* and doesn't see the word *Color.*

Be extremely careful to balance your quotes. If you start a piece of text with a quote, you must supply a corresponding end quote. Furthermore, you must be sure not to include any extra quotes. Improper use of quotes is deadly to Java-savvy browsers and may cause them to crash!

Both the following examples would wreak havoc with the browser:

- ✔ **Missing quote:** <PARAM NAME="speed" VALUE="500>
- ✔ **Extra quote:** <PARAM NAME="speed" VALUE="500"">

Avoid the use of curly quotes like the plague when creating hyperlinks for your Web pages. Browsers don't recognize curly quotes (sometimes called *smart quotes*) as real quotes, so using them prevents your hyperlink from working properly.

Although you don't have to place quotes around numeric parameters, do yourself a favor and surround all numbers and strings with quotes. Quotes don't do any harm when they surround numbers or strings that don't have spaces, and they ensure that you never make the mistake of omitting quotes where you really do need them. I highly recommend always surrounding non-numeric values with quotes, too. With applets, you're better off quote-rich than quote-poor!

Case matters! When supplying the name of an applet file, be sure to type the name exactly, matching each letter case for case. For example, if an applet is named Marquee, you must specify that name exactly in the CODE attribute. If you type in **marquee** (lowercase "m") instead, the browser won't be able to find the applet.

A class act

Almost all applets are stored in files having a .class extension. When programmers create Java applets, the final step involves converting human-readable Java code into computer-readable code (see the sidebar "Cracking the code"). Once converted, the resulting file has the .class extension.

As a result, the Marquee applet is actually stored in a file named Marquee.class. Although you're free to include the .class extension when specifying your applets, you don't have to. Java-savvy browsers know to look for a file with that extension. You must, however, provide the extension if it is anything other than .class. Thus, the following opening <APPLET> tag is functionally equivalent to the one shown previously in the "Placing the required attributes" section, although slightly more precise when it comes to the applet filename:

```
<APPLET CODE="Marquee.class" HEIGHT=25 WIDTH=450>
```

Attribute alley

At a bare minimum, all opening <APPLET> tags must contain the three attributes shown in the preceding sections: CODE, HEIGHT, and WIDTH. These are known as *required attributes* (see Table 4-1) because you can't include applets in Web pages without them. In addition to the three required attributes, you can use a number of *optional attributes* to control how an applet appears in your pages.

Table 4-1	Required Applet Attributes
Attribute	*Description*
CODE	Specifies the name of the applet file
HEIGHT	Specifies the height of your applet in pixels
WIDTH	Specifies the width of your applet in pixels

You may also include optional attributes, listed in Table 4-2, anywhere within the opening tag. I recommend that you specify optional attributes after the three required ones in order to increase the readability of your HTML source code as the following snippet of code illustrates:

```
<APPLET CODE="Marquee" HEIGHT=25 WIDTH=450
ALT="This is a cool applet — too bad you can't see it!"
HSPACE=10
VSPACE=25>
```

Cracking the code

Applets are tiny programs written in the Java programming language by software developers. The special instructions a developer writes with this language is known as *source code*, which can be thought of as an applet recipe.

After a developer writes the source code for an applet, the applet goes though a special tool known as a compiler. The *compiler* converts the human-readable source code into a form that the computer can read, known as *bytecode,* which results in the creation of the

applet. (Think of a compiler as an oven; it bakes the source code "ingredients" into a delectable treat known as an applet, a rather amazing process explained in Chapter 13.)

The resulting applet bytecode file is really what you weave into your Web pages; you specify the name of this file in the CODE attribute of the opening <APPLET> tag. When you use the word CODE to identify the applet in the opening tag, you tell the browser the name of the applet bytecode file to look for.

Table 4-2	Optional Applet Attributes
Attribute	**Description**
ALIGN	This attribute specifies where your applet is placed on the page in respect to the text around it; it may have one of the following nine alignments (refer to Figures 7-7, 7-8, and 7-9): left, right, top, texttop, middle, absmiddle, baseline, bottom, and absbottom.
ALT	This attribute gives Java-savvy browsers alternative text to display if they are incapable of executing the applet for some reason. This text is seen only by Java-savvy browsers because it falls within the opening <APPLET> tag. (Non-Java browsers skip over this tag because they don't know how to deal with applets.) If you want to communicate with non-Java browsers, do so by using *alternate HTML* — plain old-fashioned HTML that appears immediately before the closing </APPLET> tag (see the section "Alternate HTML" for more details).
CODEBASE	This attribute specifies the URL for your applet, or in other words, it describes where the applet file is located. The applet must be located relative to this URL. If you don't specify CODEBASE, the applet is expected to reside in the same directory as the Web page.
HSPACE	This attribute specifies the horizontal space surrounding your applet.
NAME	This attribute specifies the symbolic name of your applet, allowing other applets embedded in the same page to locate your applet by name. You only use this attribute when applets on a page communicate with one another, something most applets don't do.
VSPACE	This attribute specifies the vertical space surrounding your applet.

After you begin adding optional attributes to the mix, the opening tag can become quite difficult to read. To further increase the readability of your HTML source code, I recommend placing any optional attributes on their own line:

```
<APPLET CODE="Marquee" HEIGHT=25 WIDTH=450
ALT="This is a cool applet — too bad you can't see it!"
HSPACE=10
VSPACE=25>
```

The browser doesn't care how the tag appears, as long as it begins with ⟨ and ends with ⟩. As a result, you can format your opening tag in any way you want.

Getting to base

Under normal circumstances, the browser expects to find the applet file inside the same directory as the Web page. In this case, you must ensure that the applet file and the Web page in which it is embedded do reside in the same directory (flip to Chapter 7 for details).

However, you can't always keep the applet and the Web page in the same directory. What if you want to use a distributed applet (see Chapter 7)? And what if you want a bunch of different pages on your Web site to use the same applet? What a profound waste of time and Web server space it would be to upload a copy of the applet into every directory containing a Web page that used it.

Why not have the applet reside in a central location on your server where all pages can get to it?

Fortunately, the optional CODEBASE tag enables you to specify a URL that points to the directory containing your applet. When a Java-savvy browser encounters the CODEBASE attribute, it automatically knows to look for the applet in whatever directory that attribute points to. The URL you supply for CODEBASE may point to a directory on your server or one on any other server on the Web:

```
<APPLET CODEBASE="http://www.mantiscorp.com/applets/"
CODE="Marquee" HEIGHT=25 WIDTH=450>
```

In this example, browsers won't look for the Marquee applet inside the same directory as the Web page containing this <APPLET> tag. Instead, thanks to CODEBASE, browsers expect to find the applet on the Mantis Development Corporation server (www.mantiscorp.com), inside the applets directory.

The CODEBASE tag is particularly helpful when a number of pages on your site use the same applet. You can place a single copy of the applet in one directory and specify the appropriate CODEBASE attribute in all pages. Upgrading the applet is a cinch with the CODEBASE tag: Simply upgrade the single applet and you're done.

The URL you supply for CODEBASE can be either relative or absolute (refer to the sidebar "Linking to relative and absolute URLs," found in Chapter 3).

Applet parameters

The second major part of the <APPLET> tag, *applet parameters,* is where you can really customize an applet. To make an applet look or act as you want it to, you use a special <PARAM> tag that has two of its very own attributes: NAME and VALUE. Although not all applets are customizable, those that are allow you to supply information by using one or more <PARAM> tags according to the following format:

```
<PARAM NAME="parameter name" VALUE="parameter value">
```

For example, an applet may allow you to provide a sound track that plays in the background when the applet is running. To tell the applet the name of the sound file to use and where that file is located, you can supply the following <PARAM> tag:

```
<PARAM NAME="sndTrack" VALUE="audio/sinatra/summerwind.au">
```

In this example, the name of the parameter is sndTrack. The value associated with this parameter, audio/sinatra/summerwind.au, is a *relative URL* (a partial URL pointing to a file or image located relative to the Web page in which the applet itself appears, described in greater deal in Chapter 3) leading to a sound file. Some applets may also accept an *absolute URL* (complete URL provided) for this parameter:

```
<PARAM NAME="sndTrack" VALUE="http://www.music.org/beatles/
                                HeyJude.au">
```

Each applet is unique in which parameters it accepts, because its author writes the programming code that allows the applet to deal with parameters. For example, another applet may also allow you to specify a sound track. Depending on how it was written, however, the applet may not understand URLs at all — the applet may insist that the sound file reside in the same directory as the applet itself, meaning that you supply only a filename:

```
<PARAM NAME="music" VALUE="nirvana.au">
```

Here, the applet just looks for the sound file named nirvana.au, expecting to find it in the same directory in which the applet resides. Not only that, but the parameter name isn't sndTrack. Because the programmer decides what features you can customize, as well as the parameter names that correspond to these features, you may find a number of different names used for the same thing. Whereas this applet uses "music" as the parameter name that corresponds to background sound track, others may use the name background, back music, sound_Track, sound, or just about anything else a programmer can think of!

Java 1.0 and Java 1.1 applets can play only sounds that are stored in a very specific format, which is why each of the sound files specified here has the .au extension. Java 1.2 applets, on the other hand, are sound maniacs by comparison; they understand how to deal with most of the common formats used on the Internet (such as WAV, MIDI, and others). For details on Java sound formats, see Chapter 5.

Good, solid values

Different applets may support any number of different parameters. It's not unusual, for example, to come across applets that support several different parameters, giving you great flexibility when it comes to configuring them. To supply more than one parameter, all you have to do is enter the parameters one after another.

The Marquee applet, for example, enables you to customize the text that scrolls across the screen. You can specify the font, style, and point size the text should appear in. All you have to do is provide a <PARAM> tag for each parameter that you wish to supply to the applet when it's executed:

```
<PARAM NAME="font_face" VALUE="Helvetica">
<PARAM NAME="font_size" VALUE="24">
<PARAM NAME="font_italic" VALUE="yes">
<PARAM NAME="font_bold" VALUE="yes">
<PARAM NAME="marquee" VALUE="Yo! The text you are now
          reading will scroll across the screen when this
          applet is executed...">
```

You can customize the preceding applet in a number of ways, although you don't necessarily have to supply a parameter for each and every parameter the applet supports. Marquee, like many applets, supplies a default parameter if you don't bother to supply one. If, for example, you don't supply any information about the font, Marquee uses Times, 18-point by default. Of course, the programmer decides whether an applet provides a default. Some applets force you to supply parameters; others are written to supply default values if you leave parameters out.

The CD-ROM that comes with this book contains the Marquee applet, so you can weave it into your own Web pages. For more details on how to configure the Marquee applet by using parameter tags, see Chapter 8.

You must surround any parameter value that contains a space character (or many spaces) by quotes. Of course, when parameters require numeric values, you don't need to use quotes at all.

Multiple values

Some applets support more than one value being associated with a given parameter name, something you'll only know for sure if you read the documentation that comes with your applet or happen to get your hands on HTML pages that contain `<APPLET>` tag examples. In cases where you're working with an applet that supports multiple values for a parameter, you must consult your documentation to find out *how* you actually supply these values. It may be true that you can supply several values at once, but you have to separate each value from the others so as not to confuse the applet. Typically, you use the | character (sometimes called the *pipe character*):

```
<PARAM NAME="sounds"
          VALUE="sinatra.au|HeyJude.au|nirvana.au">
```

In this case, the applet receives three sound files as one parameter. Although the | character is the most common separator, the applet's developer may decide to have you supply a different character. Don't be surprised to find commas, colons, semicolons, and even spaces used to separate multiple values:

```
<PARAM NAME="sounds"
          VALUE="sinatra.au,HeyJude.au,nirvana.au">
<PARAM NAME="images" VALUE="shark.gif:pig.gif:tiger.au">
<PARAM NAME="images" VALUE="shark.gif;pig.gif;tiger.au">
<PARAM NAME="speeds" VALUE="100 355 23 0 535">
```

You typically create the pipe character (|) by pressing the shift key at the same time as the backslash key \. Isn't it nice to know that this character has its own little name, and that you have an excuse to use it? Go ahead, give the pipe character a shot.

Alternate HTML

You can supply what's known as *alternate HTML* — HTML code that's displayed by non-Java browsers— in a special area that follows any parameter tags that you may use, but is before the closing `</APPLET>` tag. Here, you may enter any amount of HTML code you want; only those browsers that can't deal with Java applets will display this code. As a result, you're able to provide an alternative to applets for those browsers that aren't Java savvy.

Alternate HTML is an important part of the `<APPLET>` tag, even though applets completely ignore it. Alternate HTML gives you an opportunity to create Web pages that are useful to Webbers regardless of the browsers they happen to use. If you don't supply alternate HTML for non-Java browsers, you run the risk of alienating users who have those browsers.

Take, for example, Figure 4-1. Here, frozen in time, is a screen shot of a Java-powered page as viewed by a Java-savvy browser. Although you can't tell by looking at this figure, the buttons on this page are all animated, courtesy of applets. When you view this page through a Java-savvy browser, each applet executes and begins animating its respective button. As a result, you're treated to a page full of living, animated buttons.

Each of the buttons on this page uses an applet tag similar to the following:

```
<APPLET CODE="LivingLinks" WIDTH=100 HEIGHT=100>
<PARAM NAME="image" VALUE="animalsButton.gif">
<PARAM NAME="effect" VALUE="ripple">
<PARAM NAME="sound" VALUE="dolphinSqueak.au">
<PARAM NAME="URL" VALUE="http://www.mantiscorp.com/">
</APPLET>
```

These buttons were brought to life with the LivingLinks applet, which you can find on the CD-ROM that comes with this book. This flexible, general-purpose applet provides you with a means to animate buttons and play sounds in your pages.

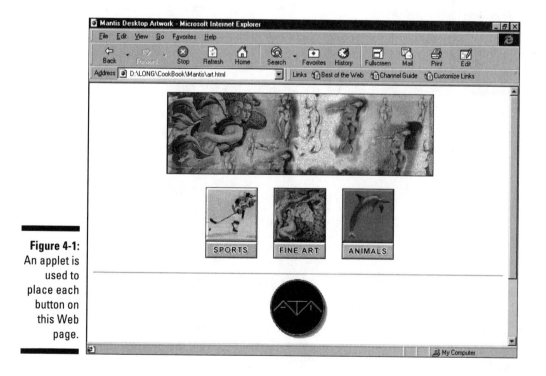

Figure 4-1:
An applet is used to place each button on this Web page.

If you view the page in Figure 4-1 with a non-Java browser, you won't see any of the applets! And because no alternate HTML is provided to compensate for their loss, you see nothing in place of these applets. The result, shown in Figure 4-2, is a pathetic excuse for a Web page: Nobody will find it useful because all the buttons are missing.

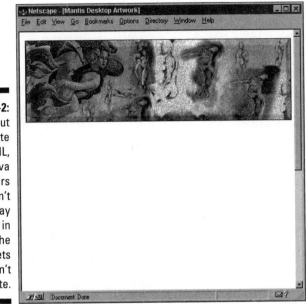

Figure 4-2:
Without
alternate
HTML,
non-Java
browsers
won't
display
anything in
place of the
applets
they can't
execute.

Fortunately, this nightmare is entirely avoidable. Just be sure to provide the corresponding alternate HTML code for each applet, and the buttons will be visible to users of non-Java browsers:

```
<APPLET CODE="LivingLinks" WIDTH=100 HEIGHT=100>
<PARAM NAME="image" VALUE="animalsButton.gif">
<PARAM NAME="effect" VALUE="ripple">
<PARAM NAME="sound" VALUE="dolphinSqueak.au">
<PARAM NAME="URL" VALUE="http://www.mantiscorp.com/">

<IMG SRC="animalsButton.gif">
</APPLET>
```

The code is easier to read if you put a carriage return between the last `<PARAM>` tag and the alternate HTML (although you certainly don't have to if you're a glutton for punishment!).

When displayed using alternate HTML (`<IMG SRC="animalsButton.gif">` in this case), the buttons aren't alive the way they are under Java's steam, but they are a far cry from having nothing at all on the Web page. In fact, because you can supply any HTML code in the alternate HTML area, these buttons can be more than mere decoration — each can be a fully functional hyperlink:

```
<APPLET CODE="LivingLinks" WIDTH=100 HEIGHT=100>
<PARAM NAME="image" VALUE="animalsButton.gif">
<PARAM NAME="effect" VALUE="ripple">
<PARAM NAME="sound" VALUE="dolphinSqueak.au">
<PARAM NAME="URL" VALUE="http://www.mantiscorp.com/">

<A HREF="http://www.mantiscorp.com/">
<IMG SRC="animalsButton.gif">
</A>
</APPLET>
```

Provide alternate HTML code for your applets whenever possible. Of course, applets do some things that you can't mimic with standard HTML. However, whenever you can provide alternate HTML code that approximates an applet's visual appearance (as in the button example in this section), users of both non-Java and Java-powered browsers will benefit from your site.

The closing </APPLET> tag

The fourth and final part of the <APPLET> tag brings the entire tag to a close. To properly form an <APPLET> tag, you must balance the opening tag with a closing </APPLET> tag. When the browser sees </APPLET>, it knows that there is no more to the applet: That's all she wrote!

Putting Your <APPLET> Tag to Work

Although many applets are quite easy to use, others are extremely complex. The only way to figure out how to construct an appropriate <APPLET> tag for a given applet is to read the information that comes with the applet (assuming that you get some sort of documentation). Otherwise, you can always look at the tag as it appears in an existing Web page (see Chapter 6 for details).

In all cases, you're free to ignore the alternate HTML portion of an <APPLET> tag when you are constructing your own tag. And, in many cases, you won't have to bother with parameter tags at all: Not all applets are customizable. However, you always need to use at least the opening and closing <APPLET> tags, regardless of the applet itself. And within the opening tag, you must supply three attributes: CODE, HEIGHT, and WIDTH.

As a result, the simplest tag looks something like this one:

```
<APPLET CODE="AnyApplet" HEIGHT=50 WIDTH=100>
</APPLET>
```

Although this example is certainly bare-boned, it's not uncommon because many applets don't support the use of parameter tags at all.

When an applet allows you to customize it, remember to use `<PARAM>` tags. Although each applet is different in the number and name of parameters it accepts, be sure to provide all of the parameters immediately after the opening `<APPLET>` tag but before the first line of alternate HTML. Although placing your `<PARAM>` tags immediately after the opening `<APPLET>` tag can make your code difficult to read, especially if you have a number of parameters, you're free to indent the code as you see fit. Personally, I prefer to indent all the parameter tags and place a carriage return between the very last one and the first line of alternate HTML:

```
<APPLET CODE="Marquee" WIDTH=500 HEIGHT=40>
    <PARAM NAME="font_face" VALUE="TimesRoman">
    <PARAM NAME="font_size" VALUE="24">
    <PARAM NAME="font_italic" VALUE="yes">
    <PARAM NAME="font_bold" VALUE="yes">
    <PARAM NAME="marquee" VALUE="Yo! I'm scrolling!">

Gee, you can't see the scrolling text can you?
That's because this page requires a Java-savvy browser...
<A HREF="http://www.netscape.com">GET ONE!</A>!
</APPLET>
```

When viewed in a Java-savvy browser, the applet comes to life and scrolls the words `Yo! I'm scrolling!` across the screen (see Figure 4-3). The screen teases those with non-Java browsers and offers a link to Netscape's home page, where they can get their hands on a Java-savvy browser (see Figure 4-4).

Java 1.1 and Java 1.2: The New
<APPLET> Tags in Town

You can easily get overwhelmed when looking at the `<APPLET>` tag from a "what's it got" view. If you look at the tag only in terms of braces, tags, attributes, and alternate HTML, you'll probably go bonkers. So don't do that, please.

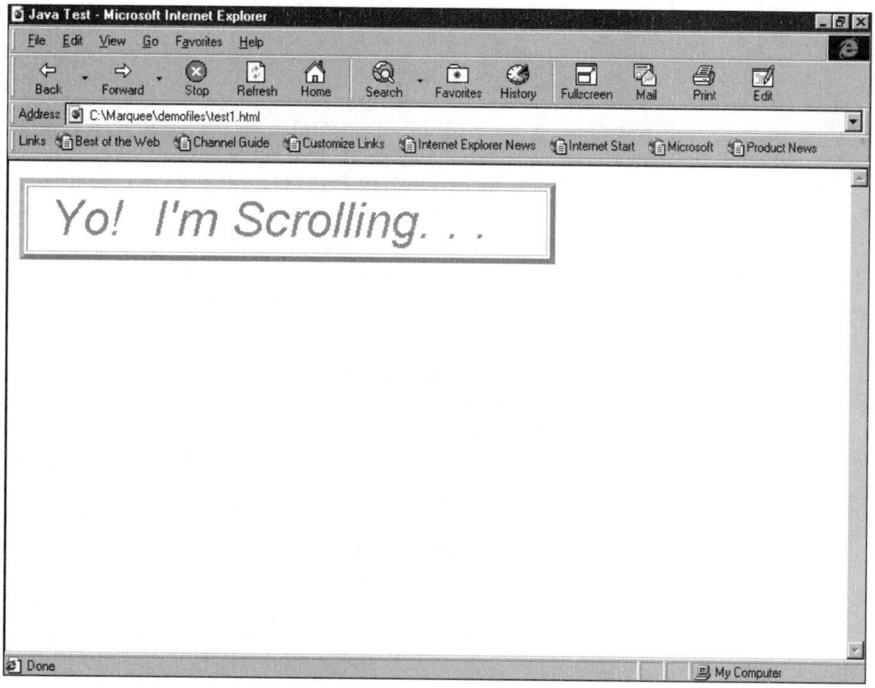

Figure 4-3:
Applets
execute
only if their
<APPLET>
tag is
properly
executed.

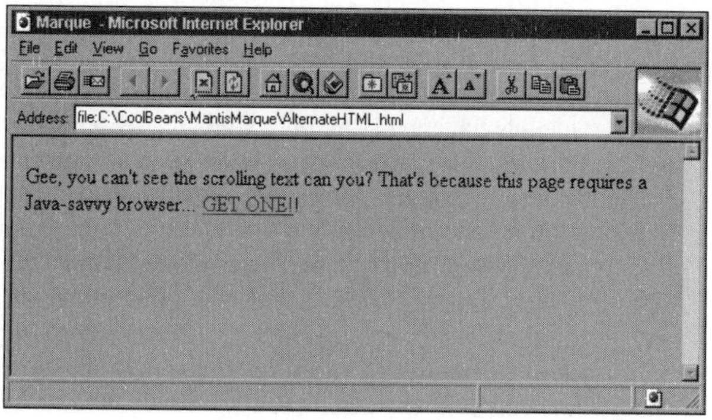

Figure 4-4:
Alternate
HTML
allows
users on
non-Java
browsers
to view
your pages.

Instead, think in terms of what the applet needs in order to operate. Don't try to memorize everything about the <APPLET> tag at once; just familiarize yourself with the parts you need to put applets into your pages. If you start with a simple applet, such as the Marquee applet (which you can find on the CD-ROM accompanying this book), you start on the ground floor and can graduate to more complicated parts of the <APPLET> tag at your own pace.

Consider the two new attributes that the Java 1.1 and Java 1.2 <APPLET> tags support, explained in Table 4-3.

Table 4-3	Java 1.1 and 1.2 Optional Applet Attributes
Attribute	*Description*
ARCHIVE	This attribute describes one or more Java archives (JARs). JAR files may contain images, sound files, or any other resources that the applet requires to operate properly. If the applet requires multiple JAR files, the files must be separated by a comma. This attribute works hand-in-hand with the required CODE attribute (see Table 4.1) because a Java archive may actually contain the class file specified with CODE.
OBJECT	This attribute specifies the name of a serialized applet file, as opposed to the non-serialized applet file (standard Java class) specified through the CODE attribute. Java 1.1 introduced *serialized* applet files which enable developers to store applet information in a way that makes it easy to send applets and their internal data over the network or save them to disk. Because serialized applet files are actually special versions of standard applets, the CODE attribute is not necessary when you use the OBJECT attribute. If you do use the CODE attribute, however, then you do not use the OBJECT attribute.
	The best way to determine whether an applet uses CODE or OBJECT is to consult the documentation that comes with it. (You may also be able to peek at an <APPLET> tag contained in a sample Web page.) Serialized applets typically have a .ser or .obj extension, as opposed to the standard .class extension in traditional applets, so you can usually determine if an applet supports the OBJECT attribute simply by looking at the applet's file extension. Of course, you'll find that your applet's documentation is worth turning to as well since simply knowing that an applet is serialized is not enough. Any applet worth weaving into your Web page comes with documentation that explains how you can take advantage of advanced features such as serialization.

Don't confuse the OBJECT attribute described here, which is part of the <APPLET> tag, with the <OBJECT> tag! See Chapter 10 for more about the <OBJECT> tag and how you can use it with the Java Plug-in.

When Java 1.0 was first introduced to the World Wide Web, it was a fresh, invigorating technology that held tremendous promise. And, as you may suspect, the <APPLET> tag was designed especially for Java 1.0.

TECHNICAL STUFF

The many faces of Java

Java 1.0, 1.01, and 1.02 are all considered "Java 1.0." Likewise, Java 1.1 plus all minor changes to that version (Java 1.1.1, 1.1.2, and 1.1.3, 1.1.4, 1.1.5 and 1.1.6 to be exact!) are considered "Java 1.1." And you can bet your booty that Java 1.2 and all minor changes to that version (Java 1.2.1 and 1.2.2, for example) are simply called "Java 1.2".

What gives? Certainly, software engineers can see that 1.1 and 1.1.1 aren't equal, so why call them the same name? To make life a little easier on you and me, it turns out.

Would you rather remember major version numbers, such as 1.0, 1.1, and 1.2, or all the major and minor versions in between? Personally, I'm happy to reserve my already feeble memory for more important things, such as when I last fed my cat Harley, and my wedding anniversary date (October 11, 1997 at 3:00 p.m., thank you — no need to send a card), and so I'm perfectly content to remember only the major Java version "families" rather than all the little itty-bitty members that come in-between.

Java 1.2 is, at the very moment I write these words, the latest and greatest version of Java. However, even as I type, another version of Java is in the works. By the time you finish reading this book, Java 1.3 may well be the latest and greatest version. As anyone who has seen Disney's *The Lion King* can tell you, this is the circle of life: Old is replaced by new, over and over and over again.

Thanks to major changes already made to Java, and others soon to come, it's no wonder that the original <APPLET> tag has been enhanced. Thankfully, you don't have to take in very much in order to take advantage of Java 1.1 applets. The enhancements to the <APPLET> tag are minor and well worth understanding because of the advantages they offer. In fact, all you have to do is figure out two new attributes. Everything else stays the same. How's that for simplicity?

Because Java 1.1 was a major enhancement to the original version of Java, Web browser manufacturers had a difficult time building support for it into their products. Thankfully, however, the most popular Web browsers in the world now understand the new ARCHIVE and OBJECT attributes that were added to the <APPLET> tag when Java 1.1 burst on the scene.

However, Java 1.1 isn't the newest kid on the block. Java 1.2 is the up and comer today. Although not as radical an update as Java 1.1 was when it arrived, Java 1.2 is no slouch by any stretch of the imagination.

Unlike Java 1.1, which introduced new functionality into the <APPLET> tag, most of Java 1.2 features are less conspicuous. That is, you don't have to learn new tag attributes to take advantage of Java 1.2 features: improved sound format support (see Chapter 5 for details), better security (discussed in Chapter 2), faster execution, and overall better performance. Simply weave Java 1.2 applets into your page as you would any other applet, and you automatically gain these benefits.

Visit Sun's Java Web site at java.sun.com/products/index.html if you're interested in finding out all about the new features and enhancements of Java 1.2 (or any other version of Java for that matter). Here you find reams of information about every major version of Java supported by Sun, as well as links to a multitude of Java-related products developed by the company that invented Java itself.

You do, however, have to wait until browsers support Java 1.2 before you can weave Java 1.2 applets into your Web pages! At the time this book went to press, no browsers in the world fully supported Java 1.2. Of course, you can always tap into the incredible Java Plug-in (see Chapter 10) to instantly add Java 1.2 support to any Java-savvy browser. In fact, the Java Plug-in is by far the best way to get your fill of Java 1.2 this very moment without waiting for browser vendors to update their products.

Catch me if you can!

Web browser vendors are always playing "catch up" with Java, which means that the latest and greatest features of the language aren't built into browsers right away. In fact, the only commercial browser that supports Java 1.2 at the time I am writing this book is Netscape Navigator 5.0. However, even Navigator 5.0 doesn't fully support all the features of Java 1.2 — it only supports a few features, so I have to wait for an upgrade to Navigator before I can be certain that all Java 1.2 applets run properly in this browser!

By the time you read this, however, Navigator may well be updated to support Java 1.2. But be warned — millions of users are likely to forgo the upgrade (for any number of reasons, not the least of which is that most folks don't realize that full Java 1.2 support isn't built into this first release of Navigator), which means that applets written to take full advantage of Java 1.2 won't work properly when these people view them. So, if you want your Java-powered Web pages to be accessible to the widest possible audience, you need to take the various Web browsers into account. Fortunately, I do just that in Appendix B, where I show you how to create Java-powered Web pages that can accommodate Web browsers of all stripes and colors.

Using the ARCHIVE attribute

A *Java archive,* better known as a JAR, is nothing more than a compressed collection of files that an applet needs in order to run. JARs are meant to make your job a little easier. Instead of dealing with a bunch of applet files, such as .class files, image files, and sound files (each of which you have to upload to your Web site to be of any practical use to a Java-powered Web page), you only need to deal with a single archive.

Because the files in a JAR are compressed, they take up less hard drive space and take less time to transfer over the network. Consequently, Webbers don't have as long to wait before an applet starts running. In many cases, JAR files cut applet download times almost in half — not bad, especially considering JAR files also make uploading applets to the Web much easier. (Wouldn't you rather upload one Java archive than a dozen or more individual files? I know I would.)

When using JAR files, you have to let the browser know what's going on — browsers aren't mind readers. Luckily, telling a browser that it needs to download a JAR file isn't very difficult thanks to the ARCHIVE attribute. Consider the following:

```
<APPLET CODE="Marquee" ARCHIVE="Marquee.jar" WIDTH=500
        HEIGHT=40>
</APPLET>
```

In this example, the browser downloads the JAR file named Marquee.jar. It then looks inside that archive for a file named Marquee.class, because that's the full name of the file specified in the CODE attribute.

The .class file extension is implied when dealing with the CODE attribute, so you actually don't have to include it. However, just for fun, take a look at the following example:

```
<APPLET CODE="Marquee.class" ARCHIVE="Marquee.jar"
        WIDTH=500 HEIGHT=40>
</APPLET>
```

This example is functionally equivalent to the preceding one — they both tell the browser to download the Marquee.jar archive file and then look inside it for an applet .class file named Marquee.class. In most cases, the JAR file contains the actual Java applet .class file, but not always. If the applet .class file isn't inside the JAR, the browser downloads it separately. Whether or not the Java archive file contains the applet .class file is entirely dependent on the software developer who creates the applet.

Developers don't have to include the .class file inside a JAR file, but doing so does make things a little easier for users because you only have to deal with one file (the JAR file) if the .class file is inside of it. If not, you have to deal with the .class file and .jar file separately.

Come to think of it, no hard-and-fast rule states what exactly goes into a JAR. Developers are free to place any files they want inside a JAR, and can even split the various files that an applet requires over more than one JAR. Consider the following variation on the theme I have going here:

```
<APPLET CODE="Marquee.class" ARCHIVE="MarqueeClasses.jar",
        "MarqueeSounds.jar", "MarqueeImages.jar"
        WIDTH=500 HEIGHT=40>
</APPLET>
```

In this example, the ARCHIVE attribute specifies three distinct JARs, each separated by a comma. Although this isn't a real <APPLET> tag (the Marquee applet on the CD-ROM doesn't have any use for images or sounds — it only scrolls a text message across the screen), it illustrates the concept that multiple JAR files are sometimes used by applets. Again, the number of JARs an applet requires depends on how the developer chooses to implement the applet.

Keep in mind that the examples you see here are merely suggestions of what your <APPLET> tag may look like if the Marquee applet supported multiple JAR files. In fact, the Marquee applet provided on CD-ROM only requires one JAR file and can even be run without a JAR file entirely because it's also available in .class form as well (that is, it's available for use with Java 1.0 and 1.1, and 1.2 browsers). However, in the interest of helping you understand how multiple JAR files are specified in the ARCHIVE attribute, I've taken the liberty of pretending that the Marquee applet supports more than one JAR file. Okay, fine. I lied. Are you happy now?

Of course, just because an applet uses JAR files doesn't mean that it can't also take advantage of the flexibility that parameters offer. In each of these examples, I intentionally omit <PARAM> tags because the focus has been on the ARCHIVE attribute. However, applets that use JAR files are just as likely to use <PARAM> tags as those that don't, as the following <APPLET> tag illustrates:

```
<APPLET CODE="Marquee.class" ARCHIVE="Marquee.jar"
        WIDTH=500 HEIGHT=40>
    <PARAM NAME="font_face" VALUE="TimesRoman">
    <PARAM NAME="font_size" VALUE="24">
    <PARAM NAME="font_italic" VALUE="yes">
    <PARAM NAME="font_bold" VALUE="yes">
    <PARAM NAME="marquee" VALUE="Yo! I'm scrolling!">
```

```
Gee, you can't see the scrolling text can you?
That's because this page requires a Java-savvy browser...
<A HREF="http://www.netscape.com">GET ONE!</A>
</APPLET>
```

A developer may specify any number of <PARAM> tags, which you can use to customize an applet. (See Chapter 8 for more information.)

Every applet supports alternate HTML in the same way, no matter who the developer is. As the preceding example shows, alternate HTML always appears just before the closing </APPLET> tag. If a Web browser isn't Java-savvy, it uses the alternate HTML. If it is Java-savvy, the applet runs.

Using the OBJECT attribute

Serialized applets are a feature of Java 1.1 and 1.2 that make life easier on the developer. *Serialized applets* are internally represented in such a way that they're easier to send over a network or save to a hard drive — they're essentially the same as normal applets, meaning you won't really be able to tell the difference between normal and serialized applets even though serialized applets are fundamentally different on the inside. On the outside, they're no different from other applets.

Serialization is a feature of the Java 1.1 and 1.2 language that relates directly to how a developer actually writes programming code — think of it as a special-purpose spice that a chef has the option of using at his discretion. Not all dishes benefit from a particular spice, and those that might aren't guaranteed to get a dash or two of it. It's the chef's choice. So it goes with serialization; not all applets need it, and the developer may not take advantage of it even if she can.

If you're interested in creating your own applets from scratch, check out *Java Programming For Dummies,* 3rd Edition, by Donald and David Koosis (IDG Books Worldwide, Inc.).

Serialization gives developers special programming capabilities, a feature that greatly advances the state of the art in applets. Fortunately, you don't have to sweat the details of serialization other than to simply use the OBJECT attribute. The programmer gets paid to work out the details of applet serialization. You just sit back and take it easy. Maybe that's why programmers are generally an edgy bunch.

The OBJECT attribute is necessary for those applets that use serialization. In fact, serialized applets have no need at all for the CODE attribute. Unlike ARCHIVE, which works closely with CODE, the OBJECT attribute replaces it lock, stock, and barrel:

```
<APPLET OBJECT="Marquee.ser" WIDTH=500 HEIGHT=40>
</APPLET>
```

If you use CODE, you can't use OBJECT, and vice versa. Of course, which attribute you use depends on the applet itself. To find out which attribute you should use for an applet, you have to either explore the documentation that comes with the applet or take a look at a sample <APPLET> tag already woven into a Web page. Alternatively, you can peek at the applet's file extension. Traditional applets that rely on the CODE attribute have the .class file extension, while serialized applets usually have a .ser or .obj extension (not always, mind you, because the extension given to a serialized applet is also up to the developer!).

Chapter 5

Designing Your Own Java-Powered Web Page

*I*f you've spent any amount of time on the Web with a Java-savvy browser, you're probably just itching to add this addictive technology to your own Web pages. After all, playing with Java-powered pages is only half the fun. Finding applets to put on your own Web pages is where it's really at. So let your hair down, kick off your shoes, slip into something more comfortable, and turn up the tunes. Prepare to get wired — it's Java time!

First, decide what you want your Java-powered pages to be like, then get your hands on the applets that will make such pages possible. After all, without applets, your thirst for Java can't be quenched. Luckily, finding Java applets is easier than locating a Starbucks coffee shop in Seattle.

To be perfectly honest, applets aren't the only route to jazzing up your life with Java. Java applications, discussed in more detail in Part III, also provide that Java jolt.

Landing the Perfect Applet

You're all ready to jazz up your Web site with some really spiffy Java applets, when you stop in your tracks and ask, "Where do applets come from?"

Time to sit down and have a little talk . . .

Don't sweat it

How you go about finding applets to use in your Web page plays a big part in your overall planning process. When you're trying to decide what Java applets to include in your Web site (as well as the overall design of your pages), you can employ either of two essential techniques:

- **Inspiration surfing:** The easiest way to generate ideas for your Web site is by looking at what other people have done. Surfing the Web, you're sure to find inspiring pages and applets. This is a process I call *inspiration surfing,* and it's the most direct and perhaps the most enjoyable way to generate ideas for your Web pages.

- **Perspiration working:** If you're a glutton for punishment, you can come up with the ideas on your own, in relative isolation, as a direct response to your site's specific requirements. This technique is much less enjoyable, requires a significant amount of mental energy, and forces Web page authors to sweat out the details of a site without taking advantage of the hundreds of thousands of hours that others have put into developing state-of-the-art Java sites.

  The worst part of this approach is that after you figure out what you want the applets to do, you have to build them or get them built. Sure, if you have a Ph.D. in Computer Nerdology, you can program your own applets from scratch (or you can take the easy way out and flip through *Java Programming For Dummies,* 3rd Edition, by Donald and David Koosis [IDG Books Worldwide, Inc.]). But if you're just starting out, you're much better off taking the easy route and customizing pre-existing applets.

Personally speaking, I'd rather be inspired than perspire. How about you?

To really get a feel for what your Web pages can and should do, you need to spend a considerable amount of time online looking at what's out there. Only after you've navigated many hypermedia documents can you really understand and appreciate good Web-page design.

Unfortunately, in an attempt to get in on the excitement, many folks rush onto the Web without truly understanding what it's all about. This eager-beaver approach leads to the condition of *perspiration working,* sweating out the details of developing Web pages for no good reason. Making this mistake can be fatal for your Web site; publishing Java-powered pages on the World Wide Web without first giving yourself the time and experience to know good page design from bad will drive a stake right through the heart of your site.

In Java, Web design is crucial because applets take a long time to load, especially if they use images and sounds (which many do). Because Java is so cool, many Webbers will hang out long enough to check out a Java-powered page. But if the site they wait around for turns out to be completely bogus, a total waste of time and money, you can bet they'll grab their surfboards and beat a path to another Web page before you can say "pork chop express." And the longer the wait, the more hostile the impression of the offending site. If, on the other hand, a site is really useful or cool, visitors will stick around — maybe even bookmarking the site for instant access later on, which means that the site gets repeat visitors.

I don't mean to suggest that you should put off hooking applets up to your own pages until you've searched the Web far and wide and distilled the quintessential Web page. In fact, honing your applet-embedding skills at the same time that you're cultivating a taste for page design is a good idea. Because you create Web pages on your local computer, you are the only one who can view them, until you upload to a Web server. Thus, your Web site can be a work in progress right on your own hard drive. You, and you alone, decide when a page is ready for prime time, so you can refine it to your heart's content in the privacy of your own home or office before uploading it to the Web for the world to see.

Getting permission to pick

When you come across an applet that you want to weave into your own page, investigate to see whether you have permission to use it. Be aware that some applets are completely out of your reach — many Web pages are chock-full of scrumptious applets that simply aren't available for the picking.

You can tell when an applet is entirely off limits to the public because the site doesn't provide any information explaining how to use the applet in your own pages. Of course, it's a good idea to navigate around the entire site before giving up. But if such details aren't provided, you have no choice but to move on.

If the Web page that contains the applet of your eye doesn't explicitly offer its applets to you, move on to another orchard. If you pilfer applets from a page that doesn't say something to the effect of, "Howdy, I'm an applet free for the taking — use me on your own Web page!" you stand a good chance of catching a shotgun blast of legal buckshot right in the rump.

Applets are little software programs, and taking them without permission is just as illegal as walking into a store and swiping a box of software off the shelf. Of course, you can always contact the author of an applet you desire and ask for permission to use it. Depending on who wrote the applet, and what the author thinks about the idea of giving away the result of his or her blood, sweat, and tears (or at least a long night at the keyboard), you may or may not get a blessing to use it. But don't let the idea of being turned down by a software developer discourage you — it's worth a shot if only to get a personal "Bug OFF!" e-mail from the author!

Fortunately, truckloads of applets on the Web are free for the taking, with bushels more arriving every day. And most of these applets describe in clear detail exactly how you can weave them into your own pages. So unless you're in the market for some exotic applet, chances are you can find exactly what you need by surfing the Web (see Appendix A).

Ordering a custom-grown applet

If you search the whole wide Web and still don't find an available applet that you like, you can always have an applet custom-developed to fit your needs (see Figure 5-1). But be warned, custom-written applets aren't cheap; depending on the work involved, you can expect to spend anywhere from $50 to $1,000 for the most basic applet!

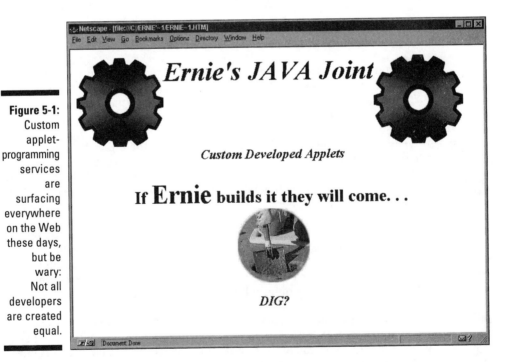

Figure 5-1: Custom applet-programming services are surfacing everywhere on the Web these days, but be wary: Not all developers are created equal.

An overwhelming number of self-proclaimed Java experts have surfaced on the Web lately, each promising to create top-notch applets at a fair price. If you decide to have a custom Java applet created for you, play it safe and follow these tips:

✓ **Choose only a firm with experience.** Look for companies with customer references and examples of their work prominently displayed on the site (or those willing to furnish these items immediately upon request).

✓ **Don't accept references at face value.** Contact each reference and ask pointed questions, such as

- What work was done?

- How long did it take?

- How much did it cost?

- Would you recommend hiring this company for my job?

✓ **Shop around.** What one company may charge $500 to develop, another company may develop for $100 or less. But keep in mind that price isn't everything; a developer's reputation is, in my opinion, the most important part of the equation.

The Web provides a forum in which all its users who have a computer and a modem can proclaim themselves Java-development experts. Don't be taken for a ride.

A Quest for the Best Applets in CyberLand

One of the most challenging aspects of injecting your Web pages with Java is choosing from the dizzying spectrum of applets available. If you take even a quick spin on the Web with a Java-savvy browser, you see exactly what I mean: At every twist and turn in the ether, new and enticing applets appear, begging to be adapted for use in your very own pages.

You can weave any number of applets into a single Web page. But don't go crazy; each applet takes time to download. As a result, anyone visiting an applet-saturated page may have to wait a long time for the applets to finally kick into high gear — which may drive folks away from your site rather than attract them. With applets, as with Web pages in general, you should consider the overall design of the page *before* you actually create it. Good Web design entails well-considered use of page elements such as text, images, sound, and, of course, applets. Bad Web design, on the other hand, is as easy to spot as an elephant at the alter: Pages are bulging at the seams because they're so crammed with elements, lending a slapped together look that's not only difficult to navigate but painfully slow to load. Go easy as you place material in your Web pages, especially when it comes to applets because they take more time to download than other page elements, and you'll come out a winner.

Setting sail in search of great applets

If you're not sure where to start your applet search, don't worry. You can begin surfing at any page, and let your mouse lead you from page to page, site to site, at any pace you choose. However, I suggest surfing slowly in the beginning because you need to cultivate a taste for Web page design.

As you surf, you begin to understand what you like and don't like, which will influence your design decisions later. What makes a Java-powered site especially strong or weak is a matter of personal taste, but a great Web site usually has the following qualities:

- ✔ **It's fresh.** The applets on the site aren't the same old applets that everybody uses. If an applet appears on half the Java sites, will your site grab anyone's attention by using it? Probably not. But if you can't get your hands on unique applets, consider configuring the ones you do have in a way that sets them apart from the pack.

- ✔ **It's attractive.** The site itself isn't overcrowded with applets, images, and so on. Faced with an ugly screen, users will probably back out of the page before you can show your magic.

- ✔ **It's cool.** Nothing beats a page that makes the surfer say, "Wow!" If you strive to make your pages unique in how they look, as well as in the content they contain, you'll almost certainly have a "Wow!" on your hands.

- ✔ **It's useful.** In addition to being attractive and cool, your page should be something that people can use. People who surf the Web love finding things they can use. If you build it, they will come.

- ✔ **It's interactive.** Finally, your site should interact with its users. If they can *do something* with the applets at your site as they play, learn, or work, the site becomes both useful and fun. After all, wouldn't you rather do something useful *and* fun more than something just useful?

Several Web sites are dedicated to exposing the worst sites and pages out there, and many more are dedicated to honoring the best ones. To find the best and worst sites on the Web, simply use a search engine (see Appendix A for details) and enter the keywords **"worst Web"** and **"best Web"** in your query.

Dropping anchor with bookmarks

When you mark your place in a printed book like this one, you may rip off a piece of paper and slip it between two pages. You may even write something on the piece of paper to remind you why you put it there. When you use the Web, you do the same thing. No, don't worry about getting out a piece of paper and a pen. Remember — this is the electronic age, so you use a virtual bookmark.

When you come upon a Java-powered Web page that appeals to you, bookmark it! Every Web browser allows you to bookmark, or *hotlink,* Web pages for instant access later on. In Netscape Navigator, the feature is called *bookmarking;* In Microsoft Internet Explorer, it's called *Favorites.* When you bookmark a page, you can return to it quickly to refresh your memory, which is certain to become clouded after you see a few hundred Java-injected pages.

As you make bookmarks for all the inspirational Web sites you find, take notes about the site, the moment you bookmark it. Fortunately, most browsers allow you to enter notes at the same time that you make bookmarks (some of my notes are shown in Figure 5-2).

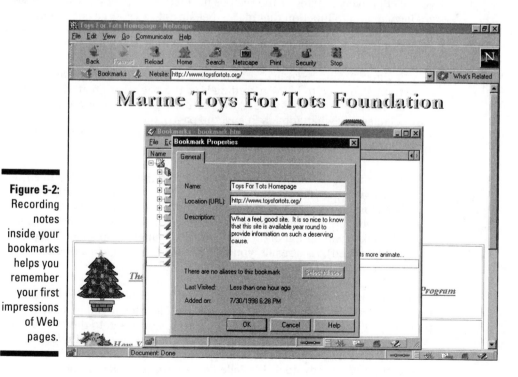

Figure 5-2: Recording notes inside your bookmarks helps you remember your first impressions of Web pages.

First impressions of a site can make or break a site; most Webbers decide within a matter of seconds whether a site is worth sticking around in or if they should head elsewhere. You need to develop a feel for what attracts and repels Webbers, and the only way you can do that is to get in touch with your inner Web child.

In addition to recording your first impressions of a site, consider ranking the site and recording its score along with your notes (see Figure 5-2). You can choose any ranking system you like, even a simple 1 to 10 scale, as long as you have a way to distinguish between the good and the bad sites. Use whatever floats your boat, as long as you can distinguish between the good, the bad, and the ugly sites.

Digging for buried treasure in source code

Setting bookmarks alone isn't enough. You also want to peek behind the curtains and take a look at the HTML code used to create the pages that turn your crank.

By taking a look at the HTML source code in the pages that inspire you, you're effectively looking at the recipes for tasty Web pages. All Web browsers have a built-in function that makes peeking at the source code behind Web pages easy: Choose either View⇨Page Source or View⇨Source, depending on which browser you use, as shown in Figure 5-3.

As you view the source code of a Web page, you can find out just about everything you need to know regarding how the page was created. You are, after all, looking at the recipe used to create the page from scratch! In particular, seeing what applets, if any, the page uses, is a simple procedure. You need only invoke the browser's Find feature and search for the word *applet.*

Keep in mind that the word *applet* may appear in the ⟨APPLET⟩ tag in either upper- or lowercase letters, though I suggest you always use uppercase when weaving applets into your own Web pages for the sake of readability. Luckily, by default, the Find feature in most browsers ignores case (if yours doesn't, look for an option in the Find window that lets you specify that case should be ignored). As a result, you find all ⟨APPLET⟩ tags in a document, whether you search for the word *applet* or *APPLET.*

Of course, just *looking at* the source of a document online doesn't do you too much good and may end up costing a small fortune in online fees if you pay for your Internet connection by the hour (as opposed to the "all you can eat for $19.95" deal that most ISPs offer). Fortunately, you don't need to have Einstein's memory to recall the specifics of the ⟨APPLET⟩ tag format; your computer already does. It's called *local storage* — better known as saving a file onto your hard drive.

Figure 5-3:
Sneaking a
peek at the
HTML
source
code used
to create
Web pages
is easy;
every Web
browser
lets you
look under
the covers
of a Web
page.

Pillaging, plundering, and bringing home the loot

When you find a page that inspires you, you can download to your personal computer the HTML source code used to create it, allowing you to view it countless times without bothering to surf the Web. After all, there's no reason to connect to the Web to peek at source code when you have the page on your very own system!

Saving the source code of a Web page is easy. All you have to do is choose your browser's Save option, which is usually under File on the browser menu. *Note:* In some browsers, you must choose the Save As option while viewing the Web page itself, because no menu options are available when viewing source code.

Give each Web page you save a descriptive name, followed by the .html (or .htm) extension, as shown in Figure 5-4. Saving the document with an extension enables you to easily recognize that it contains Web-page source code. Also, be sure to save the Web page in HTML format, if given the choice; otherwise, you may end up saving the document as plain text instead of as source code! (Although some browsers automatically default to HTML format when you save Web pages to disk, other browsers may not.) If you're unsure of what format your browser is saving a page in, simply open up the document with a word processor (or any program capable of viewing plain text files). If the format is HTML, you see the source code right off the bat. If not, return to your browser and save the page again — this time using the HTML format.

As with any document, you have to choose a location on your hard drive to store a Web page. And be sure to make a note of where you place it so that you can find that useful source code when you want it. Personally, I prefer to create a new directory for each site I pluck pages from.

You can view the source code of the Web pages you save using your browser to access the appropriate option under the File menu — usually something like Open or Open Page.

You can bookmark a Web page residing on your computer just as you do a Web page that exists online. And, just as with Web pages in cyberspace, you can use your browser to view the source code of the pages you save on your computer without having to rush yourself, concerned about tying up your phone line. With Web pages stored in local files, there is no online time.

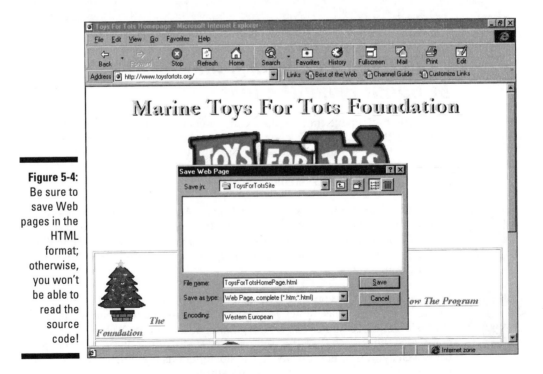

Figure 5-4:
Be sure to save Web pages in the HTML format; otherwise, you won't be able to read the source code!

Don't let your thirst for Java put you behind bars!

Although the idea of millions of Web pages floating around in cyberspace (with source code and images seemingly free for the taking) may seem like just the ticket to get your site up and running in record time, be careful; what you download may not be "free" at all. Using these materials in your own site without permission could end up costing you a small fortune in lawyers' fees!

The contents of most Web pages are intended for access only through a Web browser, not for downloading to your personal computer. However, as long as you download such information for your own personal use and don't republish it, you're safe. The second you publish (on the Web or elsewhere) words, images, sounds, music, or applets created by other people without their express permission, you're in danger of being slapped with a copyright infringement lawsuit.

For this reason, I strongly suggest that you download Web page source code and images only to learn how others went about creating them. Think of source code and images as digital blueprints: You're free to use the source as the basis for your own work, as long as you substitute your own text and images. But never (ever!) use the text or images created by another in your own pages, no matter how tempting, unless you first receive permission from the author or know for a fact that what you're using is in the public domain or falls under the legal umbrella of fair use. In a nutshell, *fair use* means that you're allowed to use someone else's property (Web pages, in this case) as long as you're not taking away profits from that person. That is, you're free to use Web pages for your own personal use, such as figuring out how to do some special trick with HTML code, as long as you're not making money off the page or detracting in any way from the original author's page. The end result: You can use other people's Web pages to try your hand at creating your own pages, but should never publish (upload to the Internet) another person's work.

Were it not for the fact that browsers intentionally provide a mechanism for saving Web page source code and images to your personal computer, I would never suggest that you do it. Lawsuits simply aren't my cup of tea, and I'm sure if the screws were put to you by a high-pressured legal dream team, you'd sing like a canary: "Aaron told me to do it. I swear!" But because browsers give you everything you need to save source code and images to disk in the blink of an eye, I'm willing to take that risk. Under heavy Spanish Inquisition-style interrogation and fear for my very life, I, too, will crack and chirp like a finch: "Netscape and Microsoft made me do it. I swear!"

Downloading More Than Source Code

When you download a page for local access, you may be surprised to find that none of the images, sounds, or applets associated with that page are available because you're only downloading an HTML file, not the elements that are displayed on it. Because Web pages are nothing more than HTML files that point to the elements that they contain, downloading a page doesn't mean that you're downloading everything you see on it. Instead, when you save a page to your computer for local access, you save only the HTML code of the page itself. That fact can make for a radical change in appearance from the page you viewed on the Web, and happens because you only downloaded the source code and nothing more. But you shouldn't have a problem because the source code of Web pages is what's most important — it's the source you use as a recipe for your own pages.

But Java-powered Web pages aren't made up of HTML source code and images alone, the way most standard pages are. Fortunately, saving Web page images to your computer is a breeze; however, saving the other elements a page may contain, such as sounds and applets, isn't so easy. In Chapter 6, I show you how to save applets and their support files.

Wouldn't it be nice to save the *entire* page (source code, graphics, sound, and applets) to your hard drive all at once? Saving *all* the elements in a page, although technically possible, is a rather tedious process compared to saving images. In fact, the way to go about saving all the elements is a fairly well-kept secret that I'm afraid I can't share. You see, not only is it unethical to retrieve an entire page to your local computer, doing so may be illegal!

The law in this area is a light shade of gray because the Web is a public entity used to publish material for the public at large. The underlying elements that make up publications, however, may not be intended for you to download and use in your own Web pages. In fact, some lawyers insist that it's illegal for you to do anything but look at a Web page, suggesting that copying any contents of a page to your own computer is grounds for a lawsuit. Because the Web is so new, this debate remains a gray area until a precedent is set, and wouldn't you just hate to be the one caught in the middle of such a high-profile lawsuit? My advice? Unless an applet is freely offered by a Web page, don't bother with it — it's just not worth the effort and risk.

Saving images

At times, you may want to save more than just the source code of a Web page to your computer. This is particularly true when you come across a page that contains images intended to be used in conjunction with Java applets, something you'll probably encounter quite often as you scour the Web in search of inspiration for your own pages.

Fortunately, Web-page images often are available free of charge and without restriction, meaning that you can use them in your own pages without fear of being slapped with a lawsuit. Look for an explicit permission stating that the images are free for the taking. Borrowing images is a real time saver and is particularly helpful, because slick-looking images are extremely difficult to create from scratch. Instead, you can pluck really cool images right off the Web for use with your Java applets, without the pain of creating images yourself.

With most Java-savvy browsers, saving images is a cinch. Normally, simply clicking an image takes you to whatever item it's linked to, assuming that the image is indeed a hyperlink. A slight variation on this theme allows you to save the image to disk:

✔ If you're a Macintosh user, the trick lies in *not* releasing the mouse after you click. All you have to do is press and hold down the mouse while your cursor is over the image and a pop-up menu appears with an option for saving the image to disk.

✔ For Windows users, simply right-click the image and a pop-up menu appears. Cool, huh?

After you click on each of the graphics in a page, using the appropriate mouse technique, choose Save Image from the menu that appears. The only fatal flaw to this plan is broken links.

Dealing with broken links

Web pages often contain images that reside in a variety of different directories on the Internet or even on different Web servers entirely. As a result, you must update the source code for the pages you download so that they can point the various images originally referenced in the page, or simply deal with these broken links ("broken" because a referenced image can't be found). You can remedy broken links by downloading all the images a page references. After you have the images on your own computer, you can then update your page's HTML source code to point to them. Alternately, you can update your page's image references so that they point to the original images on the Web (in this case, you'll only be able to see the images in your page when you're connected to the Internet).

Your options are either to update the source code or to create a directory structure on your computer that parallels that of the Web site from which the source came. I recommend updating the source code. To change the source code, load the HTML into a text editor, such as the Windows Notepad or the Macintosh SimpleText application, and update the HTML references. If you're not comfortable working with HTML, take a peek at Chapter 3 first!

Alternately, you can use the built-in Web page editor that comes with modern browsers. As Chapter 2 explains, the latest versions of Netscape Navigator and Internet Explorer feature visual page editing tools. Thanks to these WYSIWYG ("what you see is what you get") tools, you can craft Web pages visually, using only your mouse.

You can deal with relative URLs (flip to Chapter 4) simply by creating the equivalent directory path on your computer. With absolute URLs, you're in over your head unless all the absolute URLs pass through the same directory as the page itself, which is highly unlikely. In this case, you have no choice but to change the source code of the page so that it uses a relative URL, because you can't mimic entire Web servers on your computer by using simple directory structures. Check out Chapter 4 for details on absolute and relative URLs.

Battling Bandwidth Bottlenecks

Getting lost in the excitement of creating Java-powered Web pages full of sophisticated animation and sounds is easy. Souping up your site with animated, high-resolution images and injecting long, heart-pounding audio clips into the mix is terribly tempting! And even though everything may seem just dandy as you develop such pages on your personal computer, you may be cruising for a rude awakening when the time comes to bring your pages to life on the Web.

You see, when you create pages locally with the HTML source code, images, applets, and support files (usually images and sounds used by the applet) on your hard drive, everything is smooth as silk. All the pieces of your page already exist on your computer, so everything loads into your browser almost instantly — no waiting for the page to download over the wire. But when you upload the page and all its parts onto the Web (as Chapter 11 shows you how to do), you're dealing with a completely different beast, the beast called bandwidth.

Anyone who visits pages that reside on the World Wide Web is at the mercy of *bandwidth* — how fast things can travel down the wire (a hip way of saying "over the network") into the user's computer. Plainly put, limited bandwidth is one of the biggest problems on the Web today. The vast majority of Webbers connect to the Internet at speeds too slow to make viewing Web pages jam-packed with images and sounds an enjoyable experience. You can surf through your own pages because they reside entirely on your personal computer, but visitors to your site will probably feel as if they're swimming in quicksand as they wait for everything to download before the fun can begin.

Because bandwidth is a major issue with the majority of Webbers, you must consider the lowest common denominator. Although you may try to convince yourself that 56 Kbps modems are the norm — perhaps with dreams of high-speed ISDN and cable modem access not far behind — many folks are connecting to the Internet at speeds of 28.8 Kbps, 14.4 Kbps, or even less! To deliver a decent experience to visitors of your Web site — offering your Java-powered pages to everyone, without penalizing those with slower access — take extra care when planning your pages: You must take bandwidth into consideration.

Although applets are quite small and come across the wire in a hurry, the graphics and audio files that applets utilize are tremendous by comparison. You can do several things to decrease transmission time and prevent serious bottlenecks when downloading these files over the network. The following sections tell you how.

Sizing up sound files

When dealing with sound files, you should be aware that the first two crops of Java applets — Java 1.0 and 1.1 — are very restricted in the types of audio they understand. Java 1.0 and 1.1 support only Sun's AU sound format. Files using this format have an extension of .au. If you have a sound file that isn't stored in this format, like a Windows .wav file, you have to convert the sound file to the AU format in a very specific way if you intend to use the sound file with a Java 1.0 or 1.1 applet.

Java 1.2 applets, on the other hand, are much more capable when it comes to playing audio, as the section "Java 1.2 sounds off" explains. Unfortunately, Java 1.2 applets are the exception rather than the rule; you bump into them much less often than Java 1.0 and 1.1 applets, which account for the vast majority of applets on the Web today.

Although the AU format creates sound files that typically are smaller in size than other formats, the sound quality isn't the best. As a result, you may have to fiddle with various sound editing functions in your conversion tool (if you own one) to try to eliminate the hiss you hear when converting higher-quality sounds to this format.

A bevy of sounds, each in the AU format, resides on the CD-ROM included with this book — giving you a wide assortment of choices for using audio in your Java-powered pages.

If you want to use your own sound files with a Java 1.0 or 1.1 applet, you first must convert them into the AU format. Plus, be sure to apply a uLaw compression to the sound in the conversion process (AU is the format, while uLaw is a special way of compressing AU sound files). Because AU files may be compressed using different uLaw settings, be careful to convert your sounds exactly as Java requires: 8-bit, 8000 Hz, single-channel (mono) AU uLaw settings.

To help you convert your existing sound files into this very specific AU format, the CD-ROM packaged with this book contains a special utility for just this purpose. Macintosh users can use the SoundApp program and Windows users can use the GoldWave utility. For details on where these files are located, refer to Appendix C.

Although the GoldWave conversion utility (for Windows users) includes a number of sound-editing features such as Smooth and Fade effects, the SoundApp program (for Macintosh users) is only capable of converting files — it can't edit them. If you're a Macintosh user and find that the sounds you convert contain excessive hissing, consider investing in a commercial-quality tool capable of both editing sounds and saving them in the AU format supported by Java. But before you run out and plunk down your hard earned shekels, check the stockpiles of Macintosh shareware that abound on the Web.

Cutting the silence

To reduce the size of sound files as much as possible when converting them for use with Java, keep only the absolutely essential portions of the sound file. Cut out any preceding or trailing silence. In doing so, you reduce the size of the file without adversely affecting the sound.

Because cutting out all preceding and trailing silence in a sound tends to result in playback that begins and ends abruptly, you may be tempted to keep a second or two of silence on either end just to make the sound more natural. Luckily, you can achieve the same effect by applying a *fade-in* to the beginning of the sound and a *fade-out* to the end. These effects give smooth transitions to a sound that may otherwise start and stop abruptly. Not only is the result a more professional and appealing sound, but you also trim precious seconds of download time in the process.

A few seconds may not seem like much, but every single second counts when it comes to bandwidth. This is especially true if you happen to use several sounds in a Web page. Seconds add up to minutes . . . which, if you're paying for every hour of time spent online, add up to dollars.

Creating sound loops

Because sound is such an effective way to grab attention and add impact to a Web page, and because Java applets make using sound so easy, many folks tend to overuse sounds on their Web pages. Unfortunately, doing so creates bandwidth bottlenecks that can turn your Web page viewers off.

Rather than playing a large number of audio clips with your Java applets, consider whether *looping* may be a reasonable alternative. When you loop a sound file, it repeats continuously until you tell it to stop. The effect can be quite powerful, especially if the sound you loop is subtle. Looping can be a great alternative to bombarding your visitors with sound after sound and sucking up bandwidth in the process.

Thanks to Java's audio support flexibility, you can play any number of sounds at once; you don't have to stop a sound loop in order to play another sound file. Unless you specify otherwise (assuming the applet you use allows you to), all sounds you play at the same time are mixed together, resulting in a rich audio experience.

Java 1.2 sounds off

As I mention earlier, Java 1.0 and Java 1.1 applets are very restricted in the audio format they support. Java 1.2, on the other hand, is sound-rich by comparison. Java 1.2 applets support the AU format introduced with Java 1.0, in addition to the following sound formats:

- ✔ AIFF
- ✔ WAV
- ✔ MIDI (specifically, MIDI type 0 and MIDI type 1)
- ✔ RMF

Because they support a wide array of sound formats, Java 1.2 applets can play audio at the same high fidelity quality of a CD player. Rejoice, my friend. Gone are the days of applets that sound like they're playing tunes from the bottom of the Atlantic Ocean.

Java 1.0 and Java 1.1 applications are entirely devoid of sound support; applications created with these versions of Java are silent. Java 1.2 applications, however, are able to take advantage of the same sound formats available to Java 1.2 applets described here. As a result, Java applications are no longer mute thanks to Java 1.2! See Chapter 13 and 14 for more about Java applications.

Making the most of images and colors

Java 1.0 and 1.1 applets support only GIF (Graphics Interchange Format) and JPEG (Joint Photographic Experts Group) images, meaning that you have limited choices when using images with these applets. However, the format you choose relates directly to the quality of images you have as Figure 5-5 shows.

Figure 5-5:
Contrasting
formats:
The image
on the left is
in GIF
format,
while the
image on
the right is
JPEG.

✔ **JPEG** format enables you to utilize 24-bit color (near photographic quality) images with your applets.

✔ **GIF** limits you to using no more than 256 colors.

Although you may be tempted to use full-color JPEG images with your applets because this format supports a much larger spectrum of colors than GIF, don't do it! Instead, try to reduce the number of colors in your images to 256 or less; in doing so, you greatly reduce the amount of time your file takes to come across the wire. Of course, getting your images down to 256 colors or less is the trick. When you accomplish this feat of minimalism, you still have to decide upon a file format to save them in: GIF or JPEG? The next section helps you decide.

Choosing GIF or JPEG

When you add images to your Web page, you eventually have to decide on a format to support. Java supports both GIF and JPEG formats, but a number of factors may make one of these formats preferable to you over the other.

Using GIF images has several benefits:

- Most graphics programs, including shareware utilities, support this popular format, so you're never at a loss for tools to help you create and edit images in this format.

- GIF is the most common graphic format in use on the Web today.

- The GIF format is highly efficient and has built-in compression that makes for relatively small images, as long as you're not dealing with photographs. (The GIF format is great at compressing cartoon-like artwork, but not nearly as good as JPEG for compressing photographic-quality images.)

- GIF supports transparency and interlacing, which can greatly enhance the visual appeal of your applet.

Getting transparency with GIF

Transparency enables the graphic artist to specify any color in an image as being transparent. When rendered on the screen, this color isn't actually displayed. Instead, whatever is underneath it shows through (typically the background color, although other images — such as Web page background images — may be placed underneath transparent portions of a GIF image, as well).

Without transparency, images are displayed using all colors in the palette, including portions of the images that you prefer to be see-through. As a result, the images are often unattractive — unless portions of the images that should be transparent are in colors that match exactly the underlying backgrounds (see Figure 5-6). Therefore, the GIF format is the only choice for images that must have see-through portions.

Figure 5-6: Transparency allows you to specify a color in an image as being see-through. The top image of this figure uses transparency; the one underneath does not.

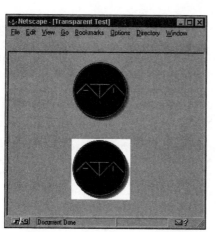

Unfortunately, not all Java applets know how to deal with transparent images. As a result, even if you've gone through the hassle of creating transparent GIF images (something you need a special graphics utility to do), your images may be displayed with the background colors showing, depending on what applets you use them with. To achieve the best visual results possible, use applets that support transparent images when you have a choice. How do you know if an applet supports transparent images? You have to ask the person who wrote the applet or check any documentation that comes with the applet. Alternatively, you can just try it out and see for yourself.

Sometimes you don't have a choice — perhaps the only applet you can find that does exactly what you want, whatever that may be, doesn't support transparent images. In this case, the solution is to use a graphics program to alter the images the applet uses, setting a background color that is exactly the same as the color of the Web page on which it will be displayed. This way, when each image is displayed, it appears to be transparent even though it really isn't.

Setting a color to be transparent and choosing a background color for your image are both functions of the graphics program you happen to use. To find out how to create a transparent image or set a particular background color for it, consult your documentation for the program or the corresponding ...*For Dummies* book.

In time, all applets will support transparent images. Because the Java programming language didn't originally provide an easy way for programmers to support transparency in their applets, many programmers simply didn't bother. Today, however, the Java programming language offers many more features than it did originally — all applets created can easily support transparent images. What a glorious time to be a Java programmer!

Interlacing with GIF

Interlacing is another feature unique to the GIF format, but unlike transparency, which is supported on an applet-by-applet basis, interlacing is supported by *all* applets. *Interlacing* enables images to be incrementally drawn on-screen as they come across the wire, so viewers don't have to wait until the entire image is transmitted. The effect is similar to watching a Polaroid photograph develop before your eyes; you have an idea of what the image is before it is completely developed.

Because interlacing gives Webbers something to watch as the image becomes clearer, viewers aren't as likely to abort the process and go elsewhere. Instead of surfing off into the sunset, some Webbers will stick around and watch the image materialize in anticipation of the final result.

Getting more colors with JPEG

Because the GIF format supports both transparency and interlacing, in addition to being the default format for Web graphics in general, it's more often than not a better choice than JPEG for your applets.

However, GIF images are currently limited to 256 (8-bit) colors. Although an update to the format is due out any day now, at the time of this writing you can't use GIF images to display any more colors than that. The JPEG format, on the other hand, supports over 16 million (24-bit) different colors. In cases where you absolutely must have more than 256 colors in an image, you must use the JPEG format.

Taking up less space with JPEG

As a general rule, keep the total amount of material to be downloaded per page (text, graphics, sound files, applets, and so on) under 250K. How do you find out how large a file is?

- ✔ Macintosh users can go to the Finder, highlight the file, and select File⇨Get Info.
- ✔ Windows 95 and Windows 98 users can go to Windows Explorer, right-click the file, and select Properties from the pop-up menu that appears.

Of course, these techniques give you the size of only one file; you have to repeat the process for each file that appears on your Web page and then add up all the numbers.

Alternatively, you can choose Get Info (Macs) or Properties (Windows) on the directory that contains your page, the applet, and all graphics and sound files it uses (assuming that they all reside in the same directory). Just be sure that the directory only contains files that are used in the page and that the size reported includes every file contained in the directory.

If you have a large number of graphics and more than 250K in total Web page material, consider using the JPEG format simply to gain the highest degree of compression possible. Because images with more than 100 colors tend to compress more efficiently in the JPEG format than with GIF, target those images with the most colors first for JPEG.

After reducing the palette and compressing each image that will appear in your page (whether as part of the standard page using HTML or to be used only by an applet), calculate the total amount of memory your page takes up. If the combined size of your page is over 250K, seriously consider reducing the overall amount of material on it. You can also reduce the dimensions of the images, cropping excess material out altogether.

How JPEG works

JPEG images use a *lossy* compression algorithm, allowing the artist to specify a trade-off between image quality and storage size. When you select the highest level of compression, some image information is lost (hence the term *lossy*) in exchange for the tightest possible compression. Future versions of the JPEG format may include support for transparency and interlacing, although, at the moment, neither is available for use with Java applets.

In fact, a new version of the JPEG format, called JPEG Progressive Download, is similar in nature to an interlaced GIF. As images in this format come across the wire, they are displayed incrementally. At first they look blurry but become sharper and sharper until finally the entire image is clearly visible. Unfortunately, this new JPEG format is not supported by Java 1.0, 1.1, or 1.2 applets.

And, of course, you can always use the JPEG format with the highest degree of compression for *all* your images. Just be aware that if you use the JPEG format, you lose both the transparency and interlacing features available with the GIF format.

Considering your visitors' systems

Your final consideration when choosing a format is the users' equipment. If you're still tempted to use images that contain more than 256 colors in your Web pages and applets, consider for a moment that the vast majority of Webbers don't have computers that display more than 256 colors. In fact, many systems connected to the Web can't even display as many as 16 colors. As a result, your beautiful full-color images will be reduced to ugly, pitiful creations on these systems. To avoid this potential disaster, take the time to reduce the palette of your images as much as possible from the very start.

Although I don't recommend that you spend a great deal of time attempting to accommodate users with really old computer systems, I do highly recommend that you assume the majority of Webbers can see only up to 256 colors. If you do so, the choice between JPEG and GIF becomes even easier.

Chapter 6
Finding the Applet of Your Eye

· ·

In This Chapter

▶ Choosing between distributed and server-bound applets
▶ Downloading the tastiest applets

· ·

*W*eb pages don't just spring to life on their own with Java; someone (maybe you!) has to weave one or more applets into the HTML code of the page. The process is very similar to that of adding graphics to Web pages: After you decide which graphic you want to add, you must obtain the graphic and then embed it into the HTML code of your Web page. Applets, however, are a bit more complicated to hook up than graphics because they often require that you configure a number of settings in the body of the <APPLET> tag before they work properly.

Just as with any aspect of Web-page development, the bulk of the work in weaving applets into your page takes place *locally;* that is, you weave applets into pages on your personal computer and upload them to the Web only after ensuring that they look and act exactly as you want them to. Depending on the applet itself and how simple or complex it is to configure, this process can take minutes or hours. Typically, however, weaving applets into Web pages takes no more than 30 minutes or so; you usually can have an applet hooked up and running before your cup of coffee cools down.

All you need in order to pour lava-hot Java content into your Web pages is a Java-savvy browser (see Chapter 2) and some degree of comfort dabbling in HTML (see Chapter 3).

Will That Be for Here or to Go?

When picking an applet, you have a choice to make: no, not golden versus red delicious — *distributed* versus *server-bound.*

If you want to add a Java-powered applet to your Web page, you have to go get the applet and put it on your page, right? Well, not necessarily. In some cases, you don't need to get the applet to make use of it on your Web page! Amazing as it may seem, you can use many applets *remotely,* without ever having to deal with them directly. All you have to do is make a reference to the applet in your Web page, specifying where the applet resides, and you're set. The browsers that people use to view your page see that the applet is located on another Web server and go retrieve it. Applets that you actually download to your own Web server are called *server-bound applets.* Applets that you can add to your Web pages without ever plucking them from their original sites on the Web are called *distributed applets.*

The distinction between distributed and server-bound applets is due to a security restriction imposed on all applets. Because an applet may access only those files that reside on the same Web server as the applet, you must upload on your own server those applets that allow you to supply your own sound and image files (hence the term *server-bound*). If an applet is self-sufficient, meaning that you don't need to provide it with your own files, it can be made available in a distributed mode. Distributed applets, however, are often provided in server-bound form as well, allowing you to upload them to your own Web site.

Distributed applets and support files

The advantage of distributed applets is obvious: You don't have to bother installing the sucker to take advantage of it. That is, you don't have to upload to your Web server the applet and its associated *support files* (any files an applet makes use of when it is executing — usually sound or image files). Because distributed applets are already installed on the Web and can be accessed remotely, the only thing you have to worry about is constructing an ⟨APPLET⟩ tag in your Web page to reference it. For the sheer ease of use alone, distributed applets are a blessing.

Although your Web pages can reference any applet on the World Wide Web, a distributed applet can't use anything other than what's on its own server. That is, you can't supply your own graphics and sounds for a distributed applet to use. Unless someone gives you special access to the Web server on which an applet resides, which is highly unlikely, there's no way for you to customize the applet with your own support files.

And herein lies the crux of your Web-page planning. Will the applets be expected to use support files (such as sound and image files) from your own server? If so, you have no choice but to install the applet on your own server. If not, you're free to use distributed applets.

Actually, everything on the Web is distributed!

If you want to be nitpicky about it, you can argue that all Java applets are distributed because they ultimately reside on the World Wide Web and are downloaded to your computer before they execute. In this sense, they are *distributed* from the Web servers to personal computers. However, in terms of categorizing the overall functionality of applets, I consider *distributed* to mean those applets that can be *invoked*, or woven into Web pages, from a remote location.

Information distribution is a fundamental capability of the World Wide Web and is not unique to applets. Think for a moment about your ability to create pages that contain graphics. Your pages can display graphics located on your own server or those that exist somewhere else. All you have to do is specify the location of the image and the browser takes care of the rest. (Check out the discussion of absolute and relative references in Chapter 3 to find out how files on the Web are referenced in Web pages.) This is the beauty of a distributed system.

Applets are subject to a security restriction that graphics aren't. Namely, applets can't access files that don't reside on the same server as they do. This restriction makes sense, considering that applets are actually little software programs that do something, whereas graphics don't do anything other than sit around and look good (not a bad gig). Therefore, all graphics, sounds, and other support files an applet requires must be on the same server as the applet.

Configuring distributed applets

When you install a Java-savvy browser, the Java runtime system, also known as the *Java Runtime Environment* or the *Java Virtual Machine,* automatically installs in the same directory. (See Chapter 13 for details on the Java runtime system.) The Java directory holds all the special programs and files that comprise the Java runtime system, which acts as a middleman between applets and your personal computer. When you download an applet from the Web, the browser hands it off to the Java runtime system. This runtime system works hand in hand with your personal computer, allowing the applet to execute as though it is just another software program on your system.

In fact, not all applets even bother with support files. Take, for example, the various ticker tape applets — little Java programs that allow text to scroll across the viewer's screen — that abound on the Web. The vast majority of the ticker tape applets available are self-contained; they don't rely on support files at all (although the `Marquee` ticker-tape applet supplied on the CD-ROM that accompanies this book does have the option of retrieving messages from text files — you can find out how to retrieve messages in Chapter 9). To customize a ticker tape applet, you need to supply only the words that scroll across the screen, as the following HTML snippet shows, along with the details of what the text should look like:

```
<APPLET
CODEBASE = "http://www.mantiscorp.com"
CODE="Ticker"
HEIGHT=25 WIDTH=300>
<PARAM NAME="message" VALUE="Welcome to my page!">
<PARAM NAME="font" VALUE="Courier">
<PARAM NAME="fontsize" VALUE="14">
<PARAM NAME="fontcolor" VALUE="red">
</APPLET>
```

In this example, the distributed Ticker applet resides on the
mantiscorp.com Web server, which the CODEBASE parameter points to with
a URL. All I do is specify the following:

- The size of the applet as it should appear on my page (25 pixels high
  and 300 pixels wide)

- The message to be scrolled ("Welcome to my page!")

- The specifics of the font to be used (14-point Courier, in a nice shade
  of red)

I make no reference whatsoever to support files because this applet doesn't
make use of them. If it did, though, those support files would reside on the
mantiscorp.com Web server so that the applet could access them. Either
way, when your browser executes the applet, it is displayed using the
various parameters that I specify (see Figure 6-1).

How you construct your <APPLET> tag is up to you. I prefer to use all uppercase letters for each tag (APPLET, PARAM, and so on) and any attributes I
supply (CODE, HEIGHT, WIDTH, NAME, VALUE, and so on). I also like to enclose
all the parameter names and values in quotes, even though doing so is
necessary only when you specify something with a space in it (such as
"background music"). For details on constructing the <APPLET> tag, refer
to Chapters 4 and 7.

Java runtime system: The applet cop

What's to stop distributed applets from using
the support files on your computer? Can't you
just tell a distributed applet where your files
are located on the server? Sure, you can try;
but it won't do any good. If the applet attempts
to access your files, the Java runtime system
smacks it with a rolled-up newspaper and
sends it off with its tail between its legs. The
Java runtime system (the underlying, invisible
system on your computer that runs the applets
your browser passes to it) simply doesn't allow applets to get files from other servers.
Period. Without the Java runtime system, your
computer is incapable of executing applets.

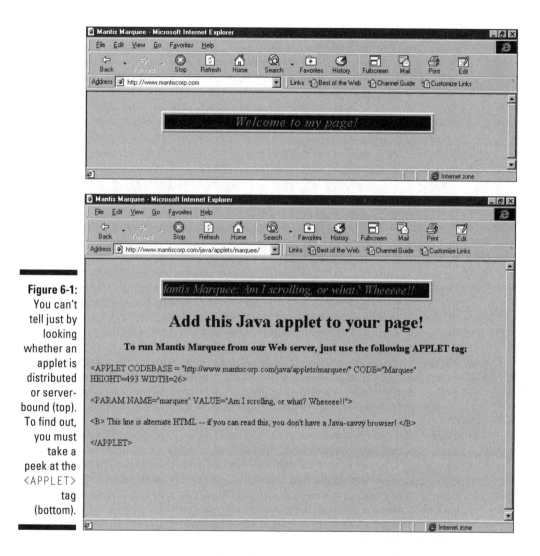

Figure 6-1:
You can't tell just by looking whether an applet is distributed or server-bound (top). To find out, you must take a peek at the <APPLET> tag (bottom).

Be careful about the fonts you choose for your text. Because you can't be sure which fonts are installed on the machines on which your applet will be executed, stick with fonts that are likely to be available on most users' systems. If you use a font that isn't installed on a visitor's computer, a font substitution will take place that may ruin the visual effect you planned. Play it safe and try to keep your font choices to a bare minimum. Times Roman, Courier, and Helvetica, for example, are good choices because they are installed on most Macintosh and Windows computer systems.

Okay, it's confession time: There really is no applet named Ticker on the `mantiscorp.com` Web server! I just said that as an example of how distributed applets work; if you try this example, it will fail. Can you ever forgive me? Tell you what — let me make it up to you by providing the Marquee applet on the `mantiscorp.com` site instead (`www.mantiscorp.com/java/applets/marquee`, to be precise) so that you can use it in a distributed fashion. Sound fair? To find out how to tap into the Marquee applet in this way, keep reading.

The pros and cons of server-bound applets

Although distributed applets are a breeze to deal with (because you don't have to bother uploading anything to your server to use them), they have one major downside: You can't rely on them to always be available. Distributed applets don't reside on your server, so you have absolutely no control over their availability. One day your page may be able to access the applet, and the next it may not. The server on which a given applet resides can become overloaded with activity, preventing browsers from making a connection. Or the applet itself may have been relocated or removed entirely. Whatever the case, you're in no position to complain.

You have much more control over server-bound applets than over their distributed brethren. You can place server-bound applets wherever you choose on your server and configure them to take advantage of your own graphics and sound files (or any other support file, for that matter).

Not only are server-bound applets more flexible than distributed applets in this respect, but you also don't have to worry about whether your pages will be able to access server-bound applets. Because they reside on the same server as the Web pages that use them, server-bound applets aren't in danger of being relocated or moved without you knowing. As a result, they won't disappear from under you the way a distributed applet might.

Despite these advantages, server-bound applets do have a minor downside: They take a bit more time to configure. As their name implies, server-bound applets must be "bound" to your server. Although the act of binding an applet to your server sounds impressive and perhaps even difficult, it's not; all you have to do is upload it to your Web server (see Chapter 11). As soon as an applet is uploaded to your Web server, it is *bound* to that server and can access only files that reside there. And, because the applet then resides on your own server, you can customize it with your own support files, which is something you can't do with distributed applets.

However, uploading an applet to your Web server is a small (if not entirely insignificant) price to pay for the benefits you enjoy in return. With server-bound applets, you're free to choose support files, such as graphics and sounds, for the applets to use. Whereas distributed applets restrict you to the support files that someone else decides to make available, server-bound applets give you complete control.

Keep in mind that all applets, whether distributed or server-bound, are capable of accessing only those files that reside on the same server as they do. For this reason, you can't customize distributed applets with your own support files, which leaves server-bound applets as the only option if you intend to use your own images or sounds. The only exception to this rule is digitally "signed" Java 1.1 and 1.2 applets which have privileges that Java 1.0 applets don't. To find out more about applet security see Chapter 2.

Making the choice

Generally speaking, I prefer server-bound applets over distributed ones (can you tell?). Not only do I get to supply my own support files with server-bound applets (an absolute necessity in many cases), but I can also rely on these applets being available 24 hours a day, 7 days a week, 365 days a year (give or take a few days here and there — Internet Service Providers aren't 100 percent reliable and occasionally become unavailable due to routine maintenance).

However, sometimes only a distributed applet will do. For example, every time the Fortune Cookie ticker tape applet runs, a new message scrolls across the screen — so every visitor to a page with this applet gets a new "fortune." This ticker tape does use a support file, unlike most of the other available ticker tapes, but it's not a graphics or sound file, as you might expect. Instead, Fortune Cookie requires the use of a plain text file containing different messages (or fortunes).

Because I don't want to bother thinking up a bunch of fortunes to place in the text file — and the whole point of a fortune cookie is that you get an unexpected message — this applet works well as a distributed applet. Someone else maintains the support file this applet uses, so I never have to bother inventing my own fortunes. As a result, a new fortune is displayed each time the applet is run, just as you'd expect a new fortune from each new fortune cookie you break open.

Having the choice made for you

Of course, the entire process of deciding whether to use a distributed or server-bound applet assumes that you have a choice. If an applet is available only through someone else's Web server (that is, if the applet program isn't made available for you to upload to your own server), you don't have a choice. Not only that, but very few server-bound applets are also available in distributed form. And it's no wonder: Giving everyone in the world distributed access to the applets on your Web server tends to put quite a load on your site.

So how do you know whether an applet you stumble across on the Web is available in server-bound or distributed form? That all depends on where you find the applet and what type of access you're given to it. You may use any applet as a distributed applet, provided that it's made available on the Web for you to reference in your own pages. In fact, I tell you how to reference distributed applets in Chapter 7. If you can download the applet, however, you can use it in a server-bound manner by placing it on your own Web site.

Just because you can get your hands on an applet doesn't mean that you can *legally* use it! If an applet doesn't come with some form of documentation clearly stating that you have the right to use it, stay far, far away. When an applet author wants you to use his or her program, they'll let you know. Simply look for a "please feel free to use my applet in your own Web page" message, or something similar, on the Web site where you find an applet. See the "Watch your step!" sidebar later in this chapter for details on how the same thinking applies to applet source code.

The CD-ROM that comes with this book contains a bunch of applets, free for the taking. All of these applets may be used as server-bound applets; that is, you can put them on your own Web site. If you want to make an applet on your Web site available to the world (distributed), all you have to do is provide information in a page on your site that tells folks exactly where it's located and how it may be configured.

If you don't find the applet you want on the CD-ROM, don't worry. Thousands of applets are available on the Web now, with more added every day. In fact, the CD has a number of hyperlinks that take you to terrific places on the Web to start your applet hunt — see Appendix C for details.

Applet Harvesting

"Great, so applets are everywhere — but how do I get them onto my own pages?" you ask. "After all, finding a cool applet on someone else's Web pages is one thing, but hooking it up on my own page is quite another."

Distributed applets are the easiest to use on your page because they remain exactly where they are — you don't have to bother downloading distributed applets to your own computer; you leave the applet on the tree, if you will. With distributed applets, all you have to do is hook up your <APPLET> tag in such a way that it *points* to the applet by providing its URL.

Server-bound applets, however, are a mite more complicated. Because server-bound applets must physically reside on the same Web server as the pages in which they are embedded, you must download the applets from the Internet onto your personal computer. When these applets are on your computer, you can weave them into your Web page and then upload the page, the applet, and any support files the applet uses (sound and image files, for example) onto *your* Web site.

Watch your step!

Many Java developers are more than happy to give away their applets; they even encourage people to use them. But giving away an applet and giving away its source code are two different things altogether. If a developer gives away an applet, you can embed it only in your own Web pages. If a developer gives away the source code for an applet, however, you can change the way the applet works internally and then redistribute your own version of it. If you use this latter approach, make sure that you always credit the developer who wrote the original source code.

Before using the source code of an applet that you find on the Web (or an application, for that matter), make certain that the author hasn't provided it as "reference only." Any available copyright information is usually at the top of a source-code file. If the source code doesn't list a copyright anywhere, and if you didn't see a copyright in any of the files that came with the applet, you can often use the code for your own purposes. If you have any doubts about an author's intent, however, your best bet is to contact that person for permission or to simply use the source code to figure out how to write your own code. Think of the code as a free tutorial, but — just to be on the safe side — make sure that you create your own code from scratch in this case.

Because applets often take a long time to develop, authors generally want — understandably — to keep their source code to themselves. If you're on the hunt for source code, trying to locate applets that fit the bill and that have the corresponding source code can be frustrating. You can always contact the applet author by e-mail to request the source code, but you're not likely to get anywhere. If the source code isn't already available, the author probably doesn't want you to have it.

When you see an applet you want to add to your Web site as a server-bound applet, and it is free for the taking, you must know how to get the applet and all its support files into your mitts and onto your page. Every Web page author has his or her own way of explaining how to go about doing this, but the process of harvesting applets is about the same, no matter what the applet.

Time to download

Whereas distributed applets are a cinch to use because you need only configure the <APPLET> tag before you're up and running, if you want a server-bound applet, you must first download it to your computer. This means that you must physically initiate a download with your Web browser, which copies the applet from the Web to your computer a little at a time. Depending on the size of the applet, this process usually takes no more than a few minutes.

The trick isn't in the downloading. Any page that offers you its applets makes downloading a snap: All you do is click the appropriate hyperlink to initiate the download and then choose the directory on your computer to place the incoming applet (see Figure 6-2). Just as with any other download, you're free to choose any location on your computer to store the applet (including the desktop).

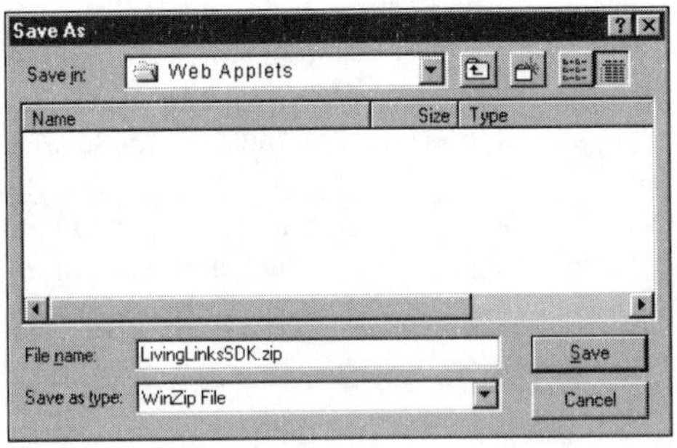

Figure 6-2:
To begin a download, first choose a place on your computer to save the file.

Save As					? X
Save in:	Web Applets				
Name			Size	Type	

File name:	LivingLinksSDK.zip	Save
Save as type:	WinZip File	Cancel

Personally, I like to place all the applets I download from the Web in a master directory on my computer called Web Applets. When choosing a location on my system to place an applet being downloaded, I simply navigate to my Web Applets directory and create a new subdirectory for the incoming applet. This way, each applet I pluck off the Web has its own little home on my computer, so I don't have to worry about it rubbing up against the others I have previously downloaded. This setup doesn't just make for healthy and happy applets, it also makes for a healthy and happy me; I'd lose my mind trying to keep track of my applets if I stored them all in the same directory!

The first step, of course, is initiating the download. That step starts the compressed files on their way, sending it a little at a time over the network until it has been completely transferred to your computer.

Downloading archives

When the compressed files, also known as a *compressed archive,* arrive, you typically need to decompress them. You can think of compressed archives as nice little bundles of goodies — packages that have been tightly wrapped to survive the journey. When a bundle arrives on your system, you need to unwrap (or *decompress*) it. Unfortunately, not all files are bundled in the same way, making the process of decompression a little more complicated in some cases.

Depending on what computer system the applet and associated files were compressed on and which compression tool was used to do the job, the archive that arrives on your computer may be in any of several formats. Although a number of formats exist, three particular types are most commonly used on the Web. You can distinguish these types by the three-character extension following the archive's filename:

- ✔ **archivename.zip:** The ZIP archive is popular in the Windows community.
- ✔ **archivename.sit:** The StuffIt (SIT) archive is popular in the Macintosh world.
- ✔ **archivename.tar:** The TAR archive is popular among UNIX users.

To decompress an archive, you must use a tool that understands the format in which the archive was created. To decompress a ZIP archive, for example, you need to use a decompression tool capable of handling the ZIP format.

The frustration comes when you finally stumble on that perfect, plump, ripe little applet on the Web, the one practically begging to become part of your site. After downloading an archive containing the applet (and any files it comes with), you realize that it's in a format that you can't decompress. You have no way to get the files out of the bundle!

Your predicament with the archive is just a temporary one, however. As soon as you find a decompression tool that understands that formula, you're back in business. The solution, of course, is to amass all the decompression tools you could ever need, building a digital war chest for just such times. If the first tool doesn't understand the format, try the second one, then the third, then the . . . well, you get the idea.

Because decompression tools are quite small by comparison to most software programs today — they typically weigh-in at a svelte 1MB or less — you can easily fit several such tools on your computer as long as you have even a smidgen of hard drive space available. And even if you went crazy and decided to download every decompression tool you could get your hands on, you'd probably only suck up around 50MB of hard drive space (you'd be hard pressed to find more than 50 decompression tools for each computing platform in use today). Of course, you don't need to download every tool you come upon. In fact, to fully round out your arsenal of decompression tools, you need only have a tool capable of decompressing the most popular type of archive formats used on the Web today.

If you choose the right decompression tool in the first place, you rarely need to fall back on others in your stockpile. A good decompression tool is like a Swiss Army Knife (complete with scissors, screwdriver, corkscrew, nail file, and jet-propulsion engine) in that it understands a variety of formats and can give you access to the vast majority of the archives you come across. So which decompression tools are the good ones?

If you're a Windows user, I suggest WinZip, by Nico Mak Computing, shown in Figure 6-3. This fantastic ZIP tool understands the TAR format as well. However, WinZip doesn't understand SIT archives. To deal with the SIT format, Windows users have to get their hands on a copy of StuffIt Expander (the Windows version of this tool, of course, as shown in Figure 6-4).

If, on the other hand, you're a Macintosh user, you should start off with the Mac version of StuffIt Expander (see Figure 6-5). This versatile decompression tool understands the SIT format as well as archives stored in CPT *(Compact),* HQX *(BinHex),* and other popular Macintosh archive formats. Because the applet orchards are thick with ZIP archives, you should also get your mitts on a copy of ZipIt, shown in Figure 6-6.

To compress, or not to compress — that is the question

In truth, not all archives are compressed. In some cases, files are just assembled into an archive to bundle them for easy transfer over the Internet. The person who assembles the archive decides what files are in it and whether compression should be used to reduce their size. The TAR format, in fact, is never really compressed; it's just a convenient way to bundle up files for distribution over the Net. You can apply compression to an existing TAR archive, however. That is, you can compress the entire archive after all the files have been added to it. ZIP compression utilities, on the other hand, compress each file as it is added to the archive. The result is a ZIP file, which you can decompress by using most utilities that handle the ZIP format.

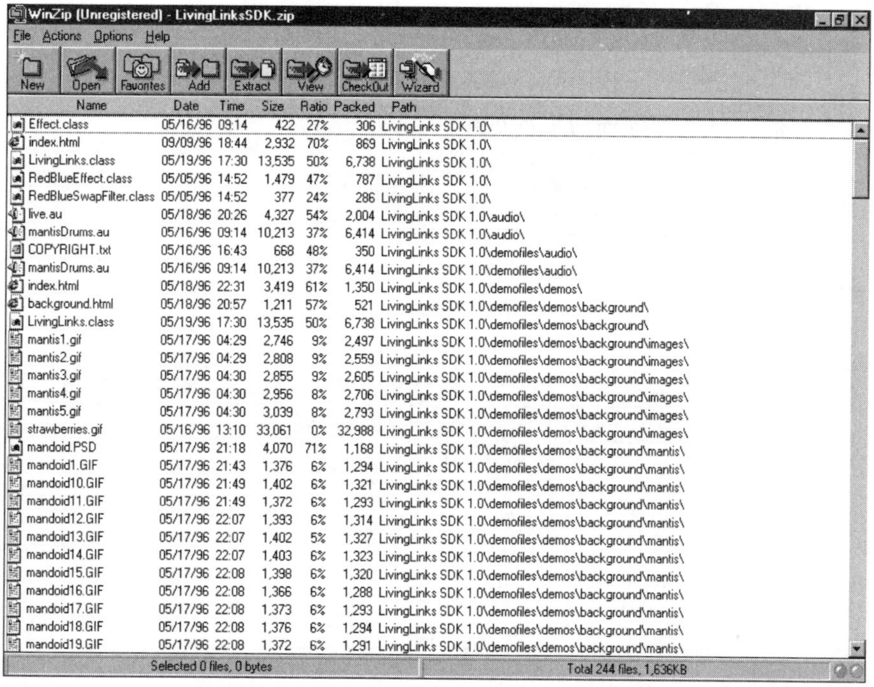

Figure 6-3:
WinZip
is an
invaluable
compression
tool that no
Windows
user should
be without.

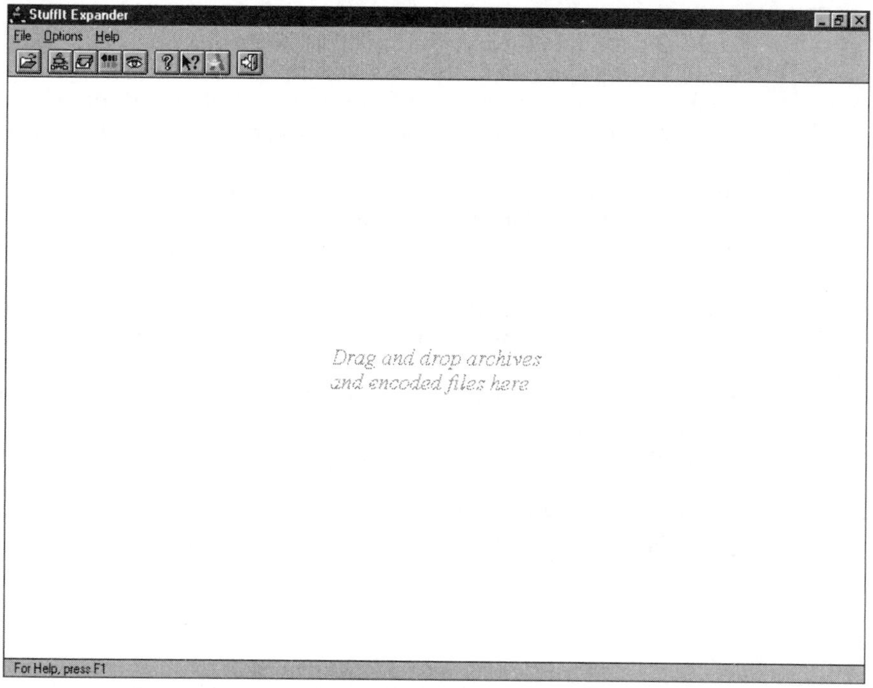

Figure 6-4:
StuffIt
Expander
for
Windows
gives you
access to
archives in
the SIT
format,
which is
wildly
popular
in the
Macintosh
community.

Figure 6-5:
StuffIt
Expander
is the
ideal de-
compression
tool for
Macs.

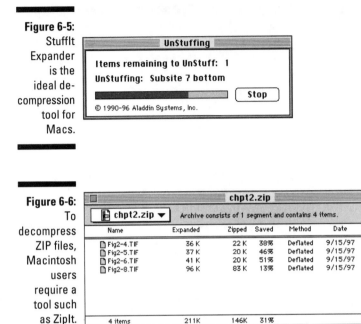

Figure 6-6:
To
decompress
ZIP files,
Macintosh
users
require a
tool such
as ZipIt.

As luck would have it, all of the utilities I mention in this section (WinZip, ZipIt, and the StuffIt Expander for Windows and Macs) are packed into the CD-ROM that comes with this book. Simply copy the Goodies directory to your computer (see Appendix C for details about the directory structure of this disc), and you're set to take on the world — or at least to decompress it.

An enhancement to StuffIt Expander, appropriately named the StuffIt Expander Enhancer, adds ZIP format capabilities to this utility. The CD that comes with this book contains a trial version of the StuffIt Expander Enhancer.

If you don't want to bother manually decompressing archives that you download from the Web, consider configuring your browser to do the decompression automatically. For details, check the documentation for your browser. Netscape Navigator users should consult the online handbook available through Netscape's home page (www.netscape.com); Microsoft Internet Explorer users can visit the Internet Explorer home page (www.microsoft.com/ie) and navigate to the Internet Explorer documentation from there. Alternately, you can use your browser's built-in help system (see Chapter 2 for details).

Although you may have a tool capable of recognizing a particular format, you may encounter different flavors of the format that the tool can't deal with. In this case, you should contact the person who made the archive available and ask which tool they recommend for decompressing it. E-mail is always the best route for contacting these individuals; hunt for an e-mail address on the Web page where you found the archive and then drop a line or two explaining your predicament. Chances are, you'll receive a reply telling you exactly which tool to use.

Decompression: Tricky, tricky

The trick to using server-bound applets isn't in the download process itself, it's in accessing the applet *after* you download it. After all, you're not just downloading an applet; you're getting a compressed archive that may contain all of the following:

- The applet
- Any support files the applet requires
- Installation instructions
- An example Web page or two with the applet woven in

Because most applets provided on the Web come with a handful of companion files such as those listed above, figuring out how to decompress the archive can be a bear. If you haven't downloaded files from the Web, the first few times can be a bit tricky. But after you have the process down, it's a breeze.

Keep your hands out of JARs

Keep in mind that when I talk about decompressing, I'm not referring to *Java archives* or *JARs* (which I talk about in Chapter 5). JAR files are a feature of Java 1.1 and 1.2 that allow applet developers to place support files in a compressed archive — and that archive is supposed to stay compressed! Don't try to extract JARs; instead, keep all the files together inside the archive they come in and use the `ARCHIVE` attribute of the `<APPLET>` tag to tell the latest crop of browsers how to deal with a JAR. (See Chapters 6 and 8 to find out how to weave JARs into Web pages.)

So, how do you find out whether you're dealing with a JAR file that's supposed to stay compressed, or a compressed archive that you're supposed to decompress after you've downloaded it? As a vintage comedian might say, "very carefully."

Actually, determining what type of archive you're dealing with isn't all that difficult. If the archive file name has the .jar extension, you're dealing with a JAR file that should not be decompressed after you get it. Any other extension is fair game, but the .zip extension may cause you problems.

If I've said it once, I've said it a thousand times: ZIP it!

If you've spent much time on the Web, chances are pretty good that you've come upon files having the .zip extension. *ZIP archives,* as they're called, are quite common on the Web because compressing and decompressing files using the ZIP technique is easy. However, as convenient as ZIP is for compressing files and sending them over the Internet, downloading applets can get a little hairy if you assume that every ZIP file containing applets should be decompressed.

You see, long before the Java 1.1 introduced JAR files (which are really just special-purpose ZIP archives created specially for applets), some developers turned to ZIP in an effort to shave time off how long it takes a browser to run their applets. Instead of using ZIP archives to give *you* easy access to the various files that comprise an applet, these developers use them in the same way that JAR files are used: To allow the Web browser to download and run the applet and its associated files as quickly as possible. As with JAR files, these particular ZIP archives are not supposed to be decompressed by you, ever! Instead, simply upload the ZIP archive to your own Web site (see Chapter 11 for details on uploading files to your site) and then construct a unique <APPLET> tag that tells the browser how to deal with the archive. Fortunately, JAR files eliminate the need for such uses of ZIP archives, so you'll probably never have to deal with this potential confusion.

As long as you pay attention to the download instructions that appear on a Web page containing ZIP archives, you'll know what kind of ZIPs you're downloading.

The private life of ZIP archives

Although I refer to ZIP as a compression technique, it's actually an algorithm, or computer "recipe," that describes the exact steps necessary to create a ZIP archive file. Conversely, ZIP archives can be decompressed with tools that apply the algorithm in reverse. If you're a computer buff, you may be interested to know that the ZIP algorithm was invented by two individuals whose last names contributed in part to the "ZIP" acronym.

Cool Beans! — hand-picked applets

If the prospect of hunting down applets on the Web, downloading them to your computer, and decompressing the archives in which they'll likely be wrapped doesn't appeal to you, take heart: Right on the CD-ROM that comes with this book, you can find a number of the hottest applets available.

To use any one of these applets, all you have to do is copy it (and any files it may require) from the CD-ROM onto your own computer. After you copy an applet to your computer, you can simply embed it directly into your Web pages (see Chapter 7), bypassing the whole downloading and decompression rigmarole.

For details regarding the applets available on this disc, check out Appendix C. There, you'll find a description of the contents of the CD-ROM along with a layout of the various directories on it. And although the Cool Beans! folder is reason enough to jam the disc into your CD-ROM drive this very moment, you'll want to click another folder as soon as the disc spins up: CookBook. The CookBook folder contains a number of Java-powered Web pages you can use as the basis for your own page.

Chapter 7

Weaving Applets into Web Pages

• •

▶ Supercharging Web pages with applets and support files

▶ Hooking up the `<APPLET>` tag

▶ Testing and troubleshooting Java-powered pages

• •

*A*fter you find the applet of your eye, as I describe in the previous chapter, you must embed it in your Web page before you can place it on the Internet for everyone to see.

Depending on the applet, the *weaving* process (how you embed and configure the applet) may take from a few minutes to an hour or more. No matter how simple or complex the applet, regardless of whether it's distributed or server-bound, you ultimately end up typing an `<APPLET>` tag into the HTML page designated to contain the applet.

Unlike Java 1.0 and 1.1 applets, which rely on the `<APPLET>` tag, Java 1.2 applets are typically woven into Web pages using the `<OBJECT>` and `<EMBED>` tags. This is due to the fact that Java 1.2 applets are brand spanking new, and so rely on the Java Plug-in in order to run inside older Web browsers. To find out how to weave Java 1.2 applets into your Web pages, or how to accommodate the Java Plug-in, take a gander at Chapter 10.

Let the Weaving Begin!

Weaving applets into Web pages breaks down into a handful of simple steps. These steps are essentially the same, whether you're dealing with distributed applets or applets bound to your own server:

1. **Obtain the applet you want to use (or a URL that points to it, if you're using a distributed applet).**

2. **Choose the page to which you want to add the applet. (If the applet will be server-bound, copy it into the same folder as the Web page.)**

3. **Construct an appropriate** `<APPLET>` **tag, typing it directly into your page's HTML source code.**

4. **Test the page.**

Without the `<APPLET>` tag, described in detail in Chapter 4, you have no mechanism for embedding an applet in your Web page. (Technically, you can rely on the `<OBJECT>` or `<EMBED>` tags, described in Chapter 10. However, only the most recent crop of Java browsers supports the `<OBJECT>` and `<EMBED>` tags, whereas all Java-savvy browsers support the `<APPLET>` tag.) The `<APPLET>` tag tells Java-savvy browsers that an applet is embedded in a page, where that applet is located, and how that applet should look and act after it's activated. Without the `<APPLET>` tag, you're weaving without a loom, stitching without a needle, sewing without thread.

Using the <APPLET> tag

The `<APPLET>` tag can range in complexity from climbing-Mount-Everest difficult to walk-in-the-park simple, depending on the applet you're dealing with. Applet *attributes* are settings you provide within the opening `<APPLET>` tag that allow you to control such factors as the applet's position on the Web page, whether references to it come from your own site (server-bound) or someone else's (distributed), and whether it can communicate with other applets on the same page. Although you can choose from a number of attributes, only three are mandatory for applets (both server-bound and distributed) created using the original version of Java (Java 1.0), and here they are:

- ✔ CODE **(or** OBJECT**):** The name of the applet file
- ✔ HEIGHT: The applet's height, in pixels
- ✔ WIDTH: The applet's width, in pixels

The HEIGHT and WIDTH settings that you provide may not affect how the applet appears or how it performs, depending on the applet and what it does. You can't be sure which of these attributes an applet needs, though, so be sure to check the documentation that comes with the applet (see Chapter 8). If the documentation doesn't note the applet's size requirements, you have to resort to the ol' trial-and-error method. Keep trying different sizes until the applet looks good. Computing height and width involves no magic formula; you just fiddle with each applet you use to get the right values for your pages (that is, you alone decide how large or small an applet looks on your Web page).

Additionally, the applets created using Java 1.1 and 1.2 may take advantage of the new `<APPLET>` tag attributes, specifically the `ARCHIVE` and `OBJECT` attributes (which I describe in detail in Chapter 7). Of course, only the most modern Java-savvy browsers understand these new attributes, which means you run the risk of alienating all other browsers unless you take the time to accommodate less powerful browsers (I describe how in Appendix B).

The only way to know whether an applet requires the `ARCHIVE` or `OBJECT` attribute is to read the documentation that comes with the applet. If you want to play it safe and not bother with the extra work involved in accommodating Java 1.0, 1.1, and 1.2 browsers, just work only with Java 1.0 applets. If you use only 1.0 applets you can rest assured that all Java-savvy browsers can run your pages, because Java 1.1- and Java 1.2-compatible browsers understand Java 1.0. If you weave Java 1.1 or Java 1.2 applets into your Web pages, however, you have to accommodate older browsers (see Chapter 10 and Appendix B for details) or face the fact that millions of people cannot experience your page.

If you just exclaimed "Jeez, dealing with all of these different versions of Java is a royal pain in the applet!" you're not alone. Fortunately, the makers of Java have recently created the *Java Plug-in* to address this version madness. The Java Plug-in, which I discuss in detail in Chapter 10, allows *any* Java-savvy browser, no matter how old, to run Java 1.1 and Java 1.2 applets. That lets you weave the latest crop of applets into your Web pages without worrying about the prospect of folks using older Java-savvy browsers being unable to experience them.

Any additional attributes that you include depend on the applet itself, as well as how you want it to look on your page. In any case, you must supply at least the opening and closing parts of the tag (`<APPLET>` and `</APPLET>`) despite how few or how many attributes you choose to weave into your Web page:

```
<APPLET CODE="Wildapplet.class" HEIGHT=100 WIDTH=350>
</APPLET>
```

Okay, the preceding tag is complete and ready to go, assuming that the Wildapplet (like many server-bound applets) requires no more than these basic components. A Java-savvy browser that encounters this tag looks for the Wildapplet applet inside the same directory as the Web page in which that applet is embedded and displays the applet in an area on that page that is exactly 100 pixels high and 350 pixels wide. What goes on inside this area is the applet's business, because an applet is free to do as it likes.

The same applet may use a JAR file, as the following example illustrates, which means you also have to include a properly configured `ARCHIVE` attribute in your `<APPLET>` tag as well. Although it might seem that the

ARCHIVE attribute is a replacement for the CODE attribute, this is not the case. Regardless of whether or not you use a JAR file, you must always include a CODE attribute to tell the browser the name of your applet *class* file. The ARCHIVE attribute, on the other hand, simply tells the browser the name of the JAR file used by the applet (that is, it compliments the CODE attribute). In the following example, the JAR file is named "wild.jar," although a JAR file can be named just about anything — the developer chooses names for both the applet ("Wildapplet," in this case) and any associated JAR files:

```
<APPLET CODE="Wildapplet.class" ARCHIVE="wild.jar"
        HEIGHT=100 WIDTH=350>
</APPLET>
```

As an applet loads and prepares to do its magic, a gray rectangle appears as a placeholder for the applet's eventual position, as shown in Figure 7-1. The rectangle's height and width match the values specified in the HEIGHT and WIDTH attributes in the <APPLET> tag.

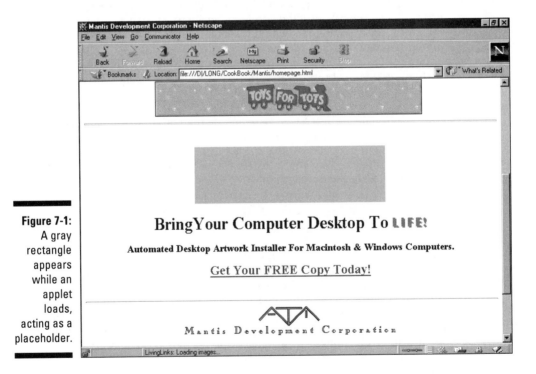

Figure 7-1:
A gray rectangle appears while an applet loads, acting as a placeholder.

Applets, whether distributed or server-bound, are stored in files that have a unique four-character *class* extension (a period separates the file name and its extension, as the file *LivingLinks.class* illustrates). When you specify an applet in the CODE attribute of an <APPLET> tag, you specify the name of the file that contains the applet. Although you don't have to include the .class extension of the file, doing so is a good idea, because it makes identifying and managing your applets easier. It reinforces the fact that applets are contained in .class files.

Sometimes you can get away with using just three basic attributes; CODE, HEIGHT, and WIDTH, but most applets require that you specify more than just their dimensions. What information an applet requires depends on its design purpose. I outline a few optional parameters that you can use to position an applet precisely in Chapter 4 (see Table 4-2).

Some applets written in Java 1.1 and Java 1.2 ignore the CODE attribute altogether. Specifically, *serialized applets* — applets which developers have designed to take advantage of features introduced in Java 1.1 that allow applets to be more easily transferred over a network or saved to a hard drive than those written in Java 1.0 — use the OBJECT attribute instead of CODE, which traditional nonserialized applets use. Applets that are serialized often have the .ser or .obj extension, making them relatively easy to identify. Only when you're dealing with a serialized applet is the CODE attribute not mandatory:

```
<APPLET OBJECT="Wildapplet.ser" HEIGHT=100 WIDTH=350>
</APPLET>
```

Whether you work with 1.0, 1.1 or 1.2 applets, one of the most important applet options isn't really an option at all — it's full-blown HTML. You can specify HTML between the <APPLET> and </APPLET> tags to appear only for people using non-Java-savvy browsers. I cover this option, called *alternate HTML,* in the next section.

Using Alternate HTML

Perhaps the most important step you can take when weaving applets into Web pages, besides configuring the applet, is to provide *alternate HTML* or *alternate context* — HTML code that appears instead of the applet when a non-Java-savvy browser loads the page. Not all Web visitors can use a Java-savvy browser to visit your Java-powered site, so many users cannot see the wonderful applets adorning your pages.

Java-ignorant browsers skip right over the opening <APPLET> tag and go on to the next tag. The browsers don't understand Java, so they ignore everything that falls between the < and > in the opening tag. The same goes for <PARAM> tags (I discuss these in Chapter 4). In fact, these browsers ignore every single tag!

However, just before the closing </APPLET> tag (which Java-ignorant browsers also ignore) is a special area, called the *alternate HTML area* (or the *alternate context area*), where you can provide HTML code. Non-Java browsers do not ignore this area. Whatever HTML code you include here appears in place of the applet, as an *alternative* to the applet, as Figure 7-2 illustrates. Any alternate HTML you want to provide for an applet that uses several parameters, for example, goes after the last <PARAM> tag but before the closing </APPLET> tags:

```
<APPLET CODE="Wildapplet.class" ARCHIVE="wild.jar"
          HEIGHT=100 WIDTH=350>
<PARAM NAME=param1Name VALUE=param1Value>
<PARAM NAME=param2Name VALUE=param2Value>
<PARAM NAME=param3Name VALUE=param3Value>
This is the alternate HTML area, which is displayed only by
          non-Java browsers!
</APPLET>
```

Figure 7-2:
You can use alternate HTML to alert those with non-Java browsers that they're missing out on something cool.

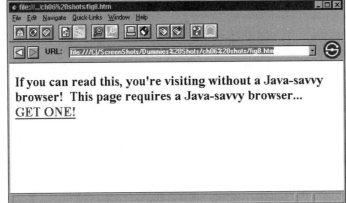

If you can read this, you're visiting without a Java-savvy browser! This page requires a Java-savvy browser...
GET ONE!

You can include any type of HTML in the alternate HTML area: plain text, hyperlinked text, and even images and hyperlinked images — basically, anything that non-Java browsers can handle. Java-savvy browsers, on the other hand, ignore this space entirely. Consequently, it's an excellent place to tell people that they're missing out on something cool:

```
<APPLET CODE="LivingLinks" WIDTH=100 HEIGHT=100>
<PARAM NAME="image" VALUE="animalsButton.gif">
<PARAM NAME="effect" VALUE="Melt">
<PARAM NAME="soundDir" VALUE="audio/animals/">
<PARAM NAME="inSound" VALUE="dolphinSqueak.au|lionRoar.au
          |rooster.au">
```

```
<PARAM NAME="links" VALUE= "Dolphins = http://anywhere.com
          |Lions = http://anywhere.com | Rooster = http://
          anywhere.com">
<B>If you can read this, you're not using a Java-savvy
          browser! <B>
</APPLET>
```

In fact, you may want to include a hyperlink to help these unfortunate souls find the truth and the light of Java. Point them to a site that offers a Java-savvy browser (such as the Netscape Navigator home page (`www.netscape.com`) or Microsoft's Internet Explorer home page (`www.microsoft.com/ie`). Then, anybody who visits your page using an inadequate browser is only a click away from nirvana:

```
<APPLET CODE="LivingLinks" WIDTH=100 HEIGHT=100>
<PARAM NAME="image" VALUE="animalsButton.gif">
<PARAM NAME="effect" VALUE="Melt">
<PARAM NAME="soundDir " VALUE="audio/animals/">
<PARAM NAME="inSound " VALUE="dolphinSqueak.au |
          lionRoar.au | rooster.au">
<PARAM NAME="links" VALUE= "Dolphins = http://anywhere.com
          |Lions = http://anywhere.com | Rooster = http://
          anywhere.com">
<B>If you can read this, you're visiting without a Java-
          savvy browser! <B>
This page requires a Java-savvy browser... GET ONE:
<A HREF="http://www.netscape.com">Get Navigator</A>
<br>
<A HREF="http://www.microsoft.com/ie/">Get Internet
          Explorer</A>
</APPLET>
```

Of course, displaying a "Shame on you! Get with it and get a Java-savvy browser" message as an alternative to your applets isn't always appropriate. You often use an applet to enhance the visual appeal of a Web page, and displaying such a message certainly disrupts the entire design of the page. Feel free to provide anything your heart desires in the alternate HTML area.

You often end up using the alternate HTML area to display whatever content the applet serves to enhance, such as animated images or image maps. But because standard HTML produces documents that are entirely static by nature, the content is no longer vibrant, dynamic, fluid — in a word, *alive* — on non-Java browsers. That's just the way the Web cookie crumbles. Just realize that users of both types of browsers will visit your site and the only way to truly accommodate (or enlighten) them is to use alternate HTML. Bring your site to life with Java, but provide for those using dead (non-Java) browsers as well.

Thanks to the following <APPLET> tag and alternate HTML, the button at the bottom of Figure 7-3 pulses with life for Java-savvy browsers. Non-Java browsers, however, cannot display the applet, so only the alternate HTML inside the <APPLET> tag appears. Viewers can still see the button and a hyperlink, but it just isn't throbbing with life for these folks.

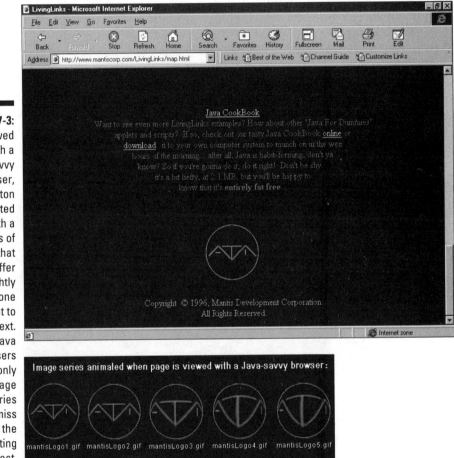

Figure 7-3:
Viewed
with a
Java-savvy
browser,
this button
is animated
with a
series of
images that
differ
slightly
from one
moment to
the next.
Non-Java
browsers
see only
one image
in the series
and miss
out on the
pulsating
effect.

```
<APPLET CODE="LivingLinks" WIDTH=115 HEIGHT=115>
<PARAM NAME="imagesDir" VALUE="images/">
<PARAM NAME="imagesName" VALUE="mantisLogo">
<PARAM NAME="imagesExt" VALUE="gif">
<PARAM NAME="imagesCount" VALUE="5">
<PARAM NAME="speed" VALUE="15">
<PARAM NAME="backgroundColor" VALUE="black">
<PARAM NAME="reverse" VALUE="yes">
<A HREF="http://www.mantiscorp.com"> <IMG SRC="images/
          logo1.gif"></A>
</APPLET>
```

Tapping into Distributed Applets

Embedding distributed applets in your Web pages is easy. All you have to know is where the applet resides and what attributes and parameters (if any) it requires. As soon as you have this information, you can tap into distributed applets.

You typically can find the information that you need to weave a distributed applet into your Web pages on the same page as you find the applet. If the information doesn't appear directly on that page, hunt around the site. If you can't find the information you need after scouring the site, the applet probably is off limits. Cut your losses and look for another applet.

Distributed applets usually come with easy to find information that tells you how to hook 'em up. Hop on the Web and visit the page at `www.mantiscorp.com/java/applets/marquee`, shown in Figure 7-4, for a good example of what I mean. There, the applet runs on-screen and you see a brief description of the `<APPLET>` tag directly below it. You don't even need to type the tag into your own page — just copy and paste it. You can always save the HTML source code of the page to your computer for later reference, a good idea if your memory is as fleeting as mine. For more information on saving the HTML source code of a Web page, check out Chapter 6.

Whether you type the `<APPLET>` tag or copy and paste it, you get the same final product. Here's the `<APPLET>` tag for the applet shown in Figure 7-4:

```
<APPLET CODEBASE="http://www.mantiscorp.com/java/applets/
          marquee/"
CODE="Marquee"
WIDTH=493 HEIGHT=26>
```

(continued)

(continued)

```
<PARAM NAME="font_face" VALUE="TimesRoman">
<PARAM NAME="font_size" VALUE="18">
<PARAM NAME="font_italic" VALUE="yes">
<PARAM NAME="font_bold" VALUE="yes">
<PARAM NAME="marquee" VALUE="Am I scrolling, or what?
          Wheeeee!!">
<B> This line is alternate HTML — if you can read this, you
          don't have a Java-savvy browser! <B>
</APPLET>
```

The most significant part of this `<APPLET>` tag (in the context of this discussion, at least) is the `CODEBASE` attribute. If a browser doesn't find the `CODEBASE` attribute, it assumes that the applet resides in the same directory as the Web page that references it. Thanks to `CODEBASE`, however, you can embed applets living on other Web sites (applets potentially located on the other side of the world!) directly into your pages.

`CODEBASE` is the key to all distributed applets; it's the only way to tell Java-savvy browsers where to find these applets. Minus the `CODEBASE` attribute, all applets would be server-bound, forced to reside in the same directory as the pages that reference them.

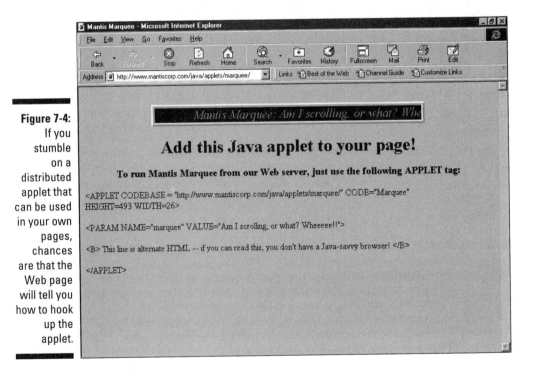

Figure 7-4:
If you stumble on a distributed applet that can be used in your own pages, chances are that the Web page will tell you how to hook up the applet.

Putting Applets in Their Place

When you weave applets into your pages, you must decide where to put them. Positioning an applet is the same as positioning an image; you decide where you want it to go and then enter the <APPLET> tag in the appropriate place in the HTML source code. An applet appears on a page based on where you enter the <APPLET> tag in the HTML source code: You put a tag at the top of the page, your applet appears at the top of the page, you put a tag at the bottom of the page, the applet appears (surprise, surprise!) at the bottom of the page.

The saving graces of CODEBASE

CODEBASE isn't exclusively for accessing applets residing on other Web sites. If you have a server-bound applet that appears in many different pages at your site, you have to upload a copy of that applet into the directory of each page that references it, right? Nope, not really. You can use CODEBASE! Just include the URL to the applet in the CODEBASE attribute of the <APPLET> tag and every page at your site references the same centrally located applet. Yippee!

Consider the <APPLET> tag used to display the Marquee applet, especially the opening tag:

```
<APPLET CODEBASE="http://
    www.mantiscorp.com/java/
    applets/marquee"
CODE="Marquee"
WIDTH=493 HEIGHT=26>
```

Which, if it happened to be a serialized applet (which it's not, but work with me here — I'm on a roll), would use the OBJECT attribute instead of CODE:

```
<APPLET CODEBASE="http://
    www.mantiscorp.com/java/
    applets/marquee"
```

```
OBJECT="Marquee.ser"
WIDTH=493 HEIGHT=26>
```

The first example actually appears in several pages of the Mantis Development Corporation Web site. It references the Marquee applet, which resides on the same server as the site (www.mantiscorp.com) but does so in a distributed manner. Now, thanks to CODEBASE, you don't need to have a copy of the Marquee applet inside the directory of each page that uses the applet. Instead, all pages reference the same one — the Marquee applet located in the directory pointed to by CODEBASE (http://www.mantiscorp.com/java/applets/marquee).

Using CODEBASE is particularly useful for managing any and all applets you have at your site. You have to keep track of only a single applet — instead of managing all the copies of the applet you would otherwise have to upload into each Web page directory referencing it. Upgrading the applet is a snap, too: Just replace the applet that CODEBASE points to and you're done!

You can include any number of applets on a Web page. However, positioning applets on a page can prove tricky if you're not comfortable writing HTML code. In particular, you must know how to position images; if you can do that, you can place applets on your page with the same precision. The only difference is that you enter applet tags instead of image tags.

To find out all about using HTML to position images, check out *HTML For Dummies,* 3rd Edition, by Ed Tittel and Steve James (IDG Books Worldwide, Inc.). Personally, I think that *HTML For Dummies* is the perfect complement to this book — the cream for your Java coffee!

Close encounters

Although you can easily position applets one right after the other, sometimes you need to get your applets closer together. For example, to give the illusion of a single, larger applet, you may need to have several applets appear side by side or one on top of the other with absolutely no space between them.

Consider the image shown in Figure 7-5. You have no idea by looking at this image that it consists of several smaller images pressed closely together. Here, different parts of the image are animated by separate applets that all work together to give the appearance of a single image that has various "moving" parts. Specifically, different parts of the image are animated by applets, giving it the appearance of a scene from a movie: The lights flicker, fluids drip into the tubes attached to the poor fella's head, and he seems to experience real pain, writhing so. When you place the mouse in different parts of the image, different sounds emanate and he twitches even more. Not only does it *look* as if he's in serious pain, but it *sounds* like it!

The key to this illusion, of course, is getting each applet to display its section of the image right next to the others, with no visible space between the applets. You must use an applet that provides these animation capabilities but doesn't place anything between the image and the edges of the applet (such as a 3-D bevel, which gives the appearance of a button by placing a thin border or a space around the animation). In addition, the HEIGHT and WIDTH attributes that you specify for each applet must match exactly the size of the images they use; otherwise, the fact that you're using several different applets becomes rather obvious when you load the page (see Figure 7-6).

To find out the exact dimensions of your images, use a graphics program. Any graphics program worth its salt enables you to easily find out the size of an image.

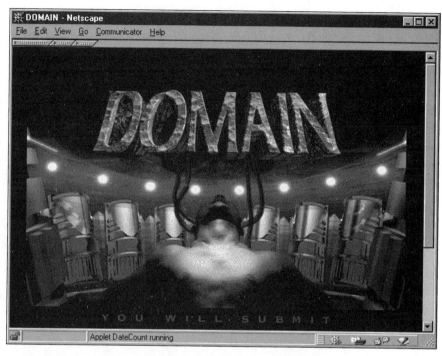

Figure 7-5:
This image is composed of four different applets, each performing a specific part of the animation.

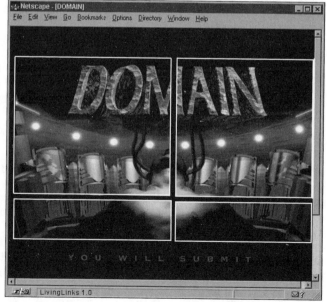

Figure 7-6:
If you don't configure your applets properly, or if they weren't meant to be positioned side by side, the effect can be ruined.

One other step you must take is to enter each <APPLET> tag, one right after the other, ensuring that no other tags come between them. If a <BR> tag, for example, appears between each <APPLET> tag, each applet appears on its own line. You want line breaks to occur only where it makes sense for the overall image — after the second applet, in this case.

Although pressing applets close together is useful if you want to create the illusion of a larger, seamless image or animation, sometimes you want just the opposite effect — to control the space between your applet and the items around it (text, images, or other applets).

The ALIGN attribute

Because applets are integral portions of Web pages, you must have some degree of control over where they appear on the page in relation to the other elements around them. In particular, you may need to place an applet in a page that has text in it.

Thankfully, you can use the <APPLET> tag's ALIGN attribute to do just that. In fact, you have nine options at your disposal:

- ✔ ALIGN=left
- ✔ ALIGN=right
- ✔ ALIGN=top
- ✔ ALIGN=texttop
- ✔ ALIGN=middle
- ✔ ALIGN=absmiddle
- ✔ ALIGN=baseline
- ✔ ALIGN=bottom
- ✔ ALIGN=absbottom

When you specify ALIGN=left or ALIGN=right inside the opening <APPLET> tag, the text following the applet falls out accordingly — to the left or right of it. When the applet is on the left, the text appears to the right. Conversely, if your applet is aligned to the right, the text appears to the left, as shown in Figure 7-7.

All subsequent text continues to flow accordingly until you force it to stop. To return the text to the way its state of alignment prior to the appearance of the <APPLET> tag, you must specify a *line break* where you want text to start flowing normally again. The break tag <BR> accepts a CLEAR attribute that allows you to specify the way for the remaining text to flow. CLEAR can be LEFT, RIGHT, or ALL. To set the text back to a normal flow, provide the following line-break tag immediately before the text you want to return to normal:

```
<BR CLEAR=ALL>
```

The best way to find out how each of the ALIGN attribute values affects the alignment of your applet is to test each one. Just provide one of the nine possible values immediately following the ALIGN attribute. For an idea of how each affects the positioning of your applets, see Figure 7-8.

Keep in mind that ALIGN is just one of several attributes you can use with the <APPLET> tag. (See Chapter 4 for a listing of each attribute you can use.) Don't forget to include these attributes in the opening <APPLET> tag, as follows. They don't do you any good outside the tag! The following line of HTML illustrates how to include attributes inside the opening <APPLET> tag. Notice how the CODE, HEIGHT, WIDTH, and ALIGN attributes appear after the word APPLET but before the greater-than character (>):

```
<APPLET CODE="LivingLinks" HEIGHT=100 WIDTH=345 ALIGN=top>
```

Figure 7-7:
The ALIGN attribute determines where an applet will be placed in the browser window and affects the flow of text following the <APPLET> tag.

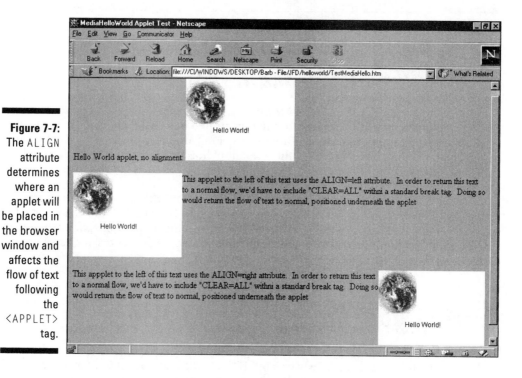

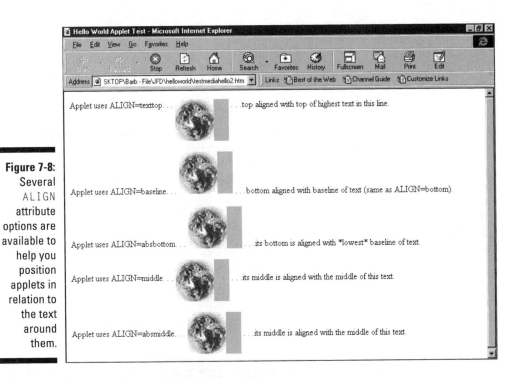

Figure 7-8:
Several
`ALIGN`
attribute
options are
available to
help you
position
applets in
relation to
the text
around
them.

Giving your applets elbow room with VSPACE and HSPACE

The VSPACE and HSPACE attributes give you even more control over the applet's position relative to the text around it. VSPACE specifies how much space appears vertically (above or below) around your applet. HSPACE, on the other hand, specifies the amount of horizontal space (from left to right) around your applet.

Whether you use them alone or in combination with the ALIGN attribute (covered in the preceding section), using HSPACE and VSPACE is a wonderful way to ensure that your applets appear with the amount of space around them that you want. For an example of how these attributes are used, see Figure 7-9.

Testing Your Java-Powered Pages

After you insert the <APPLET> tag into your Web page, you need to test the results. Save your newly created HTML code and open it in a Java-savvy browser. If all goes according to plan, a gray box appears in the the applet's ultimate position, and the applet begins running a few moments later.

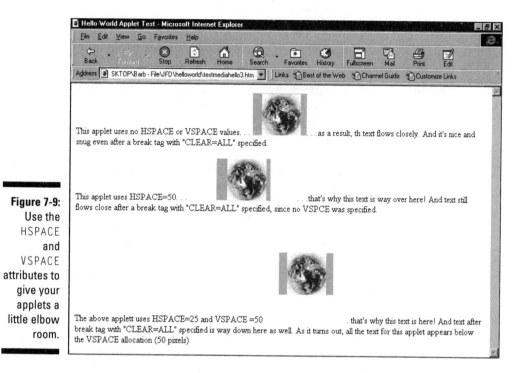

Figure 7-9:
Use the
HSPACE
and
VSPACE
attributes to
give your
applets a
little elbow
room.

If the applet doesn't appear, give it a few more seconds before you panic. If it still doesn't appear, panic now. To know that something's definitely wrong, keep your eye on the status area of the browser window. If a message informs you that the browser can't load the applet, it means that the browser can't find the applet file and one of four things is going on:

✔ The applet file (or the JAR file, if you specified one) isn't in the same directory as your Web page (assuming that you're working with a server-bound applet). If the applet file (or JAR) is intact, you could be experiencing a problem with a serialized applet if that's what you've woven into your Web page.

If the applet file is serialized, it requires the OBJECT tag instead of CODE, and most likely has the .ser or .obj file extension. If the applet is traditional (non-serialized), it uses the CODE attribute and has the .class extension. Be careful to use the correct attribute for your applet and make sure that the applet file (whether traditional, serialized, or included in a JAR) is where it should be.

In either case, make sure that the files that your <APPLET> tag refers to are, in fact, where they belong. To see if a file is where it should be, simply look inside the corresponding folder on your computer (that is, look wherever the <APPLET> tag says it is!). If the applet file is missing, copy it into the same directory as your Web page (or into the directory specified by `CODEBASE`). Likewise, make sure that any support files that your applet uses (such as sound, image, and data files) are also where they should be and copy them to the appropriate location if not.

✔ The `CODEBASE` attribute is incorrect or you're not currently connected to the Internet (assuming that you're working with a distributed applet). In this case, make sure that you're actually connected to the Internet and double-check to make sure that `CODEBASE` points to a valid applet file.

✔ The applet file or JAR is unavailable (in the case of a distributed applet) or possibly corrupt (if the file is in the same directory as your Web page). To fix the latter problem, simply upload a fresh copy of the applet or JAR file into the directory containing your Web page (or the directory pointed to by the `CODEBASE` attribute, if you're using that). When dealing with distributed applets, however, you don't have the luxury of fixing the problem yourself. The best you can do is contact the owner of the distributed applet (I suggest e-mail) and ask if there's a problem with the applet, and, if so, kindly suggest that he or she fix it for you.

✔ The applet is attempting to perform an action it does not have the right to, such as reading a file from your computer or making a connection to a computer on the Internet other than the one the applet itself resides on. In this case, you see a message like A security exception has occured or NullPointerException encountered in the status area of your browser. To remedy the problem, you can simply grant the applet the right to do whatever it's trying to do. Be careful though! Granting applets security privileges can be dangerous, as Chapter 2 explains.

Before assuming the worst, double-check whether your `<APPLET>` tag references the applet by name exactly, matching all uppercase and lower-case letters. In the case of distributed applets, make sure that the URL is correct. Usually, you find the typo; problem fixed. Simply fix the error, save the change in your source file, and reload it in your browser. If the applet still doesn't work, make sure that Java is enabled for your browser. (See Chapter 2 for how to find out whether Java is enabled on your browser and how to turn it on if it isn't.)

If Java is enabled and your tag is constructed exactly but the applet doesn't work, the file may be corrupt. (In the case of distributed applets, the server on which it resides may not be available; try again later. If the problem persists, use e-mail to contact the individual who made the applet available and explain your dilemma — the applet may have been moved or renamed.) The archive may not have made it across the wire intact, in which case, you have to download the applet and start anew.

If the applet loads okay but the status area reports that the applet couldn't initialize itself, the <APPLET> tag probably isn't configured properly. Perhaps the parameters aren't valid or the support files (sound files and graphics, for example) aren't available. Make sure that everything is where it belongs and make any necessary changes. Then reload your page and see if it flies. If it doesn't, you might be the victim of a piggish browser (one that gobbles down the first <APPLET> tag you feed it but refuses to recognize any changes that you make to the tag unless you quit and restart the browser itself). Then again, the issue may run deeper still. Consult Chapters 12 and 18 for details on the most common errors you can encounter and how to resolve them.

Chapter 8

Preparing to Customize Your Applets

In This Chapter

▶ Diving into documentation

▶ Configuring applets to suit your needs

▶ Folding in JAR files

▶ Tweaking `<PARAM>` tags

*T*hink of each Java applet as a zippy little sports car. When you first slip into the driver's seat, the car seems to have been built just for you. Sooner or later, though, you want to add your own personal touches. These personal touches may be as insignificant as a set of beaded seat covers or a pair of fuzzy dice, or as radical as a racy paint job, tinted windows, monster tires, and chrome rims.

The extent to which you can customize your car depends on two factors:

✔ **Your car:** How much can it be customized?

✔ **Your resources:** Do you have the cash, the equipment, and the skills required to turn your Volkswagen Rabbit into a makeshift Dodge Viper?

The same concerns apply to customizing your Java applets:

✔ **Your applet:** Does the applet support customizing?

✔ **Your resources:** Do you have the support files, the software, and the HTML skills required to customize your applet, in essence turning a run-of-the-mill applet into a Web page wonder?

Tune-Up or Overhaul?

As with automobiles, you can customize most applets to some extent. Other applets, however, are *infinitely* customizable. You can spend months souping up these puppies and barely scratch the surface of their capabilities. Just as different cars appeal to different drivers, your Java applet requirements vary from the applet requirements of your neighbors in the cyberhood. Your applet may work great right out of the box, or it may require regular maintenance to keep pace with your demands.

Depending on the applet itself, you may be able to customize any or all of the following characteristics:

✔ Images

✔ Sounds

✔ Text

✔ Colors

✔ URLs

While Chapter 9 tells you everything you need to know to add these features, you must first determine what features the applet you're using actually supports. To do this, you need to consult the documentation that came with the applet — you need to get your hands on the *owners* manual.

Do You Have an Owners Manual?

The most important thing you can get your hands on, aside from the applet itself, is an owners manual. Not the kind that comes with a new car or with the software programs you run on your computer, mind you, but something similar. In order to customize an applet, you need a guide that tells you what the applet can do and how the applet can do it. Sometimes an applet comes with the documentation you need. Unfortunately, this isn't always the case.

If you don't have documentation, you may have to connect to the Web and see how others have hooked up the applet. Although looking at sample HTML source code is just fine in many cases, it doesn't give you much to go on. Simply looking at the `<APPLET>` tag that someone else has constructed (see Chapters 4 and 7 for details) gives you no detailed information about the internal workings of the applet. At best, you get a general idea about how the applet works and enough information to start fiddling around with it on your own. At worst, you may never learn how to configure the applet to its fullest extent. Consider, for example, the LivingLinks applet.

The following code listing is for the LivingLinks applet as it's used in the Who We Are button on the top left of the Demon Systems CookBook page, included on the CD-ROM that comes with this book. While this snippet of code is taken directly from a Web page on CD-ROM, it could just as easily have come from a Web page residing on the Internet. Regardless of where you find them, peeking at ⟨APPLET⟩ tags woven into Web pages is very helpful when it comes to figuring out what applets can do. However, ⟨APPLET⟩ tag examples alone aren't a replacement for good documentation because some applet capabilities may not be obvious when viewing ⟨APPLET⟩ tags, as the following illustrates:

```
<APPLET CODE=LivingLinks.class WIDTH=214 HEIGHT=140>
        <PARAM NAME=imagesDir VALUE="console/who/">
        <PARAM NAME=imagesName VALUE="who">
        <PARAM NAME=imagesExt VALUE="gif">
        <PARAM NAME=imagesCount VALUE="5">
        <PARAM NAME=URL VALUE="http://www.demonsys.com/
        who.html">
        <PARAM NAME=backgroundImage VALUE="console/who/
        top.gif">
        <PARAM NAME=backgroundColor VALUE="black">
</APPLET>
```

From the preceding code, you can tell that the LivingLinks applet uses images. The big tip-off, of course, is that four of the parameters begin with the word "images"! But what does each parameter correspond to? Without any documentation, such as the LivingLinks documentation provided in Chapter 7 and later in this chapter, you have to monkey around with these settings. Assuming that the applet and its associated Web page are already on your hard drive, tinkering with the settings isn't too tough. Just open the folder or directory that contains these files on your computer and begin exploring. (See Chapter 6 for more information on how to get an applet to your computer.)

You can find LivingLinks (the applet I use in this example and throughout this chapter) in the Cool Beans! directory of the CD-ROM that comes with this book. For details on how to find LivingLinks on the CD-ROM, refer to Appendix C. If you want to work through the examples in this chapter, now is the perfect time to copy this applet to your personal computer.

By opening up the folder that contains the applet and taking a look around, you can see right off the bat that the only things it contains are an HTML file that uses the LivingLinks ⟨APPLET⟩ tag listed earlier, the applet it refers to (LivingLinks.class), and a directory called *console,* shown in Figure 8-1.

Figure 8-1:
To figure
out how to
configure
your
<APPLET>
tag, look
inside the
folder
containing
the applet.

Keep in mind that all applets end with the .class extension, even though you don't have to include that extension when referencing the applet. (Java Archive files, or JARs, are another matter — more on those in the section entitled "The JARing Truth.") In fact, you don't even need to use quotes around the applet name — you use quotes to surround text items that contain spaces. Applet names never have spaces, thanks to the way applets are compiled during the development process. As a result, any of the following four examples is an acceptable way to reference an applet:

```
CODE="LivingLinks"
CODE=LivingLinks
CODE="LivingLinks.class"
CODE=LivingLinks.class
```

Although Macintosh users always see the .class and .html extensions on filenames (and all other extensions, for that matter), these extensions may be hidden from Windows 95 and Windows 98 users.

A feature of Windows 95 and Windows 98 allows all extensions to be hidden, keeping them out of your way. Although different icons generally represent each type of extension, if you can't see the extension, the only surefire way to find out a file's document type is to actually open the file and see whether it contains the information that you're looking for. As a result, you may eventually rip out your hair in frustration. If you can't see the filename extension, how can you be sure which is myFile.html, myFile.class, or any other myFile file? To unhide the filename extensions, do the following:

1. **From Windows Explorer, choose View⇨Options. (Choose View⇨Folder Options if you're using Windows 98.)**

   The Options dialog box opens.

2. **Uncheck the Hide MS-DOS File Extensions For File Types That Are Registered check box. (Windows 98 users choose the Hide File Extensions for Known File Types option under the View tab.)**

Filename extensions are displayed from that point on.

In the LivingLinks example, you have very little documentation on how the applet may be used except for the ⟨APPLET⟩ tag itself. By closely examining the tag inside the HTML file, you see that one of the parameters, ⟨PARAM NAME=imagesDir VALUE="console/who/"⟩, actually specifies an image directory. The next logical step is to open the path that the directory points to and see what's inside (first open *console,* then open the *who* directory inside it). All you find, in this case, is a number of images, because the "imageDir" parameter does nothing more than point to a directory containing images.

On further examination of the contents of the *who* folder (see Figure 8-2) and the remainder of the ⟨APPLET⟩ tag, you discover that yet another parameter, ⟨PARAM NAME=imagesName VALUE="who"⟩, corresponds to the files inside of it. By stepping through the code and trying to relate each parameter to the files that come with an applet, you can deduce quite a bit about the parameters and how you can customize them to your personal preferences.

Figure 8-2:
Compare the contents of each folder to the ⟨APPLET⟩ tag and find the parameters that support files such as images and sound clips.

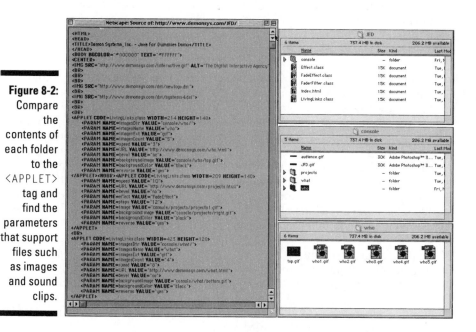

In this example, notice that a total of four parameters supply the applet with the series of images it uses in the animation. You can't tell just by looking at this applet's parameters that the animation is created by flipping through each image in the series (which produces the illusion of movement), and usually you don't know exactly what an applet does merely by looking at the HTML source code. Read on to discover a much easier way.

To find out exactly what an applet does when properly configured, simply use a Java-savvy browser to open the HTML file provided with the applet! In this case, the images inside the folder are animated on-screen. By opening the HTML file and seeing the animation in action, you know what the applet does and you have a better sense of each of the parameters. For example, if you have questions as to whether the applet is using the files in the images directory, just open the files with a graphics program to confirm your suspicions. Because you can see the animation running, you know right away whether these are the images being used, further cementing your confidence in how a corresponding <APPLET> tag is constructed.

Not every applet you get off the Web comes with a sample HTML page that shows the applet in action; sometimes all you get is the applet file and nothing more! Therefore, be careful to note where you get each applet (bookmarking is the fastest and most reliable way), and save to your computer for later reference any HTML source-code pages that use the applet. In this way, you can use source code on your computer to find out how the <APPLET> tag is constructed, and you can connect to the site later to see the applet in action, if necessary. For more information on finding applets to weave your own Web pages, see Chapter 6.

You don't have to use a graphics program to open the images associated with an applet. Instead, you can use the browser itself. After all, browsers know how to display images contained in Web pages. All you have to do is choose File➪Open and make sure that the file type (appearing in a pop-up menu at the bottom of the dialog box) is set to open *any* file, not just HTML files (which is the default). As long as the image you try to open is in the GIF or JPEG format (two common image formats supported by Java and almost all browsers), your browser will have no problem displaying it. If the file isn't in one of these two formats, however, the browser tries to pass off the file to a *helper application* (an application that knows how to deal with files stored in uncommon formats).

And so, after a little detective work, you know that with the LivingLinks applet you can specify a directory containing the images you want to display, the first name and file extension of each image, and the total number of images to use in the animation. By doing nothing more than hunting around the <APPLET> tag, you can now configure a similar applet for your own animation (see the next section).

Souping It Up

Some applets require that you follow specific rules for naming the files used with the applet. These rules, or *naming conventions,* help the applet find the files you use to customize the applet (such as image or sound files, for example). How do you find out what the naming convention for a given applet is? You have to read the documentation, ask someone who uses the applet, or experiment a little.

Take the LivingLinks applet as an example. LivingLinks uses a naming convention that requires all images used in an animation to have exactly the same name (*myFace,* for example) with the addition of a number indicating their respective sequence in the animation (1, 2, 3, 4, and so on). In addition, each image must have the same extension (such as .gif or .jpg). Knowing this, I can use any images I want in an animation, as long as I name them accordingly. For example, I can put any number of myFace images (myFace1.gif, myFace2.gif, myFace3.gif, and so on) in a directory called narcissist, as shown in Figure 8-3, and expect LivingLinks to find them, as long as I set the corresponding parameters (imagesDir, imagesName, and imagesExt). But how many images will LivingLinks load? Ah, yet another LivingLinks parameter to be aware of: imagesCount.

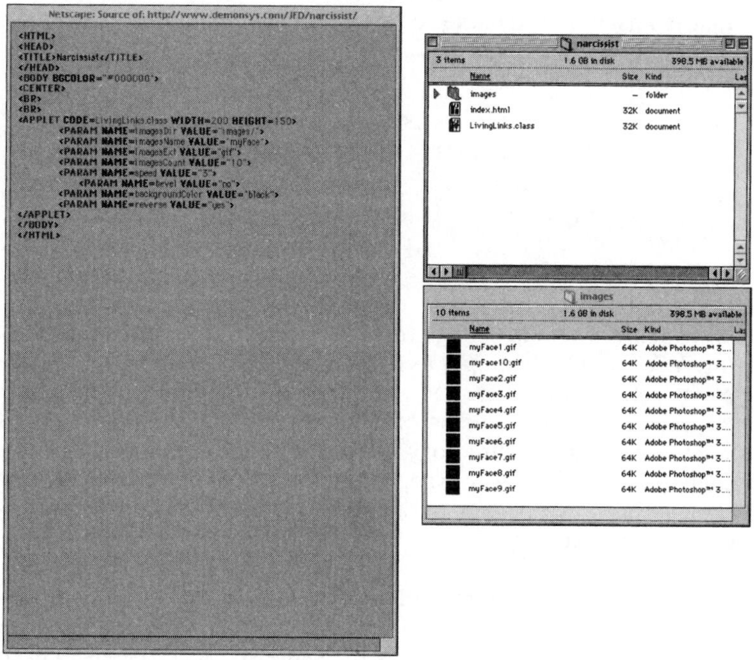

Figure 8-3:
You can
configure
an applet to
use your
own files,
as long
as you
tweak the
<APPLET>
tag
accordingly
and use the
file naming
conventions
it expects.

Although figuring out all these parameters without documentation is difficult, it is possible if you have a sample applet to work with (I discuss LivingLinks applet parameters in considerable detail later in this chapter). If you don't have a sample, hang it up: You'd be lucky to guess any one of the parameters, let alone all four!

When you have sample HTML code to check out, however, life is a breeze. All you have to do is tweak the tag you're given, customizing it for your own purposes. Consider, for example, the following <APPLET> tag. In order to customize this snippet of HTML code for your own purposes, all you have to do is change those parameters that don't apply to your particular situation.

```
<APPLET CODE=LivingLinks.class WIDTH=200 HEIGHT=150>
<PARAM NAME=imagesDir VALUE="images/">
<PARAM NAME=imagesName VALUE="myFace">
<PARAM NAME=imagesExt VALUE="gif">
<PARAM NAME=imagesCount VALUE="10">
</APPLET>
```

The images you wish to animate may be stored in a directory called Images, meaning you don't have to change the imagesDir tag in this example, but chances are pretty high that your images aren't named "myFace1.gif", "myFace2.gif", "myFace3.gif", and so forth. Instead, you may have ten images based on the name "chickenLips", which requires you to customize the above <APPLET> tag as follows:

```
<APPLET CODE=LivingLinks.class WIDTH=200 HEIGHT=150>
<PARAM NAME=imagesDir VALUE="images/">
<PARAM NAME=imagesName VALUE="chickenLips">
<PARAM NAME=imagesExt VALUE="gif">
<PARAM NAME=imagesCount VALUE="10">
</APPLET>
```

All you have to do is change the imagesName parameter value from "myFace" to "chickenLips" as shown, and ensure that the various images you're referencing (chickenLips1.gif, chickenLips2.gif, chickenLips3.gif, and so on) are stored in a folder named "images", itself located in the same directory as the Web page containing this tag and the LivingLinks applet. Of course, if you don't have ten images to animate, change the imagesCount parameter to reflect the actual number of images you do have. No biggie.

Keep in mind that you must change the WIDTH and HEIGHT attributes of the <APPLET> tag to match the width and height of your images. If you don't, and if your images aren't *exactly* the same size as those used in the example, one of three things happens:

✔ Your animated images appear cut off, or cropped, because they're larger than the dimensions specified in the WIDTH and HEIGHT attributes.

✔ Your animated images are surrounded by extra space because they're smaller than the dimensions specified.

✔ Your animated images are stretched, or *scaled,* to fit the dimensions specified in the WIDTH and HEIGHT attribute.

As you may suspect, your images actually don't have to be in the GIF format as they were in the original example. Since all Java applets know how to deal with both GIF and JPEG images (see Chapter 5 and Chapter 9 for details on using images with applets), you're free to use either format when weaving images into your <APPLET> tag. In this example, you can further customize the applet by providing your images in JPEG format. If you use JPEG images instead, simply set the imagesExt parameter to the .jpg extension, the default extension for files stored in the JPEG format (note that LivingLinks doesn't require a period when specifying an image extension such as .jpg or .gif, although other applets do):

```
<PARAM NAME=imagesExt VALUE="jpg">
```

Be sure to use the proper lowercase and uppercase letters for any parameter that you supply; myFace.gif is not the same as myFace.GIF, or myface.gif! Java applets are sensitive to character case, so be precise when supplying parameters and naming any files they use. This is true for all parameters, not just images.

The animation looks about the same whether you use JPEG or GIF images, depending on how much compression is applied to your images (see Chapter 5). Changing the format that an applet's images are stored in isn't the type of customization that has the same visual impact on the applet as does changing the actual images used in the animation. However, by using a different set of images each time you weave this applet into your pages, you can produce radically different results from the same applet.

When you customize an applet, you're really changing the way the applet looks, sounds, and feels. Although the look and the sound are pretty obvious, the feel of an applet is a little more elusive. An applet's *feel* is how the applet interacts with the Webber (see Chapter 1 for details on interactivity).

Merely changing the type of image format you use doesn't affect the overall *look* of the applet as much as it impacts the applet's *feel.* If the format you choose significantly alters the total *weight* (the combined size of each file, discussed in detail in Chapter 5) of the material that must be transferred from the Web to the browser, you can radically alter the feel of the applet. And this, in turn, affects how much or how little folks appreciate your Java-powered pages.

After all, which applets are more appealing to you — those that load quickly and begin doing something right away (such as an animation or playing sound), or those that take forever to download the files they need and then run sluggishly when they finally execute? By customizing an applet with your own sound and image files, you have the final say in how much material comes down the wire, and, ultimately, how taxed the applet is when it uses these files.

The JARing Truth

The LivingLinks example I use throughout this chapter features a plain and simple `<APPLET>` tag, one that conforms to the original Java standard. That is to say, the `<APPLET>` tags you've seen previously weave only Java class files into Web pages (as described in Chapter 4). Many applets, however, are distributed in Java Archives, known as JARs for short (Chapters 4 and 6 also discuss JARs), rather than as class files. JAR files help you manage applets (especially if those applets are comprised of a bunch of class files), and can greatly decrease the amount of time an applet takes to transfer over the Web to the end user's computer — *JAR files* are compressed archives containing any number of files that the applet needs to run properly, and are generally about half the size they would be if uncompressed.

While everything so far in this chapter applies to traditional (non-JAR) applets, the concepts also apply to applets compressed into JARs. The LivingLinks applet, for example, is available on the CD-ROM that accompanies this book, both in traditional and JAR form. Both forms of this applet support the same PARAMs, and are exactly the same in that respect. The only difference between the two, in fact, is that the JAR version contains all the .class files, which enables you to deal with only one small archive rather than many different class files.

The LivingLinks applet is comprised of several Java class files, each of which gives the applet special capabilities. The JAR version of LivingLinks simply compresses these various class files into one neat and tidy little package, making it a tad easier to manage than the non-JAR version.

To use this version of the applet, or any other applet that uses a JAR file, for that matter, you need to supply the appropriate name of the JAR when specifying the `ARCHIVE` attribute in the opening `<APPLET>` tag. For example, to use the JAR version of LivingLinks rather than the traditional one, specify the following opening `<APPLET>` tag:

```
<APPLET CODE=LivingLinks.class ARCHIVE=LivingLinks.jar
        WIDTH=200 HEIGHT=150>
```

More is not always better

In selecting images for an animation, avoid including too many images or images that are too large in physical dimensions or storage requirements. In addition to taking a great deal of time to download, using a lot of images (or a few very large ones) often adversely affects the applet. Applets struggle to draw each image on-screen fast enough, which may result in rough, jerky animation.

As a general rule, keep the total amount of material (images, sounds, text, and anything else your pages contain that must be downloaded to the browser) to 250K or less. Exceptions to this rule exist. For example:

✔ Using larger pages is justified if you provide enough information to give

visitors something to view immediately while the rest of your material comes across the wire.

✔ 250K may be far too much for your page, depending on the speed of your Web server and its connection to the Internet (which together determine how fast your page delivers the material to Webbers).

Of course, the only way you can know for sure whether the amount of information on your Web page is too little, too much, or just right is to upload the whole ball of wax to the Web (after you've crafted it on your personal computer) and then test it rigorously! For details on testing your applets, see Chapters 11 and 18.

With this opening ⟨APPLET⟩ tag in mind, then, the following code is a complete ⟨APPLET⟩ tag constructed for the JAR version of LivingLinks:

```
<APPLET CODE=LivingLinks.class ARCHIVE=LivingLinks.jar
          WIDTH=200 HEIGHT=150>
<PARAM NAME=imagesDir VALUE="images/">
<PARAM NAME=imagesName VALUE="myFace">
<PARAM NAME=imagesExt VALUE="gif">
<PARAM NAME=imagesCount VALUE="10">
</APPLET>
```

Everything but the new ARCHIVE attribute is exactly the same as it is in the traditional version of the applet. The only difference is that the archive contains all the classes that make up the LivingLinks applet, meaning that you don't have to bother with each class file individually. Just make sure that the LivingLinks.jar file is in the same directory as your Web page, and you're good to go!

JAR-style applets aren't supported in all browsers. As a result, any applets that you weave into your Web pages really should be traditional (non-JAR) if you expect all makes and models of Java-savvy browsers to see 'em!

In Appendix B, I explain how to weave both styles of applets into a single page by using JavaScript, allowing your pages to dynamically display the appropriate version for each browser that visits (that is, traditional applets for older browsers, JAR-style applets for newer ones). However, unless you take the time to specifically support both types of applets (as I explain in Appendix B), I highly recommend sticking with the traditional applets because they're supported by all versions of Java-savvy browsers.

While both versions of the LivingLinks applet support exactly the same features, the same isn't necessarily so with other applets. In truth, many applet developers add extra capabilities to their JAR-style applets. To find out what features any applet supports, whether traditional or JAR-style, you must consult the documentation that comes with the applet. To find out how, read on.

The Right Stuff

If it's so easy to figure out applet parameters just by examining the ⟨APPLET⟩ tag and tweaking it to suit your needs, why bother with real documentation? In today's ultra-sophisticated world of mouse-driven programs, clicking around to explore the various features should be enough, right? Nope! Unlike many of the software programs on your computer, you can't just click on an applet, select an Options or a Preferences menu, and configure the applet to your liking. At least, you can't today unless you spend a hefty sum of money on a visual Web page development tool, such as Sun's Java Studio. However, these programs are pretty darned expensive (several hundred dollars, which translates roughly into fifty cups of coffee at Starbucks), and generally are difficult to learn. For the time being, you're much (much!) better off learning how to tweak ⟨APPLET⟩ tags manually by typing applet parameters yourself. Hey, that's how real Web developers do it anyway! We don't need no stinkin' visual tools!

In the near future, Web page generation tools will come down drastically in price and become even easier to learn. Until then, however, it's a good idea to configure your applets by using plain old HTML. Of course, there is nothing stopping you from downloading a free trial version of these visual tools. To find a few useful links to visual Web development tools that also support Java, see www.mantiscorp.com/java.

So what's the big deal with tweaking ⟨APPLET⟩ tags manually? Does typing in applet parameters manually also mean that you need documentation? Unfortunately, yes. Because you don't have a nice, comprehensive set of visual controls for setting parameters, you really have no idea exactly which parameters an applet accepts or which values you can supply for those parameters. Perhaps you're thinking, "No big deal — I'll just sneak a peek at the HTML source code to see how to configure my applets."

That's just fine, if you don't mind eating ice cream from the bottom of a cone. Consider the LivingLinks applet. By peeking at the <APPLET> tag that I provide earlier in this chapter, you can figure out a few of the parameters this applet uses and what those parameters correspond to. As a result, you can now configure that applet to animate your very own images, making for an infinite number of cool pages. As long as you supply different images each time you configure the tag, each animation looks different and so, too, do your pages. Pretty nifty, considering this feat took all of ten minutes to figure out, huh?

But by looking only at the <APPLET> tag, you miss out on some of this applet's other juicy options:

- ✔ Did you know that LivingLinks has an option to reverse the animation when it reaches the last image, yo-yo style?

- ✔ Did you know that you can change the speed of the animation in response to the mouse? The animation can run at one speed when the mouse is outside the applet and at an entirely different speed when the mouse is inside. Did you even know that you can set a speed for the applet?

- ✔ Did you know that you can supply a background image, which optionally can be tiled end to end like wallpaper, to display your animation on?

- ✔ Did you know that you can link sounds to the animation, adding an entirely different dimension to the applet? You bet. Not only that, but you can specify sounds to play based on the mouse position!

- ✔ Did you know that this applet allows you to loop sounds, instead of having them stop after they're done playing? In fact, you can even specify a timer for the sounds, if you don't want them looping from start to finish. Instead, you may prefer to have sounds played once every ten seconds. And, yes indeed, you can set up a timer for more than one sound, and even mix sounds to play on top of each other rather than having each play by itself.

- ✔ Did you know that you can choose different special effects to apply to a single image instead of just flipping through a bunch of slightly different-looking images as an animation? You can specify just one image and have it fade in and out, have different colors inside the image blink on and off, or have the whole image melt, warp, or shatter!

- ✔ Did you pick up on one of the most wicked-cool features of the product: multiple-choice hyperlinks? Before LivingLinks, the Web supported only one link per image; you click on a hyperlinked image and navigate to the single URL associated with that link. With LivingLinks, you can specify any number of URLs to appear in a pop-up menu for the Webber to choose from!

LivingLinks is a rich, decadent treat, with scoop after scoop of luscious ice cream loaded with your favorite toppings! But by looking only at the `<APPLET>` tag, and not the documentation for the applet, you have no idea what the applet is really capable of. Instead, you get a small taste of its potential — a trickle of flavor leaking out of the bottom of the cone.

Sure, as you visit more and more pages on the Web that use a particular applet, such as LivingLinks, you find out more about the applet and how to configure the features it offers (such as animation, sound, colors, interaction with Webbers, and so forth — see Chapter 9 for more details). But that's a slow, painful process. And how do you know when you've learned all there is to know about the product?

Instead, why not take a look at the menu, so to speak, and see exactly what ingredients you have to work with? By looking at the documentation, you know the capabilities of your applets right from the get-go, giving you all the ingredients you need to whip up sumptuous, irresistible Web pages.

Menu, Please

Configuring an applet without checking its documentation is like ordering food without looking at a menu. Aside from looking at the `<APPLET>` tag on other pages, the best you can do is guess at the names of parameters you *think* the applet might accept. And that, my friend, is a complete shot in the dark. You're better off playing the lottery.

Unlike standard software programs, such as your word processor, spreadsheet, and graphics packages, documentation for applets usually doesn't come in printed form. Instead, the information you need in order to make the most of these tiny programs comes electronically — typically as a Web page or a plain text file. Although there's no standard way of organizing applet documentation, what you get almost always has two major parts to it: a usage guide and a parameter listing.

Usage guide

An applet's *usage guide* is really nothing more than a description of what the applet can do, and may be as detailed or as abstract as the author, or developer, of the applet wants. Some applet usage guides are thoroughly detailed, explaining each and every facet of the mini-program and how you can weave it into your pages. Other guides may be nothing more than a paragraph or two summarizing the applet's capabilities, perhaps even leaving out some features for you to discover on your own by looking at the parameter listing (see the next section).

But in almost all cases, the user guide includes a sample ⟨APPLET⟩ tag to get you started. And in the case of documentation that appears in Web page format, the applet may actually be running right then and there. Personally, this is my favorite form of documentation; not only do you get the information you need to use the applet, but you also see the applet running at the same time (see Figure 8-4). What a bargain!

Parameter listing

Although a usage guide is a real help, a comprehensive *parameter listing* is downright essential. Along with the name and description of each parameter, these listings tell you what values (strings or numbers) each parameter accepts and what constitutes a legal entry. Without such a listing, you have no idea what parameters to insert in the ⟨APPLET⟩ tag.

For example, some parameters that accept string values take a URL, whereas others expect the name of an image. A parameter that accepts numbers, on the other hand, may require whole integers in a certain range (1 to 100, for example), or decimal values (such as 1.5353). And in the case of those parameters that accept more than one value, you often are told what *separator character* to use in between each value you supply. Although the most popular separator is a pipe (|), some applets ask that you use a colon, semicolon, comma, or even spaces to separate each value (see Chapter 4 for details on parameters and values).

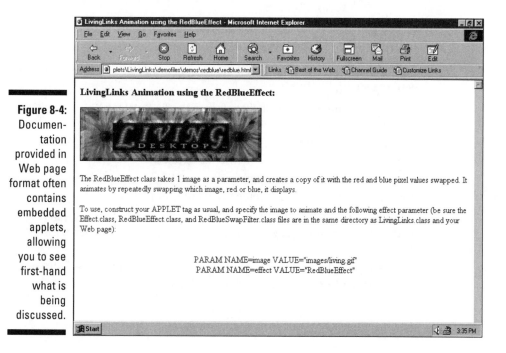

Figure 8-4: Documentation provided in Web page format often contains embedded applets, allowing you to see first-hand what is being discussed.

Just as usage guides vary from applet to applet, the way in which parameters are listed varies, too. Some programmers document their parameters by using little more than a list, as shown in the following code, whereas others use a table format (shown in Table 8-1 at the end of this chapter). Of course, the form really isn't all that important — having the information is what counts! As long as you get your hands on a comprehensive parameter listing (one that covers all parameters the applet uses), you have all you need to customize the applet.

Although a quick glance at Table 8-1 gives you all the information you need concerning the parameters of the LivingLinks applet, this program is so comprehensive that understanding exactly what each parameter does is difficult. As a result, this applet is an ideal candidate for a comprehensive user guide in Web page format, where examples of the applet can execute alongside the documentation.

Although many applets don't support parameters at all, most do. Take, for example, the following example. Here we see a list of parameters from the Celebrity Painter applet, provided (courtesy of Jeff Orkin, one of the original LivingLinks developers) on the CD-ROM that comes with this book:

```
<APPLET CODE=CelebrityPainter.class WIDTH=300 HEIGHT=200>
<PARAM NAME=brush1 VALUE="Drew Barrymore">
<PARAM NAME=brush2 VALUE="Jim Carrey">
<PARAM NAME=brush3 VALUE="Bill Clinton">
</APPLET>
```

As you can see from the preceding list, you can add as many celebrities as you want. To add celebrities, follow these steps:

1. **Add a parameter that includes the next sequential brush number and a name string.**

   To add a David Letterman brush, insert the line **<PARAM NAME=brush4 VALUE="David Letterman">**.

2. **Provide a 160 x 200 JPEG image of the celebrity, with a filename that matches the name string, but with no spaces.**

   For example, place a 160 x 200 JPEG image called DavidLetterman.jpg in the same directory as the Celebrity Painter applet.

3. **Provide a 40 x 50 JPEG image of the celebrity, with a filename that matches the name string, but with no spaces and the characters BR at the end.**

   For example, place a 40 x 50 JPEG image called DavidLettermanBR.jpg in the same directory as the Celebrity Painter applet.

The Celebrity Painter applet figures out the file names based on the preceding naming convention. You specify the name string `"David Letterman"`, and the applet knows to look for DavidLetterman.jpg and DavidLettermanBR.jpg. Celebrity Painter's documentation describes these special naming conventions.

Although applets such as LivingLinks and Celebrity Painter are complex enough that both a usage guide and a parameter listing are necessary, some applets are much easier to understand. For example, you really don't need a usage guide to figure out the Marquee applet (also provided on this book's CD-ROM). Because the Marquee applet uses a relatively small number of parameters, just a quick glance at the parameter listing gives you a pretty good idea of what the applet can do. Here's an example of the Marquee applet being used to scroll the message "Hello World!" across the screen:

```
<APPLET CODE="Marquee" WIDTH=500 HEIGHT=24>
<PARAM NAME="shift" VALUE=2>
<PARAM NAME="delay" VALUE=20>
<PARAM NAME="font_face" VALUE="geneva">
<PARAM NAME="font_size" VALUE="20">
<PARAM NAME="font_italic" VALUE="no">
<PARAM NAME="font_bold" VALUE="yes">
<PARAM NAME="back_color" VALUE="255 255 255">
<PARAM NAME="text_color" VALUE="0 0 0">
<PARAM NAME="marquee" VALUE="Hello World!">
</APPLET>
```

The JAR-style version of Marquee, as you may guess, supports exactly the same suite of parameters, yet requires that you properly specify the archive attribute in the opening <APPLET> tag, like so:

```
<APPLET CODE="Marquee" ARCHIVE="Marquee.jar" WIDTH=500
        HEIGHT=24>
```

And, just as with the traditional version of this applet, you're free to exclude the quotes when specifying either CODE or ARCHIVE (and CODEBASE, if you choose to use this attribute — see Chapter 7 for details). Just be sure to enclose inside quotes the PARAM names and values that you supply if a space character is needed (such as the space between Hello and World in the marquee PARAM). Or, play it on the safe side and enclose all PARAM names and values in quotes:

```
<APPLET CODE=Marquee ARCHIVE=Marquee.jar WIDTH=500
        HEIGHT=24>
<PARAM NAME="shift" VALUE=2>
<PARAM NAME="delay" VALUE=20>
<PARAM NAME="font_face" VALUE="geneva">
<PARAM NAME="font_size" VALUE="20">
<PARAM NAME="font_italic" VALUE="no">
<PARAM NAME="font_bold" VALUE="yes">
<PARAM NAME="back_color" VALUE="255 255 255">
<PARAM NAME="text_color" VALUE="0 0 0">
<PARAM NAME="marquee" VALUE="Hello World!">
</APPLET>
```

Keep in mind that the `CODE` and `ARCHIVE` names aren't always the same. It's up to the applet developer to choose names for the class file(s) and JARs (assuming JARs are used) — Chapter 4 has more on this. It's entirely possible, for example, to have an opening `<APPLET>` tag like the following:

```
<APPLET CODE=Marquee ARCHIVE=ABC.jar WIDTH=500 HEIGHT=24>
```

Because there's no law saying the `CODE` and `ARCHIVE` names must be the same, you often run into JARs that don't have the same name as the class file specified in the `CODE` attribute. In fact, it's entirely possible to have more than one JAR for a single applet. In this case, you must separate each JAR with a comma when constructing the opening `<APPLET>` tag, as the following theoretical example illustrates:

```
<APPLET CODE=Marquee ARCHIVE=ABC.jar, XYZ.jar, Yentil.jar
        WIDTH=500 HEIGHT=24>
```

The traditional (non-JAR) Marquee applet provided on this book's CD-ROM is made up of two class files, Marquee.class and MarqueeFile.class, both of which are required in order for the applet to run properly. The JAR version of Marquee, on the other hand, requires only one file: Marquee.jar. If you want to use the non-JAR version of Marquee, be sure to place both Marquee.class and MarqueeFile.class in the same folder as the Web page in which you weave the applet. To use the JAR version of Marquee, on the other hand, you need only place Marquee.jar in the folder containing your Web page since it contains both class files in compressed form. For more details on weaving the Marquee applet into your Web pages, see Chapter 9.

Defaults: If you don't say it, I will!

In some cases, certain parameters must contain a value to properly config-ure an applet. For example, an applet that does nothing more than display a scrolling message, such as Marquee, requires you to provide it with the text to scroll. But what if you don't?

Take, for example, the following configuration for Marquee:

```
<APPLET CODE="Marquee" WIDTH=500 HEIGHT=40>
</APPLET>
```

In this example, no parameters are used at all! Fortunately, the Marquee applet falls back onto *default* parameters that allow the applet to run even when you don't give it the proper information. Exactly what an applet does when you don't supply it with a required parameter is up to the programmer who created it; in the case of Marquee, it scrolls a little message across the screen to tell you that the applet wasn't properly configured (see Figure 8-5).

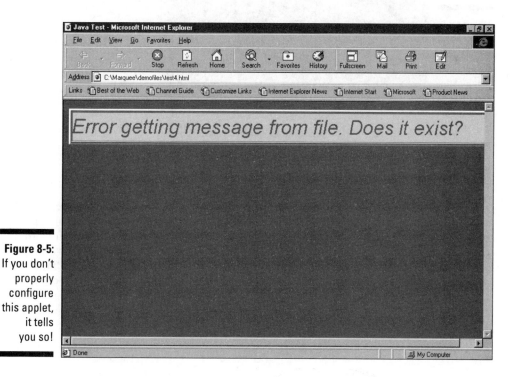

Figure 8-5:
If you don't properly configure this applet, it tells you so!

LivingLinks, on the other hand, can't do much of anything if you don't at least supply it with an image (or a number of images) to animate. In this case, LivingLinks doesn't use a default image — instead, it displays an error message in the browser's status area to let you know something is wrong (see Figure 8-6).

Figure 8-6:
Most applets use the status area of the browser to report problems.

Error message

In fact, many applets use the status area to keep you informed in case something goes wrong. As a result, be sure to keep your eye on this part of the browser each time you test your applets. Not only do applets use this area to display messages, but the browser itself does too. If, for example, the browser has difficulty locating, downloading, or executing an applet, it displays a message in the status area to let you know there is a problem.

Not all applets list the default values they use when you don't supply your own values. As a result, the only way to know what happens is to actually omit a parameter and see how the applet reacts when executed. Because every applet is different, default procedures vary greatly. In the case of ticker-tape applets, for example, some may not even run if you omit the text to be scrolled. Even those that run are likely to display a completely different message as the default.

Params that need params are the luckiest params in the world

As with people, some parameters just can't live without constant companionship. That is, some parameters require that one or more additional parameters be specified at the same time. You can find examples of these codependent parameters in both the Marquee and LivingLinks applets.

Short of checking these parameters into group therapy, you have no way of dealing with them individually. If you specify a codependent parameter, you must also supply its companion parameters when constructing the applet tag. Depending on the applet itself, the number of dependents vary.

LivingLinks is an example of an applet with several codependent parameters, as shown in Table 8-1 (at the end of this chapter). The most critical of LivingLinks' codependent parameters are the ones that specify a series of images to animate. To animate a series of images with LivingLinks, you must configure four different parameters: imagesDir, imagesName, imagesExt, and imagesCount. These four parameters are all codependent; all four must be specified in order to give the applet enough information to find the images to animate. The following snippet of HTML code shows each parameter as it might appear in your Web page:

```
<PARAM NAME=imagesDir VALUE="images">
<PARAM NAME=imagesName VALUE="myLogo">
<PARAM NAME=imagesExt VALUE="gif">
<PARAM NAME=imagesCount VALUE="5">
```

If you omit any one of the preceding four parameters, LivingLinks won't know what files to use. Without all four parameters, none of the images appears on-screen, and an error message (Error Loading Images) appears in the status area of the browser, as shown in Figure 8-6.

Not all codependent parameters are required

Although LivingLinks won't run unless you properly configure all four of its codependent parameters discussed earlier in this chapter (`imagesDir`, `imagesName`, `imagesExt`, and `imagesCount`), other codependent parameters aren't as critical. The `bevelWidth` parameter is one of these. Used alone, this parameter doesn't add (or subtract) anything from the LivingLinks applet. It's powerless without the parameter it depends on: `bevel`. However, `bevel` is *not* a codependent applet: You can use it by itself, as in the following line of code:

```
<PARAM NAME=bevel VALUE="yes">
```

If you use the `bevel` parameter alone, you have to settle for the default bevel: a thin,

2-pixel edge surrounding the applet to give it the appearance of a button. But you can add the `bevelWidth` parameter to make the bevel thicker (or even thinner). The following line of HTML code, when used with the preceding one, places a 5-pixel, 3-D bevel around the applet:

```
<PARAM NAME=bevelWidth
    VALUE="5">
```

Unlike some codependent parameters (such as those that specify a series of images to animate), LivingLinks doesn't produce an error message if you use the `bevelWidth` parameter without the `bevel` parameter in tow. The applet works just fine, but it won't display a bevel.

Plug-in support

Some applets support what are known as *plug-ins* — special files that extend an applet's capabilities. Although plug-ins are associated most often with graphics programs, such as Adobe Photoshop, you can also design applets to take advantage of plug-in modules.

Don't confuse applet plug-ins described here with the Java Plug-in; they're two completely different beasts! For details on the latter, refer to Chapter 10. To find out more about the former, read on, dear friend.

Using a plug-in adds new functionality or features to an applet. In the case of LivingLinks, plug-ins provide special animation effects that the applet alone doesn't know how to perform. You can, for example, use a plug-in called Fade to give your LivingLinks animation a *fade* effect, allowing it to fade in and out, much the way a television show fades to black before going to commercial. To use a LivingLinks plug-in, all you have to do is properly configure the `effect` parameter.

Plug-ins really are just little programs, much like applets, that come with their own set of parameters. Depending on the plug-in, you may have to supply a number of additional parameters to configure it properly, or no parameters at all. As with applets, it's entirely up to the developer of the plug-in to decide what parameters you must use to configure it. As a result, plug-ins often come with their own documentation telling you how to use them. The documentation for the Fade plug-in, for example, is a short description of the Fade effect itself and the parameters it accepts. You simply set the `effect` parameter appropriately and supply the corresponding parameters that tell the plug-in how to behave:

```
<PARAM NAME=effect VALUE="FadeEffect">
<PARAM NAME=image VALUE="images/logo.gif">
<PARAM NAME=steps VALUE="25">
<PARAM NAME=backgroundColor VALUE="white">
```

Fade requires one image and the number of "steps" to fade to the background color you supply in the `backgroundColor` parameter. Fade makes a number of copies of the image, as determined by the `steps` parameter, in which each copy is a step closer to the background color. The plug-in then animates these faded images by rotating back and forth through each of them.

Plug-ins generally are written by programmers other than the ones who wrote the applet itself; the whole idea behind plug-ins is to allow other developers to extend the functionality of the applet to meet their needs. Typically, plug-in authors are given credit for the work they do. To see the credits for LivingLinks' plug-ins, for example, place your mouse over the running applet for a few seconds and keep your eyes on the status area of your browser window.

Because plug-ins come with their own set of parameters, you need to supply them in the `<APPLET>` tag just as you do the parameters for the applet itself. Take, for example, the LivingLinks Fade effect plug-in. When you use this plug-in, you specify its parameters right alongside the applet's parameters:

```
<APPLET CODE=LivingLinks.class WIDTH=209 HEIGHT=140>
<PARAM NAME=speed VALUE="10">
<PARAM NAME=URL VALUE="http://www.demonsys.com/
            projects.html">
<PARAM NAME=effect VALUE="FadeEffect">
<PARAM NAME=steps VALUE="12">
<PARAM NAME=image VALUE="console/projects1.gif">
<PARAM NAME=backgroundImage VALUE="console/right.gif">
<PARAM NAME=backgroundColor VALUE="black">
<PARAM NAME=reverse VALUE="yes">
</APPLET>
```

The preceding tag comes from another button on the Demon Systems Web site — Our Projects. The complete page this tag comes from is provided in the CookBook folder on the CD-ROM that comes with this book if you want to see it in person!

LivingLinks has no idea what the steps parameter means; it's unique to the Fade plug-in. This is true for most plug-ins — the parameters they use are usually independent of those used by the applet. As a result, plug-ins often don't use the same name for parameters as those used by the applet itself. Or if they do, both the applet and the plug-in share whatever value you supply. For example, if both an applet and its plug-in accept a parameter named steps, any value you supply for this parameter is used by both the applet and the plug-in. Of course, how each uses the parameter is up to its respective developer; steps doesn't have to mean the same thing to both!

Several LivingLinks plug-in effects are provided on the CD-ROM that comes with this book, with others available on the LivingLinks support site (www.mantiscorp.com/LivingLinks). For details, see Appendix C.

Because each parameter has a unique name, the order in which you supply parameters doesn't matter at all. So, although the following parameter example is more difficult to read than the one that follows it, both work just the same.

```
<PARAM NAME=backgroundColor VALUE="white">
<PARAM NAME=steps VALUE="25">
<PARAM NAME=image VALUE="images/logo.gif">
<PARAM NAME=effect VALUE="FadeEffect">
```

The parameters this plug-in uses come after the plug-in is specified:

```
<PARAM NAME=effect VALUE="FadeEffect">
<PARAM NAME=image VALUE="images/logo.gif">
<PARAM NAME=steps VALUE="25">
<PARAM NAME=backgroundColor VALUE="white">
```

Personally, I prefer to group my parameters logically: I place codependent parameters with the ones they are dependent on, and supply plug-ins last, followed by whatever parameters they require. This makes constructing the <APPLET> tag easier, and also helps to make the source code of the Web page in which the applet appears easier to read.

Table 8-1   **The LivingLinks Applet Parameters**

Parameter	Description	Default	Dependent on	Example
imagesDir	A URL (absolute or relative) pointing to a directory containing images to animate.	None	imagesName, imagesExt, imagesCount	"images/logos/mantis/"
imagesName	Base name of each image in the animation series.	None	imagesDir, imagesExt, imagesCount	"mantis Logo"
imagesExt	The extension of each image in the animation series.	None	imagesDir, imagesName, imagesCount	"gif" or "jpg"
imagesCount	The number of images in the animation series.	None	imagesDir, imagesName, imagesExt	5
image	A URL (absolute or relative) pointing to a single image to animate by using a plug-in effect (see effect). May be in GIF or JPEG format.	None	None	"images/logos/Logo.jpg"
imageTop	Top-corner coordinate where the animation should appear within the applet.	Centered in applet	Image (or image series)	100
imageLeft	Left-corner coordinate where the animation should appear within the applet.	Centered in applet	Image (or image series)	20
effect	This optional parameter describes a special effect plug-in (such as Fade, Warp, Shatter, and so on) to be applied to an image. When specified, the plug-in effect file(s) must reside in the same directory as the Living Links applet.	Each effect may use its own parameters.	None	"Fade"

(continued)

Table 8-1 *(continued)*

Parameter	Description	Default	Dependent on	Example
resize	If set to "yes", the applet is resized to the size of the animation, regardless of the HEIGHT and WIDTH values specified in the <APPLET> tag. (*Note:* Some browsers, such as Netscape 3.0, do not support dynamic resizing such as this.)	"no"	None	"yes"
speed	Speed of the animation on a scale of 1 to 100, where 1 is the slowest animation possible and 100 is the fastest (see inSpeed).	1	Image (or image series)	45
URL	Navigation URL. This parameter specifies the Internet address (URL) where users are sent when they click an animation.	None	Image (or image series)	"http://www.anywhere.com"
links	List of destination URLs (and descriptions of each) to appear in a pop-up menu when the mouse is clicked inside the animation. JavaForDummies	None	Special Format: name = url Separator: |(pipe character) "Mantis Home page = www.mantiscorp.com"	Java For Dummies = www.mantiscorp.com/
poster	Image to display while others in a series load.	First image in animation series	None	"images/Image logos/mantis-Logo5.gif"
background Color	Background color of the applet, specified as a color's name or hex value.	None	None	"white"

(continued)

Parameter	Description	Default	Dependent on	Example
background Image	URL (absolute or relative) pointing to a GIF or JPEG background for animation.	None	None	"images/back paper.jpg grounds/"
background Tile	If "yes", the background image is tiled end to end like wallpaper. If "no" (the default), the background image is *not* tiled.	"no"	background Image	"yes"
random Delay	Provides support for "randomness" between frame painting, allowing users to create animations with non-precise, or random, frame rates (particularly useful for creating blinking "neon light" animations). A random delay value (in milliseconds) from 0 to randomDelay generated between every frame, results in random frame rates.	0	None	15
clear	If "yes", animation is cleared before each image is displayed.	"yes"	Image (or image series)	"no"
reverse	If "yes", animation images are animated forward, and then backward (1,2,3,4,3,2, 1,2,3...) If "no", animation loops (1,2,3,4,1,2, 3,4,1,2,...).	"no"	Image (or image series)	"yes"
bevel	If "yes", a 3-D bevel is drawn around the applet, giving it the appearance of a button (see bevelWidth).	"no"	None	"yes"
bevelWidth	Width of the 3-D bevel drawn around the applet.	2	bevel	5
inSpeed	Speed of animation when the mouse is inside the animation (see speed).	Same setting as speed	None	100
inMessage	String shown in the browser status bar when the mouse is in the animation.	"URL" if URL param is specified	"Living Links" multiple-choice links param is used	"Click me, baby..."

(continued)

Table 8-1 *(continued)*

Parameter	Description	Default	Dependent on	Example
soundDir	A URL (absolute or relative) pointing to the directory containing AU/uLaw format sounds (.au files).	None	None	"sounds/horns/"
outSound	String containing any number of uLaw format sounds (.au files) to be played when the mouse exits the applet; sounds are separated with | (pipe character) and no spaces.	None	soundDir	"horn.au|whistle.au|bang.au"
inSound	String containing any number of uLaw format (.au files) to be played when the mouse enters the applet; sounds are separated with | (pipe character).	None	soundDir	"horn.au|whistle.au|bang.au"
outSoundLoop	If "yes", out sounds loop when played (see outSound).	"no"	outSound	"yes"
inSoundLoop	If "yes", in sounds loop when played (see inSound).	"no"	inSound	"yes"
outRandomSound	If "yes", out sounds are selected randomly, rather than played in the specified sequence (see outSound).	"no"	outSound	"yes"
inRandomSound	If "yes", in sounds are selected randomly, rather than played in a specified sequence (see inSound).	"no"	inSound	"yes"
mixSounds	If "yes", sounds are mixed instead of playing one at a time.	"no"	inSound or outSound	"yes"

(continued)

Parameter	Description	Default	Dependent on	Example
clickStop Sound	If "yes", clicking inside the applet stops all sounds (clicking inside the applet again turns the sounds back on).	"no"	inSound or outSound	"yes"
outSound Timer	Number of seconds to wait before replaying the out sound (see outSound).	None	outSound	5
inSound Timer	Number of seconds to wait before replaying the in sound (see outSound).	None	inSound	45

Chapter 9

The Main Ingredients —
Customizing to Taste

*A*lthough some applets work exactly the way you want them to right out of the box, most Web site authors want to customize their Java-powered pages by using their own images, sounds, and text with the applets they've woven into their site. To customize a Java applet to your liking, you need to get under the hood and tinker with things a bit. You can customize applets in six main ways, using:

✔ Images

✔ Sounds

✔ Text

✔ Color

✔ URLs for navigation

✔ Data files

Have you ever heard the saying "no two snowflakes are alike?" Well, applets are the same way (just not as likely to melt on your nose). Some applets may support customization in all six categories; others may support just a few kinds of customization, or perhaps only one. And a few applets you can't customize at all!

Although you customize each applet differently, all applets that support images, sounds, text, color, URLs, or data files do so in a similar fashion. As a result, when you know how to customize one applet by using these features, doing the same with other applets is usually a breeze. The most you have to do is find out what parameters to specify, and you're home free.

Cooking Up Images

Without a doubt, images are the most compelling way to enhance a Web site. Although many Java applets allow you to use images, merely displaying these images is no big deal; the exciting part lies in animating them. And depending on the applet, you may have several ways to bring your images to life.

TIP

Reversing animation

Consider LivingLinks, a powerful, multipurpose applet provided on the CD-ROM that comes with this book (see Chapter 8 for more about LivingLinks). Along with a raft of cool features, such as sound effects and multiple hyperlink navigation, LivingLinks brings your Web pages to life with sophisticated animation.

To animate a series of images, simply supply LivingLinks with two or more images to display in rapid sequence. By default, when the last image, or *frame*, in an animation is drawn, LivingLinks starts anew with the first one. As a result, the animation plays from start to finish and repeats itself continuously. This behavior, known as *looping*, is extremely useful, and thus is often the default for applets that are capable of animating images.

In many cases, you have the option of *reversing* the animation instead of looping it. By reversing an animation, you prevent it from repeating the sequence when it reaches the last frame. Instead of starting over with the first image and looping through each one in the same order again, the applet reverses the order in which it displays the images.

For example, an animation loop consisting of five frames displays each in order (1, 2, 3, 4, 5), and then repeats itself when it reaches the last frame (1, 2, 3, 4, 5). An animation with the reverse option, however, starts out in the same fashion (1, 2, 3, 4, 5), but reverses direction when it reaches the last frame — the fifth image, in this case — and proceeds to animate backwards (4, 3, 2, 1), rather than repeating the starting sequence over again. Each time the animation displays the last frame in a sequence (either frame 1 or frame 5, in this example), the direction reverses.

Even if looping is the default for an animation applet, the applet may also support the reverse option. To get the reverse effect from the LivingLinks applet, use the following parameter:

```
<PARAM NAME=reverse
    VALUE="yes">
```

Frame-based and single-frame animation

The most impressive use of images is through animation, an effect you can accomplish in a few different ways. Perhaps the most popular animation method is to "flip through" a number of individual images, as you would a cartoon flip-book, where each image in the series differs slightly from the previous one (see Figure 9-1). This technique, sometimes called *frame-based animation* (where each image is like a frame in a cartoon), can produce wonderful results, depending on the images you choose.

Figure 9-1:
Frame-based animation creates the illusion of movement.

Although animating a series of images can be quite impressive, it's also a tremendous bandwidth hog! Every image in the sequence must be sent over the wire, consuming time and money in the process (see Chapter 5 for details on bandwidth issues). *Single-frame animation,* on the other hand, uses only one image to do the job. Rather than flipping though a sequence of images to produce the illusion of movement, this technique actually alters the image you specify to produce a desired effect.

Take, for example, the LivingLinks Fade plug-in effect, which I mention in Chapter 8. (You can check out LivingLinks, a powerful multipurpose animation applet, on the CD-ROM.) The LivingLinks applet itself can animate a series of images by rapidly flipping from one to the next to produce the illusion of movement. You can also use LivingLinks in combination with any of a number of plug-in files (such as Warp, Shatter, Fade, and Kaleidoscope) that modify a single image to produce special effects.

Therefore, when you use LivingLinks in combination with the Fade plug-in effect, you only specify one image for the applet to use. Working hand-in-hand with LivingLinks, the plug-in makes several copies of the original image and then modifies each copy by adding progressively deeper shades of the color that you specify in the `backgroundColor` parameter (see Figure 9-2).

Figure 9-2:
Single-
image
animation
produces
the illusion
of move-
ment by
modifying
the same
image.

Keep in mind that every applet handles parameters differently. Although LivingLinks accomplishes single-image animation by using the applet's image parameter in conjunction with a plug-in effect (such as Fade), other applets use different parameters to do the job and may not use plug-ins at all. As a result, you really must read the documentation and review the parameter list for every applet you use in order to know how to properly construct its <APPLET> tag.

Fading an image is only one of a number of possibilities with single-frame animation. Terribly cool effects, such as warping, melting, shattering, and more are all possible; all you have to do is get your hands on the applet or plug-in that makes these effects possible.

LivingLinks (which is on the CD-ROM that comes with this book) provides a few plug-in effects, such as Fade, FireWorks, Raindrop, Warp, Shatter, and Twist. If these alone don't satisfy your craving for cool effects, you can always get the latest and greatest plug-ins right off the Net for free at www.LivingLinks.com.

The need for speed

To control the appearance of an animation, most applets (at least those that deal with animation) offer a *frame rate* parameter. Regardless of whether you use a series of images or a single image to produce the animation, the speed at which the animation operates is known as the animation's frame rate. The idea is quite simple: A period of time passes before each new frame in the animation is drawn on-screen.

How fast is too fast?

In the United States, television broadcasts are displayed at 30 frames per second, whereas other parts of the globe use slightly slower frame rates. The term *full motion* describes any animation (or broadcast) that approaches 30 frames per second — 24 fps is usually the cut-off to qualify as full motion. Unfortunately, most computers aren't powerful enough to display more than 10 to 15 frames per second! Keep this fact in mind when specifying a frame rate for your animation; if you're lucky enough to have a computer capable of displaying full-motion animation, remember that almost everyone else is limited to 10 to 15 frames at best.

In general, try to keep the speed of your frames as low as possible so that they can easily play back on a wide range of systems. Depending on the applet you're using and the machine it's running on, either the computer or the applet may skip frames in an animation if they keep up with the rate you specify. To reduce the risk of skipped frames, keep the frame rate low (10 frames per second is a good number to aim for).

A slow frame rate results in a slow-moving animation. For example, a frame rate of 5 frames per second, or 5 fps, means that a total of five new images are drawn in the space of a single second. Higher frame rates result in faster animation.

The frame rate you choose for your animation depends on the overall appearance you're trying to achieve — and largely on the images or effect that you use. If the frame rate is too slow, the animation appears choppy and unrealistic. If it's too fast, the animation may become little more than a blur. To find out what's right for your animation, experiment with different frame rates.

Some applets don't use the words `frame rate` to refer to the parameter that controls the speed of animation. LivingLinks, for example, calls this parameter `speed` instead. The lower the speed, the slower the animation. You can, in fact, set two different speeds for the animation you create with this applet: `inSpeed` and `outSpeed`. These parameters correspond to the location of the user's mouse, allowing the user to interact with the animation by moving the mouse in and out of the applet (see Table 8-1 at the end of Chapter 8).

Depending on the browser you're using, changing the frame rate (or any parameter for that matter) may not affect the applet unless you quit the browser and start it again. In many cases, once an applet executes, the browser won't recognize any changes you make to the `<APPLET>` tag, even if you click the browser's Reload button. As a result, you can change all the parameters you want and still see the exact same applet in your browser, leading you to believe that there's a problem with the applet when in fact the browser's at fault.

Sizzling Sounds

Although animating images is by far the most popular way to spruce up Web pages, sounds are another wonderful way to inject life into otherwise dead content. You can easily add sound to your Web pages by using LivingLinks, which offers a number of ways to play sounds. To customize LivingLinks in this way — as with most applets that use sounds — all you have to do is provide your own sound files and set the appropriate parameters to tell the applet where they're located (see Table 8-1 at the end of Chapter 8 or check out the LivingLinks examples provided on the CD-ROM).

The first two crops of Java applets that hit the Web, Java 1.0 and 1.1 to be precise, only supported sounds of a very specific AU format, requiring a special compression scheme known as uLaw (pronounced "mu-law"), as I describe in Chapter 5. Sounds in this format have the .au extension. As a result, anytime you see a file with this extension specified in an <APPLET> tag (or anywhere else, for that matter), you know that you're dealing with a sound file.

TIP

Force feeding applets to your browser

If you use Netscape Navigator, you can try a few tricks to force Navigator to display applets with their new parameters before pulling the plug and restarting the program from scratch. The first trick is to hold down the Shift key and press the Reload button at the same time, which forces the page to reload. However, due to Navigator's finicky nature, the page doesn't always reload the files from the server, but instead simply gets them from the disk cache.

A better solution is to clear the cache by using the Clear Disk Cache and Clear Memory Cache options — choose Edit⇨Preferences⇨ Advanced⇨Cache. As with the previous trick, however, this one doesn't always work with Navigator, although the Microsoft Internet Explorer browser is usually responsive to such maneuverings. But take heart; you can use a few other ways to force the browser to recognize your changes, although they are a little more complicated to explain. For a detailed account of how you can force your browser to accept your applet parameter changes, point your Web browser to www.mantiscorp.com/java and look for the Manhandling Java-Savvy Browsers hyperlink.

While the latest and greatest flavor of Java, Java 1.2, allows applets access to a variety of sound formats, it'll be years before 1.2 applets take over the Web and supplant their earlier 1.0 and 1.1 brethren. As a result, the vast majority of Java applets you encounter are quite rigid in the AU format they can use. And so, unless you're using Java 1.2 applets (see "Jammin' with Java 1.2" later in this chapter), you must first convert sounds of other formats to AU format if you want to use them with your applets. Here's how:

1. ***Downsample*** **the sound (that is, reduce the amount of data used to represent the sound) to 8 kHz.**

   If you recorded the sound from CD, then it probably was originally sampled at 44.1 kHz — CD quality. Notice how huge the original sound file is? Of course, this size will never work within the bandwidth constraints of the Internet. Downsampling the sound to 8 kHz drastically reduces the file size. The tradeoff is that the sound quality is also drastically reduced. To downsample a sound, all you have to do is save it in the uLaw format; all excess sound information is removed automatically from the file.

2. **Reduce the file to mono and 8 bits.**

   Reducing to *mono* and *8-bit* refers to how many channels the sound uses (stereo has two channels, mono uses only one) and how many bits per channel you'll be using. Don't worry too much about what all that means — it basically comes down to the fact that you'll end up saving more disk space. Depending on the software utility you use, you may or may not have options for converting a sound to a mono 8-bit form. If you're a Windows user, you have these options when saving (or exporting) sound files with the GoldWave utility that's provided on the CD-ROM that comes with this book. If you're a Mac user, the uLaw program provided for that platform enables you to simply save a sound file in the uLaw format; the program automatically converts the file to a mono channel 8-bit format.

3. **Save the file in NEXT/Sun AU (.au) format with uLaw compression.**

   As with each of the preceding steps, how you execute this step depends on the utility you use. Most sound-conversion tools enable you to specify precisely what format you convert a given sound file to, while others (such as the Macintosh uLaw conversion utility) choose a format for you. To find out for sure, consult the documentation that comes with the utility. (If you choose to use one of the utilities provided on the CD-ROM, the documentation is in a text file along with the utility or it is built directly into the tool via a Help command.)

You're done! The work is well worth the effort; nothing quite compares to a powerful, thumping background soundtrack when you visit a Web site.

Adding and changing sounds

If an applet supports sounds, as does the LivingLinks applet provided on the CD-ROM, you can easily customize it to use your own sounds, assuming that you know the proper parameters to tweak. This process is very similar to adding images; you must tell the applet where to find your sound file and its exact name. If you give it that much information, an applet can find and play your sounds (assuming, of course, that it was designed to play sounds in the first place — you can't get blood from a stone, or sound from an applet that doesn't know how to deal with it).

What an applet does with sounds is completely up to the programmer who created it in the first place. Some applets simply play a sound you give it, and that's that. Others may give you more control, such as the ability to play a sound repeatedly (see the "Looping sounds" section in this chapter), or may even allow you to play a number of different sounds.

You can customize the LivingLinks applet to do something extremely simple such as play a single sound when it first runs, or much more. If you want to, you can configure this applet to play different sounds depending on the position of the mouse. If the mouse is outside the applet, the sounds you specify in the outSound parameter play. If the mouse moves into the applet, the sounds you specify for the inSound parameter play. By default, the sounds play in the order you specify, but as an alternative, you can tell LivingLinks to randomly choose the sounds it plays (see Table 8-1 in Chapter 8 for a listing of all the parameters LivingLinks supports).

Just as with the images the LivingLinks applet uses, you must specify in which directory the sounds can be found. However, you don't have to be so precise and rigid about the individual names of the sound files — you can use different names for each:

```
<PARAM NAME=soundDir VALUE="sounds/">
<PARAM NAME=outSound VALUE="Orbit.au|boo.au|Clang.au">
<PARAM NAME=inSound VALUE="horn.au|Bell.au|gong.au">
```

When specifying multiple sounds with LivingLinks, do not include any spaces before or after the | (pipe character) separator; otherwise, only the first sound will play. Also, be sure to type the names of your sound files precisely; bell.au is not the same as Bell.au — applets know the difference between uppercase and lowercase characters!

In the preceding snippet of HTML code, I specified sounds for the "in" and "out" mouse positions. Each sound plays in the order that it is supplied, unless you explicitly tell the applet to choose the sounds in each category at random. When the last sound in a category plays, the sequence begins again from the beginning. If you prefer that the sounds be selected at random use the following:

```
<PARAM NAME=outRandomSound VALUE="yes">
```

Here, the sounds corresponding to the "out" position of the mouse are selected at random, while those played in response to the mouse moving inside the applet are still played in the order they are specified. You can, however, tell the applet to choose these at random as well:

```
<PARAM NAME=inRandomSound VALUE="yes">
```

By default, most applets simply play sound from start to finish and then stop. If this is what you want to occur, then you're finished setting the parameters. However, if you want the sound to repeat, resulting in a continuous soundtrack that repeats itself over and over, read the following section on looping sounds.

Looping sounds

If you want the sound in your applet to repeat, looping is the only way to go.

You can find several examples of Web pages that use looping sounds on the CD-ROM that comes with this book, each powered by the LivingLinks applet (versatile little applet, no?).

Adding sound looping to the LivingLinks applet is just a matter of setting the appropriate parameter. This, in fact, is true for all applets that support sound looping — if the sounds an applet plays don't loop by default, you have to set a parameter to tell the applet to do so! If you don't, the sounds will never loop. Of course, the parameter you use varies from applet to applet, so you must consult the documentation that comes with the applet or nose around for an example of the applet in action.

Any given applet may support concurrent, or simultaneous, playing of more than one sound loop. With LivingLinks, for instance, you can loop the "in" and "out" sounds independently of one another, because a parameter is supplied for each:

```
<PARAM NAME=inSoundLoop VALUE="yes">
<PARAM NAME=outSoundLoop VALUE="yes">
```

Actually, looping isn't the *only* way to repeat sounds. Some applets, like LivingLinks, enable you to play a sound based on a timer. Technically speaking, applets that loop sounds have no way of pausing for a period of time before playing the sound again (due to a limitation in the Java programming language). As a result, if you want to repeat a sound at a certain interval (such as every 30 seconds), you have to use a timer; a standard loop doesn't give you such control.

Sir Mix-a-lot

Due to the way the Java programming language works, most applets that support sound also enable you to mix sounds. When an applet plays more than one sound, *mixing* allows them all to play at once.

Mixing sounds is a capability that's built into the Java language itself, and not something the applet programmer has to spend any time figuring out. In fact, keeping track of which sounds are playing and stopping each one before the next can begin takes more effort than mixing sounds. As a result, mixing sound is par for the course when it comes to applets that support sound.

Of course, mixing may be something you don't want, and so some applets turn this feature off until you request it. LivingLinks, for example, won't mix sounds until you set the `mixSounds` parameter. Other applets, however, mix sounds by default until you turn the mixing parameter off! That's one more good argument for getting your hands on documentation for the applets that you use.

The CD-ROM that comes with this book contains a healthy dose of sounds, along with utilities to help you convert your own files for use with applets. For details, see Appendix C.

Jammin' with Java 1.2

If Java 1.0 and 1.1 applets run lean and mean in terms of the audio formats that they support, Java 1.2 is pump and juicy by comparison. Unlike the first two crops of applets, Java 1.2 applets support uLaw (.au format) sound files and a whole lot more. In short, Java 1.2 applets rock.

As I explain in Chapter 5, Java 1.2 supports all of the most popular sound formats available on the Web today, including WAV and MIDI to name just two. Of course, not all Java 1.2 applets support these new sound formats, nor do they all support the original uLaw format. Simply put, an applet is under no obligation to play sound. Each applet developer must choose to give the applets she creates a voice or to render them mute for all eternity.

Java 1.2 applets that support sounds that you may customize require you to use parameters. And, as Chapter 8 explains, each applet uses different PARAM names and value settings. As a result, you must consult your applet's documentation in order to find out *how* to take advantage of the new sound formats that Java 1.2 offers.

Due to the sad but true fact that today's most current Web browsers are behind the times when it comes to Java, you won't be able to see or hear Java 1.2 applets in action without the Java Plug-in. See Chapter 10 to find out how the Java Plug-in takes Web pages to an entirely different level.

Sprinkling On Text

Applets that support text usually let you specify the font face (TimesRoman, Courier, and so on), point size (10, 24, 72, and so on), and style (such as plain, bold, or italics) in which the text will be displayed. The Marquee applet, for example, lets you specify all three:

```
<APPLET CODE="Marquee" WIDTH=250 HEIGHT=30>
<param NAME="shift" VALUE=3>
<param NAME="delay" VALUE=5>
<param NAME="font_face" VALUE="courier">
<param NAME="font_size" VALUE="16">
<param NAME="font_italic" VALUE="yes">
<param NAME="font_bold" VALUE="yes">
<param NAME="back_color" VALUE="255 255 255">
<param NAME="text_color" VALUE="0 100 0">
<param NAME="marquee" VALUE="Howdy! I'm scrolling...">
</APPLET>
```

Although ticker-tape applets such as Marquee use these types of settings to display text as it scrolls across the screen, you can do many other things with the text in your applets:

- ✔ The LivingLinks applet, for example, supports a plug-in effect known as WildWords. This plug-in animates the text you provide by drawing each character in a slightly different location on the screen in a variety of colors and speeds. As a result, the text you specify comes to life, dancing up and down as if hopped-up on caffeine. And rightly so — it's full of Java.

- ✔ An applet that displays bar charts, for example, may allow you to choose the text that appears on the X and Y axis, or for each element appearing in the chart itself; a spreadsheet applet may allow you to choose the size and style of the font in which its numbers will appear.

✔ Some applets let users select items from a menu. A good example of this type of applet is Celebrity Painter, which lets you specify the name of the "brushes" to use when painting. To choose a different brush, you simply make a selection from a menu. Because each brush in the menu is customizable, you can specify whatever names you want to appear in the menu (see the Celebrity Painter example earlier in this chapter).

As always, the applet developer decides what parameters you can and can't configure. And, as always, the only way to find out what you can do with an applet is to read the documentation that comes with it. However, as a general rule, those applets that allow you to specify text also allow you to specify the characteristics of the font in which the text appears.

Don't go crazy when choosing a font face for your applets! Not every computer has the same fonts installed on it as your computer, so the text on your pages may not appear to others the same way it does to you. Be conservative with your font choices and pick those available across a wide range of systems. Times Roman, Courier, and Helvetica are good examples of fonts installed on many users' computers.

Pouring On Color

Many applets, especially those that deal with text, enable you to set parameters to control the color of the content that appears on-screen (such as text, background, buttons, and other visual elements that an applet may utilize). The Marquee applet (on the CD-ROM that comes with this book), for example, lets you set the color of the scrolling text and the color of the banner on which the text scrolls. LivingLinks, on the other hand, doesn't deal with text itself (although plug-ins can provide a variety of text capabilities). As a result, this applet only allows you to set the background color on which an animation is displayed. Other applets, depending on what they do, may provide different color settings that you can customize through `<PARAM>` tags.

Because all applets are different, the approach each takes to dealing with colors differs. The most user-friendly of applets, however, lets you specify color by name:

```
<PARAM NAME="anyColorSetting" VALUE="black">
```

The `"anyColorSetting"` parameter in the preceding code isn't a real parameter — it's just an example. To find out the proper parameters for your applets, consult the documentation.

Contrast the preceding tag with one from an applet that requires you to specify colors by using three numbers to represent the separate red, green, and blue components of a color:

```
<PARAM NAME="anyColorSetting" VALUE="255 255 255">
```

Here, each number specifies how much or how little red, green, or blue to mix into the overall color. By specifying how much of each color to use, you can get just the shade of color you're looking for (if you have the patience to figure it out!). This method of representing color is called the *RGB model* — you tell the applet how much *r*ed, *g*reen, and *b*lue to mix together to produce the final color.

In this example, the color specified uses exactly the same amounts of red, green, and blue: 255. As a result, the color you end up with is white. White?! But in kindergarten you learned that mixing together the same amount of red, green, and blue results in black — what gives? Unfortunately, all you ever needed to know about colors you did *not* learn in kindergarten.

Computers work the opposite of finger paints. Instead of taking a blob of paint and putting it on a piece of paper, your computer shoots out three beams of colored light (a red beam, green beam, and blue beam) from behind your monitor. At an astonishing rate, each *pixel* (dot) on your monitor is, in turn, lit up from behind by the beams of light. Depending on how much intensity of color each beam contains, the pixel that is lit up is a different color. Basically, your computer is mixing the beams of light to make a color.

Actually, not all computer monitors display color by shooting three beams of colored light at the pixels; there are a few different ways to go about creating color on-screen. But in the end, they all mix light together to come up with the colors that you see.

Because all computers create color by mixing light (not absorbing light, as finger paints do), combining the same intensity of red, blue, and green produces white, not black. To create black by using the RGB model, you have to lower the intensity of each beam of light to nothing:

```
<PARAM NAME="anyColorSetting" VALUE="0 0 0">
```

In the RGB model, the highest value you can supply is 255, and the lowest is 0 (sorry, no negatives!). As a result, black is always formed by zero values for red, green, and blue, and white is always formed by lighting up the pixels so much that you can't see any color (255, 255, 255). With this in mind, you can create a nice shade of gray by taking the middle ground — not too light, not too dark, but right in the middle:

```
<PARAM NAME="anyColorSetting" VALUE="128 128 128">
```

Cool, huh? But what if you want other colors, say a nice bright red? Well, then all you have to do is specify the red component at 100 percent, and the others at zero:

```
<PARAM NAME="anyColorSetting" VALUE="255 0 0">
```

Got a case of the blues? Just turn up the knob on blue, and dim the others to nothing:

```
<PARAM NAME="anyColorSetting" VALUE="0 0 255">
```

And, of course, if you're after a nice, soothing green, try this value:

```
<PARAM NAME="anyColorSetting" VALUE="0 255 0">
```

You can make a less intense shade of each color merely by reducing the amount of light you use from 255 on down. The lower you go, the darker the color becomes. If you want to create other colors, all you have to do is add different amounts of red, green, and blue. How about a nice shade of pink? Aqua? Sky blue? Okey-doke:

- **Pink:** `<PARAM NAME="anyColorSetting" VALUE="255 192 203">`
- **Aqua:** `<PARAM NAME="anyColorSetting" VALUE="0 255 255">`
- **Sky blue:** `<PARAM NAME="anyColorSetting" VALUE="135 206 235">`

Armed with the RGB color model, you can now set any color you want for the Marquee background and the text that scrolls across it. How about forest green on hot pink? Coming right up:

```
<APPLET CODE="Marquee" WIDTH=250 HEIGHT=30>
        <PARAM NAME="shift" VALUE=3>
        <PARAM NAME="delay" VALUE=5>
        <PARAM NAME="font_face" VALUE="TimesRoman">
        <PARAM NAME="font_size" VALUE="12">
        <PARAM NAME="font_italic" VALUE="yes">
        <PARAM NAME="font_bold" VALUE="yes">
        <PARAM NAME="back_color" VALUE="255 105 180">
        <PARAM NAME="text_color" VALUE="39 134 34">
        <PARAM NAME="marquee" VALUE="Am I an annoying
        ticker or what?">
</APPLET>
```

TECHNICAL STUFF

Throwing a hex wrench into the works

The RGB color model makes sense, even though it may take a little getting used to. But you're in for a doozie with some applets. A few cruel applet developers in the world like to think that you spend as much time behind the soft glow of a scientific calculator as they do. These heartless souls create their programs to accept colors by using hexadecimal numbers.

Because I care about you, I'm not even going to try to explain these nasty little numbers. Black and white are no problem to represent in hexadecimal form, but things get pretty ugly from then on. Here's just a sample:

black	000000
red	ff0000
green	00ff00
blue	ffffff
pink	ffc0cb
aqua	00ffff
sky blue	87ceeb
hot pink	f0fff0
forest	228b22

If you've dealt with hexadecimal numbers before, this all makes perfect sense. Technically, these numbers are represented in hexadecimal triplet form: Each component for red, green, and blue is represented with a separate hexadecimal value. However, if this representation is new to you, don't bother trying to figure it out. Instead, what you need is a utility or chart to convert the color you're looking for into hexadecimal triplet form. Fortunately, one exists at the following URL:

```
www.mantiscorp.com/java
```

Connect to this site, and look for the Color Chart hyperlink. Here, you'll find a table containing a wide range of colors, giving you a name, RGB color, and hexadecimal triplet setting for each. Save yourself the pain and agony of dealing with hexadecimal numbers — if you ever run into an applet that requires them, come here for help. Heck, for that matter, download the chart to your computer — that way, you'll always have it handy, just in case you need to convert from RGB to hexadecimal in an emergency. Hey, it could happen.

TIP

Mac users have a nifty shareware utility called WebColor, thanks to Patrick Bores. With this utility, you can use the Mac's standard color wheel to select colors and receive the corresponding hexadecimal value. WebColor is available on most shareware archives and at www.shareware.com. If you find that the WebColor shareware program is worth paying for, drop ol' Patrick a few bucks. What could be better than test driving software without having to pay up front? Nothing, bubbie.

Cookin' with URL

Depending on whom you talk to, you'll hear URL pronounced either as a word, "earl" (sounding slightly like "oil" with a southern drawl), or by sounding out each letter in the acronym ("U-R-L," which stands for Uniform Resource Locator, described in Chapter 1). You say "tomato," I say "tomahtoe," you say "potato," I say "French fries in the larva stage."

However you say it, URLs have one purpose in life: to locate information on the Web. Every item that lives on the Web has a unique URL associated with it. Web pages, image files, sound files, data files, and everything else that exists on the Web has its very own URL. As a result, you can always find whatever you're looking for as long as you have its URL.

Because applets live on the Net, many of them (not surprisingly) accept URLs as parameters. Typically, applets use URLs in one of three ways:

✔ To find files on the Web

✔ To find directories on the Web

✔ To navigate the Web

As with every other parameter that you specify, URLs must match the item they refer to exactly. If you want to provide your applet with a file that exists at `www.mantiscorp.com/java/images`, for example, then that's exactly what you must type, including all punctuation, and using all lowercase letters.

Although some applets don't deal at all with URLs, others make heavy use of them. The LivingLinks applet, for example, has several parameters that accept URLs. One of these, in fact, is actually named `URL` (see Table 8-1 at the end of Chapter 8). Another parameter, `links`, allows you to specify multiple URLs instead, each separated by a pipe character (|). You use both of these parameters for navigational purposes, and both come into action when the Webber clicks the applet.

But this applet uses several more URLs to access directories and files. You can provide URLs to tell LivingLinks in what directory on the Web it will find the sounds and images you tell it to use. Or you can use a URL to load just one image for the animation, if you prefer. You can also use a URL to specify an image to use as a background, on top of which the animation will appear. As with many applets, LivingLinks is chock full of parameters that accept URLs:

```
<PARAM NAME=links VALUE= "Mantis Homepage = http://
        www.mantiscorp.com | For Dummies Homepage =
        http://www.dummies.com">
<PARAM NAME=soundDir VALUE="sounds/animals/mammals/">
<PARAM NAME=imagesDir VALUE="images/mantis/">
<PARAM NAME=backgroundImage VALUE= "http://
        www.mantiscorp.com/images/mantoid.gif">
```

As with most applets, LivingLinks accepts both relative and absolute URLs (see the sidebar, "Linking to relative and absolute URLs," in Chapter 3), which means that you can refer to files and directories residing inside the same directory as the applet itself or one halfway around the world! But before you go nuts hooking up your applets to use files from a distant directory, keep in mind that most applets can only access files that reside on the same server as their own (specifically, those of the original Java 1.0 variety — see Chapter 2 for details on security restrictions of applets).

As a security precaution, the creators of Java made it impossible for Java 1.0 applets to load files from anywhere else but the Web server from which they come (see Chapter 2). Consequently, all URLs you specify to access files or directories must point to somewhere on your own Web server when you're using Java 1.0 applets.

Dicing Data Files

Although most applets allow you to specify all the information they need right inside the `<APPLET>` tag by using parameters, others require (or give you the option to use) data files instead. *Data files* are nothing more than, well, files full of data! What the data consists of, however, is another story.

Just as applets differ in what they do, how they look, and the parameters they accept to get the job done, they also differ in what data they expect to find inside their files (assuming, of course, that they even use data files). Applets that track the stock market, for example, use data files that have stock market information inside of them. Applets that display pie charts and graphs, however, expect entirely different data.

So where do the data files come from that some applets allow you to use? Again, this depends on the applet. Applets that use images and sounds are the most common, and they may come with their own image and sound files. But if you really want to customize these applets, you can supply your own data files. You can even use a graphics page or a sound utility to create your own sounds and images.

You can usually use a `<PARAM>` tag to tell the applet where to find its data files, although some applets (such as Marquee) require that the file reside in the same directory as the applet itself.

Text data files

Marquee is an example of an applet that gives you the option of using a data file to obtain the text that it scrolls:

```
<APPLET CODE="Marquee" WIDTH=400 HEIGHT=34>
<PARAM NAME="shift" VALUE="2">
<PARAM NAME="delay" VALUE="20">
<PARAM NAME="font_size" VALUE="24">
<PARAM NAME="font_italic" VALUE="yes">
<PARAM NAME="font_bold" VALUE="yes">
<PARAM NAME="back_color" VALUE="255 255 240">
<PARAM NAME="text_color" VALUE="72 61 139">
<PARAM NAME="marquee_file" VALUE="bible.txt">
</applet>
```

The preceding example shows a Marquee applet that uses the file bible.txt — a file that happens to reside inside the same directory as the Web page that uses it. Other applets allow you to use URLs to point to data files.

The CD-ROM includes a few examples of text files (jokes, famous quotes, horoscopes, fortune cookie messages, and Bible verses), along with the Marquee applet. Of course, you can always add to these files or create your own — just make sure that you save the files you intend to use with Marquee in the plain text format.

Marquee uses the file you specify to randomly choose one line of text to display. But for the applet to know when it reaches the end of a line, you have to be sure to place a carriage return at the end — just press Return (or Enter), and voilà — a new line begins. This feat certainly isn't a big deal, but so many text-editing programs automatically wrap text around to the next line when you reach the end of a line, that you may rarely type a carriage return. If you omit carriage returns, Marquee thinks that what you entered is just one giant piece of text and displays the whole thing.

This carriage return requirement for Marquee is exactly the type of thing you need to be careful of when dealing with data files, and why reading the documentation that comes with your applet is crucial. If the applet's creator doesn't provide any documentation, you may have to wing it and try to figure out the file format yourself. If you have an existing file, you'll probably have no problem. Simply open the file with a text editor and see how it's organized. Then you can try to create your own by using the same basic layout of the original one, and see if it flies. It may take a few tries and some patience, but you'll probably figure it out in time.

If you don't at least have a data file to work with, then you may as well be driving without headlights down a winding country road at midnight. If the format of the data file is complex, you'll end up driving though fields and into trees, perhaps never to find the road again. Instead, get your hands on the applet's documentation. It's a lot less painful.

Although everyone still hopes for the day when computer files are truly cross-platform, that day isn't today or even tomorrow. As a result, you still don't have a good and easy way to share files among Windows and Macintosh computers without investing in special file translation software. A text file created on a Windows 95 or Windows 98 system, for example, generally appears garbled when viewed on a Macintosh, and vice versa. The problem is that these two computer platforms use different techniques to represent carriage returns. In order to properly view text files on your system when copied from a different platform, you'll likely have to use a word processor rather than the bare-boned text editor that comes with your system (Notepad on Windows, SimpleText on the Mac). A good word processor can accommodate the differences between the two platforms, but be sure to save any changes you make to a text files back out to a plain, old-fashioned text file (not a word-processing document). Applets that support text files don't have a clue how to handle word-processing documents!

Sound and graphics data files

LivingLinks is an example of an applet that allows you to use image and sound files (which are data files that happen to contain sounds and images) that exists elsewhere; all you have to do is supply the appropriate parameters. Most applets specify sound and image files with URLs. But keep in mind that, for security reasons, any data files you specify for your applets must reside on the same server as the one your applet lives on (see the preceding section on URLs and Chapter 3 for details).

When you're dealing with graphics and sound, all you have to do is save what you create to a file in the right format — GIF or JPEG format for images, AU/uLaw format for sounds (see Chapter 5 for details). The program you use to create the file takes care of all the details of organizing the information in the correct format. In fact, that's all a *format* really is — a way of organizing information.

Dipping into databases

Although text files are a simple, easy-to-use mechanism for storing information that your applet needs (such as text messages needed by the Marquee applet), they can't hold a candle to databases. Unlike text files, which are meant only to store small amounts of text, databases are specifically built for fast and flexible access to massive amounts of data of all shapes and colors (text, sound, images, and even movies can be stored in databases). If you've ever used a database program such as Access, Oracle or Filemaker, you can appreciate the many advantages these monstrously powerful databases have over text files.

It stands to reason, then, that some applets may need to tap into databases. Fortunately, Sun has devised a special Java technology to connect applets and applications to databases (see Chapter 13 for details on Java applications).

The Java Database Connection, more commonly known as JDBC, allows Java applets and applications to dip into databases in much the same way they extract data from text files today. However, the JDBC isn't an inherent part of all applets and applications simply because the need to access information residing in a database is relatively small. As a result, the JDBC is an optional *add on* technology that applets and applications are free to take advantage of if needed.

As with all applets, those that support databases do so by using customizable parameters. And, as you see in this and previous chapters, the PARAM settings that you deal with are entirely dependent on the applet you're using. For this reason, you must consult your applet documentation to find out how to configure the parameters of your JDBC-savvy applets if you wish to dip into databases.

To learn more about the JDBC, visit Sun's Java site at java.sun.com/ products/. You find links to the JDBC home page, which contains sample applets that dip into databases courtesy of this optional feature. In addition, you find links to the entire suite of Java products created by Sun Microsystems, the makers of Java.

Chapter 10

Plugging into the Java Plug-in

- -

In This Chapter

▶ Discovering the Java Plug-in

▶ Installing your Java Plug-in

▶ Exploring the ins and outs of the Java Plug-in

▶ Weaving Plug-in powered pages

▶ Plugging in with `<EMBED>` and `<OBJECT>` tags

- -

*I*f my zeal for Java seems, well, zealous, that's because it is. I'm absolutely tickled with Java and simply can't get enough. But that doesn't mean I'm looking through life with Java-colored glasses. Heck no! There's definitely a down side to Java, and I'm here to tell you about it.

Perhaps the biggest drawback Java faces is its own success. Like a child prodigy, Java exploded on the scene and seized the Web culture by the throat. It promised to change everything, and in many ways it has. But Java's own success has become one of its biggest shortcomings. In fact, if Java hadn't grown at such a blistering rate, I wouldn't be writing this chapter today. On the other hand, if it weren't for Java's blistering success in the first place, I probably wouldn't be writing this book at all; although that's another story for another time. At the moment, I consider why Java's own rapid growth led to something known as the "Java Plug-in."

Too Fast, Too Soon?

In a world that moves as fast as ours does, is it possible to grow too fast too soon? Both Microsoft and Netscape have been improving their Web browsers at break-neck speed since day one, and only now have begun to slow down and smell the roses. Although the concept of a Web browser is only a few years old, both vendors are approaching the fifth major upgrade to their products. That is to say, Version 5.0 of Microsoft's Internet Explorer and Netscape's Navigator products will soon be available — a pretty heady achievement when you consider that Microsoft's flagship word processor, Word, took about a decade to reach Version 5.0!

However, it's relatively simple to add new features and make significant enhancements to software products in the first few versions. Just as a human learns fastest and most easily as a child, software products advance by leaps and bounds within the first few versions of their digital lives. After a few major versions are released, it becomes more complicated to add new features and improve the already existing ones.

By the time Version 3 of Internet Explorer and Navigator rolled around, browsers were starting to mature. To put it in plainer terms, browsers started to get long in the tooth, with new features and enhancements becoming more and more difficult to add with every subsequent release.

Just as the Web browser industry began to mature, marked by longer periods of time between new releases, Java was hitting its stride. When Java 1.0 was first released, Internet Explorer and Navigator were both relatively "young" (both at Version 2). Immediately following Java 1.0 came a few incremental updates (Java 1.01 and Java 1.02, to be precise, which were rapidly followed by a major upgrade to the Java language, Java 1.1. (See Chapter 4 for details on how to read Java version numbers.)

Java 1.1 represented a quantum leap forward in the Java technology, as I describe in Chapter 2, and it came right on the heels of Java 1.0, 1.01, and 1.02. Browser vendors struggled under the pace of the new Java releases. Not only was the browser industry maturing by the time Java 1.1 rolled around, making it inherently more difficult to add support for this new version of the technology, but Java itself was growing at such a rapid pace that it was, practically speaking, a moving target. By the time browser vendors added support for 1.1 into their products, Java 1.1.1 was available, which was immediately followed by Java 1.1.2.

The intense pace at which the Java technology was upgraded by Sun, coupled with the fact that browser development cycles were already growing longer than they had once been, made it impossible for browsers to fully support the latest and greatest versions of Java. Instead of completely supporting Java 1.1, for example, today's most current versions of Internet Explorer and Navigator (4.0 and 4.5, respectively) understand only a portion of Java 1.1.

Clearly, browser vendors such as Microsoft and Netscape had a problem. Java 1.2 was on the way, and browsers couldn't even manage to fully support Java 1.1! Recognizing this problem, Sun devised an elegant yet powerful solution called the Java Plug-in.

What's the Java Plug-in?

Sun's *Java Plug-in* is a special piece of software that gives browsers the ability to understand the most recent versions of Java without requiring an ounce of extra effort on the browser vendor's behalf. Thanks to the Java Plug-in, which is provided free of charge, both Internet Explorer and Navigator can fully support Java 1.1 and even Java 1.2.

The Java Plug-in is, in essence, a standard browser plug-in that knows how to deal with Java content. Although the Java Plug-in doesn't *replace* your browser's ability to process Java-powered Web pages, it does *enhance* it greatly. Essentially, the Java Plug-in hands Java applets over to a more sophisticated runtime environment (also known as a *Virtual Machine,* or VM) than the one available inside your browser.

In allowing Java applets to be processed by Sun's own Java Runtime Environment, or JRE, (Chapter 13 for details) instead of the less capable runtime environment supplied by your browser, the Java Plug-in simply bypasses the limitations of today's Java-savvy browsers. By giving browsers access to the most current Java technology free of charge, the Java Plug-in allows browser vendors to focus on adding new features and enhancements to their products instead of struggling to keep up with Java. In the end, everyone's a winner, especially you.

If you're wondering why I haven't discussed the Java Plug-in sooner, you'll be happy to know that it's not essential. A modern browser such as Internet Explorer or Navigator gives you a great deal of Java without your ever having to think twice about the Java Plug-in. In time, however, you're likely to stumble upon applets that are simply too new for your browser to handle. When this happens, you must either turn to the Java Plug-in or turn away from the Web page containing the more advanced applets.

Fortunately, installing the Java Plug-in is a breeze, and it's free. Easy and free? This is starting to sound like a late-night infomercial, isn't it? Maybe. But the Java Plug-in is no gimmick and won't cost you a penny to install outside of the standard Internet connection rates you pay. What more could you want? Perhaps a bamboo steamer or a nifty set of steak knives?

If you're leery of freebies such as the Java Plug-in, don't sweat it. There's no reason to install it if you don't need it, and it's easy enough to know when you need it: If your browser displays every applet you encounter, you don't need the Java Plug-in. You can always choose to ignore those applets that explicitly require the Java Plug-in anyway.

In fact, because the Java Plug-in is brand spanking new, it'll be a while before Web page developers begin to take advantage of it. Until you run into pages designed with the Java Plug-in in mind, you're probably just as well off not installing it. After all, today's Web browsers already handle a great deal of Java.

Installing the Java Plug-in

When the day comes that you're confronted with either installing the Java Plug-in or missing out on the applets that take advantage of it, you must make the decision to either download and install the Java Plug-in or walk away. Personally, I'm the kind of guy who can't wait to get his hands on new goodies, so I've already installed the Java Plug-in even though there's not a great deal of content on the Web that requires it. Then again, I'm the kind of guy who has a closet full of gizmos and a freezer packed with new flavors of ice cream.

Happily, installing the Java Plug-in is a cinch. All you have to do is load a Web page that requires the Java Plug-in, and you'll be asked to install it. If you allow the installation to proceed, your browser does the rest. It's that easy. You can cancel the installation, of course, if you decide that the Java Plug-in isn't for you. Just don't expect to drop by my house for a taste of "Raspberry Coconut Almond Chip" ice cream anytime soon. That flavor's reserved for my like-minded friends.

Naturally, you're now wondering how you can get in on my private stash of wacky-flavored ice creams, aren't you? All you have to do is install the Java Plug-in, and then swing by. I'll have a bowl and spoon waiting.

Supported platforms and browsers: Can you plug into the Plug-in?

Because the Java Plug-in is relatively new, it's not available to everyone. As sad as it may sound that not everyone has access to the Java Plug-in, you're one of the lucky people who can get your hands on it today because you're reading this book. Sun has created the Java Plug-in for Windows and Solaris platforms, as Table 10-1 illustrates, while versions for the Macintosh and Linux systems are on the way (see the section "Future directions" later in this chapter).

Assuming you fall somewhere in the grid depicted in Table 10-1, and as long as your computer is up to par (see the "Java Plug-in system requirements" sidebar), you're good to go with the Java Plug-in. If not, you may have to wait until Sun designs a version of the Java Plug-in for your system or until you upgrade your computer.

Table 10-1	Java Plug-in Platforms and Browsers			
	Internet Explorer 3.02	*Internet Explorer 4.0*	*Navigator 3.0*	*Navigator 4.0*
Windows 95		X	X	X
Windows 98		X	X	X
Windows NT	X	X	X	X
Solaris/SPARC			X	X
Solaris/x86			X	

The first time you encounter a Web page that requires the Java Plug-in, you have to take the time to download and install it. This simple process, which I explain in detail in the following section, happens only once. From then on, any applets you encounter that require the Java Plug-in are seamlessly passed to the plug-in now residing on your computer (meaning you'll be none the wiser since they run without requiring you to do a thing).

The Java Plug-in installer is approximately 5MB in size, meaning it will take from three to ten minutes to download over most networks. If you're connected to the Internet over a modem, however, expect to wait much, much longer!

Java Plug-in system requirements

The Java Plug-in hardware system requirements for the users of Windows 95, Windows 98, or Windows NT 4.0 are:

- ✔ Pentium 90 MHz or faster processor

- ✔ 10MB free hard disk space (recommend 20MB)

- ✔ 24MB system RAM

Following are the Java Plug-in hardware system requirements for the users of Sun Solaris 2.5 or 2.6:

- ✔ Sun SPARC or Intel x86 microprocessor

- ✔ 10MB free hard disk space (recommend 20MB)

- ✔ 32MB system RAM (recommend 48MB)

Future directions

Currently, only users of Windows and Solaris systems can take advantage of the Java Plug-in created by Sun. There is, however, a non-Sun option available (or coming down the pike!) for Linux and Macintosh users:

✔ **Macintosh:** Apple Computer, Inc. has stated that it will create a special version of the Java Plug-in for Macintosh computers. While Apple's Java Plug-in for the Macintosh was not available at the time of this writing, it should be available any day now. For details, fire up your Web browser and visit Apple's own Java development Web site at devworld.apple.com/java/.

✔ **Linux:** A special version of the Java Plug-in for Linux systems is currently available at www.blackdown.org/java-linux.html and www.blackdown.org/activator/index.html.

Plugging in with Internet Explorer

If you're an Internet Explorer user, take a moment or two to rejoice — you have it easiest when it comes to installing the Java Plug-in. The Internet Explorer browser automatically downloads and installs the Java Plug-in without requiring much more than an "Okay, go ahead and do it!" confirmation from you, so there's very little for you to do after you hit a Web page that requires the Java Plug-in.

In fact, attempting to view a page enhanced with the Java Plug-in is actually the best way to install the Java Plug-in. Simply visit a Web page that requires the Java Plug-in, such as java.sun.com/products/plugin/1.1.1/demo/ Clock/1.1/example1.html. If you don't already have the Java Plug-in installed, a dialog box similar to the one shown in Figure 10-1 appears. All you have to do is ensure that the installer uses a language you understand (select your language of choice using the Locale and Region drop down lists), and then click the Install button.

After you click the Install button, Internet Explorer takes over and begins to download the Java Plug-in installer as seen in Figure 10-2. Depending on how fast your connection to the Internet is, this step may take a few minutes or a few hours!

After Internet Explorer completely downloads the Java Plug-in installer, it runs the installer. When running, the Java Plug-in installer window (which you'll recognize as a standard software installer) appears, as shown in Figure 10-3 (for details on installers, see Chapter 13). In keeping with the fact that the Java Plug-in installer is nothing more than a standard software installation utility, you must then follow the installation instructions that appear (all software installers lead you through the installation process in this manner; the Java Plug-in is no different). After all is said and done, the installer places the Java Plug-in on your computer and configures your browser to use it from here on out.

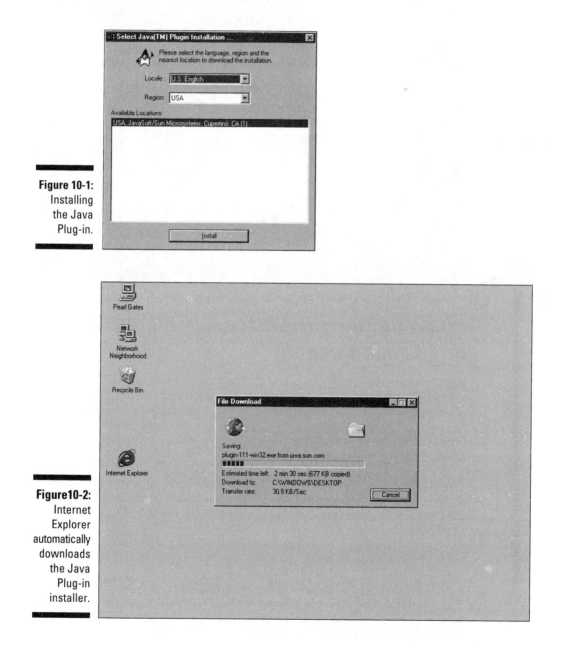

Figure 10-1:
Installing
the Java
Plug-in.

Figure10-2:
Internet
Explorer
automatically
downloads
the Java
Plug-in
installer.

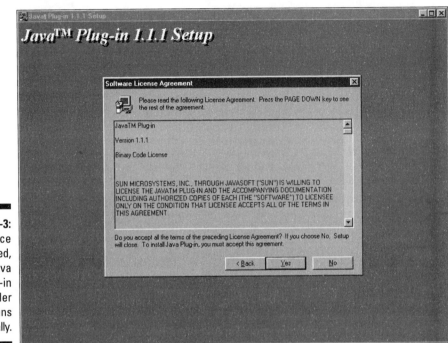

Figure 10-3:
Once
downloaded,
the Java
Plug-in
installer
utility runs
automatically.

Plugging in with Netscape Navigator and Communicator

Installing the Java Plug-in for use with Navigator (as well as the Netscape Communicator product) is just slightly more involved than the process I describe for Internet Explorer in the previous section. I say "slightly" because Navigator and Communicator users see one or two more dialog boxes during the installation process than folks who use Internet Explorer, although the process is nearly identical.

To install the Java Plug-in for use with Navigator or Communicator, simply point your browser to a page that requires the Java Plug-in. To make things easy, point your browser to the same page I suggested to users of Internet Explorer:

```
java.sun.com/products/plugin/demo/Clock/1.1/example1.html
```

If you haven't already installed the Java Plug-in, your browser realizes that it's not properly equipped to display the applet embedded in this page. As a result, you're prompted to get the plug-in as shown in Figure 10-4, which you should do if you'd like to get your hands on my ice cream.

As with Internet Explorer, after Navigator and Communicator download the Java Plug-in installer, your browser runs it. At this point, you have to advance through the various dialog boxes that appear in exactly the same way as the ones in Internet Explorer.

Playing with Your New Plug-in

After you install the Java Plug-in, it's time for a little fun. After all, why bother installing the Java Plug-in in the first place if you don't intend to use it? My sentiments exactly, which is why I'm a staunch advocate of playing with your plug-in. Just keep it clean, won't you?

Browsing Java Plug-in powered pages

Browsing the Web for Java Plug-in powered pages is the first thing you should do to test your new plug-in, beginning with the example pages provided on Sun's own site:

```
java.sun.com/products/plugin/1.1.1/demo/applets.html
```

Here you find a number of Web pages designed specifically for use with the Java Plug-in. Simply choose one of the examples provided, such as the Tic Tac Toe game found at `java.sun.com/products/plugin/1.1.1/demo/TicTacToe/1.1/example1.html`, then sit back and wait for the applet to load. If all goes according to plan, you're treated to a cute little game of Tic Tac Toe as shown in Figure 10-5. If you're not, see the next section, "Problems in Plug-in land?"

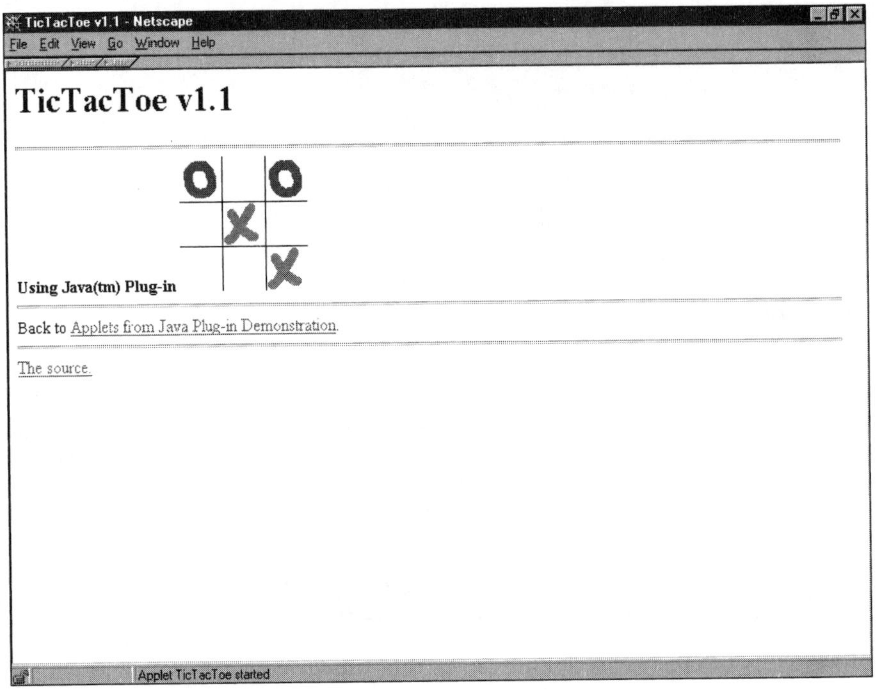

Figure 10-5:
Java
applets
appear
inside
your Web
browser
even when
run by
the Java
Plug-in.

After exploring the various example pages on Sun's own Java Plug-in site, it's time to hit the high seas of the Web and set sail for parts unknown. Start your journey by taking a peek at Chapter 16, where you find a number of great starting points when it comes to surfing for applets. You're sure to bump into plenty of Java Plug-in powered pages along the way.

Problems in Plug-in land?

Assuming everything goes according to plan, you'll be off and surfing with your new friend the Java Plug-in only moments after installing it. However, things don't always go according to plan, and if your Java Plug-in doesn't install properly, you may be in for a rough ride.

Although it's unlikely, there's a chance that the Java Plug-in won't install on your system correctly. Hey, this is software; something's bound to get screwed up sooner or later! Fortunately, Sun has compiled a very comprehensive list of Frequently Asked Questions (FAQ) related to the Java Plug-in, which you can turn to just in case things don't go exactly as you expect.

The Java Plug-in FAQ is available online at `java.sun.com/products/plugin/plugin.faq.html`. It contains a comprehensive list of the most common questions asked about the Java Plug-in.

In many cases, the Java Plug-in FAQ directs you to the "Java Plug-in Control Panel." This helpful little utility allows you to control various aspects of the Java Plug-in.

Exploring the Java Plug-in Control Panel

Along with the Java Plug-in, a utility known as the Java Plug-in Control Panel installs on your computer as well. You can access the Java Plug-in Control Panel, shown in Figure 10-6, by selecting Start⇨Programs on Windows systems. On Solaris systems, the Java Plug-in Control Panel is available at `<home>/.netscape/java/ControlPanel.html`, where `<home>` is the user's home directory.

Although it may not seem impressive at first glance, the Java Plug-in Control Panel packs a wallop. You can control just about every aspect of the Java Plug-in through the Control Panel, making it an extremely powerful tool. The various controls offered by the Control Panel are available through three tabs: Basic, Advanced, and Proxies.

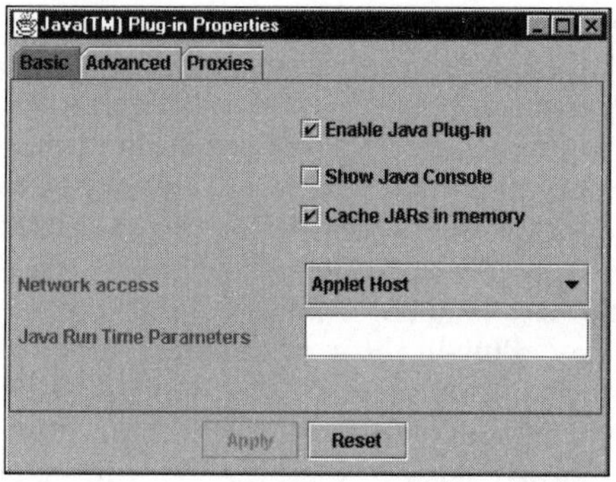

Figure 10-6:
The Java
Plug-in
Control
Panel lets
you control
various
aspects of
the Java
Plug-in.

Java(TM) Plug-in Properties

| Basic | Advanced | Proxies |

☑ Enable Java Plug-in
☐ Show Java Console
☑ Cache JARs in memory

Network access — Applet Host ▾

Java Run Time Parameters

Apply   Reset

Basic tab

The Basic tab contains three check boxes that enable you to control three fundamental aspects of the Java Plug-in:

✔ **Enable Java Plug-in:** When checked, this option permits the Java Plug-in to intercept applets encountered by your Web browser. If this option is unchecked, the Java Plug-in is inactive and will make no attempt to run applets (leaving them, instead, for the browser's own Java Runtime Environment to deal with). This option is enabled by default.

✔ **Show Java Console:** This option allows you to view a Java Console window, which is useful when troubleshooting applets that aren't running properly. The Java Console window displays error messages that you would otherwise not see. It is useful for debugging problems. This option is disabled (not checked) by default.

✔ **Cache JARs in memory:** When checked, this option allows applets that you've viewed to be *cached,* or stored, on your computer, for reuse the next time the applet is viewed. Caching, which I discuss in Chapters 9 and 12, allows applets to be run faster and more efficiently than if they had to be downloaded from the Internet each time they are needed. This option is enabled by default.

In addition to these three fundamental options, the Basic tab offers two other pop-up menu options that may come in handy:

✔ **Network Access:** This option allows you to set the level of network access privileges your applets have (see Chapter 2 for detailed explanation of security privileges). By default, applets are only able to make network connections to the host on which they reside, which is why the Network Access pop-up option is set to Applet Host. You can, however, use this pop-up menu to grant applets one of the following two privileges other than Applet Host:

  • **None:** Meaning your applets can't make any network connections whatsoever (not even to the host on which they reside).

  • **Unrestricted:** Meaning your applets get total and unrestricted access to the network. Applets with unrestricted access to the network are free to connect to any host on the Internet, which could cause you tremendous grief if you're not entirely sure what you're doing. See Chapter 2 for details on security hazards poised by applets with unrestricted access before touching this setting!

✔ **Java Run Time Parameters:** This option allows you to override the default settings of the Java Plug-in through the use of command line parameters. Although this option appears in the Basic tab, it is more advanced than you might imagine and is actually something software developers are more likely to use. See Chapter 14 for more about command line parameters.

Advanced tab

You use the Advanced tab of the Java Plug-in Control Panel to control the Java Run Time Environment (JRE), the Just In Time Compiler (JIT), and debugging settings. (See Chapters 13 and 14 to find out more about JRE and JIT.) As you may suspect, these settings shouldn't be played with unless you know precisely what you're doing. Or, as they say in war, "Run for your life!"

Proxies tab

The Proxies tab allows you to override the proxy address and ports used by your browser and isn't for the faint of heart. Unless you're already comfortable with proxy servers, port numbers, and other networking jargon, you'd be better off walking naked into a cage filled with starving lions than fiddling with these settings. Just stay away, my friend.

Weaving Your Own Plug-in Powered Pages

After playing with the Java Plug-in, chances are pretty good that you'll want to create your own Plug-in powered pages. As luck would have it, you have two ways to do just that. Method number one is an easy no-brainer, thanks to a special utility that converts your existing applet-powered pages into Java Plug-in powered-pages. Method number two, on the other hand, is a horror show that involves writing hairy gobs of HTML code line by line. Can you guess which I prefer?

The Easy Way: Using the Java Plug-in HTML Converter

Bingo! There's no easier way to create Plug-in powered-pages than to convert your existing applet-powered pages into a form that allows them to take advantage of the Java Plug-in; and there is no easier way to do that than with the Java Plug-in HTML Converter provided for free by Sun.

Although the Java Plug-in HTML Converter automatically installs on your computer when you install the Java Plug-in, you can also download it separately at java.sun.com/products/plugin/1.1.1/.

The Java Plug-in HTML Converter, or HTML Converter for short, automatically converts Web pages containing applets into a form recognizable by the Java Plug-in. There's no magic to what the HTML Converter does, really. It scans through Web pages looking for <APPLET> tags and converts any it finds into a tag the Java Plug-in can understand.

The Java Plug-in doesn't understand the standard <APPLET> tag. Instead, it requires applets to be woven into Web pages by using either the <EMBED> or <OBJECT> tag as described in the section, "The Hard Way: Rolling your own HTML code."

A simple one-window interface appears when you run the HTML Converter, (see Figure 10-7). From this window, you can convert your existing applet-powered Web pages in one of two ways:

- **One page at a time:** To convert a single Web page, select the One File radio button. You can now type in the directory path leading to the file you'd like to convert, or better yet, you can click the Browse button that corresponds to this option.

- **A bunch of pages at once:** To convert a number of Web pages at one time, select the All Files in Folder radio button. You can now type in the directory path leading to a folder full of Web pages that you want to convert, or alternatively, you can click the Browse button that corresponds to this option and visually select a folder full of files to convert. Immediately below the directory path of the folder that you choose is a list of the file extensions to convert. By default, all files having the extension *html, htm,* and *asp* will be converted, although you're free to add or remove extensions as needed. You should also note that by checking the Included Subfolders check box you can convert any Web files contained in subfolders found in the main folder you've selected (this option is enabled by default).

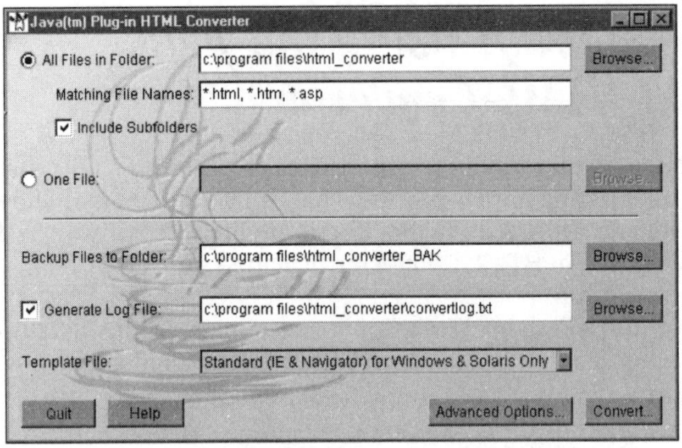

Figure 10-7:
The Java
Plug-in
HTML
Converter
allows you
to create
Plug-in
powered
Web pages.

After selecting either a single Web page or an entire folder full of Web pages to convert, you're ready to roll. Simply click the Convert button to start the conversion process, and a dialog box similar to the one shown in Figure 10-8 appears. When the conversion is complete, you're presented with a tally indicating how many files successfully converted. What could be easier?

Figure 10-8:
A dialog
box shows
the results
of your
HTML
conversions.

Progress...

Processing...   Done

Folder:

File:

Total Files Processed: 1

Total Applets Found: 1

Total Errors: 0

Done

By default, the HTML Converter converts ⟨APPLET⟩ tags into a combination of ⟨EMBED⟩ and ⟨OBJECT⟩ tags that both Internet Explorer and Navigator understand. You can, however, use the Template pop-up menu option to choose different conversion options. But, unless you have a good reason to choose a different conversion method, stick with the default Template selection of Standard (IE and Navigator) for Windows and Solaris.

Although the files you select for conversion do indeed change, meaning they no longer contain the ⟨APPLET⟩ tag they once did, HTML Converter is considerate enough to create a new folder containing a copy of your original files. The name of the folder containing backups of your newly converted files is listed to the right of the Backup File to Folder text box. You can choose a different folder if you'd like, rather than using the default created by the utility. To do so, select the Browse button that corresponds to this option and choose the folder of your liking.

The Hard Way: Rolling your own HTML code

If using the HTML Converter is a charm, the alternative is an utter nightmare. The only other way to convert an ⟨APPLET⟩ tag into a form that Internet Explorer or Navigator can use is to do it manually, something I strongly urge you not to do. However, in the interest of open and honest conversation, I'd like to show you the pain and suffering the HTML Converter spares you.

Keep in mind that you never, ever have to suffer though manually converting an ⟨APPLET⟩ tag. Thanks to the HTML Converter, ⟨APPLET⟩ tags are automatically converted into a format Internet Explorer and Navigator understand, which, as a result, allows the Java Plug-in to step in and take over when it comes to running the applet. All you have to do is fire up the HTML Converter, choose the Web pages you want to convert, and then select a template corresponding to the browser you'd like to use.

By default, the HTML Converter converts `<APPLET>` tags for use in both Internet Explorer and Navigator. In a moment I take a look at what this entails, but first consider a very basic `<APPLET>` tag used to weave the LivingLinks applet into a Web page:

```
<APPLET CODE=LivingLinks.class WIDTH=150 HEIGHT=150>
          <PARAM NAME=imagesDir VALUE="images/">
          <PARAM NAME=imagesName VALUE="mantis">
          <PARAM NAME=imagesExt VALUE="gif">
          <PARAM NAME=imagesCount VALUE="5">
          <PARAM NAME=speed VALUE="10">
          <PARAM NAME=reverse VALUE="yes">
</APPLET>
```

LivingLinks is a multipurpose applet that supports animation, sound, special effects, and navigation. In this example, however, the `<APPLET>` tag takes advantage of only a few parameters, which results in a very simple animation.

Because the Java Plug-in doesn't understand the `<APPLET>` tag, the tag is converted into an `<OBJECT>` tag that Internet Explorer understands, or an `<EMBED>` tag that Navigator can deal with.

Internet Explorer

The Internet Explorer browser knows how to deal with any `<APPLET>` tag it encounters. However, if an applet needs to go through the Java Plug-in for processing, the `<OBJECT>` tag is needed. Following is what the LivingLinks `<APPLET>` tag example looks like when converted by the HTML Converter into the `<OBJECT>` tag that Internet Explorer requires:

```
<OBJECT classid="clsid:8AD9C840-044E-11D1-B3E9-
          00805F499D93"
WIDTH = 150 HEIGHT = 150
codebase="http://java.sun.com/products/plugin/1.1/jinstall-
          11-win32.cab#Version=1,1,0,0">
<PARAM NAME = CODE VALUE = LivingLinks.class>
<PARAM NAME="type" VALUE="application/x-java-
          applet;version=1.1">
<PARAM NAME = imagesDir VALUE ="images/">
<PARAM NAME = imagesName VALUE ="mantis">
<PARAM NAME = imagesExt VALUE ="gif">
<PARAM NAME = imagesCount VALUE ="5">
<PARAM NAME = speed VALUE ="10">
<PARAM NAME = reverse VALUE ="yes">
</OBJECT>
```

Not too bad, huh? With a little concentration you can see where the various elements of the original <APPLET> landed. Of course, because the <OBJECT> tag is completely new, a lot of new information such as "classid" and "type" that isn't in a standard <APPLET> tag is included. And, if you look even harder, you notice that the "codebase" attribute of the <OBJECT> tag is quite a bit different than the one we use in our <APPLET> tags. What gives?

Well, that's a good question, one I'm afraid would take another chapter or two to adequately explain, which I'd be happy to do, mind you, if I thought you'd ever have to do this stuff by hand. Thanks to the free HTML Converter utility that I mention earlier, you'll never have to write an <OBJECT> tag like this unless you want to. And if you want to roll your own Java Plug-in <OBJECT> tags, don't go it alone. Instead, take a stroll over to Sun's Java Plug-in Web site where you'll find all the help you need.

Sun's Java Plug-in Web site contains a wealth of information for those interested in writing <OBJECT> tags by hand. Visit java.sun.com/products/plugin/1.1.1/docs/tags.html to see just how hairy these tags can get!

Navigator

Unfortunately, Navigator doesn't understand the <OBJECT> tag as Internet Explorer does. As a result, you have to convert <APPLET> tags into <EMBED> tags because that's what Navigator expects. Talk about petty:

```
<EMBED type="application/x-java-applet;version=1.1"
          java_CODE = LivingLinks.class
          WIDTH = 150 HEIGHT = 150
          imagesDir = "images/"
          imagesName = "mantis"
          imagesExt = "gif"
          imagesCount = "5"
          speed = "10"
          reverse = "yes"
pluginspage="http://java.sun.com/products/plugin/1.1/
          plugin-install.html">
<NOEMBED></NOEMBED></EMBED>
```

When Navigator sees an <EMBED> tag such as this, it knows the applet woven inside of it is supposed to be run by the Java Plug-in. If the Java Plug-in is not already installed, Navigator takes a quick trip over to the Web page listed in the "pluginspage" setting and begins the Java Plug-in installation process.

Again, you can probably see where the various <APPLET> tag elements appear in our newly constructed <EMBED> tag. But why hurt yourself? Let the HTML Plug-in do the grunt work. You deserve a break anyway, don't you? If not, and you're feeling the need to suffer a little more for your sins, swing by Sun's Java Plug-in Web site to find out how you can construct `<EMBED>` tags by hand.

Combo Deal: Internet Explorer and Navigator

Because Internet Explorer uses the `<OBJECT>` tag to hand off applets to the Java Plug-in, while Navigator uses the `<EMBED>` tag, both must be included in a Web page if both browsers are to be supported. Not surprisingly, there's a way to do it. As with most HTML tags, the `<OBJECT>` and `<EMBED>` tags can be nested as follows:

```
<OBJECT classid="clsid:8AD9C840-044E-11D1-B3E9-
        00805F499D93"
WIDTH = 150 HEIGHT = 150 codebase="http://java.sun.com/
        products/plugin/1.1/jinstall-11-
        win32.cab#Version=1,1,0,0">
<PARAM NAME = CODE VALUE = LivingLinks.class >

<PARAM NAME="type" VALUE="application/x-java-
        applet;version=1.1">
<PARAM NAME = imagesDir VALUE ="images/">
<PARAM NAME = imagesName VALUE ="mantis">
<PARAM NAME = imagesExt VALUE ="gif">
<PARAM NAME = imagesCount VALUE ="5">
<PARAM NAME = speed VALUE ="10">
<PARAM NAME = reverse VALUE ="yes">
<COMMENT>
    <EMBED type="application/x-java-applet;version=1.1"
            java_CODE = LivingLinks.class
    WIDTH = 150 HEIGHT = 150
    imagesDir = "images/"
    imagesName = "mantis"
    imagesExt = "gif"
    imagesCount = "5"
    speed = "10"
    reverse = "yes"
    pluginspage="http://java.sun.com/products/plugin/1.1/
            plugin-install.html">
<NOEMBED></COMMENT>

</NOEMBED></EMBED>
</OBJECT>
```

In this example, the `<EMBED>` tag is nested inside of the `<OBJECT>` tag. As a result, each browser gets what it needs: Internet Explorer finds the `<OBJECT>` tag and ignores the `<EMBED>` tag, while Navigator sniffs out the `<EMBED>` tag and politely passes over `<OBJECT>` tags. Cordial competitors, imagine that!

Chapter 11

Bringing Your Applet to Life on the Web

. . . .

In This Chapter

▶ Creating an applet directory structure on the Web

▶ Uploading Java-powered Web pages, applets, and support files

▶ Getting to know FTP tools

. . . .

Although Java-powered Web pages reside on your personal computer during the developmental stages (see Chapter 6), you'll eventually want to place them on the Internet for everyone to enjoy. After all, what good are Java-powered pages if you're the only one who can access them?

Luckily, when you have your applet-powered pages running in a local environment (that is, residing on your computer, not on the Web), you're only a hop, skip, and a jump away from placing them on the World Wide Web. In essence, you simply create on the Web an exact copy of the folder (directory) structure in which your local pages exist and then transfer the files from your computer to their new home on the Web. These remote folders are basically exact copies of the local ones on your personal computer that contain your Java-powered pages and the applets that are embedded in them. That's really all there is to it.

A cinch, to be sure, but here's the rub: You have to use a special software program to create the folders you need on the Web. Then you use that same software program to actually upload all the files that your applets require into the corresponding Web-based folders. Dealing with folders and files on the Internet is a bit more complicated than doing so on your personal computer. But after you get the basic process down, you can whip up Java enhancements to your Web site in no time.

Taking Your Pages to the Web

To move from creating Java-powered pages on your local system to hooking up those pages for the world to enjoy, you create a remote directory structure — a Web-based copy of the folders containing the Java-savvy pages located on your local computer system. Your Web site must have the same directory structure as your personal computer in order for the applets you use to make sense of their new home on the Web. If creating a parallel directory structure on the Web sounds intimidating, you'll be happy to hear that you don't have to duplicate your entire hard-disk directory structure, just those parts of it that your applets use.

Web pages and the applets embedded in them typically reside in the same directory (unless you're using the CODEBASE attribute, which I describe in Chapter 7). Quite often, however, an applet requires support files (such as sound or graphics files) which are stored in different directories. For example, sound files may be stored in a directory called *audio,* and graphics files may be stored in a directory called *images.* Depending on the capabilities of the applet and on your own organizational style, subdirectories containing support files often are located inside the directory that contains the Web page and the applet (see Figure 11-1).

Figure 11-1:
Support files usually live in sub-directories in the same directory as the applet and Web page.

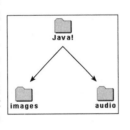

When you create a directory for the Web, you need to ask yourself the following questions:

- ✔ Does the Web page reside inside the same directory as the applets it uses? If so, you need to create only one directory on the Web in which to upload the page and any applets embedded in it.

- ✔ Do the Web page and the applet reside in separate directories? In this case, you have to create two directories on the Web, one for each file.

   ✔ If the applet requires support files, does the applet look for these files inside the same directory as the applet or in separate directories (such as an *images* or *audio* directory)? If the applet looks for the files in separate directories, you must create these directories as well.

Although this may sound like a lot to worry about, it's really not. When you have the applet running on a Web page locally (that is, running on a page located on your own computer — not one that's actually located on the Web), most of the work is behind you. You don't have to go far to know exactly what directory structure you need on the Web because the Web directory should be an exact mirror of the one you created locally. When you know which directories you need, creating them on the Web is a snap — something you can do in four short steps:

1. **Establish an FTP (File Transfer Protocol) connection to your Web server (enter a password if one is required to log on to the server).**

2. **Determine the location (URL) for your Java-powered Web pages.**

3. **Create the main directory that will contain your Web pages.**

4. **Create each subdirectory that the applets require for their support files.**

Making the Connection

To create a directory on your Web site, you must first establish a connection to the Web server on which your site is hosted by using the *File Transfer Protocol* (FTP), the standard protocol (a fancy way of saying "technique") used for sending files across the Internet. A Web server is simply a special-purpose computer, connected to the Internet, that is responsible for hosting — or *serving* — Web pages to browsers. (To find out more about protocols, hosts, and servers, pick up a copy of *The Internet For Dummies,* 5th Edition, by John R. Levine, Carol Baroudi, and Margaret Levine Young.) If you've uploaded files to the Web before, you already know the ropes. If not, don't worry; it's almost as easy as browsing the Web. You need only three things:

   ✔ An FTP tool

   ✔ The FTP address of your Web site

   ✔ The password needed to access your site via FTP

Without an FTP tool, you can't put up your site on the Web. Without the FTP address of your Web server, you have nowhere to put your site. Without a password, you'll be turned away when you get there. But when you have all these things, you have the horse to ride on, the directions to the kingdom, and the keys to unlock the door when you arrive.

In truth, you can upload files to the Web using protocols other than FTP. Integrated Web tool suites, such as Netscape Communicator, often allow you to upload files over the Hypertext Transfer Protocol (HTTP), meaning you can use a browser to upload files to the Web. Unfortunately, today's crop of HTTP-based Web browser uploading tools generally aren't as powerful or flexible as FTP tools. As a result, I prefer to use FTP tools to manage my Web site folders and files, and leave navigating the Web to my browser.

Choosing an FTP tool

If you've created Web pages before, chances are that you used an FTP tool to copy them from your personal computer onto your Web server. If this is the case, feel free to use the same FTP tool to create a directory structure on the Web and upload your pages and Java files. It really doesn't matter what FTP tool you use because applet files don't require special treatment when zooming across the Internet.

You can use whatever FTP tool you want, but for the purposes of this discussion, I use the WS_FTP utility provided on the CD-ROM that comes with this book. If you're a Windows user who doesn't already have an FTP tool, I recommend that you use the WS_FTP utility because all the screen shots and examples in this chapter are based on it. (For details on how to install WS_FTP, see Appendix C.) If you're a Macintosh user, on the other hand, I suggest using the wonderful Fetch utility. Although this utility isn't provided on this book's CD-ROM, a hyperlink to it is available at www.mantiscorp.com/java, so you can download it with your Web browser.

Obtaining your FTP address

Don't mistake the URL of your Web site with the FTP address that you use to upload files to the Web! Heavens, no; these are two different beasts altogether. *URLs* are Web addresses, which are something Web browsers use to locate sites on the World Wide Web. *FTP addresses,* on the other hand, are what FTP tools use to locate servers, directories, and files on the Internet. In a limited sense, Web browsers make use of FTP addresses; the browsers can download files to which FTP addresses point, just as an FTP tool does. But FTP tools also enable you to upload files to the Web, assuming that you have the FTP address of the site to which you want to upload the files.

FTP addresses are usually either a series of words separated by periods, such as ftp.haviland.com, or a series of numbers separated by periods, such as 201.101.19.7. Although both forms are equally effective, words are usually easier to remember. The form you use depends on how your Web site is configured by your Internet Service Provider (ISP) or Web server administrator (read on to find out about Web server administrators).

Because you're using an FTP tool to create directories and to upload files, you need to supply your Web server's FTP address to the tool. But how do you know the FTP address for your Web server?

The most straightforward way to obtain the FTP address of your Web server is to call your *Web server administrator.* This individual, or group of individuals, is responsible for keeping your Web server up and running. How you locate this person or group depends largely on how your Web site was established:

✔ If your Web site is provided through an Internet Service Provider (ISP) and you have access to the files residing in the account using FTP, you call the ISP directly. If you're not sure whether you have FTP access, give your service provider a holler and explain that you want to upload files to the Web. Your service provider can help you out and give you the details you need to access the account via FTP.

✔ If you don't have access to Web files via FTP or if your employer maintains the Web site internally, calling the ISP directly won't get you anywhere. In this case, you have to track down someone in your company who is responsible for granting access to the Web server.

✔ If you connect through a commercial online service such as America Online, CompuServe, or Prodigy, you have to use the tools provided for those services. In this case, contact the good people in the technical support group of your service provider and explain what you're doing — they'll give you all the information you need to get your Web site up and running.

You should note, however, that some commercial online services don't offer Java-savvy browsers to their members! This doesn't mean that the pages developed by these site members can't be Java-powered, mind you, it just means that viewers can't see them in action when using the service's built-in browser. Luckily, such service providers typically allow their members to configure their account for use with Java-savvy browsers, such as Netscape Navigator and Internet Explorer.

After you track down the powers that be, explain that you want to create folders on your Web site and then upload Web pages and Java applets into them. Make sure that the person you talk to understands that you want to publish Java-powered pages, to be made available for World Wide Web access. Although it shouldn't make a difference that you're uploading Java-powered pages, it's always a good idea to ask the folks at your service provider for their advice; they may point out special rules, such as where you can place the files or what types of applets you can use. Or they may offer some time-saving advice. Regardless, be sure to let your service provider know what you plan to do; one question now can save you hours of aggravation later on.

Why you need an FTP tool in the first place

Why must you bother with an FTP tool when you have a perfectly good Web browser? After all, Web browsers already know how to deal with the File Transfer Protocol (FTP), right? Well, sort of.

Unfortunately, Web browsers are designed to *get* information off the Web, not *put* information up there. When you visit a Web page, your browser retrieves the information contained (or referenced) in the page and downloads it for your viewing pleasure. How that information gets transferred really doesn't matter to your browser because it can accommodate just about every available protocol, including FTP.

When you create pages to publish on the Web, the information must travel in the opposite direction. To publish on the Web, you must create directories that didn't previously exist and then upload files into them. This process isn't something typical browsers are equipped to do, but it's something every FTP tool does quite well.

In time, all Web browsers are likely to include capabilities for both browsing and publishing. In fact, Netscape Navigator Gold and the Composer component of Netscape Communicator already feature the capability to upload files to the Web. Unfortunately, neither product is as flexible as an FTP tool when it comes to creating directories and uploading files. For this reason, you need to spend a little time getting comfortable with an FTP tool.

Before your Web server administrator tells you what FTP address to use, be prepared to provide detailed account information to confirm your access privileges. Web server administrators commonly require details such as your username and password before furnishing you with an FTP address. However, assuming that you have the authority to create Web pages on the server, you shouldn't have to spend more than a few minutes on the telephone with the administrator before you have an FTP address.

You can always request your FTP address using e-mail, assuming that you have your Web server administrator's e-mail address. But if you use e-mail, don't send sensitive details of your Web server account (such as the password) unless you're 100 percent certain that the transmission is *secure* — that is, that what you type will be encrypted, rendering the message completely unreadable from the moment it leaves your computer until it reaches the person to whom you're sending it. Astonishing as it may sound, the vast majority of e-mail systems are unsecured, so unless you know otherwise, assume that yours is, too.

Getting your FTP password

In addition to an FTP address, you need a password in order to put your page on the Web. When your Web server administrator gives you your FTP address, be sure to ask for your FTP password as well. In most cases, this password is the same as the one you provide to the administrator to validate your access to the Web server in the first place. But depending on how your Web server is administrated, you may get a separate password to use when uploading files to the server with FTP.

Generally, you can't access a Web server via FTP without a password. And for good reason; after you have the FTP address and password for a site, you can add and remove files and directories at will! If no password were re-quired, anyone with an FTP tool could alter your Web site. Imagine how surprised you would be to wake up one morning and find all the text on your home page replaced with dirty limericks: "There once was a man from Nantucket . . ."

As a general rule, you should change your FTP password every few months. Don't make the mistake of choosing an obvious password, such as your name, the name of your pet, or your license plate number. Be sure to choose an obscure word, number, or better yet, a combination of both letters and numbers that only you can easily remember.

Firing up your FTP tool

With your Web site FTP address and password in hand, making the connec-tion is a cinch. You simply launch your FTP tool as you would any other program and enter the FTP address to which you want it to connect.

The process of connecting to a site and uploading or retrieving files via FTP is often called *FTPing* by those in the know, as in "I'm FTPing to my site. I'm hip." Toss that bit of Internet jargon around from time to time, and you're sure to impress friends and family alike.

The way you enter the FTP address varies depending on which tool you use. If you happen to use WS_FTP, as I do in this chapter, you simply enter the address in the Host Name box, as shown in Figure 11-2. In fact, you may be able to enter the password at the same time you enter the FTP address, as I've done here, killing two birds with one stone. If your FTP tool doesn't allow you to enter a password along with the address, don't worry: You get your chance when your FTP tool tries to make the connection.

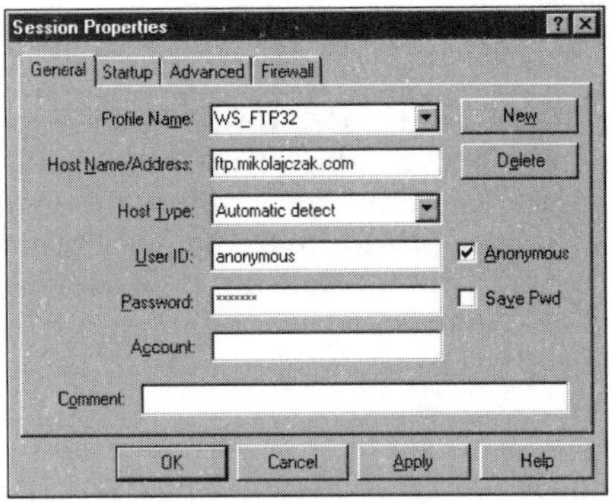

Figure 11-2:
Entering
an FTP
address
and
password
using
WS_FTP.

Connecting to a Web site via FTP is very similar to using a browser, with the exception of the password. In most cases, you never have to enter a password when browsing the Web. When using FTP to connect, however, you supply both the address for the site and the password, and the tool does the rest. You merely click the OK button or your tool's equivalent (look for Connect, Go, Do It!, or something similar) and sit back for a few seconds.

The FTP tool attempts to make a connection to the address you give it and prompts you for a password (if you haven't already provided one). Assuming that you enter the correct address and password, the FTP tool displays a list of all the directories and files located inside the top-level directory of your site (a top-level directory contains a site's home page, along with all subdirectories the site may be comprised of; because Web sites are unique creations, the names of subdirectories found in top-level directories vary greatly). If this doesn't happen, make sure that you've entered the information exactly as your Web server administrator gave it to you, matching all uppercase and lowercase letters.

Many FTP tools assume that you're already online when you use them and report an error if you aren't. In this case, you have to get online before you start your FTP tool. The easiest way to do this is to start your Web browser. When your browser begins to load a page from the Web, you're online, and your FTP tool is able to make its connection.

Although FTP tools are similar to browsers in many ways, they are nowhere nearly as graphical and elegant in their presentation of information. Remember that Web browsers go to great lengths to hide the mess of directories and files behind a visually pleasing display of graphics, text, and hyperlinks. FTP tools do just the opposite: They allow you to view the bare-boned site, as it existed on your personal computer — you're *supposed* to see all the directories and files so that you can navigate through them as you do on your own computer (see Figure 11-3).

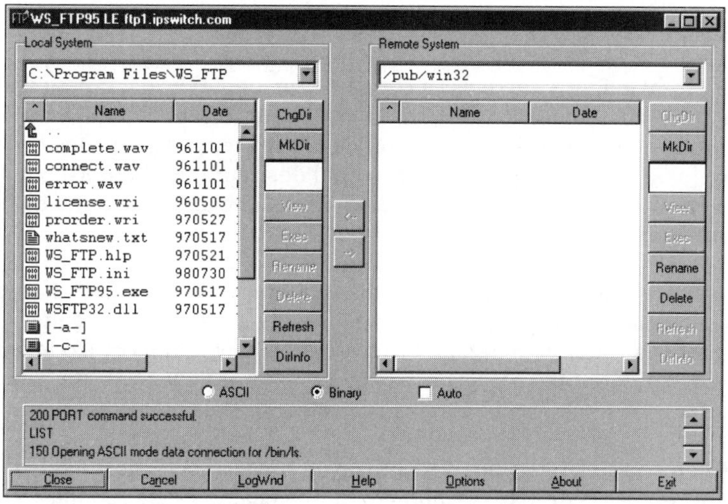

Figure 11-3:
With an FTP tool, you can see each site's directories and files.

Depending on the FTP tool you use, you may be able to save your site's address and password as a permanent *bookmark* for easy access the next time around. But be careful; if someone else uses your computer (or if your computer isn't located in a secure area), you're in danger of letting others access and alter your site. All someone has to do is launch the FTP tool and select the bookmark for your site to have full access to the directories and files!

Finding Your Own Little Piece of the Web

Where on your server you put your Java-powered Web page is largely a personal issue. Unless the page happens to be the home page for your entire site, it can go just about anywhere you choose and be named anything you want. If you're uploading the home page for your site, however, you really don't have much choice about the location or the name of the file.

Typically, your home page *must* be located in the top-level directory of a Web site, and it must be named index.html (or index.htm, if the Web server your site is running on doesn't support filenames having more than three characters in the extension). You should receive your top-level directory when your Web server administrator gives you your FTP address, or navigate to it once connected if you don't automatically log on to that directory.

Giving your pages a home

Don't take lightly the task of choosing the name or location of your Web pages. Unless you're uploading these pages to the Web temporarily (for example, just to see whether you can or for testing purposes only), assume that you're choosing each page's final destination. The reason for this assumption is simple: Where you place the page dictates the URL others will use to access it!

Suppose that your name is Matilda and that your Web site's home page is accessible on the Web by using the URL www.peanutz.org. If you were to enter the URL www.peanutz.org alone, you would most likely get the home page for your Internet Service Provider — not your own site. You need to enter www.peanutz.org/matilda to get to your home page.

When you FTP into your site, however, the FTP tool most likely takes you to your top-level directory (*matilda,* in this case). If not, you may have to specify an initial directory for the tool to use. From there, you can use the FTP tool to navigate into additional directories within your site, or perhaps move up one directory level to see the directories of all other Web sites maintained by your Internet Service Provider (see the sidebar, "Sneaking around" later in this chapter). In fact, depending on what FTP address your administrator gives you, you may come in at your service provider's base level and then have to navigate directories to get to your *matilda* directory.

Regardless of what directory the FTP tool initially takes you to, you want to end up in the directory that contains the home page for your site. If you aren't sure where this directory is located, take a look at the URL for your home page, which is the starting point for your site. In this example, the URL is www.peanutz.org/matilda, which means that you want to FTP into the *matilda* directory on the www.peanutz.org server. If you have problems finding your home directory, don't panic. A simple call to your service provider's technical support team is all it takes to get back on track.

Keep in mind that Web addresses and FTP addresses are two different beasts. To connect to the www.peanutz.org server, you may use an FTP address that bears no resemblance whatsoever to this URL. The FTP address you use may consist of numbers separated by periods, such as 234.35.35.6, or names separated by periods, such as ftp.peanutz.org or doubletree.hotdog.com.

Sneaking around

Depending on how your Internet Service Provider handles security issues, you may or may not be able to use FTP to access the files of other Web sites on your server. If you do have access, it's likely to be *read-only* access: You can download files from these sites to your local computer, but you can't delete them or upload your own (except when you're dealing with your own directory). However, with read-only access, you're free to roam around and grab files that might be confidential! Though doing so may be tempting, don't — most service providers can see (to use Sting's words) every step you take and every move you make.

Be aware that if you can poke around other people's sites, they can do the same to yours. If this is the case, don't put anything confidential on your server unless the material is encrypted with a password. This way, even if someone does grab sensitive information off your site, that person won't be able to read it. Contact your Internet Service Provider for details on security and what tools your provider recommends to password-protect files on your site.

Branching out with other pages

Any pages (in addition to your home page) you add to your top-level directory have the same URL but with a slash followed by the filename tacked on to the end. For example, if you upload your resumé into the top-level directory and name it resume.html, the URL to access this page directly is `www.peanutz.org/matilda/resume.html`.

Placing all your pages in the top-level directory isn't an efficient way of organizing your site. Think of your Web site as nothing more than a hard disk available to the world. Do you place all your files in the top-level directory of your hard disk? Certainly not; you create subdirectories that contain files, and often you create other subdirectories below that. Your computer's hard disk is organized using a hierarchy of directories, beginning at the top level and spreading out like the roots of a tree when depicted graphically, as shown in Figure 11-4.

Typically, you create subdirectories for your Web pages with an FTP tool by following a simple, three-step process similar to the way in which you create directories on your hard disk:

1. **Open the directory on your Web site that you want to place the new subdirectory in.**

2. **Issue a Create Directory command.**

3. **Give your new subdirectory a name.**

Figure 11-4:
Web sites,
much like a
personal
computer
hard disk,
are orga-
nized in a
hierarchy
that
resembles
tree roots.

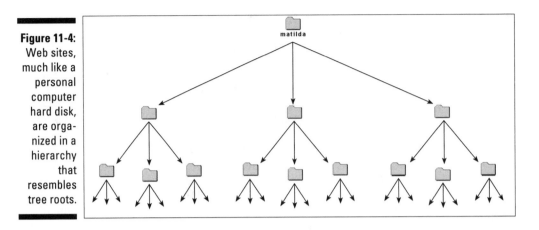

Because your Web site is really nothing more than files stored on a hard disk connected to the Internet, you should feel free to organize it however you want, adding new Web pages and directories as you see fit. You may, for example, want to store your Java-powered pages in a directory called *coolstuff,* located one level down from the top-level directory. If this directory doesn't already exist, use your FTP tool to create it (see the section "Structuring Your Web Page Directory," later in this chapter). Or you may want different directories to contain different pages. It's up to you to choose where your pages find a home on the Web.

Now, suppose that the Java-powered page that you are about to upload is named waltzing.html. By placing this file inside the *coolstuff* directory, you change the URL to `www.peanutz.org/matilda/coolstuff/waltzing.html`. This Web address is the one you give to friends, relatives, colleagues, and anyone else you think may want to learn how to waltz Matilda-style.

If you give out your page's URL and then move or rename the page, the integrity of your site suffers. Webbers hate to go through the hassle of typing a URL only to see the all-too-familiar `File Not Found` message rather than the Web page they're anticipating. If a page in your site is accessible *only* through hyperlinks in your other pages rather than directly through a URL, the consequences of moving it aren't as drastic (assuming you update all your hyperlinks accordingly). But even then, what if Webbers bookmarked your page for fast access later on? When you move or rename a page, all bookmarks to that page instantly become invalid.

To keep Web surfers happy and keep them coming back to your site, minimize the likelihood that you'll want to move or rename your pages later — carefully consider where to put your pages and what to name them *before* you put them on the Web. And in cases where you have no choice but to move a page once you've already made it available on the Web, consider leaving a *forwarding* page in its place (that is, leave a simple page that contains nothing more than a link to the relocated page).

Structuring Your Web Page Directory

How you structure your Web site's directory is a decision you should make when you first weave applets into the pages on your hard disk (see Chapter 7). When you're ready to upload your Java-powered pages to the Web, the directory structure should be pretty much set. Here are just two things to consider when creating your directory structure:

- ✔ Even with the simplest of applets, you'll likely want to create a sub-directory or two to hold the support files. Do you *have* to? Certainly not. However, if you keep all your sound files in one directory and your images in another, you always know where to find the support file you need. This assumes, of course, that the applet itself is flexible enough to allow you to place support files where you want them. Not all applets are!

  - • LivingLinks, for example, is flexible enough that you can place sound or image files wherever you choose, provided they are on the same Web site as the LivingLinks applet itself. You can organize the sound and image files used by LivingLinks in any way that makes sense to you and then tell the LivingLinks applet where they are by using the appropriate parameters (see Chapter 8 for details on parameters).

  - • Marquee, on the other hand, is not so accommodating: The text files you use with this applet (to randomly supply a scrolling message) must reside inside the same directory as the applet itself.

- ✔ Sometimes, different applets may need to access a single sound file, or all your applets may need to use a single image file, such as a trademark image. In either case, you may want to place all your sounds and images into two centrally located subdirectories that all your applets can access.

  Again, this assumes that the applet allows you to choose where such files will reside. Some applets do (LivingLinks, for example) let you choose while others don't (such as Marquee, which is very inflexible when it comes to the location of the text support files it can utilize).

Remember that applets are creatures of habit. In most cases, the Java-powered pages you configure on your personal computer expect the *exact same* directory structure after you upload them to the Web. If, for example, you configure an applet on your hard disk to use sound files located in a directory called *audio* that resides in the same directory as the page itself, the applet looks for this exact directory when it lives on the Web. You're free to choose where the page is located, but you must organize any support files required by the applets in that page in exactly the same way they are organized on your hard disk. If the *audio* directory on the Web, for example, doesn't exist in the same location relative to the page on the Web as it does on your hard disk, how will your applet find it?

An exception to the rule requiring that your hard disk directory match your Web directory comes into play when you use the CODEBASE attribute. In this case, the applet doesn't reside in the same directory as the Web page in which it appears. You may not even need a directory structure on the Web — if the applet resides on a server other than your server, it can't use your files anyway due to security restrictions imposed on applets (see Chapter 2). However, if CODEBASE points to an applet residing on your own site, you have to take care to arrange the directories and files it uses accordingly. CODEBASE can be a tricky little devil to master, so I suggest avoiding it until you're comfortable with the whole process of creating Java-powered pages and uploading them to the Web. For more details about CODEBASE, see Chapter 7.

You can think of the upload process as merely copying a directory from your hard disk to the Web server. That's really all that's happening. Therefore, all the subdirectories and files your page relies on must be in their same relative positions on the Web after they're uploaded as they were on your hard disk. To make life easier, most FTP tools let you upload an entire directory, including all its subdirectories and files, from your hard disk to the Internet. WS_FTP and Fetch, for example, take care of the whole issue of subdirectories by allowing you to copy everything wholesale. These two tools can automatically create subdirectories for you and upload the appropriate files into those subdirectories as you (and your applets) expect.

For more information on creating subdirectories for support files, please read the (appropriately named) section "Creating subdirectories for support files," later in this chapter.

In many cases, the directory for your Web page already exists, so you can move right on to uploading the page itself or creating any subdirectories the page requires. The following list describes some situations in which you don't have to worry about creating a Web page directory:

  ✔ If the page is a home page, use the top-level directory that your administrator gave you when you established your FTP address. In cases where you're *replacing* an existing Web page with a red-hot Java version, the Web page directory will be in place already.

  ✔ Even if you're uploading a brand-spanking-new page, the directory in which you ultimately want it to reside may already exist. For example, you may (for some reason) want to store all your pages in your top-level directory. In this case, you don't need to create a directory for your Web page.

However, if the directory in which you intend to place your Web page does not exist already, you create it by using your FTP tool. Simply navigate to the directory in which the new subdirectory should appear and invoke your FTP tool's Create Directory command.

Suppose that I want to upload a Java-powered page called lightning.html to my company's Web site (`www.mantiscorp.com`). Furthermore, I want to place this page inside a directory called *storms* located inside a directory called *weather,* which is located in the site's top-level directory. In this case, when all is said and done, the URL to the page becomes `www.mantiscorp.com/weather/storms/lightning.html`.

So what happens if the *storms* directory doesn't already exist? Clearly, I have to create the *storms* directory, perhaps along with the *weather* directory if that one doesn't exist either. If I have to create both, I navigate to the top-level directory and create the *weather* directory first. After creating *weather,* I next navigate into, or open, the *weather* directory (by choosing Open) and create the *storms* directory. If *weather* already exists, I can simply open *weather* and create *storms.*

How you create a directory depends on the FTP tool you use, but the concept is pretty much the same regardless: You click a button or choose a menu item to tell the tool to create a directory, and then you give the new directory a name. With WS_FTP, for example, one click on the button named MkDir does the trick. With Fetch, you choose Directories➪Create New Directory. In both cases, as soon as you choose the command, you type a name for the new directory (see Figure 11-5).

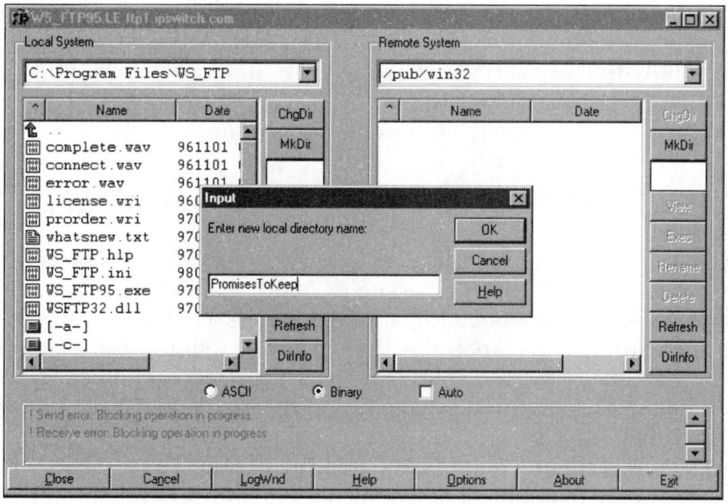

Figure 11-5:
With WS_FTP, the local hard drive (Local System) appears on the left, and the Web server (Remote System) is on the right. To create a directory on the server, click the MkDir button.

If your FTP tool supports bookmarks, consider bookmarking the main directory for each of your Java-powered pages. Doing so saves you from the hassle later of manually navigating into directories; simply choose a bookmark, and you rocket straight to the corresponding directory.

With the main directory for your page in place, you're faced with a decision about what to do next: Create the rest of the directory structure or upload the support files that should go inside the main directory you've just created. This is another one of those personal choices — either option is fine.

I prefer to create the entire directory structure first and then upload the various files that each needs. This way, if I happen to change my mind at the last minute about where the main directory for the page should be located, I have to delete only the directories I've created thus far. However, if I've also uploaded the files for each directory, I have to delete those files, too.

To delete a file or directory using an FTP tool, select the file or directory you want to delete and issue a Remove (or Delete) command. How you issue this command varies from tool to tool; some use a button, others a menu command. Although all FTP tools allow you to delete items, many don't let you delete a directory that contains files. If you have problems deleting a directory, open it up and delete any files inside; then try again.

To remove a directory by using the WS_FTP tool, for example, highlight the directory you want to blow away and then click the RmDir button. To remove a file, highlight the file and press Delete. With Fetch, you use menu items rather than buttons. This tool uses a single menu item to delete both files and directories. Highlight the file or directory you want to delete and choose Remote⇨Delete File or Directory.

Creating subdirectories for support files

After you create (or identify, if it already exists) the main directory for your Web page and the applets it contains (both reside in the same directory, unless you use the CODEBASE attribute discussed in Chapter 7), you must also create any subdirectories that an applet requires for its support files. Any subdirectories you create are, of course, merely reflections of those the applet used when it was originally configured on your hard drive (see Chapters 6 and 7 for details). Remember, you're simply copying a directory from your computer's hard disk onto the hard drive of a Web server. You must be sure to maintain the same directory structure on the Web as the one the applet-powered page used on your hard disk.

Although manually creating a directory structure on the Web, as described here, isn't difficult, it does take time and concentration. If you have the choice, consider transferring everything to the Web at one time by using your FTP tool, a process I describe earlier in this chapter. If your FTP tool supports such a thing, as both WS_FTP and Fetch do, all directories, files, and subdirectories are uploaded for you. Just be sure to use the correct transfer mode, as described in this section, and you'll be all set. Not only is this approach faster, it's more accurate because your FTP tool does all the work, creating and naming directories and subdirectories required by your applet-powered pages.

Typically, applets require only a few subdirectories at most. These subdirectories store the support files, such as graphics and sound files, that the applet uses. Where these subdirectories are located in relation to the main directory depends entirely on the capabilities of the applet and how you've configured the ⟨APPLET⟩ tag (described in Chapters 5 and 7). Because many applets allow you to reference support files relative to the applet itself or the Web page in which it is embedded, you should create the subdirectories accordingly:

- ✔ If an applet loads files relative to itself, the subdirectories you create to hold these files should reside in the same directory as the applet.

- ✔ If an applet loads files relative to the Web page it's woven into, on the other hand, the subdirectories and the files they contain must be created in the same directory as that page.

Suppose that your Web page embedded the LivingLinks applet by using the following ⟨APPLET⟩ tag:

```
<APPLET CODE="LivingLinks" WIDTH=150 HEIGHT=75>
<PARAM NAME=imagesDir VALUE="images/">
<PARAM NAME=imagesName VALUE="button">
<PARAM NAME=imagesExt VALUE="gif">
<PARAM NAME=imagesCount VALUE="5">
<PARAM NAME=speed VALUE="10">
<PARAM NAME=backgroundColor VALUE="white">
<PARAM NAME=reverse VALUE="yes">
<PARAM NAME=soundsDir VALUE="audio/">
<PARAM NAME=inSound VALUE="harp.au">
</APPLET>
```

Because the LivingLinks applet loads files relative to itself and not to the page in which it is embedded, each of the directories specified in the preceding tag (and the files they contain, of course!) must be located in the same directory as the applet. However, in this case, because the applet and

Web page reside in the same directory anyway, you don't have to do anything special — just create the directories and upload the files into them, and you're done. So how can you tell whether the applet and the page must reside in the same directory? Take a close look at the opening <APPLET> tag.

In the previous code example, the <APPLET> tag doesn't use the CODEBASE tag attribute (described in Chapter 7), so the Web page and applet must reside in the same directory. As a result, the *images* directory specified using the imagesDir parameter must also be located inside the same directory as the Web page. The same goes for the *audio* directory. All the directories and files this <APPLET> tag specifies are located in the same directory as the page itself because the CODEBASE attribute isn't used to specify otherwise.

However, the files this particular applet uses don't *have* to be in subdirectories inside the same directory as the applet. That's just how this particular tag was constructed. Because the directories are specified by using relative URLs, they're expected to be located relative to the applet. If, on the other hand, an absolute URL is used to specify a directory, the files this applet uses can be located elsewhere. Consider, for example, the following:

```
<PARAM NAME=imagesDir
          VALUE="http://www.mantiscorp.com/graphics/logos">
```

In this case, an absolute URL is used to specify the directory the images come from (see Chapter 3 for more about absolute URLs). As a result, the images are loaded from the *logos* directory, which is a subdirectory located inside the *graphics* directory on the Mantis Web server (www.mantiscorp.com). But because the applet can access files only from its own server, that is, the server on which the applet itself resides, the LivingLinks applet in this example has to be located somewhere on the Mantis server as well. If the applet resides on a different server, for example, it can't load images residing on the Mantis Web server due to security restrictions described in Chapter 2. As a result, the applet doesn't run properly!

If the subject of the file locations seems confusing, just remember these three things:

✔ If an <APPLET> tag doesn't specify CODEBASE, the applet and the Web page must reside in the same directory.

✔ In most cases, applets load files relative to themselves. But if CODEBASE isn't used, the way the applet loads the files is a moot point because the applet and the Web page are in the same directory anyway!

✔ Some clever applets, such as LivingLinks, let you use absolute URLs to load files. In such cases, files can come from anywhere on the same Web server as the applet itself resides, meaning the files don't have to be located relative to the applet.

However, the graphics and sound files this applet uses are a different story. Because the HTML code in the preceding example specifies a unique directory for each type of file (*images* for graphics and *audio* for sounds), you must create these subdirectories. But where?

First, check to see whether the HTML code specifies *where* these directories should be located, perhaps using an absolute location such as `www.peanutz.org/matilda/images`. If, as in the preceding example, the code does not specify the directory location, you have to find out more about the applet. Specifically, you have to know whether the applet looks for the images in subdirectories that are relative to the directory location of the applet or the Web page. How do you find this information? Usually, you have to check any documentation that came with the applet, or ask the applet's author (see Chapter 8 for details on applet documentation).

✔ If your `<APPLET>` tag doesn't contain a `CODEBASE` attribute (indicating that the applet class files — or JAR files if they're used — and Web page reside in the same directory), all you have to do is create the subdirectories in the Web page's directory. Simply navigate into the directory where you plan to put the Web page and applet, issue a Create Directory command once for the *audio* and again for the *images* directories (to replicate the directory structure on your hard disk), and pat yourself on the back. Your entire directory structure is complete.

✔ If your `<APPLET>` tag uses the `CODEBASE` attribute, you have to create the *images* and *audio* subdirectories in the appropriate directory: either the one the applet resides in or the one the Web page resides in (which one depends on how the applet was created — and to find that out, you have to consult the applet's documentation.

Uploading the files

After your directory structure is complete, you can upload the files that your page requires into their respective locations. This step is a breeze, because all you have to do is navigate to the directory into which you want the file uploaded and then select the button or choose the menu option that begins the transfer. Some tools, such as WS_FTP, don't even require the use of a button or menu — by simply double-clicking a file displayed in the Local System window, the upload begins.

Of course, this process can be tedious when uploading a bunch of files, so you may opt to highlight them all and upload 'em all together as I usually do. With WS_FTP, simply highlight the files and then press the arrow button pointing to the side of the window in which the Web server files are displayed. With Fetch, you have to choose the Put Folders and Files option from the Remote menu and then select the files to upload by using a standard Macintosh file dialog box.

Regardless of whether you upload all files at once or one at a time, you must be sure to do one very important thing: Use the proper transfer mode. Files are uploaded to the Web in different ways, or *modes,* depending on the type of information they contain. When dealing with Java-powered Web pages, be sure that you upload the applet and any non-text support files it uses (data files are typically in text format) by using a non-text transfer mode, such as the *binary* mode. Text transfer modes are designed to ensure that text files are uploaded to the Web with carriage returns and line breaks preserved. That system is great for text files, but quite another story for the applet and its non-text support files. If you're unsure of the transfer mode to use, consult the documentation that comes with your transfer tool.

When in doubt, choose the *raw* transfer mode, if it's available. This mode railroads the file through your modem, over the phone lines, and onto the Internet without treating it in any special way. This plain, or "raw," transfer approach is often the best choice if you're not sure what transfer mode to choose.

A potential side effect of uploading files to the Web is the mangling of filenames, which usually is experienced only by Windows 95/98 users who are transferring files with an outdated FTP tool. When this type of tool gets through with your perfectly good filename, you wind up with a shortened name and extension — and a worthless applet. If this happens to you, you must wait until the transfer is complete and then rename the file to what it should be. Even if you don't use Windows, or if you use a Windows FTP tool that preserves filenames during transfers, you should always double-check all the filenames of your support files after transferring them to the Web. Then, fire up your Java-savvy browser and enter the URL of your Web page. If all goes according to plan, your page loads and comes to life as it did on your computer. If you experience difficulties, consult Chapter 18.

Chapter 12

Troubleshooting: Shaking the Bugs Out

. . . .

. . . .

*W*hen you upload a Java-powered Web page to the Internet, along with all the Java files it requires (class or JAR files, and any support files such as sounds and images), chances are that you actually want to see it in action. But then again, maybe not. Perhaps you're the type of person who's simply too bashful to drink in the splendor of your own Java creation? Well, don't be, friend. Sit back and admire your Web masterpiece.

In reality, something will probably go wrong somewhere in the process. Although the plain old HTML pages that you spin into a Java-powered work of art may look like a million bucks when you view it on your computer hard drive, a lot can happen on the way to the Web. Plainly put, chances are high — really high — that something will go awry as you try to upload your creation to the Internet. And until you figure out what went wrong, you can't fix it and therefore can't give your applet a nice, happy home on the Web (see Chapter 18 for a list of the top ten technical tragedies you're likely to encounter).

Of course, I'm clearly assuming that *something* will go wrong *somehow.* Don't make me the bad guy here; I'm really not a doubting Thomas by nature (or a doubting Aaron, for that matter). The truth is that I've been around the block a few times (shhh, my mom doesn't know) when it comes to getting Web pages to really work on the Web. It's one thing to weave an applet into your page when the page and applet reside on your computer. It's quite another to upload the whole shebang to the Web for everyone to see.

But, hey, you're no ordinary person. You're charming, good looking, and smell great. How could anything possibly go wrong on the Web when you've got so much going for you in real life already? That's what we're going to find out. C'mon!

Testing, Testing

The only way to know for sure if your Java-powered page is uploaded to the Web fully intact is to actually view it with a Java-savvy browser. To do so, simply fire-up your browser and type in the URL leading to your page. If all goes according to plan, your baby appears bright-eyed and full of life. However, you're dealing with computers after all, so don't expect things to go according to plan the first few times around.

Instead, brace yourself for, as Zorba the Greek might say, a spectacular failure. Or perhaps just a sad, lonely little Web page that somehow lost its jolt of Java in the process of uploading from your personal computer to the Internet.

If the applet you wove into your page locally (see Chapters 6 and 7) doesn't appear on the copy you uploaded to the Web when you visit its new home with your browser, you've got problems, bubbie. Don't be hasty, of course. Wait a few minutes after the page first appears, just to make sure that the applet has enough time to make the trip from its new home on the Web to your computer, but prepare for the worst. Even the best-smelling folks sometimes fail to succeed on the first go-around.

Rather than breaking out the bubbly to celebrate what you'd hoped would be a momentous occasion, you need to figure out what went wrong. Fortunately, your browser is equipped for just such times. When testing your Java-powered pages, pay particular attention to two areas on your browser:

- ✔ Status area
- ✔ Java console

What, when, where, and why: The status area

The *status area* displays short messages related to the task at hand. If you move your cursor over a hyperlink in a Web page, for instance, the address of that link appears in the status area. In this way, the status area can help you better understand what that link is all about (assuming that such an address is actually of interest to you). At the very least, it's helpful to know if clicking the link takes you to an entirely different site on the Web, or merely takes you a little deeper into the same site you're already visiting.

The status area typically is located in the lower-left corner of your browser window. Make sure that your browser's status area is visible — you may be surprised how often folks forget that a status area even exists, simply because it isn't visible.

Thankfully, Netscape Navigator doesn't allow you to hide the status area. Older versions of the browser did, however, and so does Internet Explorer 4.0 — although Explorer uses the term *Status Bar* instead of status area — to enable the status area when using these browsers, make sure that the item named status area (or Status Bar) located under the View menu has a check mark next to it.

The status area provides helpful pieces of information regarding the links appearing on a page. The browser uses the status area to inform you of problems it encounters while attempting to run an applet. If the browser can't find the applet files that a Web page needs, for example, the status area displays an `applet not found` error message. Assume for a moment that you upload a LivingLinks-powered Web page to the Internet, but don't upload the LivingLinks class files. In that case, browsers can't find the applet files that your page requests, and so display a message in the status area something along the lines of `applet LivingLinks not found`.

Even if an applet runs just fine, it may take advantage of the status area to tell you important things while it's running, such as `Click now and sub-scribe to the Pickle of the Month Club`. Clearly, watching the status area for useful messages is a good idea when first viewing your applet. In fact, the LivingLinks `inMessage` parameter enables you to display any message that you need in the status area, as users move their mice over a running applet (see Chapter 8 for details on the `inMessage` parameter, and all other parameters supported by the LivingLinks applet).

The status area is useful for viewing short pieces of information. Sometimes, however, the information in the status area just isn't enough. If your Java-powered page fails to run when uploaded to the Web (or when you're viewing it locally on your own computer, for that matter), there's a good chance that the information displayed in the status area simply won't be informative enough. If this is the case, it's time to turn to your browser's Java console.

Finding consolation in the Java console

Most Java-savvy browsers on the market today enable you to open a *Java console* window to view the inner workings of applets. The Java Console window has a great deal of leg room when it comes to screen real estate. Unlike the status area, which is very small and can accommodate only brief messages, the Java console is an independent window that browsers and applets alike can use to display messages of any length to the user.

The Java Console window looks just like any other window (see Figures 12-1 and 12-2) that you may see on your computer. But this window is especially for Java applets, and contains information directly related to the applets running inside the Web pages you visit. If you have problems getting your Java-powered Web page to run after uploading it to the Internet, and the status area doesn't contain descriptive-enough messages to help you solve the problem, turn to the Java console. Here, you're much more likely to find detailed information related to the problem at hand.

Of course, finding out how to actually display the Java Console window can be a problem in its own right. Because all browsers are a little different, each has a different command for opening the Java console. Just poke around for a little while, and find a command with the word "console" in it.

Regardless of how you manage to open the Java Console for your particular browser, be sure to take a peek at it if you have problems with your Java-powered pages. Between the Java console and the status area, you have all the information you need to figure out why your carefully sculpted Java-powered masterpiece falls apart when it hits the Web. And after you have a few rounds of the fascinating game I call "assessing the askew applet" under your belt, you'll probably come to find that most problems with Java-powered pages are the result of only a handful of mistakes, listed in the next section.

The Java Plug-in, discussed in detail in Chapter 10, offers its very own console window. To view the Java Plug-in console window (assuming you've already installed the Java Plug-in), select Show Java Console from the Basic tab found in the Java Plug-in Control Panel (see Chapter 10).

Fixing Problems with Spit and Glue

Fortunately, most of the mistakes you're likely to make when it comes to uploading your Java-powered page to the Web fall into the "Band-Aids and bubble gum" category: They don't take much effort to fix, and just a few extra minutes of chewing on the problem can make you and your browser happy campers.

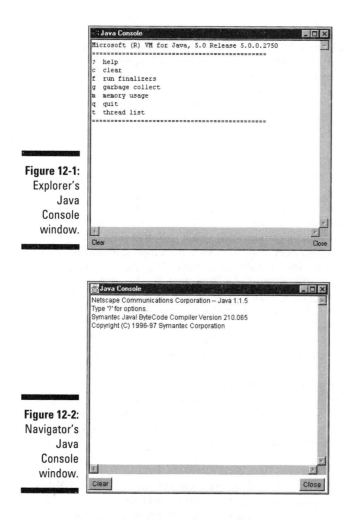

Figure 12-1:
Explorer's
Java
Console
window.

Figure 12-2:
Navigator's
Java
Console
window.

Upload upheaval

The most common mistake you're likely to make when uploading your Web page, applets, and support files to the Web is one just about everyone makes the first few times: forgetting to upload one piece or another of the puzzle.

When you first begin creating Java-powered Web pages, you may forget to upload an image that an applet needs, or a sound file, or even an applet itself. If you're working with a traditional applet comprised of more than one class file, chances are good that you'll overlook one of those class files when uploading. JAR files make this omission much less likely because all the classes are bundled together in one easy-to-swallow package, but some applets require several JAR files, and forgetting to upload one of these essential ingredients is easy. (See Chapters 4 and 8 to find out more about JARs.) This is especially true when you're dealing with support files that reside in their own directories. The more files an applet requires, and the more directories these various files may span (one directory for images, another for sound files, for example), the greater your chances of making the mistake of omitting a file, or even an entire directory, during the upload process.

When you work with LivingLinks or Marquee for the first time, take extra care to upload all the .class files associated with these applets. Marquee, for example, requires that both the Marquee.class and MarqueeFile.class files reside in the same directory on the Internet to work properly. LivingLinks, on the other hand, requires only the LivingLinks.class file if you do *not* take advantage of a special effect (such as Fade, Warp, Shatter, Blur, and so forth). If you use a special effect, however, you must also upload the corresponding Effect.class file, along with any class files that make up the special effect itself (such as Fade.class and FadeFilter.class, in the case of the Fade special effect). Neglecting to upload all the necessary class files is the leading cause of applet failure when it comes to multi-part applets, such as LivingLinks and Marquee, and nothing to be ashamed about. Just give your Internet directory a careful look-see before throwing your hands up in disgust, and you'll probably realize that an applet class file or two is missing.

Fortunately, fixing this problem is easy enough. All you have to do is use your FTP tool to compare the structure and contents of every directory associated with your Java-powered page. Simply ensure that all files residing on your local hard drive have been uploaded to the Internet, and that each file resides in its proper corresponding folder on the Net, and you'll be just fine.

Netscape Navigator features a Page Info command in the View menu. When you select this item (View⇨Page Info), the entire directory structure of a Web page displays, giving you a comprehensive overview of the various filenames and locations of files (even applets!) that a page uses. If you have difficulty figuring out what files you've uploaded to the Web, or want to take a closer look at the structure of your Java-powered page, give Page Info a whirl.

The name game

Another leading cause of applet failure lies in the naming of the files after they've been uploaded, something I like to call the "name game."

Assuming that you've successfully uploaded to the Web all the files that your page requires, your applet should run like a charm. If it doesn't, take a closer look at the name of each file involved. In many cases, FTP tools shorten (or *truncate*) long file names during the upload. What was once LivingLinks.class becomes LivingLi.cla, while MarqueeFile.class mysteriously becomes MarqueeF.cla, effectively blowing your hopes of Java bliss out of the ether.

In these cases, you actually need to rename the files on the Internet by using your FTP tool. (Every FTP tool enables you to rename a file that you upload. Simply select the file and click the Rename button, or a similarly named button or menu if Rename doesn't exist in your tool.) If an applet name is supposed to be LivingLinks.class, by gosh that's what you need to rename it! The same goes for all support files — any file associated with an applet must have exactly the same name when it lives on the Internet as it does when living on your own personal computer. If your LivingLinks applet expects to use an image named MyBigNose.gif, then you need to make sure that the file named MyBigNose.gif resides on the Internet in the folder that the applet expects to find it in (such as *images*), and that it has exactly the same spelling and case.

If I sound a bit harsh about naming your Internet-bound files exactly as they appear on your local computer, it's just because I care. I've seen far too many loved ones hurt as a result of improper file naming, and can't bear to see you go through the same pain. Seriously.

If you use an FTP tool that shortens long file names, hunt around for an option in the tool that disables this problematic feature. Chances are pretty good that you can find a check box option that enables you to turn off the automatic shortening of long file names during uploads; if it doesn't, consider using a more considerate FTP tool such as WS_FTP or Fetch.

Get off my case

Some FTP tools tend to change the case of the characters in filenames: LivingLinks.class is not the same as livinglinks.class, or even LIVINGLINKS .CLASS, for that matter!

If you use Most FTP tools have settings that enable you to specify what to do with file names during uploads. If your file names are constantly being cut up, or the case of the names changes, hunt around in the settings of your FTP tool to see if it has options for disabling such features. Many years ago, it was acceptable to truncate file names or change the case when a file was uploaded, especially when uploading to DOS-based Web servers, which can't handle long file names. But today, things are different. Java-savvy browsers (and the applets that run inside of them) expect file names to be precise in both length and case. And so should your FTP tool.

Case matters, my friend, even when it comes to file extensions (like .class, .gif, and .jpg), and your browser is the first to complain when it tries to find an image called MySmallEars.gif, yet only MySmallEars.GIF is available (or vice versa; an applet may be configured to use images having the .GIF extension, in which case images having the .gif extension simply won't do). *You* may be able to understand that the extensions .GIF and .gif are really the same thing when it comes to describing an image format, but your *browser* isn't so smart. Here, you'd either have to rename the file's extension to .gif, or configure the applet to look for MySmallEars.GIF instead of MySmallEars.gif, and things would be just ducky.

Cache conundrums

Caching is a technique that Web browsers commonly use to speed up Web page loading. When caching is enabled, your browser stashes away content (such as images, sounds and applets) into a special folder on your computer known as a *cache* (pronounced "cash"). Content is then cached, or stored, on your hard drive.

The next time that content is needed (the next time you visit a Web page), your browser is smart enough to take the images, sounds, and applets it's looking for from the cache rather than downloading them from the Web again. The result is a significant decrease in the amount of time it takes to load a page, thanks to the fact that it's faster to load a file off your computer's hard drive than it is to download it over the Internet.

Unfortunately, caching can also cause problems. Although it's rare, on occasion a cached applet can become damaged or corrupted (damage can occur to any file on your hard drive, including applets, for a number of reasons including viruses, bad hard drive media, and so on). Because damage to applets is difficult to detect, your browser may not realize the problem! As a result, your browser continues to use the damaged applet residing in your cache rather than reloading a fresh copy from the Web as it should.

Each browser maintains its own cache, meaning Netscape Navigator stores the files it caches in a different folder on your computer than the one Internet Explorer uses for its cached files. While Navigator uses the word *cache* explicitly, Internet Explorer uses the term *temporary files*. Thus, flushing Internet Explorer's cache is more commonly referred to as "deleting temporary files."

Fortunately, it's easy to clear out, or *flush,* your browser's cache, as the sidebar "Force feeding applets to your browser" in Chapter 9 explains. In fact, whenever I'm confronted by a browser problem that I can't explain or fix, I flush my cache, effectively forcing my browser to load every Web page from scratch. Clearing your cache guarantees that you receive a fresh copy of each piece of Web page content, including applets.

Turn to Chapter 18 to learn more about common problems that have easy solutions. In that chapter, you find out how to quickly and effectively snuff out applet fires, including security glitches and jittery Just In Time (JIT) compilers.

Performing Major Surgery

While the majority of problems you may experience when trying to get your Java-powered pages to live on the Web fall into the "Band-Aids and bubble gum" category, sometimes you won't be so lucky.

On the road to nowhere: Uploading files to the wrong directory

In some cases, you realize only after uploading an entire directory of files to the Web that you've mistakenly uploaded them to the wrong place. If, for example, you upload all your images into the wrong directory (the sound directory, for example, or even the directory the applet itself resides in, which is a problem if the images must reside inside their own directory) all you can do is delete the ones now on the Internet, move to the correct directory, and try again. Don't be ashamed. It happens to everyone now and again, even after years of working with Java (am I blushing?).

Dangerous dancing: The transfer mode two-step

In other cases, you may turn blue trying to figure out what's wrong with your Java-powered Web page, because nothing obvious jumps out at you. If all the files your page requires are uploaded to their proper directories, and the files are properly named, as are the directories themselves (a directory named images is not the same as one called image — that little "s" counts!), it can be truly maddening to figure out what's wrong. Everything looks exactly as it should, and the files and directory are all in place, but the browser complains that it can't find the applet files or support files even though you know they're there. What gives?

Firewalls can cause problems when you upload files to the Web and can also prevent you from viewing executable content (such as Java applets) with your Web browser. *Firewalls* are special security programs that watch all the data traffic flowing between your computer and the Internet; they prevent suspicious or questionable information from reaching its destination. If a firewall thinks that the files that you're attempting to upload to the Internet are potentially dangerous, it prevents the upload. Likewise, firewalls can prevent you from running applets in your Web browser. If you can't upload files to the Web, or have problems viewing applets in your Web browser, consider contacting your Internet Service Provider (ISP) or network administrator to see if a firewall is the cause.

If this is the case, chances are exceedingly high that you uploaded your files to the Internet using the wrong file transfer mode. File transfer modes, as explained in Chapter 11, tell your FTP tool how to break apart a file, send it over the network, and reassemble it on the other end. Think of your FTP tool as a primitive transporter of sorts, just like you'd see in any self-respecting science fiction movie (except without the big metal door and psychedelic lights). If your transporter isn't set to the right mode, things can get ugly. Did you ever see the modern remake of *The Fly* starring Jeff Goldblum? Enough said. When you use the wrong mode, you have no choice but to blow away the files you've already uploaded (that is, delete them) and try again. Simply delete the files you suspect were corrupted during the transfer from your computer to the Internet by using your FTP tool, and upload the original files from your hard drive once again. But this time, make sure that your FTP tool's file transfer mode is properly set (see Chapters 11 and 18 for advice on setting file transfer modes for various types of files).

Generally speaking, applet files get corrupted during the upload process more often than support files. If you suspect a corrupt file is causing your problems, try deleting applet class files (or JARs) first and then re-upload them from scratch using a different transfer mode. After you replace the applet files, test your page again. If this process doesn't do the trick, move on to the support files (such as images and sounds).

Finding a new home

In the worst situations, you may find out only after you've jumped through a number of fiery hoops that your problem runs much deeper than simply renaming a few files or having to upload a file you forgot to include in the first place. You may, amazing as it may seem, actually find out that your Web site doesn't support Java in the first place!

Although it's very rare, some Internet Service Providers (ISPs) out there don't allow Java-powered pages to run from the Web space they supply. In this case, all you can do is look for another service provider, one that actually supports Java (check out the AT&T WorldNet ISP kit provided on the CD-ROM that comes with this book; I personally guarantee that this ISP supports Java).

The same may even be true if you're using a corporate or educational Web site; your company or school may not want you to use Java. Because Java is powerful, it places extra demand on the computers that run a Web site (the computers are known as *hosts*). Not only does the computer hardware have to work a little harder when dealing with Java, so do the network pipes that connect the Web site to the Internet itself; they have to deliver more information than typically associated with a plain, old-fashioned Web page.

Also, the staff running the Web site has to work a little harder to support Java. Hey, something this cool doesn't come for free — somebody, or many bodies, have to support it! As a result, ISPs, companies, and even schools exist that don't want you to use Java because Java-powered pages are more demanding than their sad, naked little friends. Traditional Web pages are much less complicated to deal with and are much less difficult to support than those with Java. But then again, they're much less exciting. Much less powerful. Much less everything, as far as millions of people are concerned.

And so, if you find yourself in a situation where your Java-powered Web pages are in need of a Java-friendly Web host, be sure to ask the quintessential question before you dive in: "Do you support Java?" If the answer is no, move on, dear friend.

Part III

Application Overdrive: Bringing Java to the Desktop

The 5th Wave   By Rich Tennant

"I don't mean to hinder your quest for knowledge, however it's not generally a good idea to try to download the entire Internet."

In this part . . .

Part III shows you how to get your fill of another flavor of Java — Java applications. Here you find out what Java applications are and how they differ from applets. This part tells you where to find Java applications, how to install them on your desktop computer, and how to customize them to suit your personal taste. In the process, you discover a little about Virtual Machines and how they make the Java world go 'round!

Chapter 13

Rumble in the Jungle: Applications versus Applets

*I*n the beginning, applets dominated the wild and woolly Java jungle. Just a few years ago, the terms *Java* and *applet* were practically synonymous. Because applets were built with Java and applets were everywhere Java was, you could interchange the terms Java and applets without raising eyebrows. As for Java programs, applets ruled. At least, that is, they did until Java applications came along.

Applets that you create by using the Java programming language are still, by far, the most popular types of programs that you create in Java. But applets are not the *only* kind of programs that you can create in Java. Today, a new kid is in town. Java *applications* have recently emerged as a powerful — some even say superior — alternative to applets.

Tell Me What's Java-app-ening

Word on the street is that Java applications are beginning to steal more than just a few rays of the limelight previously showered on applets. And for good reason: Java applications, which live and run on desktop computers just as traditional applications do, are inherently more powerful than their Web-bound applet brethren in a number of areas. But why?

"Anything you can do I can do better!"

If Java applets sparked a revolution on the World Wide Web, what's so special about Java applications? After all, the revolution is over, right? Hundreds of thousands of Web pages around the world are alive and kicking thanks to Java applets, which electrify lifeless pages with jolts of animation, sound, and interactivity. How much better can Java applications possibly be than applets?

Alrighty, my fellow applet zealot, you have a point. Java applets are largely responsible for ushering in an entirely new class of Web pages, and I'd be hard pressed to say outright that applications are better than applets. Heck, I love those little guys. Who doesn't?

In truth, you're more accurate saying that applications and applets are simply *different* flavors of Java that excel in *different* areas. Java applications have their strong and weak points, just as applets do. However, when it comes to accessing files on your computer or connecting to various Internet sites, it's clear that applications can do anything applets can do and much more as this chapter shows. But that doesn't mean that applications are necessarily better than applets. Not by a long shot.

Think of applets and applications as two different children born to the same parents; each has unique gifts and qualities that sets one apart from the other, which makes loving one more than the other difficult. But isn't the adorable newborn baby always the one who gets the most attention? You bet your sweet bippy. And applications are brand spanking new compared to applets, which may explain why everyone is goo-goo ga-ga over them today.

Applications: The late bloomer of the Java family

Despite how tempted one may be to say that Java applications are "new," they've really been with us as long as applets. (Okay, I admit it. I may be misleading you in the preceding section by calling Java applications "brand spanking new," knowing full well that they're just as old as applets.) What I mean to say is that applications are "new" in terms of mind share; everyone knows about applets, while applications lurk in the shadow of their more popular Java siblings, coming late to the popularity game for a variety of reasons:

✔ **Java applications are more complicated to install and use.** Unlike with applets, which live and die in Web pages, you install Java applications on your computer just as you do any other application. As a result, you don't simply point a Web browser to a page and see Java applications in action. Quite the contrary, in fact.

✔ **Java applications require you to go through a potently thorny installation process.** To use a Java application, you must first install it on your computer as you would any other software program. This takes time, effort, and serious consideration compared to the relatively care-free act of Web browsing.

✔ **Applications demand "up front" time and consideration.** Because they reside on your desktop computer, living entirely outside of the Web, applications aren't as free-love-hippie-dippy as applets are. With applets, you can love 'em and leave 'em by the bushel. Heck, that's a big part of the appeal of applets. Applications are a different story; you can't just fire up your browser and experience a bunch of applications one after another. Java applications require a significant commitment from both you and your computer, which translates into time and effort: You have to carefully consider each application that you install well before you actually install it! Keeping this fact in mind, no one should express any surprise that applets got all the attention at first. The Web rocketed to popularity by virtue of the fact that it was fast, easy, and painless. As applets hitched their wagon to that rising star, applications were left behind, for the most part, in the dust.

Time, however, has a funny way of smoothing out life's little inequities. Java applets are now giving way to applications, largely because of the fact that applications are completely unrestricted in what they can do in comparison to applets.

Stepping out of the sandbox

Security is the area where Java applications most clearly outmuscle their Web-bound counterparts. In Chapter 2, you see a great number of restrictions imposed on applets. And for good reason! How can you make sure that every applet you bump into on the Web is a friendly one?

If Web pages consist of nothing more than text and images, they're a pretty safe place to visit. But toss in executable content, such as Java applets, and things can get pretty ugly pretty fast. Think, for a moment, what may happen if every applet you come across can access the files on your computer. What sensitive and personal information could the person or group of people sitting on the other side of the Java-powered Web pages tap into?

Worse still, what if applets could delete files from your computer? One minute, you may be playing an innocent game of Hang Man on the Web, and the next, you may consider tying a sturdy rope around your own neck after realizing that every file on your computer was systematically and permanently deleted.

For just such reasons, Java designers literally cripple their applets by forcing them to play inside an imaginary sandbox: your browser. As Figure 13-1 shows, your browser considers every applet that it encounters a potential threat and treats the applet as an "untrusted" program that may prove harmful. As a result, the browser prevents the applet from reaching out and looking at or touching the files on your computer. Unless you specifically give an applet access to your files, as I describe in Chapter 2, it has no power outside the browser and, therefore, can't damage your system.

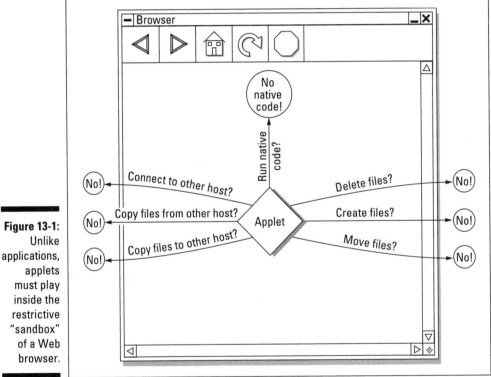

Figure 13-1:
Unlike applications, applets must play inside the restrictive "sandbox" of a Web browser.

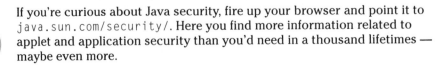

If you're curious about Java security, fire up your browser and point it to `java.sun.com/security/`. Here you find more information related to applet and application security than you'd need in a thousand lifetimes — maybe even more.

Keep in mind that only those applets that you can trust may obtain access to your computer. And not all applets even *want* you to trust them. In fact, the vast majority of applets are content to play inside the browser sandbox. All Java 1.0 applets, for example, must remain in the sandbox for eternity because that version of Java simply didn't provide for applets with the capability to step out of the sandbox. In Java 1.1 and 1.2, however, applet developers found the tools they needed to design "trustworthy" applets that had power outside the sandbox. For details, refer to Chapter 2.

Unlike applets, which suffer restrictions from the get-go, Java applications have full and unbridled access to your computer system, as shown in Figure 13-2. In particular, applications obtain the following three forms of access that applets typically don't:

✔ **File System Access:** Java applications have complete access to the files on your computer, while applets receive access only to files on the host computer on which they live (see Chapter 2). Applications can read, delete, and reorganize the files on your personal computer. In addition, applications can create new files on your computer whenever they want. Talk about presumptuous!

✔ **Network Access:** Whereas applets can access only the host computer on which they physically reside (see Chapter 2), Java applications are free to make network connections to any computers on the network that they want. This capability means that Java applications can download files from computers on the network and upload files as well. As a result, applications can reach out onto the Internet and upgrade themselves with new capabilities, install new software on your computer, or even copy files from your computer to the Web. Makes ya sort of nervous, doesn't it?

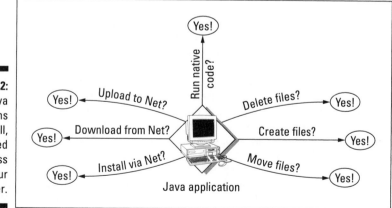

Figure 13-2:
Java applications have full, unrestricted access to your computer.

✔ **Native Code Access:** Unless you give them explicit permission to do so, as I describe in Chapter 2, Java applets can't reach out beyond the browser and access *native code* on the computers they ultimately run on. Native code refers to programming code that is written in a language other than Java. Traditional applications are written entirely in native code, while Java applets and applications are written in the Java programming language. While applications are free to run native code, applets don't have this luxury because of the restrictive browser "sandbox" in which they run.

Applications, on the other hand, can fiddle around with the innards of your computer if they so desire, meaning that they can directly access native code. This capability gives applications great power, because they can invoke platform-specific features to which applets aren't privy, such as a computer's built-in Find feature or the capability to run or quit other applications residing on a computer. Yet even applications face their own restrictions. (See the sidebar "100 percent pure Java: As good as it gets," later in this chapter, for details.)

Runtime Environments and Virtual Machines

Because they can play outside the browser sandbox, applications are clearly unrestricted in what they can do in comparison to the intentionally hamstrung applets. But why? How can two different types of programs (applets and applications) that you create by using the same programming language (Java) have such different capabilities? The answer lies in the *Runtime Environments,* or *Virtual Machines,* that ultimately govern the behavior of all Java programs.

One of the hallmarks of Java is its cross-platform nature, which enables a single Java program to run on many different computer platforms without modification (including Macintosh, Windows, and UNIX, as I describe in detail later). This capability is possible because Java applets and applications don't run directly on your computer, as other software programs do. Instead, Java programs first pass through a *Virtual Machine* that translates the platform-neutral code of which they consist into a form that can then function as a traditional program. (See the section "Java Runtime Environment (JRE)," later in this chapter.)

Java applets consist of *bytecode* instead of the machine code that traditional programs consist of. Not surprisingly, Java applications also consist of bytecode. Although the terms *bytecode* and *machine code* are more technical than you may prefer, stick with me: To understand the difference between bytecode and machine code is to understand the difference between Java programs and their traditional counterparts.

WARNING!

Tread lightly and carry a humongous stick!

Clearly, Java applications possess capabilities that applets don't have, unless you take the time to grant the latter special powers (see Chapter 2). And with these powers come danger, as you've probably sensed. Java applications are every bit as powerful as traditional applications, meaning that you must take extreme care in installing them on your computer.

Just as with traditional applications, you absolutely must know who created a Java application and you must actually trust that developer and the application itself before you install it on your computer. One wrong step and, well, things could be all over for your computer.

Fortunately, a number of software vendors are out there whom you can trust for Java applications. The most significant of these I list in Chapter 17, which points you to a number of Java applications that aren't going to wreak havoc on your computer if you install them.

In time, however, you'll come across sources of Java applications other than those that I mention in this book. As you do, make sure that you exercise extreme caution! Unless you're completely confident that the person or vendor supplying a Java application is entirely trustworthy, don't risk it. In installing software on your computer, you're better off safe than sorry. Unless, of course, you're the type of person who doesn't mind at all should a rogue application happen to delete all the files on your computer at once, after first publishing them on the Web for everyone to see. Hey, it can happen.

Programmers develop traditional software programs for a specific type of computer platform, meaning that they ultimately deliver those programs in a form that a specific type of computer can understand. The programs they write in programming languages such as C or Pascal are converted from a human readable form that the programmer understands into a form called *machine code* that only the computer understands. Machine code ties directly to one computing platform and can't run on other computers, which, in turn, limits the types of computers a traditional program can be run on.

A traditional word processor program, for example, consists of machine code that runs on a specific type of computer. A traditional word processor that one creates for Windows 98 computers consists of machine code that only those computers understand, while Macintosh word processors consist of a completely different machine code. As a result, you can't run a traditional Windows 98 word processor on a Macintosh computer and vice versa.

Java programs, on the other hand, are platform independent because they consist of bytecode rather than machine code. You can think of bytecode as an intermediate step between human-readable Java code and machine-readable code. The biggest advantage bytecode has over machine code is that every computer can read it.

Of course, computers don't magically understand Java bytecode. You must first equip them with a special interpreter than knows how to convert bytecode into machine code. To run a Java program consisting of bytecode, something must first convert the bytecode into that machine code that your computer can understand. That something is a *Runtime Environment,* or more precisely, a *Virtual Machine.*

What's a Virtual Machine (VM)?

A *Virtual Machine* (*VM*) is simply a catchy name for describing the mechanism that you use to convert Java bytecode into the native machine code that your computer requires to run a program. If you think of bytecode as cake batter, a VM is merely the oven that cooks up the bytecode batter before serving it to your computer (it's actually a software program, not an oven, but you get the point). Your computer doesn't understand batter; it just likes to eat cake. The VM enables your computer to eat cake by cooking up the bytecode batter into a form that the computer can digest (machine code). Yum!

HotSpot: The need for speed

If you're concerned about the effect that converting bytecode to machine code has on Java's performance, join the crowd. Just as baking a cake from scratch takes more time than simply buying a precooked cake, Java applets and applications take more time to run than do regular programs because they must pass through a Virtual Machine program before running on your computer.

The performance hit isn't drastic, but it's noticeable. If you compare them to traditional programs, Java programs run anywhere from 10 percent to 30 percent slower on average. And although that difference may not seem a big deal for many programs, in speed-critical situations, it's forever.

To speed up Java applets and applications, many browsers and Runtime Environments employ what's known as a *Just In Time (JIT)* compiler. JIT compilers give Java programs a significant boost by optimizing certain portions

of their bytecode for speed. Unfortunately, JIT compilers alone don't solve Java's speed problem.

Instead, Java applications are eagerly awaiting *HotSpot.* Under development by Sun, the HotSpot technology promises to radically speed up applets and applications. Unlike a JIT compiler, HotSpot is a fundamental improvement to the Virtual Machine and, in effect, enables it to "cook" bytecode batter into cakes faster than ever. You can think of HotSpot as a convection oven that offers drastic speed improvements over conventional ovens; both can cook a cake, but HotSpot does it lickedy split!

By the time you read this book, HotSpot may be available. To find out how it can help speed up your applets and applications, point your browser to java.sun.com/products/hotspot/index.html.

To stretch this cooking analogy a little farther, you can think of the Java programming language as a list of raw ingredients that chefs (programmers) can choose from to create batter (bytecode). The batter that a chef creates is a direct result of the ingredients he chooses to mix together. After all is said and done, the batter is in an intermediate form that isn't quite ready for a computer to eat; it's no longer raw ingredients, but it's not quite a cake either. A Virtual Machine must first cook it before serving it to a computer. Figure 13-3 shows you this cooking analogy.

Now, to beat the cooking analogy into the ground, I'm going to take it one step farther. What are the benefits of batter over cake? Why would you want to deliver a program as bytecode rather than as machine code? Well, good buddy, the answer all boils down to *platform independence* — that is, the ability for a program to run on a variety of different computer platforms.

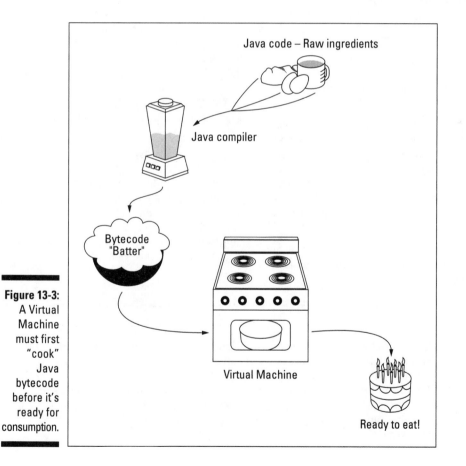

Figure 13-3:
A Virtual Machine must first "cook" Java bytecode before it's ready for consumption.

100 Percent Pure Java: As good as it gets

Although Java applications can "reach out" and tap into the native code of the platform on which they run, as I describe in the section "Stepping out of the sandbox" earlier in this chapter, that capability is not always an advantage. Consider, for a moment, what happens if an otherwise cross-platform Java application attempts to run native code.

Because native code is actually machine code that's unique to each platform, a Java application must invoke the appropriate native code for each of the platforms on which it runs. The native code for the Find command on Windows computers, for example, is very different from that for the same command on a Macintosh, both of which are different from the native code for the Find command on UNIX systems.

As a result, a Java application that reaches out and runs the native code for the Find command on a Windows computer must also be smart enough to reach out and run the corresponding code on every platform it encounters. If it doesn't, the application is no longer cross-platform; it's fully functional only on the platforms for which it understands the native code.

Sadly, the powerful capability to invoke native code is also the Achilles' heel of Java

applications. To be completely cross-platform, an application must either shun native code entirely or go to great extremes to support all platforms in running native code. And, because time is money, most developers who use native code in their Java applications don't take the time to support all platforms. Instead, they typically design the application to support only the most popular computer platforms, which limits the application to only those computer systems on which it can run.

Understanding this dilemma, Sun has launched a "100 Percent Pure Java" initiative to uphold and enforce the cross-platform nature of Java. Only Java programs that follow the 100 Percent Pure Java guidelines can sport the official logo, which tells the world that these programs are up to snuff in supporting the high cross-platform standard set forth by Sun.

And because all Java applications on which the 100 Percent Pure Java logo appears pass muster with Sun (and you can check out the rigorous requirements at java.sun.com/100percent/), you can rest easy that the application is entirely safe to install on your computer. Think of this logo as the Good Housekeeping Seal of Approval for Java.

Java applets and applications are, thanks to bytecode, cross-platform in nature. As bytecode "batter," you can ship them around the world and "cook" them up on any type of computer that has a Virtual Machine "oven." Traditional programs, by comparison, can be thought of as precooked, store-bought "cake" that has a limited shelf life — they can only be run on certain computers since they've already been "cooked" for a particular type of system.

Unlike traditional programs, which are tied to specific platforms, Java programs remain in an easily transported batter form until just before you "eat" them — or, more correctly, run them on your computer. As soon as you tell your computer that you're ready to consume, or run, a Java application, your computer pops the bytecode batter it's made of in the Virtual Machine oven. Moments later a piping hot application is served up, regardless of what platform it's on. Think of it as Betty Crocker's Easy Bake Oven for software.

Virtual Machine Madness: Installing Your Very Own VM

If the entire notion of a Virtual Machine is somewhat abstract to you, this section makes the concept more concrete by showing you several ways to soup up your own computer by installing a Virtual Machine. After you install a Virtual Machine, your computer can use it to cook your bytecode batter into a complete Java cake. That is to say, you can run Java applications on your computer after you install a Virtual Machine (see the preceding section to make sense of my ongoing batter and cake analogy). Who knows — you may already have a Virtual Machine installed on your computer without even knowing it.

Browsers

Surprise! If you install a Java-savvy browser on your computer, you inadvertently install a Virtual Machine at the same time. You may not be aware of what you're doing, but you do it anyway. So admit it: You installed a Virtual Machine on your computer at the time that you installed your Java-savvy browser. There. That wasn't so bad, was it?

You see, for a browser to support Java applets, it must first know how to convert the bytecode of an applet into machine code that your computer can run. The process is just that simple. Without a Virtual Machine, no such thing as a Java-savvy browser can even exist.

But this chapter isn't about Java applets. It's about Java applications. So simply accept the fact that a Virtual Machine is slaving away behind the scenes every time that you visit a Java-powered Web page, as shown in Figure 13-4, and we're sure to get along just fine.

Sadly, the Virtual Machine that your browser uses is only good for running applets. Instead, you need a Virtual Machine such as the one that comes with the Java Development Tookit (JDK) or Java Runtime Environment (JRE) if you want to run Java applications.

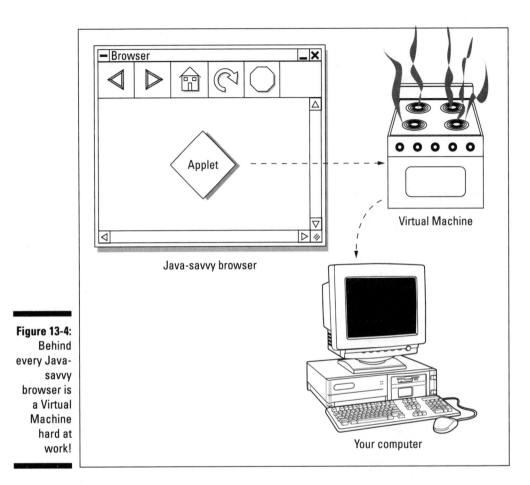

Figure 13-4:
Behind
every Java-
savvy
browser is
a Virtual
Machine
hard at
work!

Java Development Toolkit (JDK)

Installing a Java-savvy browser isn't the only way to install a Virtual Machine. And it's a good thing, too, because your browser's Virtual Machine isn't worth a pinch of salt when it comes to running Java applications. Instead, you need an industrial-strength Virtual Machine to run Java applications. Fortunately, there are a few around.

If you're a software developer, you may already know that the Sun Java Development Toolkit (JDK) comes with everything you need to create Java applets and applications, including a Virtual Machine. Unlike Java-savvy browsers, which do everything they can to hide the fact that a Virtual Machine is running under the covers, the JDK is specifically for software developers who want to create applets and applications from scratch. As such, the JDK makes no effort to hide its Virtual Machine from you.

As you install the JDK, you're fully aware that you're also installing a Virtual Machine. In fact, you also get a suite of utilities that run on top of the JDK's Virtual Machine and that help you develop applets and applications. Of course, the JDK is specifically for software developers and not your average end user, so it's a pretty hairy tool with which to deal.

Unfortunately, in the early years of Java, you had no choice but to deal with the JDK if you wanted to run Java applications. Because Java-savvy browsers are capable of running only applets, you had no choice but to install and master the complicated JDK if you wanted to run Java applications.

Fortunately, that was a lifetime ago in Web time (or just a few years ago in regular time). Today, we have a number of options for installing a Virtual Machine other than the ones that come with Java-savvy browsers. Interestingly, the most important of these is a direct descendant of the JDK. The Sun Java Runtime Environment (JRE) offers the Virtual Machine that comes with the JDK at a fraction of the complexity; you don't need to be a software developer to use the JRE. Best of all, it's a cinch to install!

Java Runtime Environment (JRE)

The Sun Java Runtime Environment (JRE) is perhaps the easiest way to install a Virtual Machine outside of your Java-savvy browser (which, as you now know, can only run applets). When Sun realized that average folks like you and me want to run Java applications, they knew that the JDK wouldn't do. What you and I really need is a painless, simple way to run Java applications, and the JDK isn't it.

Happily, Sun was quick to respond. By taking all the complexity out of the JDK, while leaving intact its fabulous Virtual Machine, Sun created the JRE. Thanks to the JRE, you can now install a Virtual Machine for your Java applications as easily as you can install a Virtual Machine for your applets. As you see in the following chapter, installing the JRE is just as easy as installing a Web browser.

Third-party Virtual Machines

As if the JRE weren't enough, plenty of other Java Virtual Machines are available out there. In fact, Virtual Machines abound. Just about every major computer software vendor now offers a Virtual Machine, which means that you're likely to bump into more than one in your Java application journey. Following are a few of the vendors who currently create Virtual Machines that you use specifically to run Java applications:

✔ Apple

✔ Hewlett Packard

✔ IBM

✔ Intel

✔ Microsoft

✔ Novell

✔ Silicon Graphics

If your eyes are bugging out wondering how to choose a Virtual Machine from this list of vendors, I must add a little drama to the scene by mentioning that this list is just a partial one. Many, many more Java Virtual Machine developers are out there, with many more to come! But with all these vendors from which to choose, where in the world do you start?

Although hooking up a Virtual Machine and installing Java applications a few years ago was about as painless as a trip to Dr. Kervorkian, today, thanks to major improvements in the Java technology over the years, installing a Virtual Machine and hooking up Java applications is a breeze. In Chapter 14, you find out all about choosing and installing Virtual Machines and Java applications. For now, however, I can ease your fears by telling you that installing a Virtual Machine and hooking up Java applications is no more difficult than is installing a traditional software program. Today, it's all a point-and-click affair.

Where Do All the <APPLET> Tags Go?!

If Java applications are more like traditional applications than applets, how do you go about hooking them up and customizing them for your own needs? After all, you must weave applets into Web pages by using the <APPLET> tag, as I describe in Chapters 7 and 8. Java applications, on the other hand, live on your personal computer just as traditional applications do, entirely outside Web pages. With this difference in mind, you may wonder what happens to the <APPLET> tag that's so fundamental to applets?

Well, I was hoping to avoid this topic, but I can see no way around it. Brace yourself, dear friend. The <APPLET> tag faces total annihilation if you're dealing with Java applications. You don't need, want, or use it. It's gone. Poof. Bye-bye.

Whew. That was painful — but true. Java applications have no need whatsoever for <APPLET> tags or any other HTML tag, for that matter, because you don't weave them into Web pages.

Similarly, you don't need to use <APPLET> tags to weave applications into Web pages, simply because you *don't* weave applications into Web pages in the first place. So what's the deal in customizing applications?

Although you're not weaving applications into Web pages, what about customizing them? Wouldn't the <APPLET> tag still prove useful for customizing how Java applications look and act, even if they're not inside of Web pages?

Yep, it would, but even better ways of customizing your Java applications exist. C'mon, get honest here. Don't tell me that you actually *like* futzing around with <APPLET> tags and PARAM attributes? You can tell me the truth. Personally, I hate it!

Customizing applications with point-and-click settings

Instead of typing all the parameters that tell a program how to behave, as you do with <APPLET> tag PARAM attributes, I prefer to use my mouse to customize programs whenever possible. Fortunately, most Java applications enable you to configure settings and customize behavior by using menus, check boxes, dialog boxes, and other graphical elements.

Naturally, you must tuck away somewhere the settings and behaviors that you customize by using your mouse if the application is to recall your preferences each time it runs. And so the fact that most Java applications store settings inside "setting" and "preference" files that you can load each time the program runs shouldn't surprise you at all.

Most Java applications allow you to use your mouse to change settings and customize the program's behavior, just as you do with any other program. You're not supposed to deal directly with the settings and preferences files as you do with applets — I discuss in Chapter 4 how you can customize applets by using HTML code to configure <APPLET> tag settings — that's the application's job.

But if you're hell-bent on getting down and dirty in customizing your applications, just as you do with applets, don't lose hope. You can customize some applications in the following ways:

  ✔ **Command-Line Parameters:** If you've lived in the UNIX or DOS worlds, you're likely to know what command-line parameters are. If your experience extends only to Macintosh or Windows 95/98 operating systems, however, you're in for a rude awakening. *Command-line parameters* are closest in nature to <APPLET> tag parameters; they're parameters that you supply in text form, on the command line (or prompt), as an application runs. The following line is a simple example of a command-line parameter passing to a Java application with the name "Sort":

```
java Sort addressbook.txt
```

In this example, you invoke the Virtual Machine by using the `java` command. Following the Virtual Machine command is the name of the Java application that you want to run — in this case, `Sort`. Of course, Sort doesn't run all by itself. Heavens, no — that would be too easy. You must supply it with the name of a file that you want it to sort, which in this case is `addressbook.txt`.

The preceding example is fictitious because Sort doesn't exist, but you get the general idea. In cases where you run an application on the command line, you may find that you can customize it by using command-line parameters. Naturally, the capability to customize an application this way depends entirely on the application itself. Fortunately, you can run most Java applications the same way that you run standard applications (that is, by double-clicking an icon instead of typing commands at a UNIX or DOS prompt). But in cases where an application executes by use of a command-line prompt, you often find that you customize the application by supplying parameters as well.

✔ **Batch File Settings:** In the unlikely event that you actually must invoke an application at the command line, you can probably just create a "batch" file containing the commands that you'd otherwise need to type manually. Unless you're already comfortable dealing with batch files, however, I see no sense in diving into the nitty-gritty details here. Just know that batch files can serve as an alternative means for customizing Java applications that you run from the command line. That much information should suffice for now.

Dealing with command lines and batch files isn't for everyone. In fact, it's for a very small portion of the world to be perfectly honest. If you'd like to be counted as one of the few who feel as comfortable at the command line as you do at the mouse, you should consider picking up the latest edition of *DOS For Dummies* by Dan Gookin (IDG Books Worldwide, Inc.). Better yet, if you have a friend of relative who knows the ancient art of batch files and command lines, why not whip up a splendid soufflé and invite her over to dinner? Chances are you'll get a freebie tutorial out of the deal. After all, who can resist your mouth watering soufflé?

Chapter 14

Hooking Up Java Applications

· ·

In This Chapter

▶ Picking a Java Runtime Environment (JRE)

▶ Installing your first Java application

▶ Customizing Java applications

▶ Caring for your applications

· ·

*A*s I discuss in the preceding chapter, Java applications have skyrocketed in popularity lately. In fact, Java applications seem to be getting more attention these days than applets. And for good reason: Java applications are typically powerful, reliable, network-savvy programs that are just as easy to install and use as traditional applications.

Java applications run entirely outside your Web browser, which means they aren't constrained in any way by the "sandbox" that intentionally cripples applets (see Chapters 2 and 13 for details). As a result, Java applications more closely resemble traditional desktop applications than they do Web-based applets, which accounts for their rising popularity. However, because they possess the ability to "reach out and touch" the Internet, thanks to being developed with the network-centric Java programming language, Java applications often combine the best qualities that traditional applications offer with the network savvy innate to applets.

In a sense, Java applications can be thought of as applets "unplugged." Java programs don't *need* the Web in order to survive, although they tend to tap into the Internet in ways that traditional applications don't. However, the ability to run Java applications on your desktop doesn't come for free. Even though you don't need a Web browser to run them, you do need a Java Runtime Environment (JRE) of some sort, as I mention in Chapter 13.

The terms Java Runtime Environment (JRE) and Virtual Machine (VM) are, for all intents and purposes, interchangeable. If you want to get technical about it, a JRE always has at its center a VM that's ultimately responsible for converting bytecode into native machine code. However, you can use the two terms interchangeably in general conversation.

Only a real geek knows that a JRE builds on top of a VM, while everyone else in the world happily accepts that they're one and the same. This fact makes it easy to spot the technodweeb lurking about at your dinner party. Simply pipe up with "Hey, aren't JREs and VMs the same thing?" Anyone who tries to explain that they're fundamentally different should be quietly led out the back door.

Thankfully, you don't have to think much (or at all) about the JRE in most cases. While it's true that in the early days of Java you had to be terribly intimate with the runtime environment your applications operated within, times have changed for the better. Today, a JRE is often installed transparently along with the application itself, meaning you won't know (or care!) where it is or how it magically converts the Java bytecode your application is made of into the native machine code that your computer actually requires. All you really have to know is that your Java applications run, and that's enough.

However, even though you may never come face-to-face with a JRE thanks to the advances made in Java over the years, it's important that, at the very least, you're familiar with the various types out there should you *eventually* come upon an application that doesn't hide the gory details from you. In fact, I intentionally dig into the guts of JREs in this chapter as I explain how to manually hook up Java applications. In the meantime, take a peek at the various shapes and colors JREs come in these days.

Doing the JRE Two-Step

As I explain in Chapter 13, Java bytecode must be converted into native machine code before your computer can run, or execute, it. This is just as true for Java applications as it is for Java applets because both types of programs consist of bytecode. The major difference between applets and applications, however, boils down to *how* and *where* the bytecode conversion takes place. In both cases, the bytecode must be converted into native machine code before a computer can run it. The question is how this conversion actually takes place, and where does the JRE doing all the heavy lifting reside?

The answer to these questions really defines the difference between applets and applications. In essence, the two general answers to the question of how and where the conversion takes place are:

- A Web browser
- A standalone JRE

As Chapter 13 explains, your Web browser converts applets from bytecode to native machine code. If it weren't for the JRE built into your Java-savvy Web browser, you wouldn't be able to see or interact with applets at all. But thanks to their built-in JREs, Java-savvy Web browsers are able to convert applet bytecode into native machine code as they are downloaded over the wire (see Chapter 2).

Java applications, on the other hand, don't have a clue about the JRE that came with your Web browser. Because Java applications live on your computer and have full access to your system, they require a more heavy-duty JRE than the one in your browser. Unlike applets, which are doomed to a life inside the "sandbox," applications are free to do things applets simply cannot. Consequently, applications demand a less restrictive JRE than the ones supplied with most Web browsers.

Thanks to the Java Plug-In, applets and applications can share the same JRE under certain circumstances. Sharing a JRE, however, is the exception and not the rule. In the vast majority of cases, your Web browser has its own JRE while your applications use an entirely different one. See Chapter 10 to find out more about the Java Plug-in and how it may be shared between applets and applications.

Version Visions: Which to choose?

In most cases, you aren't given a choice when it comes to the JRE you use with your Java applications. Typically, each Java application comes with its own JRE, meaning you don't have to consciously ask yourself, "Hmmm . . . which JRE should I install in order to run this application?"

The day may come, however, when you come across some Java applications without their own JREs. In such cases, you have no choice but to get your mitts on a JRE capable of running the program. If you don't, the application will never run because there's no way for the bytecode it's made of to be converted into machine code that your computer requires.

Fortunately, this problem has an easy solution. Whenever you're forced to get your own JRE, you're always safe choosing the most recent JRE available. Sure, this sounds like a wise guy bit of advice, but it's really not. Let me explain.

JRE freebies

You see, Sun Microsystems, the makers of Java, gives away JREs. Yes indeed, in a world overrun by price-gouging software developers, Sun actually gives away several different, world-class JREs free of charge. It's an offer you really can't refuse, if you know what I mean. The question is: Which JRE should you choose?

When you visit Sun's Java Web site, home of Java as well as JREs, you're presented with different versions of the JRE from which to choose (such as JRE Versions 1.0, 1.1 and 1.2). Unless you have good reason not to, I highly recommend the highest version you can get your hands on (presently JRE 1.2). But why?

Aside from being a red-blooded American boy who simply loves to get the latest and greatest goodies, I recommend getting the most current version of the JRE for a few practical reasons also.

- **Bug fixes.** The most current JRE has the fewest number of bugs, because the problems and issues found in earlier versions are usually ironed out before this version. This isn't to say that the most current JRE is bug-free (hey, this is software after all!), it simply means that the known bugs are squashed.

- **New features.** The most current JRE supports the latest and greatest features of the Java programming language, which means you can run the most advanced Java applications in the world. If you don't use the most current JRE, however, chances are pretty good that you won't be able to run newer applications (see the sidebar "Backwards compatibility" for details).

- **Performance improvements.** The most current JRE is usually the fastest, meaning it can run your Java applications faster than older versions. As a result, Java applications running under the most current JRE run faster and smoother than they do under an older JRE.

Backwards compatibility

Keep in mind that Java applications and applets are created with the Java programming language, which itself has a version number that corresponds to the version number of a particular JRE (Java 1.2, for example, corresponds to JRE 1.2). While newer versions of the JRE can always run older versions of Java programs, the reverse is not true. You can't, for example, expect a Java program written with Java 1.2 to run under JRE 1.0 because the program may use new features of the 1.2 programming language not understood by the 1.0 runtime environment. You can, however, rely on JRE 1.2 to run Java 1.0 programs perfectly well (known as *backwards compatibility*, because the newer JRE is compatible with older versions of the Java language). This small but significant fact gives you yet one more reason to use the most current JRE to run your programs, ensuring that the runtime environment is up to snuff when it comes to new features of the Java language.

Manually installing the JRE

Even though most of the Java applications you install come with their own
JREs (or at least make the installation of a JRE invisible to you, as the
section "The easy way" explains later), at some time you may need to
manually install your own JRE.

Sun's Java Web site, `java.sun.com`, is the best place to get a fresh JRE.
Simply point your Web browser to Sun's Java site, or to Apple's Java site at
`www.apple.com/java/` if you're a Macintosh user, because Sun doesn't
make a JRE for the Mac. In either case you'll be able to download the most
current JRE with the click of your mouse. But be warned! The JRE is by no
means small; depending on the version you choose, it ranges in size from
2.5MB to more than 8MB in size. Unless you have a fast connection to the
Web, or a lot of patience, the download will seem to take an eternity. Because the JRE takes a long time to download, be certain that you actually
download the appropriate version for your needs. Nothing's more frustrating than spending an hour or more downloading a file only to find out that
you got the wrong one (except, perhaps, buying slacks a few sizes too small.
That always gets my knickers in a bunch).

Fortunately, in most cases, the only thing you need to pick out your new JRE
is a Web browser. As Figure 14-1 illustrates, your Web browser allows you to
choose the platform and version for your new JRE.

As you select your new JRE, you typically need to specify two important
pieces of information in a standard Web page request form before you can
download it from Sun's JRE Web page. Fortunately, the two pieces of info
aren't all that difficult to provide:

✔ **Platform.** Unlike Java programs, which are comprised of platform-
    independent bytecode (see Chapter 13), JREs are traditional programs
    bound to a specific platform. When you choose a JRE, be sure to get
    one that runs on your computer. A Windows 95 JRE, for example, won't
    run on a Macintosh computer, and vice-versa.

✔ **Version.** When choosing a JRE, you must also choose the version
    number. Although you have several different versions to choose from,
    it's usually a good idea to pick the most current version available for
    the reasons described earlier. If you're not sure how to read version
    numbers, take a gander at the sidebar, "Backwards compatibility," first.

Once you specify these two pieces of information, the appropriate JRE
downloads to your computer (or is copied to your computer, as the case
may be if you're choosing a JRE from CD-ROM).

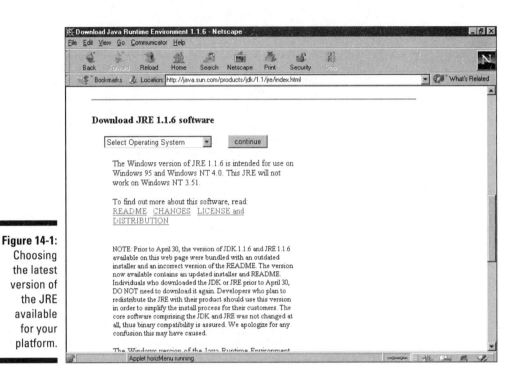

Figure 14-1:
Choosing
the latest
version of
the JRE
available
for your
platform.

Sun doesn't offer a JRE or JDK for the Macintosh platform. As a result, Macintosh users should go to Apple Computer, Inc. to get their hands on a Java Runtime Environment. Visit Apple's Java site at www.apple.com/java/. Here you'll find the Macintosh Java Runtime (MJR), Apple's own version of the JRE.

Installing Your First Java Application

Despite how riveting the concept of installing a JRE to run your Java applications is in theory, it really isn't much good until you actually *do it*. Theory, after all, is just that: an idea. And while the notion of Java applications running like the wind under the power of a JRE is exciting to talk about, it's high time you got your hands dirty. That is, it's time that you actually install your very own Java application and a JRE to power it.

As luck would have it, the CD-ROM that comes with this book has a nifty Java application on it just for you. Living Desktop, an automated desktop artwork program, is a Java application developed using Version 1.1.6 of the Java programming language. This means you need to install JRE 1.1.6 or greater in order to run the application (see the "Backwards compatibility" sidebar for details).

When it comes to installing Java applications and the JREs necessary to run them, there are, fundamentally, two ways to go about it: the "easy way" and the "hard way." Come to think of it, just about anything you do in life can be done in one of these two ways, can't it?

The easy way or the hard way. Just hearing those words reminds me of my old high school football coach, a cankerous cuss if there ever was one. He'd strut around the field like a general, yelling at the top of his lungs, "You can leave this practice field the easy way or the hard way, and either way's fine by me!" Of course, coach was a madman. But that's a different story for a different time. Now, where was I?

The easy way

Naturally, the easy way is the best way when it comes to installing *any* kind of software. I can't imagine you arguing with me here (unless, of course, you're a sadist like coach, in which case you should feel free to skip ahead to "The hard way"). After all, I don't know many people who enjoy tackling software installations head on. By this I mean manually copying files into their proper locations, monkeying with program settings and preferences, or dealing with any number of other issues involved with properly installing software.

Rather than dealing with all the particulars involved with an installation, a good installer utility does all the work for you. All you have to do is fire it up and sit back. Sure, you may have to answer a few simple questions posed by the installer utility now and again, but overall it's a cinch. In a few minutes your application and JRE will be up and running. Assuming, of course, that the Java application you want to install comes with it's own installer utility and also with it's own JRE. For example, Install Anywhere serves as one of the installer utilities for Living Desktop (see Figure 14-2).

Figure 14-2:
The Install Anywhere installer utility.

What's up, Docs?

Before you dive headlong into any software installation, be it a Java application or a traditional one, it's a good idea to read the documentation (or "docs" as they're fondly known) that comes with the program. If you don't, chances are pretty good that you'll wind up in hot water somewhere along the way. However, if you invest just a few minutes of your time reading the docs up front, you'll come out smelling like a rose when all is said and done. Let's be honest here, who doesn't want to smell like a rose?

As luck would have it, just about every application you're likely to come across will be accompanied by documentation. Whether in the form of a printed manual, a Web page, a word-processing document, or an old fashioned "README!" text file, get your hands on the docs, my friend. After you find the documentation for your program, be sure to read the section related to installation long before you try to actually install the program on your own computer. This section tells you what special needs, if any, the application has, or if it'll even run on your computer.

The documentation provided with Living Desktop comes in the form of a Web page, as well as in a text file named README. You can open either with your Web browser, or, alternately, you can open the README text file with a text editor (such as Notepad or SimpleText) or your word processor. Refer to Appendix C for details about the various programs provided on the CD-ROM that comes with this book, including Living Desktop and the documentation that accompanies this Java application.

When it comes to Java application documentation, you're almost certain to find a reference to *Java Runtime Environment* (JRE) or *Virtual Machine* (VM). In some cases, entire sections of documentation are dedicated to JREs and VMs, which is a good thing. For this is the material that tells you whether or not your program comes with its own JRE, or even its own installer utility for that matter.

In addition, the documentation for a program often includes step-by-step installation instructions, telling you precisely how to go about installing your new application from start to finish. When you find this information in your docs, you've hit the jackpot. As painful as it might be for me to admit, I'm just here to give you general directions when it comes to installing Java applications. If you spend a little time reading the documentation that comes with your applications, however, you'll turn up glorious nuggets of advice that I couldn't possibly give you (unless you invite me over, in which case I'd be delighted to spend a little time getting to know your Java applications on a more personal level).

Running the installer utility

After you cozy up with your Java application docs and confirm that your application does indeed come with an installer utility that does all the dirty work, the next step generally involves running that utility. Typically, the installer utility is named something mysterious and cryptic, such as "Installer" or "SetUp." Furthermore, the installer utility often sports an icon that cloaks its true nature, such as one found in Figure 14-3.

Figure 14-3: An icon for one of the installers for Living Desktop.

Okay, so I'm being a wee bit sarcastic here. In truth, installer utilities are pretty easy to spot; they have very obvious names and are graphically depicted with icons that make perfect sense. Sure, I could have said that right up front, but what fun would that have been?

After you locate the installer utility for your Java application, you run it by double-clicking its icon. This starts in motion the installation process. Or does it? If simply double-clicking your installer utility doesn't start the installation process automatically, perhaps you're not dealing with a real installer after all. I discuss this relatively common problem in the following section.

When is an installer not an installer?

Sometimes, what you think is an installer utility is actually nothing more than a compressed archive *containing* the real installer utility. As I mention in Chapter 13, *compressed archives* are bundles of files smooshed into one single file. The result is an archive file that you have to decompress before you can access its actual contents, which, in this particular case, is the installer utility.

Such is the case with Living Desktop. You can install this application directly from the CD-ROM, as the documentation that comes with it explains, or you can copy a compressed archive containing the installer to your personal computer. If you choose the later route, you have to decompress the archive (a simple task, really, because this particular archive is self-extracting — all you have to do is double-click it!) as illustrated in Figure 14-4.

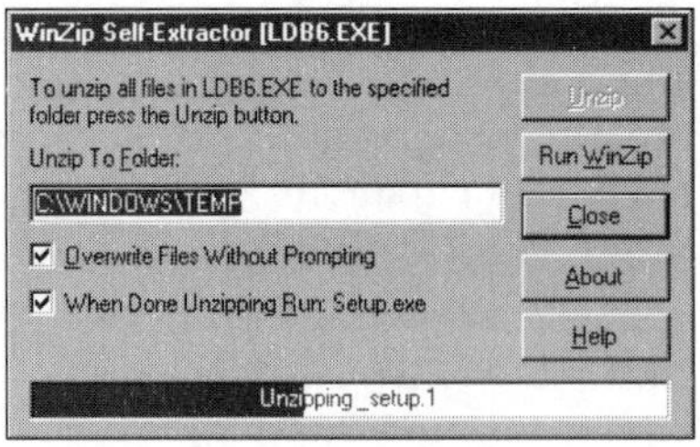

Figure 14-4:
Installer
utilities
are often
trapped
inside
compressed
archives,
and must be
extracted
before you
can use
them.

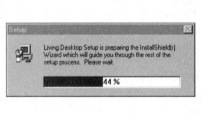

After you extract the installer utility and any associated files, you're free to
run it as described earlier in the "Running the installer utility" section. As
shown in Figure 14-5, the Living Desktop installer utility comes with a fair
number of companion files that the installer needs. All of these files, including the installer itself, are bundled into the same compressed archive. At
this point, I'm sure you're wondering why, aren't you?

Figure 14-5:
Installer
utilities
contain all
the files
needed to
install an
application
on your
computer.

In most cases, you can download Java application installers from the
Internet directly onto your computer.

In some cases, the installer utility actually installs the application while
you're downloading it. Usually, however, you must download the entire
installer utility to your computer, then run it.

Doesn't it make more sense to download a single, compressed archive
containing all the files you need, rather than downloading each file individually? Sure it does, which is why the various files that comprise an installation are often bundled snugly together into one little archive that you can

decompress after you download it. After it's decompressed, you have direct access to the installer utility and can run it as described earlier to initiate the actual installation.

"License and registration, please"

After you begin an installation, the first thing you're likely to see is a "splash screen" that usually consists of the name and logo of the product you're installing or the company that makes it. As you can see in Figure 14-6, the Living Desktop installer is no exception; the first thing you see is a splash screen showing the logo of the Mantis Development Corporation, the company that develops the product.

Figure 14-6: Installer utilities usually display a nifty splash screen before actually installing anything.

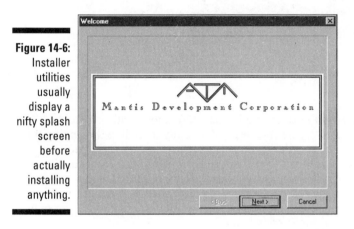

The next screen you see during the installation process typically consists of copyright and license notices, each of which you must acknowledge and agree to uphold before you're allowed to continue. In the good old days, when software came in boxes, you had to physically rip open a package containing the diskettes or CD-ROM you purchased. On the outside of the package, a license agreement of some sort was attached. More often than not, the license agreement actually sealed the envelope containing the diskettes or CD-ROM. That license agreement, known commonly as a "Shrink Wrap License," had to be physically torn or ripped by you, the licensee, the act of which constituted your agreement to the terms set forth in that license.

Because software downloaded over the Internet isn't transported in a physical container (such as an envelope or box), it's impossible to include the physical Shrink Wrap License agreements so common in the world of commercial software. Instead, Java applications typically come with what's known as a "Click Wrap License," the digital equivalent to a Shrink Wrap License. Instead of ripping open the license to indicate acceptance of the terms, you simply click a button to continue with the installation (see Figure 14-7).

Figure 14-7:
Installer
utilities
display
"Click Wrap
License"
agreements
which
govern the
terms under
which you
may use the
software
being
installed.

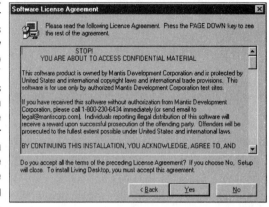

Options galore

Following the copyright notices and license agreements, all hell breaks loose. At this point, you're on the verge of actually installing the application on your computer. But in order to do this, the installer may ask you a number of questions. And while answering the questions may seem like an annoyance, don't simply dismiss the questions without first understanding what the implications are. If you're quick to click the OK, Next or Continue buttons on the screen, chances are pretty good that you'll end up agreeing to something that you don't really want.

Instead, take the time to read each of the items your installer presents to you, such as the one shown in Figure 14-8. Answering these questions thoughtfully is another example of investing a small amount of time up-front in exchange for a larger payoff down the road. Following are just a few of the types of questions your installer may ask:

✔ Who should the software be licensed to?

✔ Where do you want to put the software programs you're about to install?

✔ Where do you want to place a shortcut (or *alias,* if you're a Macintosh user) to the application?

✔ Would you like the full installation, or just a portion of the actual program installed?

✔ What portions of the program do you want to install?

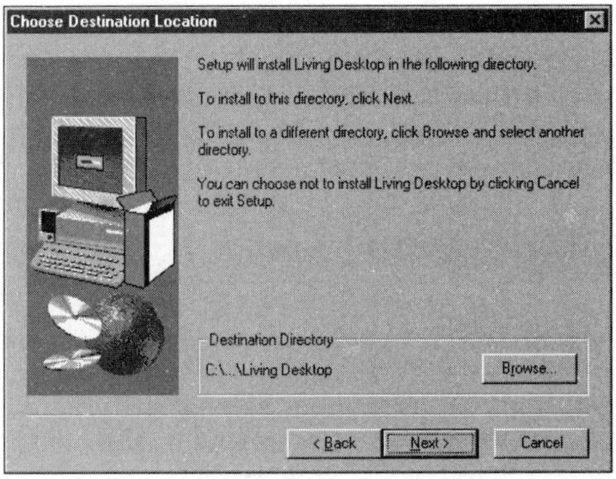

Figure 14-8:
Be sure to
read and
understand
each of the
questions
you're
asked
during the
installation
process.

> **Choose Destination Location**
>
> Setup will install Living Desktop in the following directory.
>
> To install to this directory, click Next.
>
> To install to a different directory, click Browse and select another directory.
>
> You can choose not to install Living Desktop by clicking Cancel to exit Setup.
>
> Destination Directory
> C:\...\Living Desktop   [Browse...]
>
> [< Back] [Next >] [Cancel]

- Can the installer delete a few unused files to make room for the new ones you're installing?

- Should this application run automatically each time your computer is started (booted)?

- Should this application run automatically immediately before your computer is shut down or restarted?

- Can I take your mom on a date?

Naturally, it's tempting to agree to anything just to get on with the installation. But what you may not realize in your zeal to get to the end of the installation is that each of the questions your installer asks *is itself* part of the installation! The answers you supply dictate a great deal of the installation process, providing a convenient and powerful means to customize your application setup to fit your needs.

Start me up!

After you answer all the questions your installer utility asks, the installation is just about done. The only thing you can do now is sit back and relax while the installer copies the various files your new program needs onto your computer. When everything is set, you're notified with a dialog box announcing that a successful installation has taken place (conversely, if the installation fails, you receive a notice explaining why it couldn't be completed).

Assuming the installation is successful, you may have to restart your computer in order for the changes to take hold. While this isn't always the case, I'd guess that about half of all Java application installations are followed by a restart. Usually, the installer is smart enough to restart your computer, although sometimes you have to quit the installer utility and restart yourself.

Run, baby, run

In any event, after you complete the installation process, it's time to run your new Java application. In most cases, this means you have to locate the program and run it yourself (either by double-clicking its icon or choosing its name from the Program or Application menu). In some cases, however, the application automatically runs when your computer starts, meaning you don't have to manually run it.

Living Desktop, for example, is supposed to run when your computer starts up. So, all you have to do to run Living Desktop is restart your computer. Not all programs lend themselves to running at startup, however, as the section, "Running at startup" explains later. In fact, some programs are supposed to run when you shut down your computer, or restart it, as a last-minute housekeeping task before your computer is turned off.

The majority of programs, however, are akin to your word processor, games, or Web browser. That is to say that they're neither startup or shutdown programs, but instead wait in the wings until you decide that *you* want to run them. In this respect, I suppose it's fair to say that most Java applications are at your beck and call, just as most traditional applications are. Is that a rush of power-induced exhilaration I'm sensing?

The hard way

Without a doubt, I prefer installing Java applications the easy way. What's not to love? All you have to do is run an installer utility, answer a few questions, and shazam! You're up and running with your new application in no time, perhaps even forgetting that a JRE was installed at the same time. But sometimes you're not so lucky. Sometimes, you have to suffer for your Java applications.

It's not often that you come across a Java application worth installing that doesn't come with its very own installer utility, but once in a while you bump into an application that has to be manually installed. In these situations, not only do you have to install the application manually, chances are pretty good that you have to install the JRE manually as well!

In such cases, the honeymoon is clearly over. The gloves come off and you find yourself slugging it out with any number of issues that an installer utility normally takes care of. If you're not careful, you'll find yourself hip deep in installation waters that you wish you'd never waded into. But with a bit of foresight, you'll come out alive and even victorious.

Round 1: Know thy enemy

If you thought I was bullish on reading documentation when installing an application the easy way (see "What's up, Docs?" earlier in this chapter), it probably won't come as any surprise that I'm utterly insane when it comes to documentation in cases where you have to manually install the application and JRE yourself.

In fact, if an application doesn't come with documentation of any sort, it's a good idea to steer clear of it entirely. Think about it. If a program isn't important enough to come with documentation explaining how to install and use it, is it worth installing in the first place? Probably not.

However, most Java applications are accompanied by documentation that tells you how to go about installing the application on your own computer. Before you even think about installing these applications, set aside a serious chunk of time to read and absorb the documentation they come with. Unlike those applications that come with installation utilities, manual installations require much more up-front consideration.

Think of reading your application's documentation as preparation for a big prize fight. If you win, you'll walk out with a brand-spanking new application on your computer, not to mention the rosy-cheeked glow that comes courtesy of the adrenaline rush sure to follow your success. If you lose, on the other hand, you'll be frustrated or perhaps even angry, and almost certainly sporting a bruised ego in knowing that a program bested you.

All around, losing is a bad scene, and I haven't even mentioned the potential risk to your computer if you're unable to pull off the installation. You can do plenty of damage to the guts of your system, which is precisely why you need to spend a good deal of time reading your Java application documentation well in advance of the actual installation.

Round 2: Flight or fight?

After you read an application's docs thoroughly, you're in a much better position to decide whether to continue with the installation. At the very least, you have a much better idea of what it takes to manually install the program, and you can call the whole thing off before it even gets started if you're getting in over your head.

If you're convinced that an application's worth the effort of installing, the documentation that accompanies it will solidify that feeling. You need only read through the docs once to be certain that you're doing the right thing; if an application's docs don't tell you how to install it, run like the wind.

Running up your application

After you install a Runtime Environment for your Java application, it's time to actually run the application. When you install an application the easy way, as I describe earlier, you generally don't have to bother with the details that follow. When you manually install an application, however, things are different. Rather than relying on a friendly installer utility to do everything for you, the "hard way" means that you have to do everything yourself. This includes actually *running* the application, because you first have to know what form your application is in before you can run it (something an installer utility knows, which is just one more reason to take the easy road if you have a choice). Fortunately, figuring out what form your application is in is a cinch because Java applications only come in one of two possible forms:

✔ **Standalone executable:** Looks like a standard application. On the Windows platform, for example, the application filename has the .exe extension, indicating that it's an application.

✔ **Class files:** Many Java applications are in the form of class files. Class files, as you may recall from Chapter 13, contain the intermediate bytecode an application is comprised of.

How you hook up your application depends on the form your Java application comes in. If the application is in standalone form, you really don't have much to do except run it as you would any other program. Simply double-click the application, and it starts up as any of your other programs do. Java class files, on the other hand, require a little extra work.

When you're dealing with class files, it's important to remember that, unlike with standalone applications, you're responsible for manually passing class files through your Runtime Environment. To accomplish this, you choose from two command line options (that is, you can run two different programs at a command line prompt):

✔ jre. This command opens a console window (refer to Figures 12-1 and 12-2) so you can see what's going on when a .class file passes through the JRE. The console window is very helpful for troubleshooting Java applications, because any problems with a program are listed in the console window. The following code illustrates how you run Living Desktop on the command line by using the jre command:

```
jre -cp . LivingDesktop
```

✔ jrew. This command runs your Java application without a console window, so it appears like a traditional application. Without the console window, you're not as likely to know if a program doesn't operate properly because you don't see any error messages. Run Living Desktop on the command line by using the jrew command:

```
jrew -cp . LivingDesktop
```

In either case, you have to type in a fair amount of information when running an application from the command line. Unlike most applications that are installed the easy way, you don't have any pretty icons to double-click. Instead, you have to manually type in the commands yourself each time you wish to run the application.

Alternately, you can create a *batch file* that contains the commands necessary to run your application. Batch files are nothing more than text files that contain commands that you would otherwise type in at the command line. You can, for example, create a plain text file that contains nothing more than the commands necessary to run the Living Desktop application. You can then double-click that text file to run Living Desktop, just as you would double-click the Living Desktop application icon if it were installed the easy way. Placing the commands that you need to run Living Desktop in a batch file saves you the effort of typing them in at the command line each time you want to run the application.

Whether you choose to pass your Java class files through the JRE via the jre command or the jrew command is entirely up to you. However, because the jre command allows you to see a console window while your application is running, I prefer to use it the first time I hook up a Java program. This way, I can easily troubleshoot my Java applications thanks to the corresponding console window. Then, after I'm sure that an application runs just fine under the jre, I usually switch to the jrew because there's no need for the console window at that point.

You omit the .class file extension entirely when executing Java applications from the command line. The jre and jrew commands, expect only the name of the application to follow, not the extension.

You may wonder what's going on with the -cp that appears between the jre and jrew commands and the program named LivingDesktop. The -cp is an *environment variable,* which brings me to my next point about manually executing Java applications from the command line. Read the following "Fiddling with environment variables" to find out what environment variables are and why Java applications require them.

If you haven't run programs at the command line before, the entire concept of a "command line" may be a bit difficult to grasp. Windows users can open a command line by selecting the MS-DOS Prompt option from the Programs menu (choose Start⇨Programs⇨MS-DOS Prompt), at which point you can type in a command such as **jre** or **jrew**. I'm assuming, of course, that you've already installed the JRE! If you haven't, the commands jre and jrew aren't available. You must first install the JRE as described earlier in order to execute the jre and jrew commands at the command line. Macintosh users, on the other hand, don't have to deal with the command line at all because the Macintosh Java Runtime (MJR) provided by Apple Computer (www.apple.com/java) enables Mac users to run Java applications directly by double-clicking class files.

Fiddling with environment variables

One of the beauties of installing Java applications the easy way is that you don't have to deal with environment variables when you want to run your programs. *Environment variables,* as the name implies, are settings that alter how your computer system (also known as a computer *environment*) behaves. Java applications rely on two environment variables in particular:

✔ CLASSPATH. The CLASSPATH environment variable tells your Java Runtime Environment where to look for the class files that comprise an application. As I explain in Chapter 13, Java applets and applications are created by using class files. What I don't mention in Chapter 13, however, is that Java technology allows class files to be scattered in different folders on your computer — or even across the Internet! — and the applet or application will still run properly. The CLASSPATH environment variable, represented on the command line by -cp, tells your Java Runtime Environment *where* to look for the various class files that make up your application. If, for example, some of the class files that make up the Living Desktop application are in a directory named "howdy," you type the following at the command line:

```
jre -cp howdy LivingDesktop
```

However, if the same directory as the application itself contains all the class files, you can use a period (.) to tell the JRE not to bother looking elsewhere:

```
jre -cp . LivingDesktop
```

This, in fact, is the correct way to run Living Desktop. All the class files that comprise Living Desktop are contained in the same folder as the application itself, so you don't have to bother setting the CLASSPATH environment variable to a special folder. Simply use the period (.) as shown above.

✔ PATH. The Java Runtime Environment is a software program that converts Java bytecode into native code before running applets and applications, as the previous chapter describes. As a software program, the JRE (or JDK, if you've installed that) resides in a folder somewhere on your computer. You can describe the exact location of any program on your computer by using what's known as a *directory path*. The Living Desktop application, for example, resides in the following directory path on my computer:

```
c:\Program Files\Living Desktop
```

Likewise, the JRE on my system can be located by its own unique directory path:

```
c:\Java\JRE
```

As you might guess, you can locate every file on your computer by using a directory path. The PATH environment variable, not surprisingly, tells your computer where applications are located on your machine. In order for the JRE application to do its magic, you must set the PATH environment variable with a proper directory path that leads to the program. Fortunately, the JRE installer utility sets the PATH environment variable for you, so you don't have to bother. It's important to know, however, what a directory path is and how it relates to the PATH environment variable in case you need to know this information at some point in the future. If, for example, you move the JRE program into a different folder on your computer, the PATH environment variable is no longer valid. As a result, you need to update PATH accordingly.

The PATH environment variable is set each time you start your computer. On a Windows system, the JRE installer utility updates the autoexec.bat batch file (typically located in the root level of your primary hard drive) with a line of text that sets PATH accordingly. If you move the JRE, you should edit your autoexec.bat file so that the PATH environment variable contains the correct directory path leading to the JRE. This is an advanced maneuver, however. Don't move the JRE program or change your PATH environment variable unless you know exactly what you're doing!

Running at startup

Although the Living Desktop application is designed to run automatically each time you start your computer, the same isn't true for other programs. Sometimes, however, you use a program so often that you want it to run automatically at startup in order to save you the hassle of running it yourself.

To run an application at startup, all you have to do is place a shortcut (or alias, as Macintosh users say) to the application in a special folder called, not surprisingly, the "startup" folder. The precise name of this folder, and where you'll find it, depends on the type of computer you use:

✔ **Windows.** The StartUp folder can be found at the following directory path (were C is presumed to be your primary hard drive):

```
C:\WINDOWS\Start Menu\Programs\StartUp
```

✔ **Macintosh.** The Startup Items folder can be found inside the System folder.

You can prevent an application from running at startup by removing it from the startup folder. To do so, simply locate the startup folder and delete the shortcut that points to the application that you don't want to run at startup time.

Windows users can quickly access the StartUp folder by choosing Start⇨ Setting⇨Taskbar & Start Menu. Choose the Start Menu Items tab from the dialog box that appears and then click the Advanced button. At this point you can explore the contents of your Start menu. Inside the Programs folder you find a folder named StartUp.

Care and Feeding of Java Applications

After you have a Java application up and running, you've already done the most difficult part. The rest, as they say, is gravy. As with traditional applications, you can now play with your new program as often as you like, and experience the features it offers.

Of course, you're likely to grow tired of your Java application in time. What was once fresh and new eventually becomes stale, old news, and you start to take your Java application for granted. When you reach this point, consider updating your application.

As with traditional applications, Java applications are developed incrementally over time. By the time you install and become comfortable with your new Java application, it may actually be outdated! Fortunately, Java applications are extremely easy to upgrade, generally speaking, because they have an intimate relationship with the Internet. Rather than trucking on out to a store to purchase an upgrade, as you might with a standard application, you can often update Java applications directly over the Internet with little or no effort.

Because every Java application is different, I can't offer a precise, standard way of updating them. What works for one program doesn't necessarily work for another. There are, however, two *general* methods that Java applications commonly use for updates. Some applications can be updated using both methods, enabling you to choose how you'll update your program, while some applications use one method or the other. Fortunately, both update methods are usually painless:

  ✔ **Dynamic updates.** Because most Java applications are Internet-savvy, many of them are capable of dynamically updating themselves. In such cases, the application knows how to reach out onto the Internet, find the files it needs to update itself, and can go about the whole process unattended. All you do is sit back in amazement as your Java application dynamically adds new capabilities to itself. Applications that support dynamic updates typically feature a button or menu item such as "Update Now" or "Check for Updates," which makes getting the latest version easy. Read the documentation that came with your application to find out exactly how (or even if) the application may be dynamically updated.

✔ **Manual updates.** Although some Java applications are capable of dynamically updating themselves, others require you to manually visit an "updating" Web site. You can usually find the location of the updating Web site in your application's documentation or in the help menu of the program (assuming your Java application has a help menu!). Once there you can download an *update utility,* which is much like an installer, except that it contains only the files needed to update your existing Java application, as opposed to the entire application itself. After downloading the update utility, you run it (just as you did the installer utility) and follow any instructions that appear. When all is said and done, you will have manually updated your Java application.

Doing a manual application update, you need to exercise a little more caution than when the application dynamically updates itself. Two areas in particular need special attention:

✔ **Keep your versions straight.** When you manually update an application, be certain that the update utility you use is the correct version for the application you're running. If, for example, you're running Living Desktop Version 1.0 for Window 98, download the appropriate update utility from the Web. An update utility designed for Macintosh won't do you any good, nor would an update utility created for Version 2.0 of the application.

✔ **Each to its own (directory, that is).** Assuming you download the appropriate update utility for your Java application, the next thing to do is run it. If you know what directory the application resides in, you can update with ease, because at some point, the update utility is likely to ask you to tell it where on your computer the application resides. If you don't know, you're in trouble! In this case, it's best to cancel the update utility and consult your application documentation to find out where on your computer the program exists. If you can't give the computer directions, chances are pretty good that the update utility won't be able to do its magic (although some update utilities are smart enough to find the application they need).

To further complicate matters, you must take great care to select the proper version of an application if you happen to have multiple versions of the same application installed. You might, for example, have Living Desktop 1.0 and 2.0 residing on your system at the same time, in which case you have to be extra careful to use the correct utility when manually updating one or the other. However, because most unique versions of an application reside in their own directories (Living Desktop 1.0 and 2.0 each have a separate directory, for example), all you have to do is tell the installer which to update and you'll be fine.

Part IV
The Part of Tens

The 5th Wave   By Rich Tennant

"You know, I've asked you a dozen times not to animate the torches on our Web page!"

In this part . . .

Ah, the Part of Tens. What would a *...For Dummies* book be without it? Take a peek at the ten hottest Java-powered Web sites, the ten best places on the Internet to find Java help, the ten liveliest applet and application sites, and the ten most common pitfalls Java users around the world fall prey to.

Chapter 15

Ten Places to Find Java Help on the Web

*A*s you travel down the road toward Java nirvana, you will no doubt have questions about this fascinating technology. Perhaps you'll even require help from time to time as your Web pages become more sophisticated and your Java applications more mission-critical. Naturally, the best place to find Java-related help is on the Web itself. In this chapter, you find ten (or so) of the best Java help sites out there, each of which contains even more links to Java-related resources and support sites.

Apple Computer, Inc.

Not one to be left out of a good thing, the folks at Apple have embraced Java as if it were their own. Apple's Java site allows Macintosh users to download and install the Mac OS Runtime for Java (MRJ), a special Java Virtual Machine for Macintosh computers. At the site, you also find links to other Apple-flavored Java pages, including the MRJ Frequently Asked Questions (FAQ) site that answers just about any question you can think of when it comes to running Java on Macintosh computers:

```
www.apple.com/macos/java/
```

IBM

IBM is one of the largest and most significant contributors to Java technology. Over the years, IBM has partnered with Sun on many different development issues related to Java. Claiming to have the most Java software developers of any company in the world, Big Blue has a mean brew waiting for you at:

```
www.ibm.com/java/
```

The IDG Books Worldwide Java Resource Center

IDG Books Worldwide, Inc., the leading publisher of computer-related materials (including the book you're reading now), is on the Web — and the site's Java-powered! Visit the Java Resource Center often to find out all about IDG Books Worldwide's current Java titles and those coming down the pike — and pick up applets and source code while you're there. At this site, you can get the latest scoop (and plenty of links!) on this constantly evolving technology. Visit IDG Books at the following Web address:

```
www.idgbooks.com/rc/java
```

Java FAQ Archives

Frequently Asked Questions, or *FAQs,* are plain, old-fashioned text documents bursting at the seams with detailed questions and their corresponding answers — well worth consulting if you have a question that you think others may have asked before. Fortunately, you can visit the Java FAQ Archives site if your question is in any way related to Java. If you have questions about cheese, however, you must look elsewhere. For those Java questions, check out the following URL:

```
www-net.com/java/faq
```

Java Life

Billed as "All The Buzz That's Fit To Click," *Java Life* is a Web and e-mail publication that keeps you abuzz with useful and interesting Java-related news and events. As a *Java For Dummies* reader, your subscription to *Java Life* is on the house, courtesy of Mantis Development Corporation. Sign up for your free *Java Life* subscription today; it's my way of saying thanks for reading this book. And visit the site at the following Web address:

```
www.mantiscorp.com/javalife/
```

JavaSoft

As the makers of Java, Sun Microsystems, Inc., is responsible for developing, marketing, and supporting Java technology. A ton of Java-related information is available here, including links to external Java sites. If you want to stay on top of this rapidly moving technology, visit often at:

```
java.sun.com
```

In addition to Sun's main Java site, you may find the online Java tutorial handy. Although it's a bit technical, the Java Tutorial is a wonderful learning tool that teaches you how to use Java step-by-step.

```
java.sun.com/tutorial
```

JavaWorld

As Olivia Newton-John may say, "Let's get technical, technical. I wanna get technical, technical. Let me hear your Java talk!" To stay on the cutting edge of Java, visit IDG's *JavaWorld,* a Web-based magazine dedicated entirely to Java, in which you can find articles, applets, applications and source code written by professional Java developers. And it's available for free! Take a trip to *JavaWorld* at the following URL:

```
www.javaworld.com
```

Microsoft

No one said life was fair, so why should you expect Netscape to have all the fun? Microsoft has waged a fierce battle in an attempt to make away with Netscape's crown jewels: the Java-savvy browser market. But while the two companies duke things out in true gladiator fashion, we're the ones who really make out like bandits with all the free information, Java applets, and slick Java-powered Web page examples that these two give away in hopes of drawing users to their sites. And why not? War is hell, so get what you can while the gettin' is good. Check out Microsoft at the following URL:

```
www.microsoft.com/java/
```

Netscape Communications

What better place to find out about Java than from the company that helped make it a star? Here you find plenty of Java-related information and links, as well as the most current versions of the world's most popular Java-savvy browser, Netscape Navigator. Visit Netscape at the following Web address:

```
www.netscape.com
```

Yahoo!

One of the first search engines to catalog the Web, Yahoo! is the place to visit if you're searching for Java sites (or anything else, for that matter). Yahoo! not only enables you to search the Web for Java resources, but it also organizes many of the better Java links for easy access.

To search by using Yahoo!, visit the following URL:

```
www.yahoo.com
```

To view Yahoo!'s Java links, surf directly to the following Web address:

```
www.yahoo.com/Computers_and_Internet/Programming_Languages/
        Java/
```

Chapter 16

Ten Rock 'n' Roll Web Sites for Finding Applets

In This Chapter

▶ Rock 'n' roll Web sites for finding Java applets

▶ Hip 'n' happening Java-powered Web sites

*W*hether you're new to Java or an old pro, you want to keep your Web pages flowing with fresh, innovative applets. Thankfully, you'll find no lack of applets on the Web — with your trusted Web browser at hand, you have everything you need to quench your thirst for Java. Here you'll find a bevy of Web sites (ten or so) overflowing with fresh and invigorating Java. Fire up that browser and take off!

AltaVista

If you're hankering for that special applet and can't track it down through any one of the previously listed sites, you can turn to the AltaVista search engine. Created and maintained by Digital Equipment Corporation (DEC), which was recently bought by Compaq, AltaVista has a leg up on its competition when it comes to Java: This search engine lets you find applets that have already been woven into Web pages by their exact name.

Thanks to this innovative feature, you can, for example, search for an applet named "FlyingPig" and be certain that only those Web pages that contain a Java applet whose name matches exactly (including the precise mixture of upper- and lowercase characters) will be referenced. After all, when you're searching for "FlyingPig," anything less simply won't do.

`altavista.digital.com`

Gamelan

The mother of all Java sites, Gamelan is a comprehensive Java repository with links to all things Java. You'll find links to tons of applets, information sites, help areas, and much, much more. If you can't find it on Gamelan, it probably doesn't exist.

```
www.gamelan.com
```

Java Applet Rating Service (JARS)

A repository with a twist: a rating system! This site has links to top-rated applets (according to a large panel of judges). When you look at the JARS Top 1% list of applets, you know that you're dealing with the cream of the crop.

But before you dive in, you should know a few things about this Java Applet Rating Service. First, it has no association with the compressed Java Archive files (JAR files) that I talk about in this book. And second, you must enter the URL that follows this paragraph *exactly* as it is shown if you intend to wind up at the site I'm talking about. There's another site out there that uses a different mix of uppercase and lowercase letters (although it has the exact same address). If you don't type the address that follows in all lowercase characters, you won't end up where you really want to go!

```
www.jars.com
```

The Java Boutique

Let's see . . . the last time you went to a boutique it was most likely quite small and overpriced, and it sported a funky-looking staff that gave off serious attitude. But then again, what did you expect from the real world? Things are a little better in cyberspace, as the Java Boutique illustrates. True, the site may be small — it houses just over 100 applets — but the applets are free and they all contain instructions for downloading and weaving them into your Web pages. What's more, you find a clear and refreshing absence of attitude. Now, if only pricey designer boutiques in the real world could be more like the Java Boutique. . . .

```
javaboutique.internet.com
```

The Java Centre

Located in the United Kingdom, The Java Centre (that's right, "centre," not "center!" — folks in the UK have swapped the "re" around just to make life interesting) is a watered-down version of the Gamelan site previously listed. That's not to say that The Java Centre isn't useful; heavens no! (Hey, some folks don't like strong coffee.) If Gamelan seems overwhelming to you, check out The Java Centre — it's visually appealing, well organized, and chock full of useful and exciting Java applets.

```
www.java.co.uk
```

jCentral

You know Java has reached epic proportions when Big Blue gets in the game. jCentral is IBM's comprehensive Java site, packed to the brim with applets, applications, source code, research papers, articles, and tons of other Java goodies. It even includes a nifty search utility that helps you track down the perfect applet. What more could you ask for from the company that practically defined the word *computer?*

```
www.ibm.com/java
```

LivingLinks

Want to add more special effects (plug-ins) to the LivingLinks applet provided on the Cool Beans! portion of this book's companion CD-ROM? How about more cutting-edge CookBook pages with recipes for some of the hottest Java-powered sites on the Web? Perhaps you want to see how sites from around the world are using this state-of-the-art applet to turn standard Web pages into dynamic, living ones? Or maybe you just want to surf the Web using LivingLinks-powered buttons? If so, then this is the site for you!

```
www.livinglinks.com
```

Mantis Java Links

This master page provides links to all Java sites I mention in this book — and many more sites — and keeps them up-to-date to ensure that you always have access even if those URLs change. In addition, all Cool Beans! applets are available for downloading through this site, including new ones that aren't on your CD-ROM. But perhaps the most tantalizing reason to fire up your browser and visit today is the free subscription to *JavaLife* that awaits. This exclusive digital publication delivers "All The Buzz That's Fit To Click" directly to your e-mail inbox, and it is available free of charge to all *Java For Dummies* readers. All you have to do is ask, so don't be shy.

```
www.mantiscorp.com/java
```

Chapter 17
Ten Kickin' Java Applications

● ●

In This Chapter

▶ Must-have Java applications
▶ Killer Java application Web sites

● ●

*U*nlike ubiquitous Java applets that seem to appear at every twist and turn on the Web, Java applications are considerably less plentiful. As a result, you have to look a little harder to get your mitts on top-notch Java applications. Making matters more complicated is the fact that Java applications have full and unrestricted access to your computer after they're installed because they don't require you to explicitly grant them security privileges as applets do. This easy access means that you have to be exceptionally careful in deciding what applications to install on your computer. Installing a malicious application on your computer is akin to letting a pit bull stand guard over a mountain of sausage — it's just a matter of time before things get ugly.

Thankfully, plenty of wonderful, trustworthy Java applications are out there if you know where to look. And that's just what this chapter is about. Stand back, my friend, and get ready to "kick apps and take names!"

HotJava

Who can resist the Web browser that started the Java craze? If you want to get your hands on the latest and greatest Java applet technology, HotJava's the browser to have. Created by Sun, the company that invented Java, HotJava is the only commercially available browser in the world created entirely with the Java programming language.

    java.sun.com/products/hotjava/

IQSuite

Despite the good-natured reputation Java applications have, they aren't all fun and games. Take IQSuite, for example. IQSuite is a powerful package of advanced Internet-based stock trading tools designed for the financial novice and genius alike. Hey, who doesn't have a closet accountant lurking inside of them? C'mon. Loosen up and show your nerd side. And while you're at it, why not make it financially worthwhile with IQSuite?

```
www.iqc.com
```

JavaStudio

JavaStudio is a visual Java programming environment for the rest of us. If you've ever wanted to create your own Java applets and applications but were too shy to start programming, JavaStudio's for you. Not only is it designed for ordinary people who don't want to write code, JavaStudio is also perfect for experienced code-jockeys who want to rapidly create prototypes, JavaBeans, and even working applications.

```
shop.sun.com/
```

JSNTP (The Application Formerly Known as "TickTock")

Do you know what time it is? Does your computer? If you had the JSNTP Java application, formally known as "TickTock," you'd both know! This clever little Java application synchronizes your computer clock with the master time clocks at the U.S. Naval Observatory. Thanks to Java and the Internet, JSNTP makes sure that your computer clock is within one second of absolute accuracy. Guess I need to come up with a better excuse for being late all the time now that JSNTP on my computer. Tick-tock . . . Tick-tock . . . Tick-tock . . .

```
www.kcmultimedia.com/jsntp/
```

LiveAgent Pro

Has the monotony of surfing the Web got you down? Tired of wasting your time loading Web page after Web page when you know that the special nuggets of information you're looking for are hidden somewhere in the bowels of the Internet? Relax! Let LiveAgent Pro do the grunt work for you. Java-based LiveAgent Pro provides an easy to use, powerful, flexible, and extensible way to automate Web activity through the use of automated agents. Gone are the days of slaving over a hot keyboard, thanks to LiveAgent Pro. Now, if I could only find an agent that would wash my dishes. . . .

www.agensoft.com/liveagentpro.html

Living Desktop

Created exclusively for you, the *Java For Dummies* reader, Living Desktop is featured in Chapter 14 and is provided free of charge on the CD-ROM that comes with this book. An automated desktop artwork utility, Living Desktop replaces your standard wallpaper with wonderful little works of art that bring your computer to life. Living Desktop will display a new selection of desktop artwork as wallpaper at any time interval you choose. (I have mine set to display a new piece of art every 10 minutes) Why slog through the day with boring desktop wallpaper when you can bring your screen to life with fine art, flora, sports, and textures thanks to Living Desktop?

As my way of saying thanks for reading this book, I've arranged for free upgrades to your copy of Living Desktop. Simply choose About from the Living Desktop menu for details, or visit the official Living Desktop Web site listed here. Tell 'em you're a reader of *Java For Dummies* and you'll get new versions of Living Desktop for free as they're developed, as well as new and fresh artwork as it's created. If that doesn't work, tell 'em you're a good friend of mine. And if that doesn't work, tell 'em you're my mom. Explain what an unruly little tyke I was, and you'll get free upgrades for life. Guaranteed.

www.LivingDesktop.com

LivingLinks Editor

Sure, weaving applets into Web pages is a blast. But wouldn't it be nice if you didn't have to do everything by hand? Now you don't have to, thanks to the LivingLinks Editor provided on the CD-ROM that comes with this book. Rather than hand-coding <APPLET> tags and typing in PARAMS by hand, let the LivingLinks editor do the work for you. This powerful utility takes the pain out of weaving the LivingLinks utility into your Web pages, and it even provides a preview window so you don't have to bother reloading your Web browser each time you change a parameter. Shave time and effort off your LivingLinks applet weaving and let the LivingLinks editor do all the hard stuff.

```
www.livinglinks.com/editor
```

Lotus eSuite

What do you get when you cross two software giants like Lotus and IBM? For starters, you get one heckuva Java application suite. Lotus, which became an IBM company in recent years, has created eSuite, a comprehensive set of Java tools and applications. eSuite is designed with the Internet in mind and is chock full of Internet-savvy programs. As an integrated suite of programs, eSuite rolls together a word processor, a spreadsheet, a calendar, e-mail, and a presentation graphics program. How suite it is.

```
eSuite.lotus.com
```

Net-It Now!

Speaking of Web automation, truck on over to the Net-It Now! Web site if you want to see the latest in document processing. With Net-It Now, you can transform your standard desktop documents into cross-platform, instantly viewable, Java-enhanced Web pages. All it takes is a click of your mouse to convert run-of-the-mill documents into killer Java-powered Web pages. Talk about taking the grunt work out of Web development. Hmmm . . . maybe if Net-It Now! teamed up with LiveAgent Pro, I'd have a shot at automating my kitchen work.

```
www.Net-It.com
```

NetResults

Can't find your wallet? Seem to have misplaced your car keys? If your life is in disarray, what makes you think finding information on your Web site is any easier? Thank goodness the organizationally impaired have NetResults. In just three easy steps, all the information on your Web site can become organized and easily navigated by visitors, so you can kiss your disorganized site of yesterday goodbye. Now, if I could only remember where I put my laptop . . . .

`www.netresultscorp.com`

NetTracker

Inquiring minds want to know. About your Web site, that is. If you're curious about the goings-on behind your Web site or suspicious that a hacker is milling around in areas that are supposed to be off-limits, you need to hire the private dick of Web pages. Let NetTracker keep an eye on things for you. NetTracker is a powerful yet easy-to-use Web tracking program that watches and analyzes visitor traffic on your Web sites. Not only is NetTracker a great deal less expensive than hiring a real-life detective, it's a darned sight less slobbery than a bloodhound.

`www.sane.com/demo/NetTracker/`

The Network Vehicle

Okay, this isn't really a Java application. But it's one doozy of an example of how innovative Java applications can be. I'm not going to ruin the surprise by telling you what the Network Vehicle is; just be sure not to miss it! Fire up your Java-savvy browser and visit Sun's Network Vehicle site or IBM's Alphaworks Java Web site, both of which are listed here. You won't be sorry, I promise.

`java.sun.com/features/1997/nov/javacar.html`

`www.alphaworks.ibm.com/networkvehicle/`

VolanoChat

If your Web site is suffering from a profound lack of interactivity, perhaps it's time to set up a chat room. With VolanoChat, you'll be up and running with multi-user chat rooms in no time. As one of the leading Java chat applications on the Internet, VolanoChat is responsible for millions of people around the world talking live with each other every day. Talk about a Chatty Cathy.

www.volano.com

Chapter 18
Ten Technical Tragedies

*I*n this chapter, I discuss the ten most likely reasons that you're having trouble getting a Java applet or application to run correctly — assuming that your browser can handle Java applets in the first place and that your desktop computer is properly equipped to run Java applications. Not having a Java-savvy browser is the leading cause of applets failing to work correctly, and not having properly installed a Java application (or a Java Runtime Environment in cases where the application doesn't come with its own JRE) is the leading cause of application failure. Thankfully, both of these are easy problems to solve as Chapter 2 and Chapter 13 explain. Following, however, are a few of the not-so-obvious technical hurdles that you may need to clear on your path to developing Java-powered Web pages and reaching true desktop enlightenment with Java application.

Missing or Misspelled Tags

HTML tags (as I explain in detail in Chapter 3) are the lifeblood of Java applets. Misspelling a tag or forgetting to include one altogether can certainly cause your Java-powered page to flop. If you experience an applet failure, check your tags for the following mistakes:

- **Forgetting the opening or closing tag.** You must always open with `<APPLET>` and close with `</APPLET>` tags.

- **Spelling tags incorrectly.** Check for tag typos such as `<APPLE>`, `<APLET>`, or`<APPLIT>`.

- **Using a backward slash instead of a forward slash.** Your closing tags should look as follows: `</APPLET>`. They should *not* look as follows: `<\APPLET>`.

- **Leaving off required tag attributes.** In all `<APPLET>` tags, you must at least specify `CODE`, `HEIGHT`, and `WIDTH` attributes.

- **Neglecting to open and close all `<PARAM>` tags.** If you forget to begin your `<PARAM>` tags with an opening less-than sign (`<`) or neglect to close 'em with a terminating greater-than sign (`>`), you're probably going to be sorry. Some Java-savvy browsers deal gracefully with a missing opening or closing tag and go on as if nothing is wrong. Others flip out, refuse to run the applet, or may even crash. Don't gamble with the life of your applet. Correctly open and close `<PARAM>` tags and you come up a winner every time.

Missing or Misspelled Information between Tags

What good are meticulously typed tags if the information inside them is full of errors and holes? If your tags look okay but your applet still fails to run, look a little deeper at the parameters and statements between the tags. Time to pull apart the chocolate sandwich cookies and check out the creamy filling inside.

You configure applets by using parameters, all of which you must supply in the form of a `<PARAM>` tag with the following basic structure:

```
<PARAM NAME="the parameter name" VALUE="parameter's value">
```

Watch out for the following applet-killers in your parameters:

- Misspelling a parameter name or value or providing incorrect information in a value prevents your applet from getting what it needs to function correctly.

- Omitting quotes from around names or values that contain spaces (or even one space) prevents your applet from getting the entire parameter. Browsers read only the characters up to the space and omit the rest.

✔ Including an extra quote (for example, `VALUE="This is the text for my ticker tape""`) is deadly and may even crash the browser!

✔ Using "curly quotes" rather than "straight quotes" prevents the browser from correctly processing a parameter. Because plain text doesn't support curly quotes, however, you shouldn't have a problem. If you happen to see curly quotes around a parameter, you're probably using a word processor to construct the tag. In that case, make sure that you save the file as *plain text* before trying to load it in your browser.

✔ Omitting a required parameter (such as an image or series of images, in the case of LivingLinks) prevents an applet from executing or adversely affects its behavior if it does manage to run.

Mistaken Identity CODE and ARCHIVE Attributes

In working with JAR files (Java Archives), you may be tempted to assume that the name you supply for a `CODE` attribute derives from the name that the `ARCHIVE` attribute specifies. And although a close relationship between the two usually exists, no law says that the two names must be identical. The developer who creates the applet gets to choose a name for both the `CODE` and `ARCHIVE` attributes, so you shouldn't try to guess one or the other. Instead, consult the documentation that comes with each applet to correctly identify the correct `CODE` and `ARCHIVE` attributes.

The JAR-style Marquee applet available on the CD-ROM that comes with this book, for example, requires the following opening `<APPLET>` tag:

```
<APPLET CODE="Marquee.class" ARCHIVE="Marquee.jar"
        WIDTH=500 HEIGHT=40>
```

Clearly a close relationship exists between the name that the developer supplies for both the `CODE` and `ARCHIVE` attributes. The company that created this applet (Mantis Development Corp.) could, however, just as easily use different names (such as Marquee for the `CODE` attribute and PickleJuice.jar for the `ARCHIVE` attribute). Mantis simply chooses to make life a little easier on you by using the same names for both `CODE` and `ARCHIVE`, although other applet developers are under no obligation to do the same. Beware.

Jarring JARs

Although applets rarely require multiple JAR files, sometimes they do. If you haven't seen applets that use multiple JARs, you may forget to explicitly list each JAR file in the ARCHIVE attribute. And even if you remember to specify each JAR file individually, you may forget to place a comma between each one. Just be sure to place a comma between the name of each JAR file your applet requires, as the following example shows, and you'll be just fine:

```
<APPLET CODE="MyApplet.class"
        ARCHIVE="MyApplet.jar","MyApplet2.jar","MyApplet3.jar"
        WIDTH=50 HEIGHT=40>
```

Each of the three JAR files in this example is separated from the other by a comma but no spaces! If you try to slip a space between the comma and a JAR file, you're asking for trouble. Some browsers can handle the space, but others can't. Play things safe and remove all spaces between the JAR files you list in the ARCHIVE attribute — and stick with commas only.

Missing Applet Files

Depending on the design of an applet, it may or may not rely on more than one *applet file* to run. Applet files can be traditional class files (files with the .class extension), newer JAR files (Java Archives, which have the .jar extension), and serialized files (applet files that are serialized, which typically sport the .ser file extension), all of which I discuss in Chapters 3 and 4. If you don't have the correct assortment of applet files for a given applet, you get nothing but grief.

The Marquee applet that I supply on that CD-ROM that comes with this book, for example, comes in two forms: One uses the original version of Java to hit the Web (Java 1.0), and another uses features introduced in Java 1.1. To distinguish between the two, I call the Java 1.0 version of the applet "traditional." If you want to weave this applet into a Web page that all Java-savvy browsers can use, you must ensure that you upload to the Web the two class files — Marquee.class and MarqueeFile.class — that make up the traditional version of this applet. If you want to support *only* newer browsers, however, you need only weave the associated Java Archive file (Marquee.jar) into your <APPLET> tag by using the new ARCHIVE attribute.

You can also opt to weave both into a single page to serve up the more efficient (and faster!) JAR version to newer browsers, while using the traditional class files if older Java-savvy browsers come knocking. To do so, use a smidgen of JavaScript to enable your Web page to "sniff" details about the browser someone's using to view your page and then construct the appropriate <APPLET> tag (as I describe in Appendix B). Just make sure that all files associated with both versions upload to the Web: Marquee.class and MarqueeFile.class, in addition to Marquee.jar.

Unlike the traditional Marquee applet, which always requires two class files regardless of how you configure it in the <APPLET> tag, the LivingLinks applet (as do many other applets) requires only multiple class files, depending on how you use it. If you don't tap into the power of a special effect, for example, you need to upload only the LivingLinks.class file. If you want to hook up a special-effect plug-in such as Fade, however, you need to ensure that the Effect.class file also uploads, along with any class files associated with that particular effect — Fade.class and FadeFilter.class, for this example. Of course, there are always exceptions to this rule. Because the Microsoft Internet Explorer browser is particularly finicky when it comes to applets comprised of multiple .class files, as LivingLinks is, you may need to include the Effect.class file when using this browser even in cases where you don't take advantage of special effects. If you try to use LivingLinks alone (without the Effect.class file) Internet Explorer may refuse to load the applet at all. If this happens, simply copy the Effect.class file into the same directory as the LivingLinks.class file and reload the page.

Relative URLs Starting with a Slash

Most applets can't process relative URLs correctly if the URL starts with a slash. You should always specify relative URLs without the leading slash. In specifying a single image to use in a LivingLinks animation, for example, the following tag is incorrect:

```
<PARAM NAME="image" VALUE="/images/logos/mantoid.gif">
```

Because the relative URL that you supply as the value for the image parameter begins with a slash, the applet can never find the support file. Instead, leave off the initial slash, as follows:

```
<PARAM NAME="image" VALUE="images/logos/mantoid.gif">
```

Absolute URLs Pointing to Another Server

Unless you use an absolute URL for navigation, the file to which it points *must* reside on the same server as the applet. For security reasons, applets can access only files that reside on the same server as they do unless you grant them permission to access files on other servers (as I explain in Chapter 2). If, however, you use a URL for navigation purposes (for example, the `URL` and `links` parameters of the LivingLinks applet), the URL may point anywhere on the Web. Applet server security restrictions apply only to URLs that you use to access files (such as images, sounds, data files, and any other file an applet may require); meaning it's perfectly fine to supply a URL for navigation purposes. (Absolute and relative URLs are discussed in Chapter 3.)

Files Incorrectly Uploaded

Depending on the tool you use to upload files to the Web and on the mode in which you choose to upload the various files you need (the applet .class file, support files such as images and sound clips, and Web pages), one or more files may fail to reach the Web server intact. Uploading files to the Web can be a tricky business the first few times you do it. You're almost certain to upload files incorrectly from time to time, rendering them useless after they arrive.

The key to a successful upload lies in choosing the correct *transfer mode* for each file you're uploading. This mode determines exactly how the file on your hard disk breaks up into tiny pieces, goes over the wire, and reassembles on the Web server. If you're unsure of what transfer mode to use, just figure out what type of file you want to upload and choose the corresponding transfer mode, as the following list describes:

- ✔ Text files (Web pages, text-based support files, and scripts): Use Text mode.
- ✔ Nontext files (applet files, sound files, and image files): Use Binary mode.

If in doubt, choose the *raw* transfer mode if it's available. This mode just crams the file through your modem, over the phone lines, and onto the Internet without trying to treat it in any special way. As a result, this plain-vanilla approach is your best bet if you're not certain which mode to use.

If you're uploading from a Macintosh computer, don't use *any* of the Apple encoding methods (special upload modes for Macintosh files), such as Apple Single, BinHex, or MacBinary II. Instead, determine the type of file you're uploading (text or nontext) and stick with the appropriate corresponding transfer mode.

Another potential side effect of uploading files to the Web, which Windows folks using older uploading tools primarily experience, is the mangling of filenames during the upload process. What starts out on your hard drive as "LivingLinks.class" may end up on the Web as "livingli.cla," making it worthless as a support file unless you rename the file to what it should be (LivingLinks.class, in this case). Even if you don't use Windows or you happen to use a Windows tool that preserves filenames during transfers, you should always double-check every file's name after transferring it to the Web to make sure that it has *exactly* the same name on the Internet as it has on your personal computer (including upper- and lowercase letters!).

Giant File Overload

At times, knowing for sure whether an applet is loading large files over the Web or is actually having problems running is tough. To find out, take a look at the lights on your modem: If they're flashing, the applet is probably busy receiving files from the Net. If not, and you wait for an excessive amount of time, the applet may have *hung* or is stalled out.

In the case of internal modems, you may have no way to know whether information is transferring. Windows 95, Windows 98, and Windows NT users can check the status of their connection by double-clicking the icon of a modem that appears on the right side of the taskbar. Mac users, however, don't have this type of indicator built into their operating system. If you need this type of tool, you may be happy to hear that a number of shareware tools are available that enable you to peek at your modem connection. Check out the utilities section of your nearest Macintosh shareware archive or use a search engine on the Web to look for such a program. (See Appendix A for details about search engines.)

As a general rule, try to keep the total amount of material on your Web pages (text, applets, support files, and sound clips, for example) down to 250K. If that's not possible, inform Webbers that the information on your site may take a while to download. Whenever possible, supply a message in the applet if you expect a lengthy file download. With LivingLinks, for example, you can specify a *poster image* (a placeholder image that appears on-screen while the rest of the images an applet uses are loading) that says something like "Quit your whinin'; I'm downloading as fast as I can!"

Out of Memory

Mac users especially are susceptible to this problem: Netscape runs out of available memory and crashes or simply does not display your applets. This problem usually happens if you have a bunch of graphics or large applets running at the same time.

If you're a Windows user, you can remedy a RAM shortage by making sure that at least 50MB (megabytes) of free space is always available on your primary hard disk — although I recommend that you reserve even more. (I like to keep 100MB or so free on my own system.)

Because Windows uses the hard disk as *swap space* if it's low on memory (transferring the contents of RAM to an invisible *swap file* on the hard disk if it needs extra RAM), keeping a hefty amount of free space available ensures that you always have room on the hard disk, even if real RAM is in short supply. This swapping process happens all the time in Windows, although things get really hot and heavy if a number of applications are all vying for the same chunk of RAM.

If you're a Macintosh user, you can allocate more memory to Netscape Navigator by highlighting the program's icon in the Finder and choosing File⇨Get Info. A dialog box appears, giving you an opportunity to set the memory requirements for the application. Depending on how much RAM you've installed (which you can easily find out by choosing Apple⇨About this Macintosh), you can boost up the preferred memory allocation as much or as little as you want — but don't ever lower it!

Dueling Runtime Environments

As I mention in Chapter 14, Java applets and applications require a Runtime Environment (also known as a Virtual Machine) to run. Specifically, applets run via the Runtime Environment that you find in Java-savvy browsers such as Internet Explorer and Netscape Navigator, while applications require that you install a more industrial-strength Runtime Environment (such as Sun's JDK or JRE) on your computer before they can run.

Although having a Runtime Environment in your browser is essential for you to run applets, as is having one outside the browser if you plan to run Java applications, you actually *can* have too much of a good thing in terms of Runtime Environments for Java applications.

Although installing a variety of Runtime Environments on your machine while installing Java applications may be tempting, avoid the temptation. Instead, install only the most current Runtime Environment available and call it a day. If you install more than one Runtime Environment while hooking up Java applications, you're likely to drive yourself batty because your applications won't know which Runtime Environment to use, meaning they (and you!) may become confused if more than one option is available. As a result, your applications may not run properly or may not even run at all. Save your sanity and avoid dueling Runtime Environment by installing only one for your applications. In doing so, your Java applications have only one Runtime Environment to execute them, which saves you a great deal of hassle in the end because you don't need to associate or coordinate your applications with multiple Runtime Environments.

In fact, unless you have good reason to do otherwise, why not go with Sun's latest and greatest Java Runtime Environment (JRE)? Sun's JRE is specifically intended for folks such as you and me, meaning that it's easy to install and simple to use (see Chapter 14). Of course, if you're a software developer, the more complex Java Development Kit (JDK) is for you, because it includes all the Java programming tools you need to start writing applets and applications, as well as an industrial-strength JRE.

Plug-in Particulars

The first time you encounter an applet that requires the Java Plug-in, you must take the time to actually install the free Java Plug-in on your computer if it's not already there (see Chapter 10 for details). Although this process is pretty painless for the most part, it's still something that you need to be aware of. Because you must download the Java Plug-in over the network before you can install it on your computer, you end up waiting a long, long time for it to arrive if you're using a slow Internet connection, such as a modem.

You must remain patient while installing the Java Plug-in. A lot of people who encounter applets that make use of the Java Plug-in never get to see them in action because they abort the installation process before it finishes, something that you shouldn't do! Be patient the first time you encounter an applet that requires the Java Plug-in; after the Java Plug-in downloads and you install it on your computer, you're in the clear from then on because you need to install it only once. Aborting the installation process, however, means that you effectively remove the Java Plug-in from your system. If you do so, you'll never have a chance to see the most advanced Java applets in action because they generally require the Java Plug-in to run.

Solving Security Screwups

As applets become more and more sophisticated, they tend to stretch the boundaries of the security "sandbox" to which they're restricted. In many cases, you must grant applets security rights (such as giving them access to files on your computer, for example) before they run correctly. But be careful!

If you give an applet security rights beyond those they receive by default (which isn't much, actually, as I describe in Chapter 2), you put your computer in a very compromising position. A number of good reasons exist for restricting applets in what they can do, and you should have just as many good reasons for enabling them do anything more.

Unless you know and trust the developer of an applet, don't grant an applet security rights. If you do grant such rights, I can almost guarantee that you're going to regret it. Sooner or later, you find yourself face to face with a malicious applet that intends to do your computer harm. If you grant such an applet access to your computer, you may wake up one fine morning to find your computer files gone or your system unusable. Such a situation is rare, but it can occur if you grant an applet privileges that it abuses. In a nutshell, you should never, ever grant an applet security privileges unless you're entirely certain that it comes from a trustworthy source.

The same goes for Java applications, of course, although you don't explicitly grant Java applications access to your computer. Because you don't restrict applications in the way that you do applets, they *inherently* have the capability to wreak havoc on your computer after you install them. As a result, you must take great care in choosing those applications that you install on your computer, just as you must take great care in granting applets security rights.

JIT Conflicts (Just-In-Time Compilers)

Although Just-In-Time (JIT) compilers give applets a significant speed boost by converting the bytecode an applet consists of into native code immediately after the applet is downloaded over the Internet, sometimes JITs can cause conflicts. On occasion, you run into applets that simply don't run if you enable the JIT in your browser. If you encounter an applet that doesn't run and you can't figure out why, try disabling your browser's JIT. Then quit your browser (to flush out any residual applet bytecode that may be lingering around) and start again from square one.

If the applet loads just fine this time around, chalk it up to a JIT conflict. In fact, you may find that the speed increase your JIT provides isn't worth the potential conflicts that it can cause as you surf the open seas of the Web. This situation is especially true in older browsers (such as Netscape Navigator 3.0 and Internet Explorer 3.0), because the earliest JITs simply aren't as reliable as the ones today. Most modern browsers, however, include JITs that are nearly conflict-free by comparison, meaning that you rarely (if ever) need to disable your JIT while using the most recent Java-savvy browsers.

Part V
Appendixes

In this part . . .

This part contains a boatload of useful appendixes. Appendix A shows you how to get up to speed with the rapidly changing world of Java by pointing you to cutting edge Web sites, newsgroups, and list servers. Appendix B shows you how to tap into Java "scripts," enabling you to create smart Web pages that can detect the make and model of browsers so that the appropriate version of an applet (1.0, 1.1 or 1.2) is delivered to visitors. Finally, Appendix C is your road map to the CD-ROM that comes arm-in-arm with this book — it contains all the information you need to locate the applets, applications, scripts, sample CookBook Web pages, utilities, online-service information, and other goodies included on the disc.

Appendix A

Resources for Staying Hip to That Java Noise

*T*he CD-ROM in the back of this book contains a bunch of applets and a few applications to kick-start your Java habit. But the CD-ROM is just the beginning. You can find literally thousands of applets and scores of applications on the Web, free for the taking — and hundreds more appear every day.

Because the number of Java-powered pages is increasing so rapidly, the demand for comprehensive Java support has gone through the roof. You now can find a number of sites dedicated to assisting Java developers and people who create Java-powered sites. To get your Java fix, you need only to look in the right places. And even if you don't know exactly where to look for that special nugget of Java information, you can always turn to traditional search engines to light the way.

In an attempt to make sense of the different types of sites you may visit on the road to Java enlightenment, I break them down into the following six categories:

✔ **List:** Special e-mail communities, similar to newsgroups, that let you share thoughts and ideas with fellow list members.

✔ **Repository:** Contains bunches (a technical term) of Java applets and applications, as well as oodles (another technical term) of hyperlinks to other Java sites.

✔ **Electronic magazine:** Generally targets Java developers and high-end users. An *e-zine* is the digital equivalent of a paperbound periodical, in which you can usually find material about the latest and greatest happenings in the world of Java.

✔ **Support area:** Web sites containing Java source code and example applets that demonstrate special features of the Java programming language. Typically targeted at Java developers.

✔ **Search engine:** Enables you to search the Web for information about any subject, from chocolate-chip cookies to Java.

✔ **Newsgroup:** E-mail groups that allow ongoing online conversations with fellow Javaites from around the world. The electronic equivalent of a town meeting.

List Servers: Online E-Mail Communities

Without a doubt, communication is the most powerful and compelling reason to use the Internet. Thanks to the Internet, the world seems to grow smaller day by day. In mere moments you can communicate with friends and family scattered across the globe using little more than e-mail. But that's just the tip of the e-mail iceberg; list servers lie below the surface.

List servers make e-mail even more powerful. *List servers,* or simply "lists" as they are commonly called, make it a cinch to communicate with entire groups of people through a single e-mail. The concept is as simple as it is powerful: Send e-mail to a single address, and your message is automatically forwarded to everyone on the list.

There are scores of lists that you can subscribe to, but the following three should be of particular interest. These lists were established especially for you, the *Java For Dummies* reader. If you have questions about *Java For Dummies* or any of the applets or applications that come on the CD-ROM, you can get help through the lists described in Table A-1.

Table A-1	Java-specific E-mail Lists
Address	*Description*
javafordummies@ listserver.tiac.net	Comprised of *Java For Dummies* readers who help each other get the most out of this book and the applets, applications, and other goodies provided on the accompanying CD-ROM.

Address	Description
`livinglinks@ listserver.tiac.net`	Comprised of readers who help each other get the most out of the LivingLinks applet provided on the book's CD-ROM.
`livingdesktop @listserver.tiac.net`	Comprised of readers who help each other get the most out of the Living Desktop applications provided on the book's CD-ROM.

To subscribe to a list, simply send an e-mail to any of the above list addresses. Don't type anything in the subject line, but be sure to type **subscribe** in the body of your message. That's it! You'll receive an automatic response welcoming you aboard within moments of sending a subscription request to a list address. You're now part of a bustling community (or three bustling communities!) that can help you become fully fluent in Java applets and applications. Who knows? True love may even find you on one of these lists. Stranger things have happened in cyberspace.

Repositories: Jam-Packed with Applets, Applications, and Source Code

If you want to get your mitts on a specific Java applet or application, make sure that you drop by a repository first. A *repository,* in essence, is a Web site containing centrally maintained links to Java applets and applications. A great deal of *source code* is also available in repositories, which is a welcome bonus if you want to know how others create the applets and applications in a repository. (Source code, by the way, is the body of computer instructions that a programmer writes to create an applet or application — consider it the DNA of an applet or application.)

EarthWeb's Java Applet Review Service (JARS)

Although Gamelan, which I mention later in this section, is a repository of immense proportions, the Java Applet Review Service (JARS) is lean and mean. JARS reduces the number of links that it maintains by employing a rating system for the applets and applications it references.

Keep in mind that the JARS I'm talking about here is simply an acronym for *Java Applet Review Service* and has no relation whatsoever to Java Archives (JARs), which is a nifty archive solution for Java that I discuss in Chapter 6.

Because a large panel of judges rates all JARS applets, you can rest assured that you see only the cream of the crop if you look at the "JARS Top 1%" applets.

Check out JARS at:

```
www.jars.com
```

Gamelan

Not many people would argue about whether Gamelan is the most comprehensive Java repository on the Web — it's the hands-down favorite of many Java developers. Gamelan is a *reference repository:* It provides links to external pages that applet, application, and bean authors maintain instead of storing and maintaining them on the Gamelan Web server. Although Gamelan may not sound like a *true* repository because it doesn't act as a central storage area, it really *is* a repository — just not in the traditional sense. If, however, you think of the Web as one gigantic hard disk (which, in a sense, is what it really is), you can consider any site that maintains links to its contents a repository.

Maintaining links is what Gamelan does best! Gamelan is a wonderful site, offering hyperlinks to tons of applets, applications, and even source code. Gamelan doesn't stop at merely providing links, however: At Gamelan, Java developers register themselves as resources — you can retrieve the profile of an individual or group who's responsible for developing a particular applet or application that you like, and you can then retrieve other Java products developed by that person. Alternatively, if you're looking exclusively for custom Java-development services, you can search the developer resource list to find that special individual or group who can meet your Java-related development needs. In this sense, Gamelan also acts as a registry of Java resources.

Gamelan is a great resource not only for locating applets, applications, beans, source code, and resources, but also for finding anything that relates to Java. Gamelan even contains links to electronic Java magazines, newsgroups, and support areas. Check out Gamelan at:

```
www.gamelan.com
```

Mantis Java Links

The Web site of Mantis Java Links, the code repository for this book (and other Java publications that the Mantis Development Corporation produces), is shown in Figure A-1. The applets and applications at this site also serve as an upgrade to the CD-ROM in the back of this book. This site is regularly maintained and updated — check it out for more new goodies at:

```
www.mantiscorp.com/java
```

The Mantis Java Links site is a self-contained repository, which means that it stores and manages all its applets and applications right on the Mantis Development Corporation server. As a result, none of the site's links depend on *external* sites, or sites other than the Mantis server. In this approach to maintaining a repository, you don't need hyperlinks to take you to an external site to view applets or applications, so you don't need to head into deeper waters unless you specifically choose to link to another repository.

Unlike other repositories, which attempt to provide as many applets and applications as possible, Mantis Java Links attempts to separate the wheat from the chaff so that you don't waste time sifting through unwanted links. For that reason, Mantis Java Links is a good place to begin your quest.

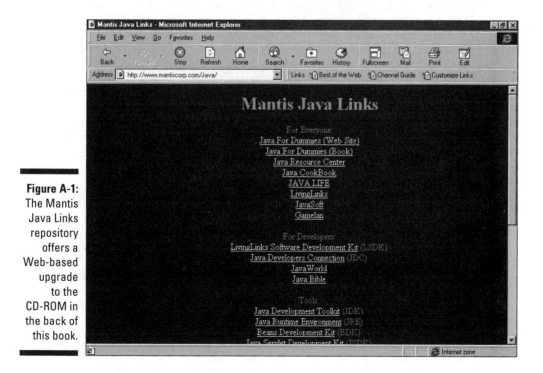

Figure A-1:
The Mantis
Java Links
repository
offers a
Web-based
upgrade
to the
CD-ROM in
the back of
this book.

Javazines: Electronic Magazines on a Caffeine High

Electronic magazines, commonly known as *e-zines,* or simply zines (pronounced "zeens"), have emerged from the woodwork over the past few years. Similar to traditional magazines, e-zines offer articles to inform you about a specific subject. In Java e-zines (or *Javazines,* as I like to call them), that subject matter revolves exclusively around — surprise, surprise — Java!

Although you can now find scores of e-zines on the Web that cover a gamut of topics, only a handful focused exclusively on Java a few years ago. Today, however, with a quick spin of your mouse, you can find scores of e-zines that cover cooking, nightclubs, macramé, and body piercing — and nearly as many that focus on Java.

You can categorize e-zines into two general groups: professional and independent. Professional e-zines are usually consistent, well-written publications that appear on a regular schedule. Independent e-zines, on the other hand, may not be as reliable, well thought out, or rich in the breadth and depth of the material they offer, but they're usually much more creative, irreverent, exciting, and visceral in their approach to delivering information.

If you're looking for something fresh and exciting to read, independent e-zines are wonderful, but they usually have a tough time attracting professional writers. In many cases, this difficulty doesn't make a bit of difference, but it does matter with Java. The caliber of content in the independent Java e-zines generally pales in comparison to their professional counterparts. I suspect that this situation is eventually going to change, however, as more and more Webbers willing to contribute to independent e-zines become fluent in Java. In the meantime, you're likely to find that the professional e-zines are much more valuable.

JavaWorld

JavaWorld is an online magazine that International Data Group (IDG) publishes. Appearing bimonthly, *JavaWorld* is full of comprehensive, well-written articles written primarily for Java developers and high-end users. Not only can you read about Java technology, but you can also see it working right in front of your face. With nothing more than a click of your mouse, you can view the source code that you need to create each applet and application that you see in action.

If you really want to push the envelope of what Java can do for you, check out this site. At a minimum, you can find articles relating to specific applications. For ambitious types, *JavaWorld* includes plenty of applet source code. Dig in and don't be shy — access it at:

```
www.javaworld.com
```

The Java Resource Center

The *Java Resource Center* flowed into the ether just a few years ago but fast became a favorite pit stop of Java junkies around the globe. IDG Books Worldwide, Inc. (the same company responsible for this very book), owns and operates the Java Resource Center, which offers information about all the company's Java publications. In addition, sample chapters, applets, applications, and other Java materials are available at this site, which you find at:

```
www.idgbooks.com/rc/java
```

Support Areas: Where Java Developers Dare to Tread

Unlike repositories, *Java support areas* aim almost exclusively at developers. Support areas attempt to provide you with the tools and information that you need to *develop* Java applets and applications — not just to use them in your Web pages. These areas may also supply applets, applications, and source code, although that's not their focus. Instead, you're more likely to find Java software development tools, documentation, technical support, Frequently Asked Questions (FAQs), and other Java-related information that programmers need to create top-notch applets and applications.

Although support areas are mainly for developers, they often contain applets and applications for the taking. With this in mind, you may want to visit these areas even if you have no intention of writing your own applets or applications. You never know where you may find that nugget that pulls your page or desktop together.

Sun's Java site

Perhaps the most popular Java support area is the Sun Microsystems Inc. Java Software Web site, the official home of Java (see Figure A-2). If you want to become a Java developer, this site is the place to begin. Here you can find everything you need to start developing your own Java applets: the Java Development Kit (JDK), Java Runtime Environment (JRE), extensive documentation, FAQ documents, source-code samples, and links to other Java resources. Be warned! The process of programming Java applets is no trivial task and requires significant software-development skills and a heavy dose of geek appeal. Even if you don't have an interest in creating your own applets, however, Sun's Java Software site may be of interest to you.

As if Java itself and all the goodies that the Java Software Web site aren't reason enough to rejoice, I have another reason to kick up my heels. Rich Burridge, the technical reviewer of *Java For Dummies,* works for Sun Microsystems Inc. An avid Java programmer, Rich is the team leader for a collaborative computing effort now going on inside Java Software. I'm delighted to have Rich's help in beating this text into submission and thought you'd sleep better at night knowing he's on the case.

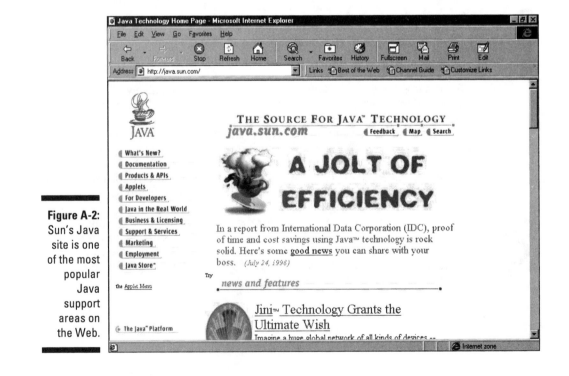

Figure A-2:
Sun's Java site is one of the most popular Java support areas on the Web.

The Java Software site also contains a large number of applets, which are available for free to anyone who visits. Unfortunately, the only way to get these applets is to install either the Java Development Kit (JDK) or the Java Runtime Environment (JRE) on your system. Both the JDK and JRE are 15MB or so in size and, depending on the speed of your connection to the Internet, can take a long time to download. (If you're using a modem, expect to put aside more than an hour!) Fortunately, both the JDK and JRE are on the CD-ROM that comes with this book, so you don't need to hock your toaster oven to pay for the connection time you'd otherwise need to download these items from the Web.

If you decide to download and install either, your reward is more than 25 nifty little applets, ranging from animation to tic-tac-toe to hangman and more. Of course, you can also get these applets directly off the CD-ROM by installing the JDK or JRE that comes for free with this book (see Appendix C for details). Regardless of how you get to them, whether online or off the CD-ROM, you can plug most of these applets directly into your own Web site, using your own graphics and sound files where appropriate, or use them as the basis for your own development efforts. If any of these goodies sound appealing to you, check out the CD-ROM that comes with this book or take a quick spin on the Java Software Web site at:

```
java.sun.com
```

Writing Java applets is no simple trick; it makes writing HTML-based Web pages seem like a carefree walk in the park on a lazy summer afternoon in comparison. If you want the full power of Java at your fingertips, however, you have no other way to go. If you want to try your hand at developing Java applets, I highly recommend that you get a copy of *Java Programming For Dummies,* 3rd Edition, by Donald J. Koosis and David Koosis (IDG Books Worldwide, Inc.) — it's a great book for picking up the ins and outs of the Java programming language without losing your mind in the process.

The Java FAQ Archives

Frequently Asked Questions, or *FAQs,* are text documents full of questions and their corresponding answers; they're a fantastic resource if you find yourself asking, well, *questions* about applets or applications.

The Java FAQ Archives is actually a FAQ document repository that maintains links to scores of different Java-related FAQs available on the Web. If you have a question about applets or applications, you're likely to find that someone else has already asked — and received an answer to — that question at the Java FAQ Archives. Because FAQs are nothing more than text documents, you can download them to your computer, where you can read through them whenever you have a question.

You can save yourself much of the time you spend scanning through FAQ documents simply by using a text-search tool (such as your browser, word processor, or the Find utility built into your computer) to search the contents of FAQ documents that you download from the Internet.

Although FAQs of all flavors exist, you may be happy to know that scores of Java-related FAQs are available from the Java FAQ Archives site. Simply connect to this site with your Web browser and then download all the FAQs you want. New FAQs appear all the time, so make sure that you return to the site often:

```
www-net.com/java/faq
```

Search Engines: Scouring the Web for Java Nuggets

Should you come up empty-handed in looking for a specific applet or application at the sites in the preceding section, you may want to turn to *search engines* — sites to help you find information available on the Web. Just visit a search engine and type a keyword or two relating to your question. The engine compares your keyword or keywords to its massive database of links and reports back to the links that it thinks match your query.

Type the keyword **applet**, for example, and a search engine shows you all the hyperlinks in its database that contain that word. The links, and a brief description of their pages, act as a table of contents for the Web as it applies to your query, as shown in Figure A-3. You can click any of the hyperlinks to visit a site.

The problem with search engines, however, lies in the vast amount of information that they return, no matter how much you limit your search criteria. (A recent search for **Java applets** in a popular search engine found several hundred thousand matches!) The biggest drawback, of course, is that you must visit each link to know for sure what it contains. For this reason alone, I rarely use search engines if I'm looking for applets and applications; I'd rather spend my time prowling around repositories, Javazines, and newsgroups.

Most search engines, however, also categorize their databases so that you can see all the best links on a specific topic (such as Java). You can then bypass altogether a standard keyword search and head directly to the category you want. Yahoo! (at www.yahoo.com), for example, offers a Java category that consists only of links to useful Java sites.

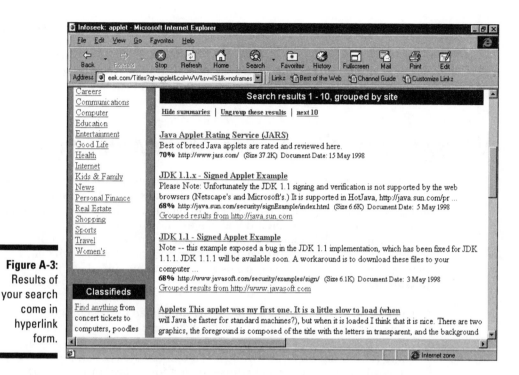

Figure A-3:
Results of
your search
come in
hyperlink
form.

One search engine, however, stands apart from the crowd in finding Java applets: AltaVista (at www.altavista.digital.com), from Digital Equipment Corporation, enables you to search for the *name* of the applet class file you want — by searching inside the <APPLET> tag (see Chapter 4 for details on the <APPLET> tag)! If you want to find all the pages containing the embedded "tickertape" applet, for example, you can search for just that name. You simply type **applet:** in front of the applet name, so that the result looks like this:

```
applet:tickertape
```

Other search engines return a link to every Web page containing the word *tickertape,* even if they have nothing to do with applets or Java. (Ticker tape parade, anyone?) Thanks to AltaVista, however, you don't need to separate the needles from the haystack — AltaVista does it for you. This feature is particularly helpful if you'd like to see a particular applet in action; simply fire up AltaVista and search for the applet tag as explained here. In mere moments you'll be surfing though all the known Web pages that contain the applet.

Although AltaVista can save you a great deal of time by looking for a specific applet, be careful as you type the applet name: AltaVista matches it exactly, including lowercase and uppercase letters! If you search for *Tickertape,* for example, AltaVista finds only 100 or so applets. Change your search to *tickertape,* however, and it reports several thousand matches.

Newsgroups: Electronic Town Meetings

If after searching the Web, you can't find the Java information you seek, you may consider joining a Java newsgroup. *Newsgroups* are online discussion groups in which people get together electronically to talk and share information. Newsgroups aren't standard Web pages, but you can access them through your Web browser by typing the newsgroup address into your browser's location area (although newsgroup addresses begin with `news:` instead of `http://`). Following are two of the more popular Java newsgroups:

- ✔ `comp.lang.java`: Although primarily populated by Java programmers, this newsgroup is worth visiting if only to hear some of the lively and often passionate debates that surface from time to time. You may also find this newsgroup worthwhile if you're interested in more technical Java discussions, especially those related to the Java programming language.

- ✔ `alt.www.hotjava`: Although less technical than the `comp.lang.java` newsgroup, `alt.www.hotjava` is still plenty technical. In this newsgroup, however, you're likely to find discussions revolving around nonprogramming related issues, such as Java-savvy browsers.

For details on joining a newsgroup, contact your Internet Service Provider or network administrator. To access newsgroups, you must configure your browser correctly, which requires special information about your connection to the Internet. Simply ask your ISP what you need to do to participate in Java newsgroups, and the people there can lead you through the process.

Don't forget to precede the newsgroups listed here with `news:` instead of `http://` when typing them into your browser. If you type in the newsgroups as listed here, without the `news:` portion of the address, your browser will think that they're simply Web pages and try to visit them accordingly (that is, your browser will automatically add `http://` to the newsgroup address).

Although newsgroups are generally a great place to congregate and ask questions if you hit a sticking point, people asking questions are currently overloading the Java newsgroups. The problem is that everyone seems to be asking questions and only a few are giving answers. As a result, many questions go unanswered and become little more than digital roadkill that newsgroup participants speed by while looking for help with their own problems.

At this point in your Java travels, however, you may consider posting a question anyway in the hope that someone may help you out. After you truly exhaust all other avenues, your question is more likely to be taken seriously. If you can't easily answer your request simply by doing a little legwork, others in the newsgroup may recognize that you aren't being lazy but are truly in need. With luck, someone may respond to your post with a solution.

Many search engines enable you to search newsgroups. If you don't want to wade manually through the messages in a newsgroup, you can use a search engine instead. In particular, you may consider visiting DejaNews (at www.dejanews.com), a search engine dedicated entirely to finding information related to newsgroups.

Appendix B
A Sip of JavaScript

* *

In This Chapter

▶ Demystifying JavaScript

▶ Weaving scripts into Web pages

▶ Forcing your applets and scripts to march in sync

▶ Spying on browsers with "sniffer" scripts

* *

*J*avaScript, developed by Netscape Communications Corp. and Sun Microsystems, is a *scripting language* for the World Wide Web. While not a full-blown programming language like Java, a scripting language isn't as user-friendly as a markup language such as HTML (see Chapter 3 for details on HTML). JavaScript, in essence, is a "light weight" programming language and falls somewhere between HTML and Java in complexity. JavaScript isn't as powerful as Java, nor is it as capable. Conversely, JavaScript is more difficult to use than HTML, but it is also more powerful that HTML.

JavaScript is the ideal language for non-programmers who have grown out of HTML yet aren't quite ready for the leap to the Java language. At the same time, JavaScript is often the perfect "glue" to bring HTML and Java applets closer together.

When first introduced, JavaScript held enormous promise for scripting Java applets, but it was only a promise because initially the language wasn't capable of controlling applets as directly as it does HTML elements (JavaScript gives you direct control over Web page elements such as text, images and sound, meaning you make them behave however you'd like in response to user activity). As of today, thankfully, JavaScript is capable of scripting applets in the latest browsers. When used within these new browsers (Netscape Navigator and Internet Explorer 4.0 or later), JavaScript can activate applets, and even fully interact with them after they are running.

With older Java-savvy browsers, however, JavaScript can only activate applets — interacting with applets isn't possible. You probably realize by now that the most powerful features of JavaScript are available only within the most powerful browsers, meaning that the scripts will "break" when older browsers load them. Fortunately, you can work around this problem with "sniffer" scripts, as you find out later in this appendix.

This appendix also shows you how you can use simple scripts to *sniff* browsers, enabling you to determine the exact browser types and versions that visit your pages. Using this information, a JavaScript-enabled Web page can dynamically accommodate any type of Java-savvy browser out there: Old browsers are fed only the scripts and applets they can handle, while newer browsers are given the more advanced scripts and applets.

Introducing JavaScript

Although Java — a full-blown programming language meant to be used by experienced software developers — is enough to cause the Fonz to lose his cool, JavaScript is a scripting language that even Potsie can handle. In terms of difficulty, scripting languages fall somewhere between markup languages, such as HTML, and full-blown programming languages, such as Java. Although programming languages are used to *create* software products (such as word processors, spreadsheets, Web browsers, applets, and the like), scripting languages let you, the end user, *control* such programs. In fact, a *scripting language* is defined as a relatively easy-to-use programming language that allows the end user to control existing programs.

Before JavaScript was born, you had very little control over the interaction between your Web pages and the Webbers who used them. Sure, you could weave applets into your pages, but applets alone don't give you the ability to *precisely* control the interactivity your pages offer. For the most part, applets were just little programs that you plugged in to make your pages look and sound cool.

Cool is good, no doubt about it. However, you can't make an applet do something it wasn't intended to do. If the applet's developer doesn't give the applet certain capabilities, no amount of parameter tweaking is going to make it do what you want it to do!

As a result, you may find yourself saying, "My Web page would be so killer if it could only. . . ." But with HTML and applets alone, you don't always have the degree of control you need to create such a site. Unless you have JavaScript, you can only do two things: Write the applets yourself or (more likely) gripe, gripe, gripe.

Satisfying JavaScript's meager needs

Writing Java applets from scratch requires a host of special software programs intended for use by experienced software developers, but JavaScript is much less demanding, and more akin to HTML in its requirements. Actually, if you're already creating Web pages from scratch, typing HTML code directly into a document, and saving the result as a plain text file, you have everything you need to write JavaScript.

If you want to create your own scripts or customize scripts created by others, you need the following:

- ✔ **A text editor:** A text editor is any program that enables you to change the contents of a text file. Every Windows computer comes with a text editor called Notepad. Macintosh users can use the SimpleText application that comes with every Mac that rolls off the assembly line.

- ✔ **A JavaScript-savvy browser:** JavaScript and Java are *not* the same thing, although they share the same gene pool. Just because your browser supports Java doesn't automatically mean that it supports JavaScript, and vice versa. Just as you need a Java-savvy browser to run Java applets, you need a JavaScript-savvy browser to run JavaScript.

    If a browser is Java-savvy, it's likely to be JavaScript-savvy as well. The reverse isn't true, however. Because JavaScript is a different technology than Java, browsers commonly support JavaScript but not Java; in fact, such is the case with Netscape Navigator 2.0 for the Macintosh. As a result, Macintosh users using Navigator 2.0 must get their hands on either Navigator 3.0 (www.netscape.com) or Internet Explorer 3.0 (www.microsoft.com/ie) or higher, if they want to access both Java and JavaScript through one browser — a move I highly recommend.

Choosing JavaScript

If JavaScript is so difficult, why bother with it? For starters, JavaScript may be difficult to learn, but it's easy to *use!* Just include a script between an opening <SCRIPT> tag and a closing </SCRIPT> tag, and you're done. At this level, using JavaScript is as easy as weaving the simplest applets into Web pages. *Customizing* scripts, however, is a different story.

When you customize a script, you actually change it. In essence, you reprogram the script to do what you want. How little or how much you alter the script depends on your needs, and how close the original script comes to fulfilling those needs. In some cases, the task is no more difficult than what you may experience in configuring <APPLET> tag parameters; at other times, altering a script gets much hairier. Luckily, how much you alter a script depends entirely upon you.

You may find that you rarely, if ever, have to bother with customizing a script. After all, thousands of scripts are available for the taking on the Web. All you have to do is find the ones that fit your needs, and you're all set. But even if you do have to get under the hood from time to time, tinkering with a script's innards until does what you need, you'll probably find the process worthwhile. When you can use existing scripts and customize them to fit your needs, your Web site will never lack for truly compelling content. (This assumes, of course, that you first obtain permission from the original owner of the scripts before you weave them into your pages — what a shame to admire your compelling site from behind bars!)

A Script Is Born

Someone, somewhere creates JavaScript scripts just as somebody writes applets. And just as applets vary in terms of what they do, scripts also widely vary in form and function.

Although JavaScript is an easier language to understand than Java, it's still complicated and intimidating until you get used to it. I won't even pretend to try to show you how to create your own scripts — that would take a whole book! In fact, a whole book is indeed dedicated to JavaScript. If you're looking to move beyond the use of existing scripts to becoming fluent in JavaScript, check out *JavaScript For Dummies,* 2nd Edition, written by Emily A. Vander Veer (IDG Books Worldwide, Inc.).

Introducing the <SCRIPT> tag

Ladies and gentlemen, children of all ages, I now give you the tags that make adding scripts to Web pages possible. Please put your hands together and give a good old-fashioned welcome to the opening and closing <SCRIPT> tags:

```
<SCRIPT attributes>
</SCRIPT>
```

Not exactly the show-stopper you were expecting? They may not make you gasp in amazement, but the opening <SCRIPT> and closing </SCRIPT> tags are truly the stars of the JavaScript show. No matter how you slice it, if you want to add JavaScript to your pages, you have to go through these two tags. Or, to be more precise, JavaScript must go between these two tags:

```
<SCRIPT attributes>
Here, inside the opening and closing script tags, is where
        the JavaScript code goes.
</SCRIPT>
```

The unsolved mystery of JavaScript attributes

One of the most interesting (if not downright mysterious) aspects of JavaScript has to do with the attributes that you may include in the opening tag. As with applet attributes, which I discuss in detail in Chapter 4, *JavaScript attributes* are simply keywords within an opening `<SCRIPT>` tag that change the way browsers treat that tag. According to the documentation that Netscape provides, you may supply two attributes inside the opening `<SCRIPT>` tag: `LANGUAGE` and `SRC`. But (here's the weird part), although you're free to supply either or both of these attributes when creating your `<SCRIPT>` tags, original JavaScript-savvy browsers, such as Netscape Navigator 2.0 and Internet Explorer 3.0, ignore them both!

That's right — despite being part of the formal JavaScript documentation, the original crop of JavaScript-savvy browsers totally ignore the `LANGUAGE` and `SRC` attributes. However, the most recent crop of browsers (Netscape Navigator 4.5 and Internet Explorer 5.0) supports both of these attributes, giving you an incentive to understand what each attribute does and how (and when) to use them.

Do you speak my language? Using the LANGUAGE attribute

Today, the most important of the two `<SCRIPT>` tag attributes is `LANGUAGE`. Even though older JavaScript-capable browsers don't use this attribute, you should take care to include it in all of your scripts anyway because most modern browsers require it. While older browsers ignore the `LANGUAGE` attribute, this attribute is important to today's most modern JavaScript-savvy browsers — or, to be more accurate, today's script-savvy browsers. But why?

Although JavaScript was the only game in town when it was originally introduced to the Web, JavaScript is no longer the only scripting language to choose from. Today, alternatives to JavaScript, such as Microsoft's JScript and Visual Basic Script, have burst on the scene and are vying for your browser's attention.

In anticipation of this recent outpouring of diverse scripting languages, the makers of JavaScript long ago decided to give you a way to tell browsers which scripting language you're actually using: The `LANGUAGE` attribute. Naturally, the most popular scripting language in use by people like you and me today is JavaScript, simply because it was the first out of the gate and is dead simple to use. But time has a way of changing leadership in the Web area! Because JavaScript already has serious competition, and other scripting languages are on the way, make sure that all the JavaScript scripts that you use are clearly identified as such. To tell a script-savvy browser which type of script falls between your opening and closing `<SCRIPT>` tags, all you have to do is set the `LANGUAGE` attribute to `"JavaScript"`:

```
<SCRIPT LANGUAGE="JavaScript">
Some nifty JavaScript code goes here.
</SCRIPT>
```

Although you're free to omit the LANGUAGE attribute in your scripts, leaving it off alienates those browsers that expect to find the scripting language specified. Additionally, future browsers may even refuse to recognize scripts that aren't explicitly identified as being written in a specific scripting language. Because the official word from Netscape is that all opening <SCRIPT> tags must set the LANGUAGE attribute to identify the type of script being used ("JavaScript", in this case), you would be wise to do so!

A source of aggravation: Using the SRC attribute

Whereas the LANGUAGE attribute may save your script from short-circuiting when modern script-savvy browsers view them, the SRC attribute may keep *you* from short-circuiting! Script-savvy browsers did not initially support the SRC attribute (which stands for *source*). Today, however, you may use the SRC attribute with Netscape Navigator 4.0 (or later) or Internet Explorer 4.0 (or later).

With these browsers, you can provide a SRC attribute that specifies a URL pointing to a file containing the JavaScript code you want to execute. With older browsers, however, you have no choice but to provide that JavaScript code right then and there, between the opening and closing <SCRIPT> tags. Writing out JavaScript code inside the tag is no problem for short-and-sweet scripts, but it's a royal pain in the attribute with scripts that span more than a half-dozen lines or so.

HTML becomes more cluttered and difficult to understand the longer the script or the more scripts you have in a page. What was once reasonable, easy-to-read HTML code can quickly become a nightmare that contains so much JavaScript code that you must scroll for what seems like an eternity to get though it all. When you have to include all that JavaScript code between your <SCRIPT> tags, page maintenance becomes much more difficult than it should be. You may spend more time swimming though line after line of JavaScript than you spend enhancing your pages.

The solution to this potential travesty of code justice lies in the SRC attribute, which enables you to separate your HTML code from your JavaScript code. Although older, script-savvy browsers don't support this miraculous SRC attribute, you're free to use it as long as the browser viewing your page is either Netscape Navigator 4.0 (or later) or Internet Explorer 4.0 (or later).

Although you can use the SRC attribute with modern browsers, older JavaScript-savvy browsers don't support it at all; any scripts that SRC points to won't run under older browsers. To deal with this situation, you can either forego the SRC attribute altogether and imbed all of your scripts inside the Web page itself, or you can use a *sniffer* script to determine exactly what browser a Webber is using each time she visits your page (see "Bait and Switch Browser Sniffing" later in this chapter). With this information, you can construct a new <SCRIPT> tag on the fly. In this way, you can support older script-savvy browsers.

To use the SRC attribute with today's latest and greatest browsers, all you have to do is provide a URL, either absolute or relative (see Chapter 3 for details on absolute and relative URLs), that points to the text file containing the JavaScript code you want to execute:

```
<SCRIPT LANGUAGE="JavaScript" SRC="MyScript.js">
</SCRIPT>
```

Quick! Hide! It's a non-Java browser

Aside from the inclusion of opening and closing <SCRIPT> tags, the most important thing to remember when constructing a tag for JavaScript is that not all browsers understand how to deal with JavaScript. In fact, millions of Webbers are still using old browsers that don't have a clue when it comes to JavaScript. Not only that, some Webbers with perfectly fine JavaScript-savvy browsers actually "turn off" this capability, or never turn it on in the first place, making it impossible for them to see JavaScript in action (imagine the nerve!). For all intents and purposes, your Web pages consider such browsers to be the same as older, JavaScript-ignorant browsers. Unfortunately, millions of Webbers hit the Web every day with browsers that can't (for one reason or another) understand JavaScript.

When a non-JavaScript browser encounters a JavaScript-powered page, it displays what amounts to garbage instead of executing the script. As a result, your well-designed pages look like a junkyard to folks who don't use JavaScript-savvy browsers. The trick is to hide the JavaScript code from these types of browsers. If a non-JavaScript browser can't see the JavaScript in a page, it won't display the garbage. In essence, you sweep this unreadable garbage under the rug when non-JavaScript browsers come to visit.

Unlike the <APPLET> tag, the <SCRIPT> tag doesn't support an area for alternate HTML, so you must use comments to hide scripts from non-JavaScript browsers.

So how can you hide your JavaScript from script-ignorant browsers and still allow JavaScript-savvy browsers to do their magic? The answer lies in *comments,* special pieces of code that exist for your benefit only. Browsers ignore comments entirely, so you can use them to help make sense of otherwise cryptic code (that is, you can "comment" on code for your own benefit since the browser doesn't see them). One of the pleasant side effects of comments' invisibility to browsers is that they allow you to hide scripts from those browsers that don't understand JavaScript.

To hide scripts from non-JavaScript browsers, you must surround the entire script with a special comment tag that begins with a less-than sign, an exclamation point, and two hyphens (<!--) and ends with two forward slashes, two hyphens, and a greater-than sign (//-->). Non-JavaScript browsers ignore anything that comes in between, such as a script. But browsers that do know how to execute JavaScript realize that they don't want to ignore what's inside the comment tag. JavaScript-savvy browsers know that a script falls between these special comments and therefore treat it with all the love and attention that it justly deserves.

To hide JavaScript from standard browsers, while still making it available to those in the know, all you have to do is surround the script with these special comment tags. However, most folks just getting started with JavaScript forget this little nugget of helpful information, and usually omit these special comment tags, even though adding them is a cinch. Before I show you how to use comment tags, take a gander at the code below that you can use to display the current date and time inside a Web page. I intentionally neglected to hide this script from non-JavaScript browsers:

```
<SCRIPT LANGUAGE="JavaScript">
todays_date=new Date();
document.write("The Current Date and Time: ")
document.write(todays_date)
</SCRIPT>
```

TIP

A snippet in code saves time

If you want to save yourself time and effort, all you have to do is use the following snippet of HTML code as the basis for all scripts you weave into your pages. Just save the following code in a plain text file, and then copy it the next time you add a script:

```
<SCRIPT LANGUAGE="JavaScript">
```

```
<!--

//-->
</SCRIPT>
```

By using this code snippet as the template for all scripts you weave into your pages, you prepare for the future while also accommodating the past.

To fix the code and prevent non-JavaScript-savvy browsers from displaying garbage, just surround the JavaScript code that appears between the opening <SCRIPT> and closing </SCRIPT> tags with the special comments previously described:

```
<SCRIPT LANGUAGE="JavaScript">
<!--
todays_date=new Date();
document.write("The Current Date and Time: ")
document.write(todays_date)
//-->
</SCRIPT>
```

That's all there is to it.

Adding Self-Contained Scripts to Your Web Pages

The most basic scripts you can find are those that exist entirely inside the opening <SCRIPT> and closing </SCRIPT> tags. Although a number of scripts are broken up into little pieces, called *functions,* and are woven into different parts of a Web page, many scripts are entirely self-contained and exist inside a single set of <SCRIPT> tags. Not surprisingly, self-contained scripts are the easiest to add to your own pages.

Adding self-contained scripts to your pages takes just a few easy steps:

1. **Find the script to add.**
2. **Copy the script (or save it to your computer).**
3. **Add the script to your page.**

Copying scripts

After you find a script that you want to add to your own page, all you have to do is copy the entire <SCRIPT> tag and paste it into your own HTML source code. Of course, you can also type the entire thing from scratch, but why bother? By simply copying and pasting it, you save both time and aggravation — and no typos!

To copy a script, just highlight it with your mouse and choose Edit⇨Copy. Or, if you want to save a little time, you can press the appropriate key combination instead (Ctrl+C if you use Windows or ⌘+C for the Macintosh). But be sure to get the whole thing! If you don't copy the *entire* script, it won't work when you add it to your page. To make sure that you copy the whole script, simply highlight all the code appearing between the opening <SCRIPT> and closing </SCRIPT> tags *and* the tags themselves before issuing the Copy command.

If you want to, you can save all the HTML source code for the page to your personal computer rather than just copying the script itself. In fact, this method is the easiest way to deal with scripts that use functions.

Pasting scripts

After you copy a script, the only thing left to do is to paste it into your own HTML source code. You can add the script anywhere you want within your Web page by simply pasting it in (choose Edit⇨Paste or press Ctrl+V if you use a Windows system, or press ⌘+V if you use a Macintosh). In fact, you can add the script to several different pages if you want; all you have to do is paste it into the HTML code for each page in which you want it to appear. Or you can add the same script in many different places inside a single page. Again, it's just a matter of pasting the code wherever you want the script to appear.

The script alteration cha-cha

Unless the scripts you add to your pages are flawless from the get-go, chances are pretty good that you'll end up making changes here and there to get the effect you want. Fortunately, you can modify your scripts until the cows come home as long as you follow what I call the "Script Alteration Cha-cha."

Whereas applets can be frustrating to configure because browsers tend to grab the first set of parameters they see and refuse to accept new ones, you can easily alter a script and immediately see the changes in your script-savvy browser. Applets require that you either quit and rerun the browser or use a few tricks to get the browser to see the changes you make. Viewing your altered scripts, on the other hand, is a simple process:

1. **Make your changes.**

2. **Save the HTML source code by choosing File⇨Save.**

3. **Switch to your browser.**

4. **Choose Reload.**

As long as you use your Web browser to open the Web page, pressing the Reload button — after saving the changes you made to the code — forces the browser to look at the page anew, reflecting any changes you made to it.

Coexisting in Cyberspace

Using applets and scripts in the same page is a breeze, and you don't need to do anything special. You merely weave the appropriate tags into your HTML code (by using <APPLET> tags to add applets and <SCRIPT> tags to add scripts), and you're off to the races. Of course, simply sprinkling applets and scripts together on the same page is just half the fun. Things really get moving when you use scripts to execute and control applets, as you're about to see.

The capability to run applets and scripts side by side is all well and good, but the real kicker is when scripts actually execute and dynamically control applets. Yes, you can design your scripts to execute applets in response to user interaction. You can even create scripts that finely control the various aspects of running applets, changing at will how your pages look and act and how they respond to user activity, giving your site the highest degree of interactivity possible on the Web today.

For example, consider the following snippet of HTML code. It doesn't look like much, but it packs quite a punch:

```
<FORM>
Would you like to see a neat Java applet?
<input type="button" name="button_one" value="Yes!"
onClick="window.open('animation.html', 'new_window',
         'width=315,height=175')">
</FORM>
```

The preceding code creates an input form consisting of nothing more than the text "Would you like to see a neat Java applet?" followed by a Yes! button.

This is no ordinary form, mind you; it's a JavaScript-powered form. The JavaScript used in this page is really an *event trigger*. Clicking the Yes! button ("onClick") triggers an event, which, in turn, opens a new window (window.open) that displays a Web page (animation.html) containing both JavaScript code and an animation applet.

The script in this new `animation.html` page sets the background color to black while the LivingLinks applet runs through a slick little animation. The HTML code is pretty simple. Here's the complete HTML source code for the entire page:

```
<HTML>
<TITLE>Animation</TITLE>
<SCRIPT>
document.bgColor = "black"
</SCRIPT>
<APPLET CODE=LivingLinks WIDTH=299 HEIGHT=155>
<PARAM NAME=image VALUE="images/features.gif">
<PARAM NAME=effect VALUE="RedBlueEffect">
<PARAM NAME=speed VALUE="15">
<PARAM NAME=backgroundColor VALUE="black">
<PARAM NAME=soundDir VALUE="audio/">
<PARAM NAME=inSound VALUE="bongoDrums.au">
<PARAM NAME=inSoundLoop VALUE="yes">
</APPLET>
</HTML>
```

Seeing this page in action is cool, but the real point here is that an applet is executed in response to an event. Although this example executes when a user clicks a button, you can use many other events to trigger the execution of applets and script functions.

We're moving through JavaScript here faster than a greased monkey at a hoe-down. To get the most out of JavaScript, you need to stop and smell the coffee beans. I highly recommend plunking a few bucks down at your local bookstore to buy yourself a copy of *JavaScript For Dummies,* 2nd Edition, by Emily Vander Veer (IDG Books Worldwide, Inc.).

Synchronizing Your Applets and Scripts

What if you want your applets and scripts to work in tandem? For example, what if you want a script's scrolling text to correspond to the applet's image below it? Suppose that you want a half-dozen or so different images displayed on-screen, one after the other, while a text message about the current image scrolls above it. When your forest-ranger applet runs, for instance, you want the corresponding text (`Where's Yogi?`) to scroll above it. In short, you want the applet and script to be *synchronized* with each other.

Unfortunately, many applets and scripts can't easily be synchronized — at least not today. In the future, when more applets are designed with JavaScript in mind, things will change. The LivingLinks applet on the CD-ROM that comes with this book, for example, is fully scriptable. It's designed specifically for use with JavaScript, and has a great number of scriptable features. LivingLinks, however, is an exception to the rule; in many circumstances, you have only two choices for synchronizing applets and scripts: Script it or hack it.

When the original crop of Java-savvy browsers hit the Web, scripts didn't know diddly about applets. JavaScript, however, is fully aware of applets and is capable of sending them messages that control their behavior. As long as the scripts and applets are viewed with a browser that knows how to deal with the more advanced capabilities of scripts and applets (such as Netscape Navigator 4.0 or later or Microsoft Internet Explorer 4.0 or later) and the applet itself is scriptable (such as LivingLinks), you can weave pages that are as dynamic and interactive as the best traditional (non-Web) software products available today.

Specifically, you can write scripts that execute, control, and terminate applets. The applets in a Web page become, in essence, objects that scripts can communicate with, just as scripts communicate with any other object.

Are you talking to me? Huh? Are you talking to me?!

Even though images of Robert De Niro always run through my mind when I think about scripts talking to applets, the interaction is relatively painless, (assuming that you're running Netscape Navigator 4.0 or later or Microsoft Internet Explorer 4.0 or later, with both Java and JavaScript capabilities enabled).

The trick to getting scripts to talk to applets lies in the `<APPLET>` tag — specifically in the NAME attribute of the `<APPLET>` tag. Using this attribute, you can give the applets in your page a name that scripts can use to talk with them:

```
<APPLET CODE=LivingLinks WIDTH=299 HEIGHT=155 NAME=Bob>
<PARAM NAME=image VALUE="images/features.gif">
<PARAM NAME=effect VALUE="RedBlueEffect">
<PARAM NAME=speed VALUE="15">
<PARAM NAME=backgroundColor VALUE="black">
<PARAM NAME=soundDir VALUE="audio/">
<PARAM NAME=inSound VALUE="bongoDrums.au">
<PARAM NAME=inSoundLoop VALUE="yes">
</APPLET>
</HTML>
```

In this example, I named the applet *Bob*. Now that the applet has a name, you can control Bob with a script. Just place the Bob object in a *JavaScript variable* — a name that you use in JavaScript to identify a piece of information, in this case an applet — and you can then use and abuse the applet. In the following line of code, because I've created a script variable named bobTheApplet to which I've assigned the applet object, I can use the variable to communicate with the applet:

```
var bobTheApplet = document.Bob
```

Not so stinkin' fast!

Armed with the most current crop of Java-savvy browsers and the preceding information, you're set to synchronize your scripts and applets, right? Well, you have to deal with *one* more little detail: Just as you must know what parameters an applet accepts to configure the applet properly, you must also know what commands the applet uses to communicate with scripts. Finding these details is a no-brainer; if an applet can communicate with scripts (that is, if it's a *scriptable* applet), the documentation that comes with the applet includes all the information you need.

Any scriptable applet will come with documentation that explains the various ways it may be controlled by scripts. Specifically, you should look in your applet's documentation to find out what *messages* your applet understands. Scripts communicate with applets by sending them messages, and so it stands to reason that the messages your applet understands dictate the messages you can send it from your scripts.

At the same time, you should peruse your applet documentation for the word *object*. Object is a word typically used to refer to a scriptable applet that can receive messages. If you find the word "object" in your applet documentation you're also likely to find a listing of the messages that applet understands.

The messages that an object understands are also known as *methods;* you *invoke the method* of an object when you send it a message. Java programmers may be interested to know that JavaScript can access all public methods of an applet, whether or not the applet was designed to be scriptable. You can therefore invoke any public method of an applet, whether or not the developer of that applet intended it to be used with JavaScript. Of course, if an applet's methods aren't documented, you are in the dark regardless — you can't invoke methods unless you know their names!

Even though you can control all applets to a certain degree by using scripts (you can execute and terminate them by using the standard start() and stop() messages supported by all applets), applets designed with JavaScript in mind from the onset are infinitely more flexible. These applets will do your bidding, provided that you write the script properly!

With JavaScript, you can access an applet's scriptable messages whenever you want. You can then orchestrate how an applet behaves and finely tune its behavior in response to a Webber's behavior. You're the puppet master; you call all the shots. For example, to change the speed at which the LivingLinks images are displayed, just insert this line of JavaScript:

```
bobTheApplet.setSpeed(100)
```

Or to stop playing sounds that may be pumping away, use this line of JavaScript:

```
bobTheApplet.stopSounds()
```

Depending on what messages an applet understands, the possibilities are truly staggering. With the right applet and a dash or two of JavaScript, your pages have the potential to become as sophisticated and powerful as any commercial piece of software on the computer store shelf, if not more so. LivingLinks alone, for example, can create sophisticated multimedia pages that include interactive games, virtual worlds, interactive music videos, and other wildly impressive features.

Bait and Switch Browser Sniffing

Because JavaScript isn't fully compatible with JScript (the Microsoft version of JavaScript), there's a good chance that some portions of JavaScript that work like a charm under Netscape Navigator will fail miserably under Microsoft Internet Explorer, or vice versa. If a browser doesn't fully understand a script, look out. At best, you get an error dialog box explaining the problem. At worst, your browser may freeze or crash, and you even may need to restart your machine. For this reason alone, you need to make sure to use JavaScript with browsers that expect JavaScript and JScript with browsers that expect JScript.

Sniff, Sniff . . .

A simple solution, however, to the JavaScript/JScript incompatibility problem is at hand — your scripts can *sniff out* each browser it encounters and supply each browser with the appropriate type of script that it requires. You can write a bit of script that detects the make, model, and version of the browser being used, and serves up an appropriate *real* script (one that does something interesting or useful, and doesn't merely sniff), contingent on the information your script sniffs out.

Of course, the trick is to create your sniffer script by using 100 percent compatible JavaScript (that is, JavaScript that can be read by JScript browsers without incident), because you don't want it to *break,* or stop working, under any browser. But that's no problem, as the following basic sniffer script illustrates:

```
<SCRIPT LANGUAGE="JavaScript">
<!--
var browserType = navigator.appName;
var browserVersion = navigator.appVersion.substring(0,5);
document.write("You're running: " + browserType +
            " version " + browserVersion);
 //-->
</SCRIPT>
```

The preceding script doesn't do anything useful, really, except detect the make, model, and version number of the currently visiting browser and then display that information on the browser window. But that information is what you're after. With a little spit and polish, you can actually turn the preceding bare-bones sniffer into something worthwhile:

```
<SCRIPT LANGUAGE="JavaScript">
<!--
var browserType = navigator.appName;
var browserVersion = navigator.appVersion.substring(0,1);
if (browserType == "Microsoft Internet Explorer") {
  if (browserVersion >= "4"){
    document.write ("You're using a new version of Internet
            Explorer!");
  }else{
    document.write ("You're using an old version of
            Internet Explorer.");
  }
}
if (browserType == "Netscape"){
  if (browserVersion >= "4"){
    document.write ("You're using a new version of
            Netscape!");
  }else{
    document.write ("You're using an old version of
            Internet Explorer.");
  }
```

```
}
if  ((browserType != "Netscape") && (browserType !=
            "Microsoft Internet Explorer")) {
  document.write ("You're NOT running Navigator OR
            Explorer!!");
}
//-->
</SCRIPT>
```

Building on the basic sniffer script, the preceding code example actually checks to see what type of browser the Webber is using, and then displays an appropriate message. The first important thing this script does is test the browserType variable to find out whether the Webber is using Netscape Navigator or Internet Explorer — if so, the script then tests the browserVersion variable to see if the browser's actual version number is equal to or greater than four, (browserVersion >= "4"). The results of this test determine what text the script displays in the browser (assuming, of course, that the Webber is actually using either Internet Explorer or Navigator). If not, the text "You're NOT running Navigator OR Explorer!!" is displayed, and no attempt is made to determine the actual browser version.

With the preceding bit of script, you can determine exactly what type of browser the Webber is using and serve up custom content based on that knowledge. All you have to do is place the JavaScript code inside the if ( ) clause that identifies the Netscape Navigator browser, and your JScript code inside the else () clause. In this way, Netscape Navigator receives only 100 percent pure JavaScript code, and Microsoft Internet Explorer is fed 100 percent JScript code, like so:

```
<SCRIPT LANGUAGE="JavaScript">
<!--
var browserType = navigator.appName;
if (browserType == "Microsoft Internet Explorer") {
  JSCRIPT GOES HERE!
}
if (browserType == "Netscape"){
  JAVASCRIPT GOES HERE!
}
//-->
</SCRIPT>
```

It's just what the doctor ordered when dealing with sticky script that isn't entirely compatible between the two browsers.

Sniffing out JARs

Similar to the sniffer scripts in the preceding section, you should try to support both the older and newer browsers when it comes to using JARs (Java Archives).

Consider the following script-sniffing example:

```
<SCRIPT LANGUAGE="JavaScript">
<!--
var browserType = navigator.appName;
var browserVersion = navigator.appVersion.substring(0,1);
var jarString = 'Supports Jar Files';
var originalString = 'Does Not Support Jar Files';
if (browserType == "Netscape" || "Microsoft Internet
          Explorer"){
          if (browserVersion >= "4"){
              document.write (jarString);
              }else{
              document.write (originalString);
          }
}else{
          document.write (originalString);
}
//-->
</SCRIPT>
```

This sniffer script still doesn't do much — it decides only whether the browser in question is Netscape Navigator or Microsoft Internet Explorer, and whether the browser is new enough to support JARs. If it is new enough, the browser displays the string Supports Jar Files. If it's either of the two browsers, but not current enough to deal with JAR files, the string Does Not Support Jar Files displays. If the browser is not Navigator or Internet Explorer, no string displays.

Keeping in mind the fact that older Java-savvy browsers don't support JAR files, consider the following sniffer script created specifically to support both Java 1.0 and Java 1.1 and Java 1.2 browsers. Using both versions of the Marquee applet that this book's CD-ROM supplies, this script dynamically serves up the appropriate <APPLET> tag depending on which browser comes a-calling:

```
<SCRIPT LANGUAGE="JavaScript">
<!--
var browserType = navigator.appName;
var browserVersion = navigator.appVersion.substring(0,1);
var jarString = '<APPLET CODE=Marquee
          archive=MarqueeClasses.jar WIDTH=400
          HEIGHT=34><param NAME=shift VALUE=2><param
          NAME=delay VALUE=20><param NAME=font_size
          VALUE=24><param NAME=font_italic
          VALUE=yes><param NAME=font_bold VALUE=yes><param
          NAME=back_color VALUE="255 255 240"><param
          NAME=text_color VALUE="72 61 139"><param
          NAME=marquee VALUE="Hello! Welcome to my JAR-
          POWERED homepage..."></APPLET>';
var originalString = '<APPLET CODE=Marquee WIDTH=493
          HEIGHT=26><PARAM NAME=font_face
          VALUE=TimesRoman><PARAM NAME=font_size
          VALUE=22><PARAM NAME=font_italic
          VALUE=yes><PARAM NAME=text_color VALUE="255 0
          0"><PARAM NAME=marquee VALUE="Mantis Marquee: Am
          I scrolling, or what? Wheeeee!! "><B> This line
          is alternate HTML — if you can read this, you
          don't have a Java-savvy browser!</B></APPLET>';
if (browserType == "Netscape" || "Microsoft Internet
          Explorer"){
          if (browserVersion >= "4"){
              document.write (jarString);
              }else{
              document.write (originalString);
          }
}else{
          document.write (originalString);
}
//-->
</SCRIPT>
```

In this example, I crammed two complete <APPLET> tags into one sniffer script! The entire <APPLET> tag for the JAR version of Marquee is stuffed into the jarString variable, while the original non-JAR <APPLET> tag is stored inside the originalString variable. The appropriate variable is then dynamically sent to the browser using the document.write() command depending on what version the browser is. The result is dramatic: Browsers receive only the <APPLET> tag that they can understand. No more, no less.

Because Version 4.0 of both Netscape Navigator and Internet Explorer are the only browsers in widespread usage that support JAR files, I've accommodated only them. However, if I wanted to support HotJava as well (Sun's very own Java-savvy browser; see Chapter 2 for details), I could just as easily modify the actual "sniffer" portion of the script to accommodate it as well.

If you want to find out more about JavaScript and JScript and their incompatibles, I strongly suggest going to the source. Turn to Netscape's own JavaScript developer's guide (`developer.netscape.com`) to find out all the grisly details of this language, or to Microsoft's JScript site to learn about that scripting language. Finally, you may consider sashaying on over to your nearest bookstore and leafing through a copy of *JavaScript For Dummies,* 2nd Edition, by Emily Vander Veer (IDG Books Worldwide, Inc.). Who knows? You may even walk out with it (just be sure to pay first).

Appendix C
About the CD

- -

*T*he CD-ROM included with this book contains a hefty amount of software to get you up and running with Java in no time flat. Designed for use with Windows 95, Windows 98, and Windows NT 4.0, Macintosh, and OS/2, this CD-ROM gives you a number of Java applets and scripts that you can weave directly into your own Web pages. In addition, the CD-ROM includes a bevy of utilities to help you get the most out of your Web travels, as well as a few utilities to help you convert your own images and sounds for use with Java.

Although the same applets and scripts are available regardless of what type of computer you use, the same utilities aren't. If you're a Windows user, you find a number of utilities specifically for use with these systems; if you're a Macintosh user, you find a separate set of utilities altogether (OS/2 utilities are not provided). However, despite these differences, the end result is the same — the disc contains utilities to help you decompress files that you download from the Web and utilities to help you convert sound and image files for use with your Java applets. This appendix is your guide to the CD-ROM, and it shows you how to install its contents on your personal computer.

System Requirements

In order to successfully use the CD that comes with this book, I recommend the following:

- ✔ For PCs: Windows 95, Windows 98, Windows NT 4.0 (or greater), or IBM OS/2. For Mac OS computers: Mac OS 7.5 (or greater).

- ✔ 100 MHz Intel Pentium processor (or compatible) for Windows-based systems, or a Motorola 68030 processor (a PowerPC processor is even better!) for Macintosh systems. A faster processor (133 MHz, 200 MHz, and so forth) will greatly enhance your Java experience but is not absolutely necessary.

- ✔ 16MB RAM at a bare minimum (32MB, or more, is much better — you can never have too much RAM).

- ✔ At least 146MB of hard drive space for Windows users, or at least 112MB of hard disk space for Macintosh, if you want to install the entire contents of the CD-ROM on your hard drive.

- ✔ A double-speed or faster CD-ROM drive.

- ✔ A Java-savvy browser (such as Netscape Navigator 3.0 or greater or Internet Explorer 3.0 or greater) is necessary if you want to see the Java applets in action. You're free, however, to browse the CD-ROM without a Java-savvy browser, in which case any browser will do the trick (for details on installing the Java-savvy browser that comes on the CD-ROM, see the "Client Software folder" section later in this appendix).

- ✔ A connection to the Internet is necessary only if you want to visit the Web sites listed in this book.

- ✔ For PCs, a sound card is not required unless you want to hear the audio played by many of the applets included on the CD-ROM. (All Macs come with built-in sound support.)

- ✔ A color monitor capable of displaying 256 colors (8-bit) or more is highly recommended, although Java applets can run under any monitor configuration (even black and white!).

If you're uncomfortable with the technobabble jargon I use to explain the recommended system requirements here or you are interested in getting the most out of your computer by upgrading what you have to a more powerful configuration, take a look at the latest edition of the ...*For Dummies* book that corresponds to your computer: *PCs For Dummies, Macs For Dummies, Windows 95 For Dummies, Windows 98 For Dummies, Windows 3.11 For Dummies,* or *OS/2 For Dummies* (all published by IDG Books Worldwide, Inc.).

How to Use the CD with Microsoft Windows

On the CD are several folders containing loads of sample applets and some great software.

Before you get down and dirty, you need to perform a short test of your CD-ROM drive:

1. **Pop the CD into your CD-ROM drive and use My Computer mode or the Windows Explorer program to show the CD's contents.**

   The first thing you see are two folders named Long and Short.

2. Open the Long folder and look for a folder named Client Software.

If you see the Client Software folder staring back at you, great. When I talk about the CD from here on, open the Long folder on the CD and fiddle with the CD from there.

If you don't see the Client Software folder, then move to the section "Whoops . . . I Don't See That Folder Name."

Whoops . . . I Don't See That Folder Name

If you see a folder named CLIENTSO or CLIENT~1 in the CD test that I describe at the start of "How to Use the CD with Microsoft Windows," then you're one of a few readers who needs to copy most of the good stuff from the CD to your hard drive using the Short folder.

Fear not, for the Short folder has everything you need to make a copy of the CD to your hard drive, where you can access almost everything that's found on the CD (except the Internet signup software and the other useful utilities — I explain that installation process later on).

Moving the folders to your hard drive

To copy the sample applets and such to a folder named Java For Dummies 3E CD on your hard drive, follow these steps.

1. **Insert the CD in your CD-ROM drive and open the Short folder on the CD.**

2. **Double-click the file ALL.EXE.**

   A message appears that tells you that the sample applet folders will be copied.

3. **Click the tiny message away.**

   The Unzip window appears.

4. **Click the Unzip button to copy the items.**

5. **Another tiny message appears that tells you that a number of items were copied. Click the message away and then click the Close button in the Unzip window to wrap up.**

On your hard drive is a folder named Java FD 3E. Inside this folder are Support Files, CookBook, and Cool Beans! folders, as well as the file Index.html and a few other small tidbits.

This process didn't copy the Goodies, Clients, and Living Desktop (LIVDESK) folder to your hard drive. You won't need to. The software can be installed from the CD.

Later on, you may twiddle a bit with the contents of the Cool Beans!, Support Files, and CookBook folders and have a need to reinstall a fresh copy of one of the folders. In the Short folder are additional installer files named roughly after these folders. To install them, follow the same instructions as above, but substitute COOKBOOK.EXE, COOLBEAN.EXE, or SUPPORTF.EXE in Step 2.

If you need to make a new copy of a CD folder but don't want to delete the contents of your original folder, be sure to type in a new folder name in the installer's Unzip window, or your original files may be erased.

How to Use the CD with a Mac

To install the items from the CD to your hard drive, follow these steps:

1. **Insert the CD into your computer's CD-ROM drive and close the drive door.**

   In a moment, an icon representing the CD you just inserted appears on your Mac desktop. Chances are, the icon looks like a CD-ROM.

2. **Double-click the CD icon to show the CD's contents.**

Like the Windows folks, you find a collection of files and folders. For a quick glimpse of what you'll find on the CD, move along to "What You'll Find."

What You'll Find

Because most folks like to dive right into new software products as soon as they get them home, I supply a quick-and-dirty tour of the CD-ROM to get you going now.

Flipping through files

The following is a brief description of each of the files within the main directory of your CD-ROM (or the main directory installed onto your hard drive, as the case may be).

The Read Me file (README.txt or Read Me First)

README.txt is a text file that's essentially an electronic version of the appendix you're now reading. It's provided on the CD-ROM to help you find the applets, scripts, and utilities the disc contains without requiring that you reference this printed book. You can view the contents of this file with any text editor or word processor.

Index.html

Index.html is a Web page that serves as your electronic guide to the applets and scripts provided on the CD-ROM — Index.html requires a Java-savvy browser to use it (see the section "Client Software folder" later in this appendix for details on Java-savvy browsers). Whereas the README.txt file merely tells you where the applets and scripts are located on the disc, requiring that you manually locate them, opening Index.html with a Java-savvy browser takes you on an interactive tour — you actually see the applets and scripts in action. (This file doesn't, however, give you access to the utilities. You must access the utilities the old-fashioned way, as described in this appendix and in the README.txt file.)

Although Macintosh users always see file extensions (such as .html, .class, and .txt), Windows users may have this option turned off, making it difficult to distinguish between files of different types that have the same name (such as LivingLinks.class and LivingLinks.html). If you're using a Windows system and the files on your CD-ROM don't have extensions, your computer has been instructed not to show file extensions. Not seeing file extensions doesn't affect your ability to use files, but you can always turn this option on, if you want to, by doing the following:

1. **From Windows Explorer, choose View⇨Options. (Choose View⇨Folder Options if you're using Windows 98.)**

   The Options dialog box opens.

2. **Uncheck the Hide MS-DOS File Extensions For File Types That Are Registered check box. (Windows 98 users choose the Hide File Extensions for Known File Types option under the View tab.)**

   Filename extensions are displayed from that point on.

Dashing through folders

Now for a bare-bones description of each of the subfolders within the main folder of your CD-ROM.

Client Software folder

In order to see Java in action, you must use a Java-savvy browser (such as Netscape Navigator 4.0 or Microsoft Internet Explorer 4.0). Without such a browser, the applets and scripts in a page never come to life. You also need a connection to the Internet if you want to surf the Web or publish your own Java-powered pages.

To help you get your hands on the most current crop of Java-savvy browsers, the Client Software folder contains Internet Service Provider (ISP) setup software and two of the world's most popular Java-savvy browsers — Netscape Navigator 4.0 and Microsoft Internet Explorer 4.0.

If you don't have a connection to the Internet (and you want one), try AT&T WorldNet Service — it provides good Internet service and gives you a Java-savvy browser. If you want to shop around for other ISPs, open the ISP.txt file with any text editor or word processor to find the names and telephone numbers of a few nationwide services that can help.

If you don't already have a connection to the Internet, you may want to join AT&T WorldNet Service, an ISP that provides you with a Java-savvy browser as well as some space to publish your Web pages. You have to pay for this service, so have a credit card ready as you install the software and sign on. You also need a modem connected to your computer. A 14,400 bps modem does the trick, but I recommend 28,800 bps or faster.

If you already have an Internet Service Provider, be aware that installing AT&T WorldNet Service software may change your current Internet connection settings.

During registration, you may be asked for a registration code. If you are an AT&T long-distance service customer, type this registration code: **L5SQIM631.** If you use some other company to do long-distance calls, type **L5SQIM632.**

CookBook folder

This folder contains a number of starter pages to help you generate ideas for your own Java-powered Web site. Using the applets and scripts provided on the Cool Beans! portion of the CD-ROM, CookBook pages are living examples of what you can do to kick your own pages into high gear with Java.

Although this folder provides a number of CookBook pages, you'll also find a hyperlink to CookBook pages on the Web. Between the pages you have on CD-ROM and the ones you can find in cyberspace, you'll never run out of great ideas for your Web site!

Cool Beans! folder

This folder contains two subfolders that are home to the coolest applets and scripts around:

✔ **Applets subfolder:** The Applets folder contains all the applets provided on the CD-ROM, along with examples of each applet in action. You can use the Index.html file (housed on the main level of this CD-ROM) to navigate through these applets, or you can open the Applets folder yourself and go straight to any of the applets you find inside of it. To use any one of these applets in your own pages, you must first copy the actual applet (a file with the .class extension, such as LivingLinks.class) and any support files it requires (image, sound, or data files) to your own computer.

✔ **Scripts subfolder:** This folder contains a number of JavaScripts (and examples of each in action) that you can add to your own Web pages. Although the Index.html file provided on the main level of the CD-ROM gives you one-click access to the contents of this folder, you're free to open it yourself and explore its contents manually.

Goodies folder

Ah, the Goodies folder. This is where you can find a small arsenal of tools to help you get the very most out of your Web experience, whether you're a Windows or Macintosh user. Here are some of the handy utilities housed in this folder:

✔ **ConvertMachine (Macintosh):** ConvertMachine (Rod Kennedy) is a batch-processing utility to convert sound format files to a desired format. It performs one or more of the following tasks without requiring user interaction: decompression, resampling (sample rate conversion), mixing (stereo to mono), and compression. You don't need to worry about what format the file is in; all you do is specify the desired output format. Freeware.

✔ **DropStuff with Expander Enhancer (Macintosh):** This shareware utility (by Aladdin Systems) gives Macintosh users the ability to create StuffIt (SIT) archives by dragging and dropping files and folders onto the DropStuff icon. And thanks to the Expander Enhancer, users of Aladdin's StuffIt Expander (also provided with this CD-ROM) can expand virtually every compression format found online that was created by Macs, UNIX systems, and IBM PCs and compatibles. You can decompress SIT, ZIP, and TAR archives, which are the most common formats you'll probably encounter when surfing for applets.

✔ **eSuite DevPack (Windows):** eSuite (Lotus) is a comprehensive set of Java tools and applications. eSuite is designed with the Internet in mind and is chock full of Internet-savvy programs. As an integrated suite of programs, eSuite rolls together a word processor, a spreadsheet, a calendar, e-mail, and a presentation graphics program. Trialware.

✔ **GraphicConverter (Macintosh):** GraphicConverter (Lemke Software) is a powerful shareware graphics viewing and conversion program. You can also make retouches, perform batch conversions for Mac and PC graphics formats, and more.

✔ **GoldWave (Windows):** GoldWave is a comprehensive digital audio editor that allows you to play, record, edit, and convert audio files on your Windows computer. In addition to the number of audio file formats GoldWave supports, it allows you to save sound files in a special *AU* format that is required by Java applets. To save files in this format, simply choose File⇨Export from GoldWave's menu, choose Sun (.au) from the Save Files as Type list box that appears, and then click OK. For more details on using sound in your Web pages, see Chapter 5.

✔ **InstallAnywhere:** Written completely in Java, InstallAnywhere Now! from Zero G Software is an ideal lightweight distribution system for your very own Java applications. With this installation tool, you can distribute Java software to Windows, UNIX, OS/2, Mac OS, or any other Java-enabled platform.

✔ **InstallShield (Windows):** InstallShield Java Edition lets you create installations for your Java applications on multiple platforms and ensures a consistent look and feel. Develop and deliver in Java with InstallShield Java Edition — create a single cross-platform installation that covers your Java deployment needs.

✔ **The Java Development Kit (Windows Version 1.1.6 Mac OS Version 1.0.2):** The Java Development Kit (or JDK for short) from Sun Microsystems provides you with the basics you need to create Java applets. Included with the installer for the JDK is an installer for the HTML-based documentation for the software. Note to Mac OS users: Your Mac may require additional software to run Java applets and programs outside of a Web browser. One option is the Macintosh Runtime for Java (MRJ) software, available from Apple Computer's Java Web site at www.apple.com/java.

Note: The JDK is © 1997 by Sun Microsystems, Inc., 2550 Garcia Ave., Mtn. View, CA, 94043-1100, USA. All rights reserved.

✔ **LivingLinks Editor (Windows):** The LivingLinks Editor (Jeff Orkin) is a Windows application that allows you to visually configure the LivingLinks applet featured in this book. Instead of manually writing HTML code to imbed LivingLinks into your Web pages, why not use your mouse? You can, thanks to the LivingLinks Editor.

✔ **Paint Shop Pro (Windows):** Paint Shop Pro (JASC, Inc) is a graphics program that offers many useful features such as image retouching, painting, and image-format conversion. In addition to enabling you to create and save images in the two graphics formats supported by Java applets, GIF and JPEG, Paint Shop Pro supports transparent and interlaced GIF images (see Chapter 5 for details on the image formats supported by Java).

- **Sound Editor 1.2 (Macintosh):** Sound Editor (David Veldhuizen) helps solve some of the problems associated with recording sound from your Mac's Sound control panel (control panels are located in the Apple menu). This utility also enables you to copy and paste portions of a sound, mix sounds together, and create special effects, such as echoes and backwards sounds.

- **SoundApp:** SoundApp (Norman Franke) is an extremely powerful freeware program that can play and convert a variety of sound formats. It understands the special Sun AU sound format required by Java applets, as well as many others, including the following: SoundCap and Studio Session Instruments, SoundEdit, AIFF and AIFF-C, System 7 sound and .snd resource, QuickTime MooV (soundtracks only, including MIDI movies), NeXT .snd, Windows WAV, MPEG audio, Sound Blaster VOC, many varieties of MODs, ScreamTracker 3 module (S3M), Multitracker module (MTM), MIDI, Amiga IFF/8SVX, Sound Designer and Sound Designer II, IRCAM, and PSION sound.

- **SoundMachine:** This utility (Rod Kennedy) allows Macintosh users to play many of the most common sound format sound files, such as AIFF, Windows WAV files, and AU files from the Internet. New versions of SoundMachine are available through updates on the World Wide Web (see the software's documentation for the Web address) so you can stay up to date as more sound formats are invented.

- **StuffIt Expander (Macintosh):** StuffIt Expander (Aladdin Systems) expands archives from the most popular archive-based compression formats found on the Macintosh: StuffIt and Compact Pro. It can also decode BinHex attachments from Internet e-mail and newsgroups. All non-encrypted archives created by any version of these products are supported, including files created with any member of the StuffIt family, such as StuffIt SpaceSaver, StuffIt Deluxe, StuffIt Lite, or DropStuff.

- **WinZip (Windows):** WinZip (Nico Mak Computing) brings the convenience of Windows to ZIP-compressed files. This versatile utility is one of my all-time favorites; it allows you to decompress (*unzip*) and compress (*zip*) file archives in the ZIP format, and it supports many other popular Internet file formats, such as TAR, GZIP, and UNIX compress. WinZip includes a powerful yet intuitive point-and-click, drag-and-drop interface for viewing, running, extracting, adding, deleting, and testing files in ZIP, LZH, and ARC files, including self-extracting archives. To install WinZip, simply copy the folder to your hard drive and then execute the winzip95.exe program (or, if you prefer, you can install it directly from the CD-ROM). Located in the Winzip folder.

- **WS_FTP (Windows):** The WS_FTP program (Ipswitch) is a file transfer protocol (FTP) utility. The user interface for this FTP client is designed with the novice FTP user in mind, yet it is extremely powerful. With this program, you can upload your Web pages, applets, and support files to the Internet one at a time or all at once (assuming they reside in the same folder on your personal computer).

✔ **ZipIt:** ZipIt (Tom Brown) is a Macintosh program to decompress (*unzip*) and compress (*zip*) files in the ZIP format. To decompress a ZIP archive by using ZipIt, choose File⇨Open and then select the archive by using the dialog box that appears. After an archive opens, use the mouse or the Edit⇨Select All command to choose the items you want to extract and then choose Zip⇨Extract to actually perform the decompression.

Living Desktop folder

You've read about it in *Java For Dummies,* 3rd Edition (that is, I hope you did). Now it's time for you to see this hot new Java application in action. To install Living Desktop:

1. **Double-click the Install LD.exe application.**

   This step assumes that your browser doesn't automatically run LD.exe for you.

2. **Follow the installation instructions that appear on your screen.**

   Restart your computer to automatically run Living Desktop or run Living Desktop from the Programs menu via the Start button.

Support Files folder

Because the most compelling Java-powered pages usually contain graphics and sounds, this folder contains a number of animations and sounds that you can use in your own Java pages. In addition, a number of special data files (jokes, fortunes, horoscopes, quotes, Bible verses, and so on) are included for use with the Marquee ticker-tape applet provided on the CD-ROM.

If You've Got Problems (Of the CD Kind)

On the CD, I've tried my best to compile programs that work on most computers with the minimum system requirements. Alas, your computer may differ, and some programs may not work properly for some reason.

If you have any trouble seeing the applets on the CD-ROM come alive, you may want to consider upgrading to Netscape Navigator 4.0 or later or Internet Explorer 4.0 or later. Earlier Java-savvy browsers — particularly those on the Macintosh platform — aren't industrial strength in their handling of Java-powered pages. I've even put the latest browsers on the CD for you — short of coming to your home and installing it myself, I don't know how much easier I can make it. (Although I'd still love to stop by some time, if you'll have me.) Take my advice: Upgrade as soon as possible.

The other two most likely problems are that you don't have enough memory (RAM) for the programs you want to use or you have other programs running that are affecting installation or running of a program. If you get error messages like Not enough memory or Setup cannot continue, try one or more of these methods and then try using the software again:

- ✔ **Turn off any antivirus software that you have on your computer.** Installers sometimes mimic virus activity and may make your computer incorrectly believe that it is being infected by a virus.

- ✔ **Close all running programs.** The more programs you're running, the less memory is available to other programs. Installers also typically update files and programs; if you keep other programs running, installation may not work properly.

- ✔ **In Windows, close the CD interface and run demos or installations directly from Windows Explorer.** The interface itself can tie up system memory or even conflict with certain kinds of interactive demos. Use Windows Explorer to browse the files on the CD and launch installers or demos.

- ✔ **Have your local computer store add more RAM to your computer.** This is, admittedly, a drastic and somewhat expensive step. However, if you have a Windows 95/98 PC or a Mac OS computer with a PowerPC chip, adding more memory can really help the speed of your computer and enable more programs to run at the same time.

If you still have trouble installing the items from the CD, please call the IDG Books Worldwide Customer Service phone number: 800-762-2974 (outside the U.S.: 317-596-5430).

Index

(continued)

(continued)

Notes

Java™ Development Kit
Version 1.1.5 Binary Code License

This binary code license ("License") contains rights and restrictions associated with use of the accompanying software and documentation ("Software"). Read the License carefully before installing the Software. By installing the Software you agree to the terms and conditions of this License.

1. **Limited License Grant**. Sun grants to you ("Licensee") a non-exclusive, non-transferable limited license to use the Software without fee for evaluation of the Software and for development of Java™ compatible applets and applications. Licensee may make one archival copy of the Software. Except for the foregoing, Licensee may not re-distribute the Software in whole or in part, either separately or included with a product. Refer to the Java Runtime Environment Version 1.1 binary code license (`www.javasoft.com/products/JDK/1.1/index.html`) for the availability of runtime code which may be distributed with Java compatible applets and applications.

2. **Java Platform Interface**. Licensee may not modify the Java Platform Interface ("JPI", identified as classes contained within the "java" package or any subpackages of the "java" package), by creating additional classes within the JPI or otherwise causing the addition to or modification of the classes in the JPI. In the event that Licensee creates any Java-related API and distributes such API to others for applet or application development, Licensee must promptly publish an accurate specification for such API for free use by all developers of Java-based software.

3. **Restrictions**. Software is confidential copyrighted information of Sun and title to all copies is retained by Sun and/or its licensors. Licensee shall not modify, decompile, disassemble, decrypt, extract, or otherwise reverse engineer Software. Software may not be leased, assigned, or sublicensed, in whole or in part. **Software is not designed or intended for use in on-line control of aircraft, air traffic, aircraft navigation, or aircraft communications; or in the design, construction, operation, or maintenance of any nuclear facility. Licensee warrants that it will not use or redistribute the Software for such purposes**.

4. **Trademarks and Logos**. This License does not authorize Licensee to use any Sun name, trademark or logo. Licensee acknowledges that Sun owns the Java trademark and all Java-related trademarks, logos and icons including the Coffee Cup and Duke ("Java Marks") and agrees to: (i) comply with the Java Trademark Guidelines at `java.com/trademarks.html`; (ii) not do anything harmful to or inconsistent with Sun's rights in the Java Marks; and (iii) assist Sun in protecting those rights, including assigning to Sun any rights acquired by Licensee in any Java Mark.

5. **Disclaimer of Warranty**. Software is provided "AS IS," without a warranty of any kind. ALL EXPRESS OR IMPLIED REPRESENTATIONS AND WARRANTIES, INCLUDING ANY IMPLIED WARRANTY OF MERCHANTABILITY, FITNESS FOR A PARTICULAR PURPOSE OR NON-INFRINGEMENT, ARE HEREBY EXCLUDED.

6. **Limitation of Liability**. SUN AND ITS LICENSORS SHALL NOT BE LIABLE FOR ANY DAMAGES SUFFERED BY LICENSEE OR ANY THIRD PARTY AS A RESULT OF USING OR DISTRIBUTING SOFTWARE. IN NO EVENT WILL SUN OR ITS LICENSORS BE LIABLE FOR ANY LOST REVENUE, PROFIT OR DATA, OR FOR DIRECT, INDIRECT, SPECIAL, CONSEQUENTIAL, INCIDENTAL, OR PUNITIVE DAMAGES, HOWEVER CAUSED AND REGARDLESS OF THE THEORY OF LIABILITY, ARISING OUT OF THE USE OF OR INABILITY TO USE SOFTWARE, EVEN IF SUN HAS BEEN ADVISED OF THE POSSIBILITY OF SUCH DAMAGES.

7. **Termination**. Licensee may terminate this License at any time by destroying all copies of Software. This License will terminate immediately without notice from Sun if Licensee fails to comply with any provision of this License. Upon such termination, Licensee must destroy all copies of Software.

8. **Export Regulations**. Software, including technical data, is subject to U.S. export control laws, including the U.S. Export Administration Act and its associated regulations, and may be subject to export or import regulations in other countries. Licensee agrees to comply strictly with all such regulations and acknowledges that it has the responsibility to obtain licenses to export, re-export, or import Software. Software may not be downloaded, or otherwise exported or re-exported (i) into, or to a national or resident of, Cuba, Iraq, Iran, North Korea, Libya, Sudan, Syria, or any country to which the U.S. has embargoed goods; or (ii) to anyone on the U.S. Treasury Department's list of Specially Designated Nations or the U.S. Commerce Department's Table of Denial Orders.

9. **Restricted Rights**. Use, duplication, or disclosure by the United States government is subject to the restrictions as set forth in the Rights in Technical Data and Computer Software Clauses in DFARS 252.227-7013(c) (1) (ii) and FAR 52.227-19(c) (2) as applicable.

10. **Governing Law**. Any action related to this License will be governed by California law and controlling U.S. federal law. No choice of law rules of any jurisdiction will apply.

11. **Severability**. If any of the above provisions are held to be in violation of applicable law, void, or unenforceable in any jurisdiction, then such provisions are herewith waived to the extent necessary for the License to be otherwise enforceable in such jurisdiction. However, if in Sun's opinion deletion of any provisions of the License by operation of this paragraph unreasonably compromises the rights or increase the liabilities of Sun or its licensors, Sun reserves the right to terminate the License and refund the fee paid by Licensee, if any, as Licensee's sole and exclusive remedy.

IDG Books Worldwide, Inc., End-User License Agreement

READ THIS. You should carefully read these terms and conditions before opening the software packet(s) included with this book ("Book"). This is a license agreement ("Agreement") between you and IDG Books Worldwide, Inc. ("IDGB"). By opening the accompanying software packet(s), you acknowledge that you have read and accept the following terms and conditions. If you do not agree and do not want to be bound by such terms and conditions, promptly return the Book and the unopened software packet(s) to the place you obtained them for a full refund.

1. **License Grant.** IDGB grants to you (either an individual or entity) a nonexclusive license to use one copy of the enclosed software program(s) (collectively, the "Software") solely for your own personal or business purposes on a single computer (whether a standard computer or a workstation component of a multiuser network). The Software is in use on a computer when it is loaded into temporary memory (RAM) or installed into permanent memory (hard disk, CD-ROM, or other storage device). IDGB reserves all rights not expressly granted herein.

2. **Ownership.** IDGB is the owner of all right, title, and interest, including copyright, in and to the compilation of the Software recorded on the disk(s) or CD-ROM ("Software Media"). Copyright to the individual programs recorded on the Software Media is owned by the author or other authorized copyright owner of each program. Ownership of the Software and all proprietary rights relating thereto remain with IDGB and its licensers.

3. **Restrictions on Use and Transfer.**

    (a) You may only (i) make one copy of the Software for backup or archival purposes, or (ii) transfer the Software to a single hard disk, provided that you keep the original for backup or archival purposes. You may not (i) rent or lease the Software, (ii) copy or reproduce the Software through a LAN or other network system or through any computer subscriber system or bulletin-board system, or (iii) modify, adapt, or create derivative works based on the Software.

    (b) You may not reverse engineer, decompile, or disassemble the Software. You may transfer the Software and user documentation on a permanent basis, provided that the transferee agrees to accept the terms and conditions of this Agreement and you retain no copies. If the Software is an update or has been updated, any transfer must include the most recent update and all prior versions.

4. **Restrictions on Use of Individual Programs.** You must follow the individual requirements and restrictions detailed for each individual program in Appendix C of this Book. These limitations are also contained in the individual license agreements recorded on the Software Media. These limitations may include a requirement that after using the program for a specified period of time, the user must pay a registration fee or discontinue use. By opening the Software packet(s), you will be agreeing to abide by the licenses and restrictions for these individual programs that are detailed in Appendix C and on the Software Media. None of the material on this Software Media or listed in this Book may ever be redistributed, in original or modified form, for commercial purposes.

5. **Limited Warranty.**

    (a) IDGB warrants that the Software and Software Media are free from defects in materials and workmanship under normal use for a period of sixty (60) days from the date of purchase of this Book. If IDGB receives notification within the warranty period of defects in materials or workmanship, IDGB will replace the defective Software Media.

    (b) IDGB AND THE AUTHOR OF THE BOOK DISCLAIM ALL OTHER WARRANTIES, EXPRESS OR IMPLIED, INCLUDING WITHOUT LIMITATION IMPLIED WARRANTIES OF MER-CHANTABILITY AND FITNESS FOR A PARTICULAR PURPOSE, WITH RESPECT TO THE SOFTWARE, THE PROGRAMS, THE SOURCE CODE CONTAINED THEREIN, AND/OR THE TECHNIQUES DESCRIBED IN THIS BOOK. IDGB DOES NOT WARRANT THAT THE FUNCTIONS CONTAINED IN THE SOFTWARE WILL MEET YOUR REQUIREMENTS OR THAT THE OPERATION OF THE SOFTWARE WILL BE ERROR FREE.

    (c) This limited warranty gives you specific legal rights, and you may have other rights that vary from jurisdiction to jurisdiction.

6. **Remedies.**

    (a) IDGB's entire liability and your exclusive remedy for defects in materials and workmanship shall be limited to replacement of the Software Media, which may be returned to IDGB with a copy of your receipt at the following address: Software Media Fulfillment Department, Attn.: *Java For Dummies,* 3rd Edition, IDG Books Worldwide, Inc., 7260 Shadeland Station, Ste. 100, Indianapolis, IN 46256, or call 800-762-2974. Please allow three to four weeks for delivery. This Limited Warranty is void if failure of the Software Media has resulted from accident, abuse, or misapplication. Any replacement Software Media will be warranted for the remainder of the original warranty period or thirty (30) days, whichever is longer.

    (b) In no event shall IDGB or the author be liable for any damages whatsoever (including without limitation damages for loss of business profits, business interruption, loss of business information, or any other pecuniary loss) arising from the use of or inability to use the Book or the Software, even if IDGB has been advised of the possibility of such damages.

    (c) Because some jurisdictions do not allow the exclusion or limitation of liability for conse-quential or incidental damages, the above limitation or exclusion may not apply to you.

7. **U.S. Government Restricted Rights.** Use, duplication, or disclosure of the Software by the U.S. Government is subject to restrictions stated in paragraph (c)(1)(ii) of the Rights in Technical Data and Computer Software clause of DFARS 252.227-7013, and in subparagraphs (a) through (d) of the Commercial Computer–Restricted Rights clause at FAR 52.227-19, and in similar clauses in the NASA FAR supplement, when applicable.

8. **General.** This Agreement constitutes the entire understanding of the parties and revokes and supersedes all prior agreements, oral or written, between them and may not be modified or amended except in a writing signed by both parties hereto that specifically refers to this Agreement. This Agreement shall take precedence over any other documents that may be in conflict herewith. If any one or more provisions contained in this Agreement are held by any court or tribunal to be invalid, illegal, or otherwise unenforceable, each and every other provision shall remain in full force and effect.

Installation Instructions

● ●

*I*n order to use the cool applets, scripts, applications, and tools on the *Java For Dummies,* 3rd Edition CD-ROM, you need to have a Java-savvy browser installed on your computer (see Chapter 2).

Note: Use of the Java Development Kit is subject to the Binary Code License terms and conditions. Read the license carefully. By opening this package, you are agreeing to be bound by the terms and conditions of this license from Sun Microsystems, Inc.

For Microsoft Windows

1. **Pop the *Java For Dummies,* 3rd Edition CD-ROM into your computer's CD-ROM drive.**

2. **Use My Computer mode or the Windows Explorer program to show the CD's contents.**

3. **Double-click the index.html file for an interactive tour of the CD-ROM, or copy the specific files that you want to install on your computer.**

   See Appendix C or the README.txt file on the CD-ROM for detailed instructions.

For Macintosh

1. **Insert the *Java For Dummies,* 3rd Edition CD-ROM into your computer's CD-ROM drive and close the drive door.**

   In a moment, an icon representing the CD you just inserted appears on your Mac desktop. Chances are, the icon looks like a CD-ROM.

2. **Double-click the CD icon to show the CD's contents.**

3. **Double-click the index.html file for an interactive tour of the CD-ROM, or copy the specific files that you want to install on your computer.**

   See Appendix C or the Read Me First file on the CD-ROM for detailed instructions.